DESTRUCTIVE BEHAVIOR
IN DEVELOPMENTAL
DISABILITIES

OTHER RECENT VOLUMES IN THE
SAGE FOCUS EDITIONS

DESTRUCTIVE BEHAVIOR IN DEVELOPMENTAL DISABILITIES

Diagnosis and Treatment

Travis Thompson
David B. Gray

editors

SAGE PUBLICATIONS
The International Educational and Professional Publisher
Thousand Oaks   London   New Delhi

For information address:

SAGE Publications, Inc.
2455 Teller Road
Thousand Oaks, California 91320

SAGE Publications Ltd.
6 Bonhill Street
London EC2A 4PU
United Kingdom

SAGE Publications India Pvt. Ltd.
M-32 Market
Greater Kailash I
New Delhi 110 048 India

Printed in the United States of America

Library of Congress Cataloging-in-Publication Data

Main entry under title:

Destructive behavior in developmental disabilities : diagnosis and
    treatment / edited by Travis Thompson, David B. Gray
        p. cm. — (Sage focus editions ; 170)
    Includes bibliographical references and index.
    ISBN 0-8039-5582-0 (cl). — ISBN 0-8039-5583-9 (pb).
        1. Mental retardation—Complications. 2. Self-injurious behavior—
    Prevention. 3. Violence—Prevention. 4. Aggressiveness
    (Psychology)—Prevention. 5. Mentally handicapped—Rehabilitation.
    I. Thompson, Travis. II. Gray, David B.
RC451.4.M47D47   1994
616.85'88—dc20   93-43673
                                            CIP

94 95 96 97 98 10 9 8 7 6 5 4 3 2 1

Sage Production Editor: Yvonne Könneker

Contents

Preface

A recent study by the National Institute of Child Health and Human Development (NIH, 1991) revealed that the annual cost of services to people with mental retardation who harm others, injure themselves, or damage property in the United States exceeds $3.5 billion per year. Self-injury and aggression are among the primary reasons for people with mental retardation being placed out of their natural families' homes into institutions. To the affected individual who displays these violently destructive behavior problems, they are inexplicable, as captured metaphorically by the poet A. R. Ammons (1968): "The wind said/You know I'm/the result of/forces beyond my control" (p. 39). Devising effective ways of diagnosing, educating, habilitating, serving, and treating people with mental retardation who are destructive is among the more challenging problems facing psychology, medicine, allied health, and education today. For the past 30 years, researchers have struggled to understand these daunting problems. Their efforts have been hampered by lack of empirical foundation on which to build, by unnecessarily impenetrable disciplinary boundaries, and by lack of funding to support research in these areas. Answers to even the most basic questions have remained elusive, including diagnostic methods, measurement approaches, and intervention/treatment alternatives and their effectiveness. Theorists largely have relied on single factors (e.g., genetic, learning, or neurochemical) that they believed would account for a wide array of problems. It has become increasingly apparent that the time has come to move beyond single-factor theories and accord proper attention to the interaction of multiple classes of variables responsible for these diverse and highly complex phenomena.

The present volume brings together many of the nation's experts actively involved in research on problems of destructive behavior in developmental disabilities. They come from an array of disciplines and backgrounds, but share a commitment to overcoming these deeply troubling problems. These investigators have strived to bridge disciplinary boundaries in the search for solutions to challenging problems. The chapters in this volume originated with a conference sponsored by the Mental Retardation and Developmental Disabilities Branch of the National Institute of Child Health and Human Development (NICHD), which was held in Minneapolis, Minnesota, in the spring of 1991 and hosted by the Institute for Disabilities Studies of the University of Minnesota. Subsequent to the conference, authors revised and updated their papers, and some were entirely rewritten for this volume.

The editors wish to express their gratitude to Dr. Felix de la Cruz, chief of the Mental Retardation and Developmental Disabilities Branch of the NICHD, and Dr. Duane Alexander, director of the NICHD, for their support. We are most grateful to Patricia Merrill and Claudia Brummel of the Institute for Disabilities Studies at the University of Minnesota, who provided invaluable support in connection with the conference. Patricia Harmon of the John F. Kennedy Center staff at Vanderbilt University assumed responsibility for communications with authors and secretarial work in connection with these final manuscripts. To her we express our gratitude. Above all, we wish to thank the authors for their scholarly contributions and their patience in seeing this project to its final form.

—Travis Thompson
—David B. Gray

References

Ammons, A. R. (1968). *Selected poems.* Ithaca, NY: Cornell University.
National Institutes of Health. (1991). *Treatment of destructive behaviors in persons with developmental disabilities* (NIH Publication No. 91-2410). Bethesda, MD: U.S. Department of Health and Human Services.

PART I

Epidemiology and Ontogeny of Destructive Behavior

1

Prevalence of Destructive Behaviors

A Study of Aggression, Self-Injury, and Property Destruction

SHARON A. BORTHWICK-DUFFY

The association between mental retardation and destructive behavior has been well documented in the literature (Bruininks, Hill, & Morreau, 1988; Dibble & Gray, 1990; Reiss, Levitan, & McNally, 1982; Stark, Menolascino, Albarelli, & Gray, 1988). Specifically, persons with mental retardation have been characterized as being vulnerable to such behaviors as self-injury, aggression, and property destruction. For example, a recent study reported that among 699 residents of a large state school, 43% displayed aggressive behavior, 28% were self-injurious, and 24% were identified as destroying property (Fovel, Lash, Barron, & Roberts, 1989). Although different aspects of these behaviors have been the subject of study for many decades, the interest in determining prevalence rates has increased in recent years, with a notable increase in large-scale survey studies (Griffin, Williams, Stark, Altmeyer, & Mason, 1986).

AUTHOR'S NOTE: This study was supported in part by grants awarded to the University of California, Riverside, from the National Institute of Child Health and Human Development (Grants HD 22953 and HD 21056).

Variability in Reported Prevalence Rates

Reported prevalence rates for destructive behaviors vary widely. For example, in a recent review of the literature on self-injurious behavior, Winchel and Stanley (1991) reported a range of prevalence estimates from 3.5 to 40% for self-injury in facilities that care for people with mental retardation. Several reasons have been suggested to help explain the variability in reported prevalence rates.

Schroeder, Mulick, and Rojahn (1980) discussed issues related to the definition of self-injury that could affect prevalence estimates. First, the selection of topographies that are included in a definition of self-injury contributes to the variability in reported rates. In fact, Schroeder et al. (1980) suggested that the term *self-injurious behavior* (SIB) may erroneously lend credibility to "a syndrome consisting of response topographies that may be only loosely related functionally" (p. 419). A related definitional problem is the lack of a widely accepted definition of SIB (Gunter, 1984; Schroeder et al., 1980). One of the early definitions of self-injurious behavior was proposed by Tate and Baroff (1966). Theirs was a rather broad definition of self-injury, describing it as "behavior which produces physical injury to the individual's own body" (p. 281). Later, Baumeister and Rollings (1976) defined self-injurious behaviors as "acts which are highly repetitive or stereotyped in character which result in direct physical damage to a person" (p. 2). The latter definition provides a more restricted view of SIB and eliminates some behaviors whose damage may be less immediate and more cumulative (Gunter, 1984). Thus whether or not an individual is identified as being self-injurious (or aggressive or destroying property) is dependent on how broadly or narrowly the behavior is defined.

A second definitional issue relates to the level of severity that classifies a person as having problems of self-injury, aggression, or property destruction. Again, a range of criteria have been used in the studies reported in the literature. Prevalence studies have used different cut-off points for deciding when a behavior is considered severe enough, how frequently it must occur, and, finally, how recently it must have occurred in order to be "counted." Although several investigators have examined levels of severity or frequency in relation to other characteristics of the individual, overall prevalence rates generally are reported for those who simply "manifest" the behavior, making comparisons of rates difficult to interpret.

Not surprisingly, prevalence rates also are affected by the characteristics of the sample on which the rates are based. As noted, the majority of prevalence studies on destructive behaviors have focused on institutionalized samples (e.g., Baumeister & Rollings, 1976; Fovel et al., 1989; Griffin et al., 1986; Maurice & Trudel, 1982; Schroeder, Schroeder, Smith, & Dalldorf, 1978). Some recent studies have presented findings on noninstitutionalized people with mental retardation (e.g., Hill & Bruininks, 1984; Rojahn, 1986) and have reported rates considerably lower than those found in institutional settings. Hill and Bruininks (1984), for example, reported differences in self-injurious behavior of 11.1% among clients in community residential facilities (CRFs) versus 17.6% of clients in public residential facilities (PRFs). Rojahn (1986) found an even lower prevalence rate for self-injury of 1.7% among individuals living in community settings. With regard to aggression, Hill and Bruininks found 16.3% of the clients in CRFs were reported to injure other people, whereas 30.3% of clients in PRFs injured others. Finally, disruptive behavior was noted among 28.8% of people in CRFs, whereas 34% of those in PRFs were identified as disruptive. These differences are not surprising because maladaptive behaviors have been identified as important criteria in the determination of residential placement, with persons with destructive behavior having an increased likelihood of being placed in larger, more restrictive settings (Borthwick-Duffy, Eyman, & White, 1987; Eyman & Call, 1977; Hill & Bruininks, 1984). Moreover, the variability between the specific community setting types selected for study may explain the rather dramatic differences in prevalence rates of self-injury found by Rojahn (1986), who studied people in schools and training centers, workshops, and group homes, and by Hill and Bruininks (1984), who did not include clients who lived with relatives or those who lived in independent living programs.

The changing patterns of residential placement also have affected differences in reported ranges of prevalence over the years, particularly in studies that have used institutional samples. Eyman, Borthwick, and Tarjan (1984) described the changing characteristics of people living in institutions in a 25-year natural history study. They concluded that the residents of institutions were evolving into a residual group of older persons with severe and profound retardation who were more likely to have organic diagnoses and concomitant behavior problems. Thus the prevalence rates of destructive behaviors in institutions would be expected to increase over time as persons with less severe problems are placed in less restrictive environments. Further, the impact of those who display milder forms of destructive behaviors and have left (or will never be placed in) institutions also will increase the prevalence of those behaviors found in community settings.

Co-Occurrence of Destructive Behaviors

An important consideration in the study of destructive behaviors is the fact that these behaviors frequently coexist, meaning that individuals who display self-injurious behavior are likely to also evince aggressive behavior and/or destruction of property (Winchel & Stanley, 1991). Maisto, Baumeister, and Maisto (1978) studied an institutionalized population and found that individuals who were self-injurious also exhibited aggressiveness with relatively high frequencies. Maisto et al. suggested that these behaviors may be functionally related, i.e., they produce a similar effect of eliciting attention. Their data supported this hypothesis in that both types of problem behavior escalated in situations where the residents were upset or felt they had needs that were unmet. Similarly, Griffin et al. (1986) noted that among the people they studied who were living in institutions and who were identified as self-injurious, 55% displayed other aberrant behaviors, including aggression toward others (55%) and destruction of the physical environment (30%). It is worth pointing out again that these proportions are likely to be higher in institutionalized groups of people whose placement in the more restrictive environment often is associated with higher levels and more combinations of maladaptive behaviors (Eyman & Call, 1977).

Prevalence Estimates Based on California Data

The preceding review provided a brief overview of important issues related to the study of the prevalence of destructive behaviors among persons with mental retardation. An attempt was made to explain differences in overall prevalence rates that have been reported for subgroups of people with retardation during the past 30 years. In the remainder of this chapter prevalence estimates of destructive behaviors are presented that are based on data recently examined from a statewide database.

The presentation of these new data does not solve the definitional caveats mentioned above. However, an important advantage of the data presented in this chapter is that the estimates are based on an administratively defined population of more than 91,164 people who were served by the California Department of Developmental Services (DDS) in 1987. The database includes people who were living in settings that represented the complete range of residential alternatives, including institutions (called developmental centers in California), parent/relative homes, community residential facilities, and semi-independent and independent living arrangements. Moreover, the database is large enough to allow for prevalence comparisons to be made among community residence types. As noted, destructive behavior has been studied most often in institutions or other public residential settings. However, because more than 60% of individuals with mental retardation who receive services from the DDS system are living with their parents or relatives, this represents a significant proportion of the population that often has been excluded from prevalence studies.

Representativeness of California DDS Sample

Because the data used in the study were obtained from the registry of people receiving DDS services from the state, the figures reported represent what Kushlick (1974) referred to as "administrative prevalences." Persons with moderate, severe, and profound levels of mental retardation are believed to be well represented by the DDS system, which provides a wide range of services such as transportation, counseling, therapies, respite care, and residential care. By contrast, those individuals with milder forms of retardation who are receiving state-reimbursed services probably represent a subset of people with mild retardation that includes those who have greater medical or behavioral needs and thus benefit from the kinds of services provided by the state.

Measurement of Destructive Behaviors

The California Department of Developmental Services requires that an annual assessment of adaptive behavior and diagnostic information be conducted on each client receiving services. The assessment is reported on the Client Development Evaluation Report (CDER, California Department of Developmental Services, 1979) and is maintained in a computerized database. The CDER is based on information provided by someone who knows the individual with mental retardation well and can respond to questions about behavior observed during the recent year. Interrater reliabilities of the destructive behavior scores used in this study have been determined to be acceptable, ranging from .60 to .72 (Harris, Eyman, & Mayeda, 1982). Other characteristics of the individual, including age, gender, residential placement, health status, level of retardation, and expressive communication, also were obtained from the computerized database.

The line of demarcation between people who are considered to have a destructive behavior and those who do not have this behavior problem usually is determined by the research investigator and varies across studies. In the present study, the criteria shown in Table 1.1 were used to identify people who had severe forms of aggression or self-injury or who destroyed property. The definitions represent item response categories found on the CDER. Serious levels of aggressive behavior were identified by "violent episodes causing serious physical injury." Two indices of self-injurious behavior were used in order to illustrate throughout the analyses the differences in prevalence rates that can emerge by using different eligibility criteria. One definition of self-injury took into account both the frequency and severity of the behavior (severe self-injury once per month and/or minor self-injury once per week), whereas the other definition considered a person to be self-injurious solely on the basis of the behavior's weekly occurrence. Serious levels of property destruction were defined by "serious destruction within the past year and/or minor property damage on six or more occasions in the past year." These cut-offs represented the most serious of the response categories for each behavior. Thus the criteria were intended to identify individuals whose manifestation of the behavior was considered to be a serious problem; those people who displayed the behavior infrequently or in a mild form were not included.

Presentation of Prevalence Data

The percentages of people who were identified as manifesting serious problems of destructive behavior are displayed in Table 1.2. The overall prevalence rates for the sample indicated that 2.1% were aggressive, 2.2% were self-injurious when taking both severity and frequency into account, 9.3% were self-injurious when considering only frequency, and 7.1% had serious problems related to property destruction. The remaining sections of Table 1.2 describe prevalence rates in terms of other characteristics such as gender and age. The chi-square values for

Table 1.1 Definitions of Destructive Behavior Used for Prevalence
Estimates

Aggressive Behavior
    One or more violent episodes causing serious physical injury (requiring immediate
    medical attention) to others within the past year.

Self-Injurious Behavior: Frequency and Severity
    Behavior causing severe self-injury and requiring physician's immediate attention at
    least once per month and/or behavior causing minor self-injury and requiring first aid
    at least once per week.

Self-Injurious Behavior: Frequency Only
    Self-injurious behavior at least once a week.

Property Destruction
    Serious property destruction within the past year and/or minor property damage on six
    or more occasions within the past year.

each characteristic were significant for all behaviors, although some
differences in rates within categories were more dramatic than others.
Note that the figures shown for the two measures of self-injury in Table
1.2 illustrate the rather dramatic differences in rates that are associated
with using different eligibility criteria.

Gender

Highly significant ($p < .001$) gender differences were present for both
aggression and property destruction; only 1.5% of females were identified as aggressive, whereas 2.6% of males displayed severe levels of
aggressive behavior. Similarly, property destruction was considered
severe for 8.5% of the males, whereas only 5.3% of females were
identified as destructive. These findings are consistent with other reports
in the literature that males are more likely to evince these externalizing
problem behaviors (Achenbach & Edelbrock, 1981).

Gender differences have been observed with regard to the incidence
of specific topographies of SIB (Baumeister & Rollings, 1976; Maisto
et al., 1978), although overall prevalence rates by gender have revealed
mixed findings (Schroeder et al., 1978). In this examination prevalence
rates for self-injury were found to be statistically different for males and
females. However, given the statistical power afforded by the sample size,
the comparison of phi coefficients, and the larger p value for serious

Table 1.2 Percentages of People With Destructive Behavior in California Service System

Category	Aggression (n = 1,899)	Frequent and Severe Self-Injury (n = 2,017)	Frequent Self-Injury (n = 8,444)	Property Destruction (n = 6,466)
Gender				
Male	2.6	2.3	9.7	8.5
Female	1.5	2.1[a]	8.7	5.3
Age				
0-3 years	1.1	1.0	5.8	1.8
4-10 years	0.9	1.1	9.6	5.7
11-20 years	1.7	1.9	10.7	7.9
21+ years	2.7	2.8	9.3	8.1
Level of MR				
Mild	1.4	0.8	3.5	4.4
Moderate	1.8	1.5	6.7	6.7
Severe	2.9	3.3	15.3	9.9
Profound	4.5	7.1	24.9	15.0
Expressive Communication				
Verbal	2.0	2.0	8.6	7.9
Nonverbal	2.9	5.2	17.0	7.0[b]
Residence Type				
Independent	0.7	0.4	1.0	1.7
Parental home	0.8	0.8	5.5	3.2
Comm. care (1-6)	1.1	2.4	6.6	2.2
Comm. care (7 or more)	1.8	3.8	17.8	9.1
ICF/health facility	2.2	2.3	9.3	9.2
Skilled nursing	2.2	2.6	12.9	11.2
Institution	12.8	12.2	31.2	29.6
Dual Diagnosis				
MR diagnosis only	1.6	1.9	8.7	6.1
Dual diagnosis	8.5	5.9	15.9	19.4
Dual diagnosis/ severe impact	14.5[c]	9.1	22.0	29.4
Total	2.1	2.2	9.3	7.1

NOTE: Table values are percentages of persons within given categories who display the behavior (e.g., 1.0 means 1%). Total sample size is 91,164. All chi-square values testing equality of prevalence rates across categories were significant at $p < .0001$ unless otherwise noted.
a. $p < .01$.
b. $p < .001$.
c. This subcategory of persons with a dual diagnosis was not included in the chi-square test.

SIB than for the other behaviors, it can be concluded that this association was not as strong. Maisto et al. (1978) found in their institutionalized sample that the prevalence of self-injury was higher among females, but that the behavior was more severe among males. One would have expected, then, that the prevalence of SIB might be greater for females using the frequency-only criteria, and for more males to be identified when seriousness also was considered. Table 1.2 shows that this was not the case, as the prevalence rates still were higher for males when considering only frequency of occurrence.

Chronological Age

Table 1.2 shows linear trends in frequent/severe self-injury and property destruction, with the prevalence of those behaviors increasing with chronological age. Aggression is most prevalent among those older than 10 years, and the prevalence of frequent self-injury rises after age 3 and remains relatively stable thereafter.

Prevalence rates for self-injury in the youngest age group may be affected by the fact that self-injurious behavior occurs in about 7 to 17% of normal children from about 7 to 8 months until the age of 5 (Kravitz & Boehm, 1971; Maisto et al., 1978; Schroeder et al., 1980). As these researchers have noted, it is important to recognize that self-injury among very young children is not always viewed in terms of pathology. Thus the identification of children with mental retardation who display self-injury involves a determination as to whether the behavior should be considered part of normal development or whether it should be viewed as a severe behavior problem.

Level of Mental Retardation

Levels of retardation reported on the CDER are based on psychological evaluations and are consistent with those found in the American Association on Mental Deficiency's (AAMD) *Manual on Terminology and Classification in Mental Retardation* (Grossman, 1983). The linear pattern of prevalence rates for aggression and property destruction supports previous reports that these problems increase with the severity of retardation (e.g., Eyman & Call, 1977; Maisto et al., 1978). Similar relationships also are found for both measures of self-injury, which means prevalence rates are higher for more severe forms of retardation.

Expressive Communication

Although a causal relationship between intelligence and maladaptive behavior has not been established, an association between the individual's reduced capacities to utilize different strategies to meet his or her needs seems to be related to a higher probability of problem behavior (Maisto et al., 1978; Padd & Eyman, 1985). A number of investigators have noted that communication deficits accompany destructive behavior (Gunter, 1984), and some suggest that problem behaviors represent attempts to communicate. The prevalence rates for verbal and nonverbal clients in this study lend support to this hypothesis, with the most dramatic differences found for both measures of self-injury.

Residential Setting

In California, community residential programs are classified according to the number and age group of the individuals with mental retardation who live in the facility, as well as by the level of health care provided. In the present study, the seven residence types examined were (a) institutions or large residential facilities, called developmental centers in California; (b) skilled nursing facilities; (c) intermediate care facilities that provide intermittent health care; (d) community care facilities for seven or more clients; (e) community care for six or fewer clients; (f) parent/relative homes; and (g) semi-independent or independent living. Residential placements should be determined on an individual basis, defining the restrictiveness of environments according to the specific needs of the person: What is least restrictive for one person might be considered more restrictive for another. Further, wide variability in terms of restrictiveness has been demonstrated within different broad residential categories (Landesman-Dwyer, 1985). Nevertheless, enough commonalities exist within residence types to justify a crude ranking by restrictiveness for an examination of destructive behaviors. The residence types shown in Table 1.2 are ordered roughly from least restrictive to most restrictive, or from independent living to institutions. Table 1.2 reveals a systematic pattern of differences in prevalence rates in the various residential settings. The results suggest a positive linear relationship between the prevalence of aggressive behavior and the level of restrictiveness in the residential placements. Although there are some exceptions (e.g., the high proportion of clients with frequent self-injury in large community care homes), prevalence rates of self-injury and property destruction also increase with the restrictiveness of the residence type. The lower rates in health facilities (intermediate care facilities, skilled nursing facilities) when compared to large community care homes probably is related to the fact that the independence of clients in health facilities is restricted due to health limitations, rather than being related to the presence of problem behaviors.

As previously noted, maladaptive behavior consistently has been shown to be associated with residential placement. It has been reported numerous times in the literature that problem behaviors such as aggression, self-injury, and property destruction keep some individuals from being placed in less restrictive settings (Hill & Bruininks, 1984) and also are responsible for what have been called placement failures, or readmissions to restrictive settings (Eyman et al., 1984; Hill & Bruininks, 1984). A different perspective suggests that certain setting types, such as institutions, are responsible for accelerating levels of destructive behavior (Ingalls, 1978; Winchel & Stanley, 1991). For example, Maisto et al. (1978) suggested that if destructive behavior is a learned behavior, then it may be one of the few forms of behavior that are reliably reinforced "in an impoverished environment, such as the typical institutional ward, where there is either a low density or irregularity of naturally occurring reinforcing stimuli" (p. 33). Although this may provide a reasonable explanation for the development and maintenance of destructive behaviors, more current research is required to determine which environments, regardless of broad setting categories, are impoverished in the way described by Maisto et al. MacMillan (1982) also pointed out that the evidence supporting the greater prevalence of aggression and other types of maladaptive behavior in institutions stems almost exclusively from research with institutionalized populations. In a study by Eyman, Borthwick, and Miller (1981), changes in behavior levels over a three-year period were examined for new cases that had been placed in community or institutional settings, controlling for preplacement maladaptive behaviors. The contention that institutions produce maladaptive behavior among their residents was not supported by the results of the study. Hence, in the absence of convincing data to suggest that institutions encourage destructive behaviors, differences in prevalence rates across residence categories that were found in the study by Eyman et al. (1981) were assumed to be primarily due to placement selection decisions that had taken problem behavior into account.

From the present data on residence types, it is interesting to note that the prevalence rate of 12.2% for self-injury (taking severity and frequency into account) is within the range of rates reported in the Baumeister and

Rollings (1976) review and is similar to later rates found in studies by Schroeder et al. (1978), Maurice and Trudel (1982), and Griffin et al. (1986). However, given the changing composition of institutionalized populations, one would expect to find much higher rates of destructive behaviors than those researchers had reported. Thus the prevalence rate in this study for self-injury as measured by its frequency of occurrence (31.2%) may be the figure that best reflects the changing institutional populations.

Psychiatric (Dual) Diagnosis

The focus on specific problem behaviors has occurred concomitantly with a growing interest in the notion of the "dual diagnosis" of mental retardation and a psychiatric disorder (Reiss, 1990). It is apparent from the literature that, although persons with mental retardation and mental health disorders are at a higher risk of developing destructive behavior patterns, these behaviors also are present among a significant proportion of people whose only diagnosis is mental retardation (Borthwick-Duffy, 1990; Borthwick-Duffy & Eyman, 1990; Bruininks et al., 1988).

In California, information on psychiatric disorders is completed only if a psychiatric diagnosis has been made by a qualified professional. Clients with a psychiatric diagnosis also are rated according to the impact (none, mild, moderate, severe) of the mental disorder on their daily functioning and need for supervision. Table 1.2 illustrates how prevalence rates for all destructive behaviors are significantly higher for people who have been assigned both mental retardation and mental health diagnoses (approximately 10% of the population). Further, prevalence rates for clients whose mental disorders are rated as having a severe impact are distinctly higher than for the dually diagnosed group as a whole. Nevertheless, it should be noted that severe forms of destructive behaviors also are present among some individuals whose only diagnosis is mental retardation.

Co-Occurrence of Destructive Behaviors

It already has been suggested that some individuals with destructive behaviors are likely to engage in combinations of those behaviors in order to communicate and seek attention or other types of reinforcement. For the figures shown in Table 1.3, the individuals studied were classified according to the combinations of serious destructive behaviors they displayed. If an individual was found to have all three destructive behavior problems, he or she would not be included in the columns representing people with two problem behaviors (i.e., an individual is represented in only one column). For the sake of brevity in this table, a person was considered to be self-injurious if he or she met the criteria for either of the two self-injury definitions.

Almost 15% of the sample displayed serious degrees of at least one of the three destructive behaviors. Most of those people (10.8%) had only one behavior problem, 3.0% evinced two of the three, and 0.6% had serious problems in all three categories of destructive behavior.

With regard to the characteristics of people who displayed more than one destructive behavior, the trends were mostly consistent with what was found for specific behaviors. Males were represented significantly more often than females in all combinations. Linear trends in age and level of mental retardation indicated higher rates with older people and more severe levels of retardation for all combinations of behaviors. Similarly, persons who were nonverbal were more likely to engage in more than one type of destructive behavior. As expected, large residential facilities (institutions) were caring for most people who displayed two or more problems, with those problems being almost nonexistent in independent living and small community care homes. Finally, two or three serious forms of destructive behaviors were more prevalent among persons with a dual diagnosis (mental retardation and psychiatric disorder) than among those with only a mental retardation diagnosis.

Numbers of Behavior Problems

The last treatment of these data was to examine prevalence rates for individuals who had different numbers of destructive behaviors. Again, self-injury was counted if the person met the criteria for either of the two measures. This allowed a comparison of distributions of people in the various categories who had no destructive behaviors with those who evinced one, two, or all three behavior problems. The trends were consistent with those reported for the other ways of grouping destructive behaviors. With the inclusion of the "no behavior" category, some differences in rates within categories were even more dramatic. As shown in Table 1.4, more than 30% of persons with profound retardation displayed at least one serious form of a destructive behavior. Although the rates decrease as the number of problems increases, proportionately more people with profound retardation are represented in all columns

Table 1.3 Percentages of People With Combinations of Destructive
            Behaviors

Category	Aggression and Self-Injury (n = 271)	Aggression and Property (n = 521)	Self-Injury and Property (n = 1,976)	Aggression and Self-Injury and Property (n = 546)
Gender				
Male	0.3	0.8	2.4	0.7
Female	0.2[a]	0.3	1.9	0.5[b]
Age				
0-3 years	0.1	0.0	0.8	0.4
4-10 years	0.2	0.2	1.9	0.3
11-20 years	0.2	0.4	2.4	0.6
21+ years	0.4	0.8	2.4	0.7
Level of MR				
Mild	0.1	0.5	0.8	0.2
Moderate	0.2	0.7	1.6	0.4
Severe	0.5	0.7	3.3	1.0
Profound	1.0	0.8	6.5	1.8
Expressive Communication				
Verbal	0.3	0.6	2.0	0.5
Nonverbal	0.6	0.2	3.6	1.3
Residence Type				
Independent living	0.0	0.1	0.1	0.1
Parental home	0.1	0.2	0.9	0.2
Comm. care (1-6)	0.5	0.0	0.7	0.1
Comm. care (7 or more)	0.3	0.5	3.1	0.5
ICF/health facility	0.2	0.7	2.1	0.5
Skilled nursing	0.4	0.7	3.4	0.5
Institution	1.9	3.8	10.6	4.6
Dual Diagnosis				
MR diagnosis only	0.2	0.4	2.0	0.5
Dual diagnosis	1.1	2.9	4.8	2.3
Dual diagnosis/ severe impact	2.0[c]	5.7	7.2	3.8
Total	0.3	0.6	2.2	0.6

NOTE: Table values are percentages of persons within given categories who display the behavior (e.g., 1.0 means 1%). Total sample size is 91,164. All chi-square values testing equality of prevalence rates within categories are significant at $p < .0001$ unless otherwise noted.
a. $p < .01$.
b. $p < .001$.
c. This subcategory of persons with a dual diagnosis was not included in the chi-square test.

for one or more behavior problems. Similarly, close to half of the residents in institutions have at least one serious destructive behavior, and 20% display more than one behavior problem. Whereas only 15% of persons with a single diagnosis of mental retardation evince destructive behaviors, 30% of those with a dual diagnosis, and almost half of persons whose psychiatric disorder was reported to have a severe impact on their daily functioning, displayed serious levels of destructive behavior.

Major Medical Problems

One question that is of interest when examining data on destructive behaviors is whether severe forms of destructive behaviors lead to higher morbidity and mortality rates. The cross-sectional data considered in this study are limited in this respect, because longitudinal data are required to examine cross-lagged causal relationships. It was possible in this study, however, to examine the prevalence of destructive behaviors among people with and without serious medical conditions. In Table 1.5 it can be seen that for all destructive behaviors the presence of medical problems was associated with higher rates of aggression, self-injury, and property destruction. Although this examination of bivariate relationships does not take into account the relationship of medical problems to other correlated factors, such as mental retardation level, which is strongly associated with destructive behavior and also with the presence of major medical problems, the presence of these higher rates suggests nevertheless that further investigation is warranted.

Mortality

Mortality was monitored for this sample from 1987 to 1990 to identify those persons who died within a three-year period. This amounted to 2.5% of the total. From a series of studies on life expectancy (e.g., Eyman, Borthwick-Duffy, Call, & White, 1988; Eyman, Call, & White, 1989) several variables have been identified that can predict death with some accuracy among people with mental retardation. The predictor variables include severe or profound mental retardation, nonmobility, and lack of toileting and eating skills. Although these may not be *causes* of death, they identify individuals who are at risk.

Persons in the prevalence study sample were categorized as at risk, not at risk, or not at risk but died during the three-year period. Because

Table 1.4 Percentages of People With Zero, One, Two, or Three Destructive Behaviors

Category	No Behaviors (n = 78,019)	One Behavior (n = 9,831)	Two Behaviors (n = 2,768)	Three Behaviors (n = 546)
Gender				
Male	83.9	11.9	3.5	0.7
Female	87.7	9.4	2.4	0.5
Age				
0-3 years	92.9	5.8	0.9	0.4
4-10 years	86.4	11.1	2.2	0.3
11-20 years	83.7	12.7	3.1	0.5
21+ years	84.7	11.0	3.6	0.7
Level of MR				
Mild	92.4	6.1	1.4	0.2
Moderate	88.0	9.2	2.4	0.4
Severe	78.0	16.6	4.5	1.0
Profound	67.1	22.8	8.2	1.8
Expressive Communication				
Verbal	86.2	10.4	2.9	0.5
Nonverbal	78.8	15.6	4.3	1.3
Residence Type				
Independent	97.0	2.6	0.2	0.1
Parental home	92.0	6.7	1.1	0.2
Comm. care (1-6)	91.2	7.5	1.2	0.1
Comm. care (7 or more)	75.6	20.0	3.9	0.5
ICF/health facility	83.0	13.5	3.0	0.5
Skilled nursing	78.8	16.4	4.4	0.5
Institution	51.2	27.9	16.2	4.6
Dual Diagnosis				
MR diagnosis only	86.9	10.1	2.6	0.4
Dual diagnosis	69.2	19.7	8.8	2.3
Dual diagnosis/ severe impact	55.8[a]	25.4	14.9	3.8
Total	85.6	10.8	3.0	0.6

NOTE: Table values are percentages of persons within given categories who display the behavior (e.g., 1.0 means 1%). Total sample size is 91,164. All chi-square values were significant at $p < .0001$.
a. This subcategory of persons with a dual diagnosis was not included in the chi-square test.

deaths still occurred among people who did not fall into the high-risk category, it seemed possible that those who died but were not high

Table 1.5 Percentages of Destructive Behavior by Medical Problems and Survival

	Aggression	Self-Injury Severity	Self-Injury Frequency	Property Destruction
Major Medical Problems				
None	1.9	1.9	8.7	6.7
One or more	5.0	8.0	19.8	14.2
Survival (1987-1990)				
Lived	2.1	2.2	9.3	7.1
Died	1.7	3.0	8.4	5.2

Table 1.6 Percentages of Destructive Behavior by Risk of Early Death

	Aggression	Self-Injury Severity	Self-Injury Frequency	Property Destruction
Risk of Early Death				
High risk[a]	1.5	2.0	6.7	1.6
Not high risk—lived	2.1	2.2	9.4	7.4
Not high risk—died	1.8	3.5	9.3	6.2

a. Severe/profound/suspected MR level, nonambulatory, nonmobile, non-toilet trained, must be fed.

risk in terms of the identified variables might evince higher than expected rates of destructive behavior. In other words, if these rates were higher it might suggest that the destructive behavior was in some way associated with the death of these individuals. Table 1.6 summarizes the differences in prevalence rates for the three groups. As might be expected for the high-risk group of individuals who were most dependent and relatively inactive, the rates of destructive behavior were significantly lower than for those who were not high risk.

The higher prevalence rates of serious self-injury among those who died but were not at risk lends some support to the hypothesis that persons who died but were not at risk might have died from behavior-related consequences. These differences were significant but not dramatic. For self-injury as defined by frequency of occurrence, no differences were found between the survivors and the nonsurvivors who were not high risk.

Discussion

The impressive size of the database used to estimate the prevalence rates in this chapter has several advantages over data that have been reported for more restricted samples. All residence types, including parent and family homes, were included in the data. Also, persons receiving service of any kind from the DDS system were examined, thus extending the study group beyond referred or clinical samples. The recency of the data provides an opportunity both to update previous reports and to study differences in prevalence rates that have emerged over time.

The updated prevalence rates based on an administratively defined population of individuals with mental retardation were consistent with much of the earlier literature. Prevalence rates of all destructive behaviors (aggression, self-injury, and property destruction) (a) are higher for males and people who are nonverbal; (b) increase as severity of retardation increases (although mild retardation was underrepresented in the data); (c) increase with age; (d) in general, are higher in residential placements that are more restrictive; (e) are higher among persons with a dual diagnosis than those with only mental retardation; and (f) are dramatically higher among persons whose psychiatric disorder is rated as having a severe impact on daily functioning. For the subgroup of individuals who have serious problems with more than one destructive behavior, the trends were consistent with those described above.

A limitation of the data is that the ratings are based on broad categories of aggression, self-injury, and property destruction: Specific topographies of the behavior categories were not examined. Schroeder et al. (1980) discussed the limitations of including all topographies in one broad category, particularly for studies of ecology and treatments. Also, the cross-sectional examination of these data did not address the issue of turnover, or chronicity of the destructive behaviors. Schroeder et al. (1978) found that although a 10% prevalence rate of self-injurious behavior was constant over a three-year period, 90% of the referrals (to institutional social workers) they studied were noted as changing status, meaning the SIB either disappeared or worsened. A longitudinal examination of data like those reported in this chapter could investigate the stability of these behaviors and provide important information for both treatment and planning.

References

Achenbach, T. M., & Edelbrock, C. S. (1981). Behavioral problems and competencies reported by parents of normal and disturbed children aged four through sixteen. *Monographs of the Society for Research in Child Development, 46*(1, Serial No. 188).

Baumeister, A. A., & Rollings, J. P. (1976). Self-injurious behavior. In N. R. Ellis (Ed.), *International review of research in mental retardation* (Vol. 8, pp. 1-34). New York: Academic Press.

Borthwick-Duffy, S. A. (1990). Application of traditional measurement scales to dually diagnosed populations. In E. Dibble & D. B. Gray (Eds.), *Assessment of behavior problems in persons with mental retardation living in the community* (pp. 147-157). Rockville, MD: National Institute of Mental Health (Information Resources and Inquiries Branch, Room 15 C 05, 5600 Fisher's Lane, Rockville, MD 20857).

Borthwick-Duffy, S. A., & Eyman, R. K. (1990). Who are the dually diagnosed? *American Journal on Mental Retardation, 94,* 586-595.

Borthwick-Duffy, S. A., Eyman, R. K., & White, J. F. (1987). Client characteristics and residential placement patterns. *American Journal of Mental Deficiency, 92,* 24-30.

Bruininks, R. H., Hill, B. K., & Morreau, L. E. (1988). Prevalence and implications of maladaptive behaviors and dual diagnosis in residential and other service programs. In J. A. Stark, F. J. Menolascino, M. H. Albarelli, & V. C. Gray (Eds.), *Mental retardation and mental health: Classification, diagnosis, treatment, services* (pp. 3-29). New York: Springer Verlag.

California Department of Developmental Services. (1979). *Client development evaluation report.* Sacramento: California Department of Developmental Services (1600 9th Street, Sacramento, CA 95814).

Dibble, E., & Gray, D. B. (Eds.). (1990). *Assessment of behavior problems in persons with mental retardation living in the community.* Rockville, MD: National Institute of Mental Health (Information Resources and Inquiries Branch, Room 15 C 05, 5600 Fisher's Lane, Rockville, MD 20857).

Eyman, R. K., Borthwick, S. A., & Miller, C. (1981). Trends in maladaptive behavior of mentally retarded persons placed in community and institutional settings. *American Journal of Mental Deficiency, 85,* 473-477.

Eyman, R. K., Borthwick, S. A., & Tarjan, G. (1984). Current trends and changes in institutions for the mentally retarded. In N. Ellis & N. Bray (Eds.), *International review of research in mental retardation* (Vol. 12, pp. 177-203). New York: Academic Press.

Eyman, R. K., Borthwick-Duffy, S. A., Call, T., & White, J. F. (1988). Prediction of mortality in community and institutional settings. *Journal of Mental Deficiency Research, 32,* 203-213.

Eyman, R. K., & Call, T. (1977). Maladaptive behavior and community placement of mentally retarded persons. *American Journal of Mental Deficiency, 82,* 137-144.

Eyman, R. K., Call, T. L., & White, J. F. (1989). Mortality of elderly mentally retarded persons in California. *The Journal of Applied Gerontology, 8,* 203-215.

Fovel, J. T., Lash, P. S., Barron, Jr., D. A., & Roberts, M. S. (1989). A survey of self-restraint, self-injury, and other maladaptive behaviors in an institutionalized retarded population. *Research in Developmental Disabilities, 10,* 377-382.

Griffin, J. C., Williams, D. E., Stark, M. T., Altmeyer, B. K., & Mason, M. (1986). Self-injurious behavior: A state-wide prevalence survey of the extent and circumstances. *Applied Research in Mental Retardation, 7,* 105-116.

Grossman, H. J. (Ed.). (1983). *Manual on Terminology and classification in mental retardation.* Washington, DC: American Association on Mental Deficiency.

Gunter, P. L. (1984). Self-injurious behaviour: Characteristics, etiology, and treatment. *The Exceptional Child, 31,* 91-98.

Harris, C., Eyman, R. K., & Mayeda, T. (1982). *An interrater reliability study of the Client Development Evaluation Report* (Final Report). Sacramento: California Department of Developmental Services (1600 9th Street, Sacramento, CA 95814).

Hill, B. K., & Bruininks, R. H. (1984). Maladaptive behavior of mentally retarded individuals in residential facilities. *American Journal of Mental Deficiency, 88,* 380-387.

Ingalls, R. P. (1978). *Mental retardation: The changing outlook.* New York: John Wiley.

Kravitz, H., & Boehm, J. (1971). Rhythmic habit patterns in infancy: Their sequence, age of onset, and frequency. *Child Development, 42,* 399-413.

Kushlick, A. (1974). Epidemiology and evaluation of services for the mentally handicapped. In M. J. Begab & S. A. Richardson (Eds.), *The mentally retarded and society: A social science perspective* (pp. 325-343). Baltimore, MD: University Park Press.

Landesman-Dwyer, S. (1985). Describing and evaluating residential environments. In R. H. Bruininks & K. C. Lakin (Eds.), *Living and learning in the least restrictive environment* (pp. 185-196). Baltimore, MD: Paul H. Brookes.

MacMillan, D. L. (1982). *Mental retardation in school and society.* Boston: Little, Brown.

Maisto, C. R., Baumeister, A. A., & Maisto, A. A. (1978). An analysis of variables related to self-injurious behaviour among institutionalised retarded persons. *Journal of Mental Deficiency Research, 22,* 27-36.

Maurice, P., & Trudel, G. (1982). Self-injurious behavior prevalence and relationships to environmental events. In J. H. Hollis & C. E. Meyers (Eds.), *Life threatening behavior: Analysis and intervention* (AAMD Monograph No. 5, pp. 81-103). Washington, DC: American Association on Mental Deficiency.

Padd, W., & Eyman, R. K. (1985). Mental retardation and aggression: Epidemiologic concerns and implications for deinstitutionalization. In A. F. Ashman & R. S. Laura (Eds.), *The education and training of the mentally retarded: Recent advances* (pp. 145-168). New York: Nichols.

Reiss, S. (1990). Special section on dual diagnosis: Introduction. *American Journal on Mental Retardation, 94,* 577.

Reiss, S., Levitan, G. W., & McNally, R. J. (1982). Emotionally disturbed mentally retarded people: An underserved population. *American Psychologist, 37,* 361-367.

Rojahn, J. (1986). Self-injurious and stereotypic behavior of noninstitutionalized mentally retarded people: Prevalence and classification. *American Journal of Mental Deficiency, 91,* 268-276.

Schroeder, S. R., Mulick, J. A., & Rojahn, J. (1980). The definition, taxonomy, epidemiology, and ecology of self-injurious behavior. *Journal of Autism and Developmental Disorders, 10,* 417-432.

Schroeder, S. R., Schroeder, C. S., Smith, B., & Dalldorf, J. (1978). Prevalence of self-injurious behaviors in a large state facility for the retarded: A three-year follow-up study. *Journal of Autism and Childhood Schizophrenia, 8,* 261-269.

Stark, J. A., Menolascino, F. J., Albarelli, M. H., & Gray, V. C. (Eds.). (1988). *Mental retardation and mental health: Classification, diagnosis, treatment, services.* New York: Springer Verlag.

Tate, B. G., & Baroff, G. S. (1966). Aversive control of self-injurious behavior in a psychotic boy. *Behaviour Research and Therapy, 4,* 281-287.

Winchel, R. M., & Stanley, M. (1991). Self-injurious behavior: A review of the behavior and biology of self-mutilation. *American Journal of Psychiatry, 148,* 306-317.

2

Challenging Behaviors Among Persons With Mental Retardation in Residential Settings

Implications for Policy, Research, and Practice

ROBERT H. BRUININKS
KATHLEEN M. OLSON
SHERYL A. LARSON
K. CHARLIE LAKIN

The needs and characteristics of people who exhibit destructive or challenging behavior can be examined in a variety of ways. The purpose of this chapter is to examine those needs and characteristics in the context of the places in which people with mental retardation live. We begin by examining the changing nature of the residential service delivery system and how challenging behavior influences residential placement patterns. We then move to a review of recent studies that examine the prevalence of challenging behaviors in national studies and a detailed description of the behavioral characteristics of people with mental retardation living in five types of residential settings. We conclude by delineating the implications of our findings for policy makers, researchers, and providers.

AUTHORS' NOTE: Preparation of this manuscript was supported in part by the National Institute on Disability and Rehabilitation Research (Cooperative Agreement No. H133B80050).

Table 2.1 Changes in Residential Placement Patterns for Persons With Mental Retardation Between 1977 and 1991

Type of Facility	1977	1991	Net Change
State MR/DD facility (16+ residents)	154,638	79,407	−75,231
Nonstate MR/DD facility (16+ residents)	52,718	48,001	−4,717
Nursing home	42,242	37,817	−4,425
State MI facility	15,524	1,594	−13,930
Nonstate group home (1-15 residents)	21,182	103,467	82,285
Semi-independent or supported living arrangement	3,658	28,292	24,634
Specialized MR/DD foster home	14,418	21,478	7,060
State group home (1-15 residents)	1,166	8,725	7,559
Total	305,546	328,781	23,235

NOTE: These data are from Amado, Lakin, & Menke (1990) and Lakin et al. (1993).

Changing Service Patterns Influencing Residential Placement Patterns

Dramatic changes in the patterns and nature of residential services are creating new opportunities for persons with mental retardation and growing challenges for providers of residential and related services. National trends away from institutional care toward community residential options have afforded many people with mental retardation increased opportunities to experience meaningful community integration. Although steady growth was seen in the population of public residential institutions through the mid-1960s, the institutional population declined rapidly from its peak of 194,650 average daily residents in 1967 to only 79,407 in 1991 (Lakin, Blake, Prouty, Mangan, & Bruininks, 1993). Almost all persons with developmental disabilities who lived in state psychiatric facilities in 1977 moved to other settings by 1991 (see Table 2.1). Somewhat slower movement from large nonstate settings and nursing homes occurred between 1977 and 1991. Increasing use of community versus institutional care is projected to continue into the 21st century (Lakin, Bruininks, & Larson, 1992).

Movement from state mental retardation/development disability (MR/DD) institutions to community settings is not the only change influencing residential placements in recent years. Major changes also have occurred in the types of community residential options used. Between 1977 and 1991, dramatic growth occurred in small nonstate- and state-operated group homes, semi-independent or supported living arrangements, and specialized MR/DD foster homes. These changes reflect the increasing use of a variety of types of smaller settings in typical neighborhoods. Although people living in formal residential settings are the most visible group of people with mental retardation, as many as 85% of individuals with mental retardation live independently or with natural or adoptive families (Amado, Lakin, & Menke, 1990). Furthermore, though the national population is increasing, the relative stability in number of persons served in residential settings suggests that increasing numbers of persons are remaining within the family home or living independently in community settings.

National statistics reflecting residential placement patterns for people with mental retardation are complimented by research findings showing greater opportunities for meaningful integration in smaller community settings. The benefits of movement from institutions to community living include improvements in adaptive skills (Larson & Lakin, 1989), increased social participation (Molony & Taplin, 1988), increased access to and participation in functional activities within the home (Felce, Thomas, deKock, Saxby, & Repp, 1985), increased opportunities for community participation (Conroy & Bradley, 1985; Conroy, Lemanowicz, Feinstein, & Bernotsky, 1991; Horner, Stoner, & Ferguson, 1988), and overwhelming satisfaction on the part of families with community living arrangements (Larson & Lakin, 1991). Despite these improvements, however, no consistent changes in challenging behavior have been associated with deinstitutionalization (Larson & Lakin, 1989).

Challenging Behavior Influences Residential Options

The presence of challenging behaviors (i.e., those that are hurtful to self, hurtful to others, or destructive to property) in persons with mental retardation adversely affects opportunities to live in community settings. Challenging behavior limits opportunities for admission to community facilities (Hill et al., 1989; Scheerenberger, 1981), contributes to failure of community placements (Hill et al., 1989), and contributes to readmission to larger public residential facilities (Intagliata & Willer, 1982; Lakin, Hill, Hauber, Bruininks, & Heal, 1983; Landesman-Dwyer & Sulzbacher, 1981; Pagel & Whitling, 1978; Scheerenberger, 1981). As a result, higher prevalences of challenging behavior exist in institutions than in community settings (Borthwick-Duffy, Eyman, & White,

1987; Eyman & Borthwick, 1980; Eyman, Borthwick, & Miller, 1981; Eyman & Call, 1977; Hill & Bruininks, 1984; Jacobson, 1982). Furthermore, at least in New York, higher prevalences of challenging behavior are found in community group homes than in smaller foster care, family, or independent settings (Jacobson, 1982).

The presence of challenging behavior not only limits placements in community settings but also limits integration opportunities for persons with mental retardation who do live in community settings. Persons exhibiting challenging behavior have fewer social relationships with other community members (Anderson, Lakin, Hill, & Chen, 1992; Larson, 1991) and have limited opportunities to participate actively in the community (Hill & Bruininks, 1984). People with serious challenging behavior living in a national sample of small (1- to 6-person) group homes participated in fewer leisure activities at home and fewer activities in community settings than people in the same type of setting who did not have challenging behavior (Larson, 1991).

In some cases, community participation for persons with challenging behavior is hampered by inadequate access to needed support services. Individuals in jeopardy of failure in community placements typically have more unmet needs for professional counseling, mental health services, and psychological and behavioral intervention services than individuals whose placements are not in jeopardy (Jacobson & Schwartz, 1983). Lower numbers of service hours from dentists, physical therapists, and teachers have been reported for persons with challenging behavior compared to others who do not exhibit challenging behavior (Jacobson, Silver, & Schwartz, 1984).

Prevalence of Challenging Behavior in National Studies

There are many important reasons for describing the nature and prevalence of challenging behavior among persons with mental retardation in residential settings. As the preceding discussion shows, the presence of challenging behavior clearly influences where and how people with mental retardation live. Knowledge of the extent and severity of challenging behaviors, particularly those of a destructive nature, is critical to the development of programs and services including personnel training and crisis support, which provide opportunities for all individuals with mental retardation, including those who exhibit challenging behavior, to enjoy the benefits of community living.

Although a few contemporary studies have identified the prevalence of challenging behavior across different types of residential settings, most used very general definitions and did not provide specific information about the frequency and severity of particular classes of challenging behavior. Very few recent studies have examined prevalence of challenging behavior among persons in small community living arrangements. This chapter addresses these needs by describing the prevalence, frequency, and severity of three classes of challenging behavior (hurtful to self, hurtful to others, and destructive to property) among persons living in the most common types of residential settings, namely, semi-independent settings, family homes, foster homes, group homes, and institutions. It includes both a review of recent literature and a secondary analysis of several databases reporting rates of these challenging behaviors. Moreover, potential support needs are identified through examination of the typical behavior management approaches of personnel used in each type of setting in responding to challenging behavior.

The literature contains wide variations in reported prevalence rates of challenging behavior among persons with mental retardation. Jacobson (1990), for example, reviewed 23 studies reporting the prevalence of behavior disorders among persons with mental retardation published between 1975 and 1987. He found prevalence estimates ranging from 7% to 70% with wide variations related to the type of study, the type of setting, the age, and the level of mental retardation of the populations sampled. Because of the dramatic changes in the residential service delivery system noted earlier in this chapter, however, many of the setting-based prevalence studies conducted even 10 years ago now are no longer valid. In recent years, residential placement patterns have shifted from a predominantly institutional model (in 1977, 62% of people in non-family settings lived with 16 or more people) to a community system in which most people in residential facilities (56.3% in 1991) live with 15 or fewer people (Lakin et al., 1993). Table 2.1 shows in somewhat more detail the "redistribution" of persons with mental retardation among different types of living arrangements between 1977 and 1991. Because persons with challenging behavior are more likely to be placed in large institutions and are less likely to leave once placed, it is likely that the proportion of people with challenging behavior in settings of various sizes has changed considerably. Given the changing utilization patterns for different types of residential options, only relatively contemporary studies can be used to estimate the prevalence of challenging behavior in residential settings today. With this in mind, this chapter uses only research with data collected in 1985 or later, but even these findings must be viewed with caution as thousands of people move from larger to smaller settings each year.

A recent national study examined the prevalence of challenging behavior in 288 large public institutions for the year ending June 30, 1991 (Lakin et al., 1993). This study noted that an average of 47.8% of people living in large state-operated facilities had an additional handicapping condition labeled behavior disorders. As shown in Figure 2.1, the reported prevalence of behavior disorders within these institutional settings ranged from a low of 23.5% in Montana to a high of 90.0% in Alaska. Clearly, challenging behavior is common among persons with mental retardation in the public facilities surveyed for this national study.

Although reports from facilities and programs provide useful broad estimates of the prevalence of challenging behavior among persons living in supervised settings, they lack the flexibility and detail to evaluate the specific behavioral characteristics of individuals in those settings. The 1987 National Medical Expenditure Survey (NMES), conducted by the U.S. Agency for Health Care Policy and Research, was an individually based survey of 3,618 persons living in mental retardation facilities throughout the United States. The subjects were drawn from a national controlled sample of 691 mental retardation facilities of all sizes except that homes where only 1 or 2 people with mental retardation lived were excluded. Findings of this survey indicated that among residents of settings with 15 or fewer people, 25.2% sometimes tried to physically hurt others, 19.4% sometimes tried to hurt themselves, and 15.0% sometimes tried to steal from others. In the settings with 16 or more people, 29.9% sometimes tried to physically hurt others, 23.6% sometimes tried to hurt themselves, and 16.0% sometimes tried to steal from others (Lakin, Hill, Chen, & Stephens, 1989). These differences between prevalence rates in large and small settings are not very sizable compared to those reported in earlier studies (e.g., Bruininks, Hill, & Morreau, 1988).

The National Medical Expenditure Survey included the largest sample to date of persons in mental retardation facilities from which to draw prevalence estimates for challenging behavior. This study overcame the inflexibility of facility-based data to provide up-to-date prevalence estimates for persons living in all but the smallest facility sizes. Its major limitation in describing the challenging behavior of persons with mental retardation was that it did not include information to judge the frequency or severity of the behavior measured. Information about frequency and severity is needed in addition to prevalence rates to begin

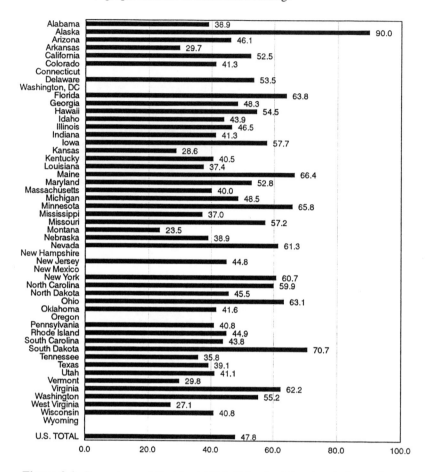

Figure 2.1. Percentage of Residents With Behavior Disorders in Large State-Operated Facilities on June 30, 1991

NOTE: Data presented in the figure are from Lakin et al. (1993).

to understand the nature and extent of supports needed by persons living in various settings. That information may best be gathered using structured individual assessment procedures. Studies summarized in the next section used such procedures to provide further detail on the nature and impact of challenging behavior in residential settings of various sizes and types.

Behavioral Characteristics Among Persons in Five Types of Residential Settings

Procedures

Secondary analyses of four existing databases were used to produce estimates of prevalence, frequency, and severity of challenging behavior classified as destructive to self, to others, and to property. These sources focused on the nature of challenging behavior among persons in five types of residential settings including institutions, group homes, foster homes, family homes, and semi-independent living arrangements.

The first source of data was a 1986-1987 national survey of small (1- to 6-person) foster homes and group homes (Hill et al., 1989). This study used a two-stage nationally representative random survey to identify 181 foster and group homes and 336 people who lived in them. Two residents per facility were selected for an in-depth mail and telephone survey of behavioral characteristics, services, programs, and other community experiences. Challenging behavior was measured using items adapted with permission from the *Inventory for Client and Agency Planning* (ICAP) (Bruininks, Hill, Weatherman, & Woodcock, 1986).

The other three databases were from the states of Montana, South Dakota, and Utah. All three states adopted the ICAP for monitoring and planning services at the state level. In Montana, all adults and children with a primary or secondary diagnosis of mental retardation or autism who were receiving services for persons with developmental disabilities were included in the sample except those living in institutions. The sample did not include children and adolescents in public school who were not receiving other nonschool services or people living in nursing homes. In all 1,239 people were included in the Montana sample. In South Dakota, the sample included all adults with a primary or secondary diagnosis of mental retardation or autism who were receiving any type of human services except those only receiving school-based services or living in nursing homes. A total of 1,612 people were included in the South Dakota sample. In Utah, all adults living in the Utah State Training School or receiving day habilitation and training services were included in the sample. A total of 1,743 people were included in the Utah sample. The entire ICAP assessment was available for each person in these databases.

The subjects from each database lived in one of five types of residential settings: independent or semi-independent living arrangements, family homes, foster homes, group homes, and public institutions. Semi-independent living arrangements included those listed on the ICAP as independent in own home or rental unit, independent with regular home-based services or monitoring, room and board without personal care, or semi-independent unit with supervisory staff in the building. Family settings included those where the person was living with natural or adoptive parents or relatives. Foster homes for the three state databases included those identified as foster homes on the ICAP. For the Foster Care/Group Home study, foster homes were defined as a residence owned or rented by a family as their own home, with 6 or fewer people with mental retardation living as family members (Hill et al., 1989). Group homes for the three state databases included group residences with staff providing care, supervision, and training. They included both ICF-MR (Intermediate Care Facilities for the Mentally Retarded) certified and non-ICF-MR certified homes. Group homes for the Foster Care/Group Home study were defined the same way but included only homes with 6 or fewer residents. Almost all group home residents lived with 15 or fewer people with mental retardation. Institutions were large publicly operated residential facilities.

Table 2.2 shows the distribution of subjects from each database who lived in each type of residential facility. The number of studies represented varied by facility type. In some studies where representative information could not be obtained about a type of facility, all persons from that facility type were excluded from this analysis. For example, neither adults nor children in Montana who lived in institutions were included in this report. One study, the 1986-1987 Foster Care/Group Home study, did not survey any people in semi-independent, family, or institution settings. Although some overlap exists between the samples for different facility types, they are not identical. For example, the foster home and group home categories included children and adults from both statewide and national samples, whereas the institution category included only adults from Montana and South Dakota. The data within each setting type should be reviewed separately, and direct comparisons among facility types should be made with caution.

Subjects

Altogether 5,338 persons with mental retardation were included in these secondary analyses. As Table 2.3 shows, just over one half of the

Table 2.2 Number of Subjects From Each Source According to Type of Facility

| | Type of Setting | | | | | |
State/Study	Semi-Independent	Family	Foster	Group	Institution	Total
Montana—Adults	332	287	66	554	0	1,239
Montana—Children	0	313	43	52	0	408
South Dakota—Adults	349	126	57	641	439	1,612
Utah—Adults	199	511	47	457	529	1,743
1986 FGH Study	0	0	138	198	0	336
Total	880	1,237	351	1,902	968	5,338

Table 2.3 Characteristics of the Sample in Each Type of Residential Setting

| | Type of Setting | | | | |
Characteristic	Semi-Independent	Family	Foster	Group	Institution
Level of Mental Retardation					
Mild	78.0	40.3	31.5	32.4	8.0
Moderate	16.6	32.4	35.0	29.9	5.2
Severe	5.2	13.7	24.6	24.5	15.6
Profound	0.2	4.9	5.7	13.0	71.3
MR, level unknown	0.0	8.7	3.2	0.2	0.0
Age Group					
0-4	0.0	9.1	5.7	0.0	0.0
5-9	0.0	8.6	6.3	0.3	0.0
10-14	0.0	4.9	5.4	1.4	0.0
15-17	0.0	2.7	5.4	1.8	0.0
18-21	6.9	6.7	10.0	8.0	10.3
22-39	59.9	57.2	38.5	55.9	60.5
40-62	30.5	10.5	23.1	28.7	25.1
63+	2.7	0.3	5.7	3.8	4.0
Gender					
Male	53.1	53.5	51.0	53.8	55.8
Female	46.9	46.5	49.0	46.2	44.2

NOTE: The numbers in this table represent percentages of individuals within a particular type of setting who have each characteristic.

people in each type of setting were male. Other characteristics varied by type of setting.

Semi-Independent

The independent/semi-independent living sample included 880 adults from Montana, South Dakota, and Utah. The majority presented mild (78.0%) or moderate (16.6%) mental retardation. Most were in the 22- to 39-year age group.

Family

The family sample included 313 children from Montana and 924 adults from Montana, South Dakota, and Utah. The majority presented mild (40.3%) or moderate (32.4%) mental retardation. Very few of the adults living with their families were more than 39 years old.

Foster

The foster home sample included a few people from each database, with the largest number drawn from the national Foster Care/Group Home study (138). Subjects were somewhat equally divided among the mild, moderate, and severe categories of mental retardation. The foster home sample had the greatest proportion of children 18 or under (23.8%) and of adults who were 63 or over (5.7%).

Group Homes

The group home sample included 1,902 people from all of the databases. The subjects were equally distributed among mild, moderate, and severe levels of mental retardation. More than 50% (55.9%) of those in group home settings were in the 22-39 age group. All the subjects except for a few from Utah lived in homes with 15 or fewer other people with mental retardation.

Institutions

The institution sample included 968 adults from South Dakota and Utah. It represented the entire public institution population in each of those states. Most people in the institution sample had profound mental retardation (71.3%), compared with a national average of 63.7% in state

Table 2.4 Staff Responses to Challenging Behavior for Persons Who Exhibit at Least One ICAP Behavior

Response Category	ICAP Definition
No response	Do nothing, or offer comfort
Verbal response	Ask client to stop, reason with him or her
	Ask client to amend or correct the situation
	Ask client to leave room, sit elsewhere (time out)
	Take away privileges from client
Nonverbal response	Purposely ignore, reward other behavior
	Structure or restructure surroundings, remove materials
Physical response	Physically redirect, remove, or restrain client
Get help	Get help (two or more people needed to control client)

institutions (White, Lakin, Bruininks, & Li, 1991). Most of the people in institutional settings were between 22 and 39 years old.

Instrumentation

The databases included in the secondary analysis used all or part of the *Inventory for Client and Agency Planning* (ICAP) (Bruininks et al., 1986) for data collection. The ICAP is an instrument for gathering individual client information (diagnostic status, functional limitations, adaptive behavior, problem behavior, and service history and needs) important to planning and evaluating services for people with disabilities (see Johnson, 1989, and Wikoff, 1989, for further review). The ICAP problem behavior section measures the frequency and severity of eight categories of challenging behavior including hurtful to self, hurtful to others, destructive to property, disruptive behavior, unusual or repetitive habits, socially offensive behavior, withdrawal or inattentive behavior, and uncooperative behavior.

Prevalence, frequency, and severity of the three categories of challenging behavior from the ICAP that are destructive in nature were examined in this study. Those categories included behaviors that are hurtful to self, hurtful to others, or destructive to property. The hurtful-to-self category included behavior that "injures own body—for example, by hitting self, banging head, scratching, cutting or puncturing, biting, rubbing skin, pulling out hair, picking on skin, biting nails, or pinching." The hurtful-to-others category included behavior that "causes physical pain to other people or to animals—for example, by hitting, kicking, biting, pinching, scratching, pulling hair, or striking with an object." The destructive-to-property category included behavior that "deliberately breaks, defaces, or destroys things—for example, by hitting, tearing or cutting, throwing, burning, marking or scratching things" (Bruininks et al., 1986, p. 8).

In addition to providing information about the prevalence, frequency, and severity of challenging behavior, the ICAP also provides an indication of the most typical staff responses to challenging behavior. These data were collected for each person who exhibited at least one of the eight ICAP categories of challenging behavior. Five categories of staff response were coded including no response, nonverbal response, verbal response, physical response, and get help. Table 2.4 defines each of these responses.

Results

Behavioral Characteristics

Three types of information were gathered about the challenging behavior exhibited by people with mental retardation living in these five setting types (see Table 2.5). First, the proportion of people who did not exhibit any of the eight ICAP challenging behavior categories was noted. Next the proportion of people who exhibited behaviors hurtful to self, hurtful to others, or destructive to property was presented. Finally, a breakdown of the frequency and severity with which each type of behavior occurred was noted. The frequency and severity ratings included only the people who exhibited the behavior.

Semi-Independent

Among the 880 adults with mental retardation living independently or in semi-independent settings, 22.4% did not exhibit any of the eight ICAP challenging behaviors. Furthermore, few exhibited the three most serious types of behavior: hurtful to others (14.1%), destructive to property (12.8%), and hurtful to self (10.0%). Of those who hurt others or damaged property, fewer than 1% did so more than once a week. On the other hand, 13.7% of those who hurt themselves did so at least once a day, and 35.3% did so at least once a week.

Table 2.5 Behavioral Characteristics of Subjects in Each Type of
Residential Setting

Characteristic	Type of Setting				
	Semi-Independent	Family	Foster	Group	Institution
% with no challenging behavior	22.4	28.7	33.0	11.3	8.5
			Hurtful to Self		
Prevalence—% Hurtful to Self	10.0	12.8	17.7	31.0	46.4
Frequency When Exhibited					
Less than monthly	36.4	21.0	27.3	26.5	15.2
1-3 per month	28.4	21.0	21.8	25.8	20.9
1-6 per week	21.6	26.9	23.6	24.9	28.0
1-16 per day	11.4	25.1	23.6	16.6	25.8
1+ per hour	2.3	6.0	3.6	6.2	10.1
Severity When Exhibited					
Not serious	27.3	11.4	18.2	16.4	10.1
Slightly serious	42.0	50.9	45.5	43.5	33.9
Moderately serious	23.9	28.7	27.3	29.0	32.3
Very serious	5.7	7.2	7.3	9.5	17.5
Extremely serious	1.1	1.8	1.8	1.6	6.3
			Hurtful to Others		
Prevalence—% Hurtful to Others	14.1	15.9	18.6	35.6	49.6
Frequency When Exhibited					
Less than monthly	75.0	54.5	56.7	53.8	29.2
1-3 per month	19.4	21.3	18.3	30.7	30.7
1-6 per week	4.8	14.9	13.3	11.8	26.7
1-16 per day	0.8	7.4	11.7	3.4	11.9
1+ per hour	0.0	2.0	0.0	0.3	1.5
Severity When Exhibited					
Not serious	16.9	18.3	21.7	14.3	14.4
Slightly serious	49.2	51.5	41.7	46.2	34.2
Moderately serious	26.6	20.8	30.0	27.5	30.1
Very serious	4.8	8.4	1.7	9.9	15.4
Extremely serious	2.4	1.0	5.0	2.1	5.8
			Destructive to Property		
Prevalence—% Destructive to Property	12.8	10.1	13.0	29.8	33.8
Frequency When Exhibited					
Less than monthly	69.6	48.4	45.5	47.3	24.3
1-3 per month	27.8	19.4	25.0	33.9	31.7
1-6 per week	2.6	21.8	25.0	14.4	27.4

Table 2.5 Continued

	Type of Setting				
Characteristic	Semi-Independent	Family	Foster	Group	Institution
1-16 per day	0.0	9.7	4.5	4.2	10.8
1+ per hour	0.0	0.8	0.0	0.2	5.9
Severity When Exhibited					
Not serious	11.3	12.1	22.7	17.0	8.9
Slightly serious	52.2	41.9	40.9	42.6	35.7
Moderately serious	27.8	37.1	29.6	31.6	32.6
Very serious	7.0	8.1	2.3	7.6	19.1
Extremely serious	1.7	0.8	4.6	1.3	3.7

NOTE: The prevalence figures represent the percentages of people in each type of setting who ever display the behavior. The frequency and severity figures are also percentages, but they are calculated using only the people in that setting who actually exhibit each type of behavior.

Family

Of the 1,237 adults and children in family homes, 28.7% never exhibited any of the eight ICAP challenging behaviors. Furthermore, few exhibited the three types of destructive behaviors considered here. The most common destructive behavior in family settings was behavior hurtful to others (15.9%). Most of the destructive behavior exhibited by people living with families did not cause serious problems. However, a small portion of individuals (about 9% of those who exhibit each type of behavior) exhibited destructive behaviors that created very or extremely serious problems.

Foster

Among the five facility types examined, the highest proportion of people without any challenging behavior (33.0%) lived in foster homes. At the same time, however, of the three smallest types of living arrangements (i.e., semi-independent, family, and foster homes), people living in foster homes were most likely to exhibit the three types of destructive behavior profiled here. Behavior that was hurtful to others was the most common challenging behavior (18.6%). Behavior hurtful to self caused the most serious problems among those in foster settings (9.1% of those who hurt themselves caused very serious to extremely serious problems in doing so).

Group Homes

The largest sample in this study was from group home settings (*n* = 1,902). Unlike people living in the three smaller types of settings, only a few (11.3%) had none of the eight target behaviors. About one third of group home residents were hurtful to themselves, to others, or to property. Behavior hurtful to others was the most prevalent form of destructive behavior (35.6%). All three types of challenging behavior caused at least moderately serious problems for about 40% of the approximately 33% of persons who exhibited those behaviors in group home settings.

Institutions

Not unexpectedly, given the findings of earlier studies, challenging behavior occurred more commonly among the residents of institutions than among those of any other type of residential setting. Almost one half of institution residents were hurtful to themselves or to others. Furthermore, most people in institutions who hurt themselves or others did so at least one to six times per week. More than 50% of institution residents who engaged in each type of destructive behavior caused at least moderately serious problems in doing so.

Although comparisons among these five types of residential settings must be made with caution, several commonalities are evident (see Table 2.5). First, across all settings, all three types of challenging behavior occurred with substantial frequency or severity among some people. On the other hand, most people in each type of residential setting did not engage in behavior that was hurtful to themselves, others, or property. Finally, the prevalence, frequency, and severity of challenging behavior was greater in settings providing more intensive care and supervision, namely institutions and group homes, than in other residential settings.

Staff Responses

In addition to the examination of the rates and severity of challenging behavior, the typical response by staff members to challenging behavior also was examined. Table 2.6 shows the responses of staff to all eight categories of ICAP problem behavior for individuals who exhibited one or more behaviors. The 8.5% (of institution residents) to 33.0% (of foster home residents) who did not engage in any ICAP challenging behaviors were excluded in these analyses. Across environments, staff members reported actively responding to more than 90% of all reported

Table 2.6 Staff Responses to Challenging Behavior in Each Type of Setting

| | Type of Setting | | | | |
Staff Response	Semi-Independent	Family	Foster	Group	Institution
No response needed	6.1	7.3	5.5	5.7	5.3
Verbal response	75.3	63.6	66.3	52.8	50.4
Nonverbal response	18.1	25.3	22.1	32.7	19.5
Physical response	0.3	3.2	5.7	7.4	23.1
Get help from others	0.2	0.5	0.4	1.5	1.7

challenging behavior. Verbal responses were the most common responses in all types of residential settings, followed by nonverbal responses. Although physical responses were used in all environments, they were used most frequently in institutions.

Discussion

As we as a society try to improve residential services to enhance the independence of all people with mental retardation, it is critical to have information about the behavioral characteristics and needs of people with mental retardation in all sectors of the service delivery system. Information about challenging behavior is needed to manage and improve services and supports for individuals with mental retardation and their families. This chapter used a variety of sources and special analyses to identify trends with important implications for improving services, practices, and supports to enhance the independence and integration of persons with mental retardation. We have used three state databases and a national survey, all of which used the same assessment tool, to make our estimates. Other states, including New York and California, also have developed databases that include information about challenging behavior of persons with mental retardation. The California database information is presented elsewhere in this volume (see Borthwick-Duffy, Chapter 1).

Although much can be learned about challenging behavior from these data, several cautions should be considered in applying this information. The process of determining the prevalence, frequency, and severity of challenging behavior among persons with mental retardation in various living arrangements is difficult at best. Observed variation in reported prevalence rates may have arisen from several sources including differing definitions of behavior challenges, variation in the time frame used to identify behavior, variation in the method of obtaining information, the use of clinical populations rather than populations representative of the community, and, perhaps most notably, the shifting pattern of residential living arrangements for persons with mental retardation and developmental disabilities. All of these factors likely influence statistical findings and descriptions of service populations in both the existing literature and, to a lesser extent, the results summarized in this chapter.

An additional caution relates to the representativeness of the groups included in this study. Although this study included all individuals who had been in formal contact with state service agencies in South Dakota and Montana, in Utah those who were not in institutions or who did not receive day habilitation services were not included. None of these samples included individuals with mental retardation who had not been in formal contact with state agencies and thus may underrepresent individuals who are living independently of formal service systems. This is particularly important for children and older adults living with family members who may draw services primarily from agencies other than the mental retardation system, if they use them at all. Another issue is that South Dakota, Montana, and Utah are states with primarily rural populations. The data from these states may or may not reflect national population characteristics.

A final caution is that although a strong association may exist between placement and behavior challenges, a causal relation should not be inferred from these data. In many instances, multiple interrelated factors influence residential placements, service delivery, and community participation. Most notable among these is level of mental retardation. In the samples examined in this study, the differences in level of mental retardation across setting types were at least as pronounced as the differences in challenging behavior. These differences likely affect both placement patterns and staff responses to challenging behavior.

Implications

Despite the limitations noted, the findings summarized in this chapter raise several issues regarding serving persons with mental retardation who have challenging behavior in various residential settings. Those issues need to be addressed by policy makers, researchers, and providers. This section highlights a few of these issues and their implications.

For Policy Makers

Because challenging behaviors are present among people in all types of living arrangements, resources to address such behavior must be available to people in a wide range of environments. This is particularly an issue for people who live with their families. Although the proportion of people with challenging behavior in family settings is lower than in most other settings, the sheer number of people with challenging behavior living with families may be higher because the total number of people living with family members is much higher (up to 85% of all people with mental retardation live on their own or with family members). Therefore, if challenging behavior is associated with higher rates of out-of-home placement, and if policy makers are interested in reducing the need for costly out-of-home placement, then the provision of support to individuals and families is critical.

The availability of resources to serve persons with challenging behavior is also an issue in all other small community settings including foster homes, semi-independent living arrangements, small group homes, schools, work settings, and recreation settings. As more and more people leave institutions and large private facilities and others are never placed there, we can expect to see even higher numbers of people with challenging behavior in community settings. This has several implications. First, if community providers are to serve increasing numbers of people with challenging behavior, staff training and technical support must be provided and improved to enable providers to successfully serve people with more intense needs. Second, crisis intervention services must be more broadly available to prevent episodes of severe or persistent challenging behavior from jeopardizing community living opportunities. As ever greater numbers of persons with challenging behavior move to community settings, the rates of reinstitutionalization related to challenging behavior must be minimized. Finally, staff wages must be increased in community settings to attract and retain qualified staff (Lakin, 1988). Currently wages are higher for staff working in institutions than for staff in community settings by a large margin (Braddock & Mitchell, 1992). Well-trained and adequately paid staff are essential to the provision of quality community services. The fact that a disproportionate number of persons with severe challenging behavior live in restrictive environments and that a leading cause of placement in restrictive settings continues to be challenging behavior suggests that the community service delivery system has not dealt successfully with challenging behavior among persons with mental retardation. As the population is redistributed across residential settings and a wide range of community environments, resources need to be allocated in proportion both to the actual number of people in each type of setting and to the severity of their needs. Because of the costs in financial and human terms, addressing the issues of wage equity and expansion of training and technical support are essential strategies to reduce public costs and expand personal independence and opportunity for persons with mental retardation who exhibit challenging behavior.

For Researchers

There are many needs for research related to serving individuals with challenging behavior in community settings. As we noted earlier, conducting research on the prevalence of challenging behavior is difficult, and many studies are beset with biases of various types. Jacobson (1990) suggested a need for less biased epidemiological methods in the measurement of prevalence rates. In addition to these methodological changes, we also suggest changes in the scope of information collected. We recommend that future studies measure not only the prevalence rates of challenging behavior but also the frequency and severity of the behavior exhibited. Ongoing controlled, unbiased studies of the prevalence, frequency, and severity of challenging behavior exhibited in various types of residential settings are needed to evaluate the changes in service needs for persons with challenging behavior as the characteristics of residential settings and placement patterns continue to evolve.

In addition to studies describing the type, frequency, and severity of challenging behavior, future research should include both demonstrations of effective service strategies and studies documenting the frustrations encountered as attempts to serve persons with challenging behavior in small community and family settings continue. Further, future research should examine the impacts of challenging behavior on opportunities for integration into typical community, recreation, and social environments. This suggestion implies increased attention to the application of treatments in normal living and community environments to increase the social validity and application of research results in typical service settings. Much research is needed to identify the critical aspects of residential and other community settings that contribute to the provision of high-quality services and the reduction of challenging behavior among persons with mental retardation. Specific suggestions related to behavioral intervention strategies, experimental methodologies, prevention strategies, staff training strategies, and service delivery issues can be found in the final report from the recent National Working Conference on Positive Approaches to the Management of Excess Behavior (Reichle, 1990).

Research to address challenging behavior among persons with mental retardation must not focus only on persons who exhibit such behavior. The supports and training provided by direct service staff members are critical to whether behavioral interventions will be successful. Unfortunately, community programs experience great difficulty in retaining and training staff members (turnover rates in community residential settings average 50% to 70% annually; Larson & Lakin, 1992). Therefore, a substantial investment must be made in researching various staff management and training strategies to reduce turnover problems in home and community settings. Research that leads to improvements in retention and training increases the likelihood that positive treatment strategies will be properly used, and that staffing problems will not so jeopardize the effectiveness of interventions that more expensive personal and social alternatives must be sought to address challenging behavior.

A final area of research relates to investigation of strategies used by staff members to address challenging behavior. In this study, physical responses to challenging behavior were more commonly reported in institutional settings than in community settings. Research is needed to examine the relative influence of the challenging behavior exhibited, resident characteristics such as IQ, available technology, staffing patterns, and staff and agency philosophy on the use of various intervention strategies. This is particularly important in small community settings because although institutions and licensed group homes have well-established systems in place to monitor the use of physically intrusive procedures, such systems are new or not yet developed for the other types of residential environments. Furthermore, with the current emphasis on the use of nonaversive interventions, monitoring and evaluation of the strategies used in different types of settings become all the more important. Careful attention to use of intrusive interventions is needed to safeguard consumers as providers serve increasing numbers of persons with challenging behavior in increasingly decentralized community settings.

For Providers

In this summary we noted that many individuals did not display destructive challenging behavior. For those people, challenging behavior will not be prominent among the factors influencing placement decisions. At the same time, however, some people in every type of residential setting do exhibit challenging behavior. For those individuals, community living arrangements are needed that can effectively meet the needs of persons with frequent or severe challenging behavior. The finding that group homes, foster homes, and semi-independent living settings now serve some individuals with frequent and severe problems is encouraging. However, it is also important to recognize that serious destructive behaviors frequently are associated with failure in family and community placements. Providers of community residential services must accept the challenge to identify and implement practices that effectively address the needs of persons with challenging behavior. National organizations and governmental agencies, therefore, should increase support for evaluating and describing programs that successfully serve persons with substantial challenging behavior.

The number of persons with challenging behavior living in community settings will continue to grow as institutions and large private facilities are closed or reduced in size. This means providers of all types of residential services will experience increased demands for trained and qualified staff to provide services to persons with challenging behavior. Providers must identify training and consultation needs of staff members so this demand can be met, and all persons, including those with challenging behavior, will have the opportunity to live in integrated community settings.

Conclusion

Manifestations of challenging behavior clearly limit life opportunities for some persons with mental retardation. But findings presented in this chapter present an optimistic picture in which many persons with mental retardation do not exhibit challenging behavior or present behavior that is relatively mild in impact. For the others, however, the presence of very frequent or very severe challenging behavior is costly in lost opportunities and service expenditures. The presence of challenging behavior among persons in service programs represents a serious concern. Fortunately, this concern is one that can be addressed through research and available training and consultation strategies. For thousands of persons with mental retardation and their families, the application of available knowledge can reduce personal and public costs resulting from challenging behavior. More important, concerted activities to address such problems of adjustment can materially reduce the costs of services and expand the opportunities for meaningful inclusion and participation of persons with mental retardation in our communities.

References

Amado, A. N., Lakin, K. C., & Menke, J. M. (1990). *1990 chartbook on services for people with developmental disabilities.* Minneapolis: University of Minnesota, Center for Residential Services and Community Living.

Anderson, D. J., Lakin, K. C., Hill, B. K., & Chen, T. H. (1992). Social integration of older persons with mental retardation in residential facilities. *American Journal on Mental Retardation, 96,* 488-501.

Borthwick-Duffy, S. A., Eyman, R. K., & White, J. F. (1987). Client characteristics and residential placement patterns. *American Journal of Mental Deficiency, 92,* 24-30.

Braddock, D., & Mitchell, D. (1992). *Residential services and developmental disabilities in the United States: A national survey of staff compensation, turnover, and related issues.* Washington, DC: American Association on Mental Retardation.

Bruininks, R. H., Hill, B. K., & Morreau, L. E. (1988). Prevalence and implications of maladaptive behaviors and dual diagnosis in residential and other service programs. In J. A. Stark, F. J. Menolascino, M. H. Albarelli, & V. C. Gray (Eds.), *Mental retardation and mental health: Classification, diagnosis, treatment, services* (pp. 1-29). New York: Springer Verlag.

Bruininks, R. H., Hill, B. K., Weatherman, R. F., & Woodcock, R. W. (1986). *Inventory for client and agency planning.* Allen, TX: DLM Teaching Resources.

Conroy, J. W., & Bradley, V. J. (1985). *The Pennhurst longitudinal study: A report of five years of research and analysis.* Philadelphia: Temple University Developmental Disabilities Center.

Conroy, J. W., Lemanowicz, J. A., Feinstein, C. S., & Bernotsky, J. M. (1991). *1990 results of the CARC v. Thorne longitudinal study.* Narberth, PA: Conroy and Feinstein Associates.

Eyman, R. K., & Borthwick, S. A. (1980). Patterns of care for mentally retarded persons. *Mental Retardation, 18,* 63-66.

Eyman, R. K., Borthwick, S. A., & Miller, C. (1981). Trends in maladaptive behavior of mentally retarded persons placed in community and institutional settings. *American Journal of Mental Deficiency, 85,* 473-477.

Eyman, R. K., & Call, T. (1977). Maladaptive behavior and community placement of mentally retarded persons. *American Journal of Mental Deficiency, 82,* 137-144.

Felce, D., Thomas, M., deKock, U., Saxby, H., & Repp, A. (1985). An ecological comparison of small community-based houses and traditional institutions II. *Behavior Research and Therapy, 23,* 337-348.

Hill, B. K., & Bruininks, R. H. (1984). Maladaptive behavior of mentally retarded individuals in residential facilities. *American Journal of Mental Deficiency, 88,* 380-387.

Hill, B. K., Lakin, K. C., Bruininks, R. H., Amado, A. N., Anderson, D. J., & Copher, J. I. (1989). *Living in the community: A comparative study of foster homes and small group homes for people with mental retardation* (Report No. 28). Minneapolis: University of Minnesota, Center for Residential and Community Services.

Horner, R. H., Stoner, S. K., & Ferguson, D. L. (1988). *An activity-based analysis of deinstitutionalization: The effects of community re-entry on the lives of residents leaving Oregon's Fairview Training Center.* Eugene: University of Oregon, Specialized Training Program, Center on Human Development.

Intagliata, J., & Willer, B. (1982). Reinstitutionalization of mentally retarded persons successfully placed into family-care and group homes. *American Journal of Mental Deficiency, 87,* 34-39.

Jacobson, J. W. (1982). Problem behavior and psychiatric impairment within a developmentally disabled population I: Behavior frequency. *Applied Research in Mental Retardation, 3,* 121-139.

Jacobson, J. W. (1990). Assessing the prevalence of psychiatric disorders in a developmentally disabled population. In E. Dibble & D. B. Gray (Eds.), *Assessment of behavior problems with persons with mental retardation living in the community* (pp. 19-70). Rockville, MD: Department of Health and Human Services, National Institutes of Health, Public Health Service, Alcohol, Drug Abuse, and Mental Health Administration.

Jacobson, J. W., & Schwartz, A. A. (1983). Personal and service characteristics affecting group home placement success: A prospective analysis. *Mental Retardation, 21,* 1-7.

Jacobson, J. W., Silver, E. J., & Schwartz, A. A. (1984). Service provision in New York's group homes. *Mental Retardation, 22,* 231-239.

Johnson, R. (1989). Review of the Inventory for Client and Agency Planning. In J. C. Conoley & J. J. Kramer (Eds.), *The tenth mental measurements yearbook* (pp. 394-395). Lincoln, NE: Buros Institute of Mental Measurements.

Lakin, K. C. (1988). Strategies for promoting the stability of direct care staff. In M. P. Janicki, M. W. Krauss, & M. M. Seltzer (Eds.), *Community residences for persons with developmental disabilities* (pp. 231-238). Baltimore, MD: Paul H. Brookes.

Lakin, K. C., Blake, E. M., Prouty, R. W., Mangan, T., & Bruininks, R. H. (1993). *Residential services for persons with developmental disabilities: Status and trends through 1991.* Minneapolis: University of Minnesota, Center on Residential Services and Community Living, Institute on Community Integration (UAP).

Lakin, K. C., Bruininks, R. H., & Larson, S. A. (1992). The changing face of residential services. In L. Rowitz (Ed.), *Mental retardation in the year 2000* (pp. 197-247). New York: Springer Verlag.

Lakin, K. C., Hill, B. K., Chen, T. H., & Stephens, S. A. (1989). *Persons with mental retardation and related conditions in mental retardation facilities: Selected findings*

48   Challenging Behaviors in Residential Settings

from the 1987 National Medical Expenditure Survey (Report No. 29). Minneapolis: University of Minnesota, Center for Residential and Community Services.

Lakin, K. C., Hill, B. K., Hauber, F. A., Bruininks, R. H., & Heal, L. W. (1983). New admissions and readmissions to a national sample of public residential facilities. *American Journal of Mental Deficiency, 88,* 13-20.

Landesman-Dwyer, S., & Sulzbacher, F. M. (1981). Residential placement and adaptation of severely and profoundly retarded individuals. In R. H. Bruininks, C. E. Meyers, B. B. Sigford, & K. C. Lakin (Eds.), *Deinstitutionalization and community adjustment of mentally retarded persons* (pp. 182-194). Washington, DC: American Association on Mental Deficiency.

Larson, S. A. (1991). Quality of life for people with challenging behavior living in community settings. *Impact: Feature Issue on Challenging Behavior, 4*(1), 4-5. [Minneapolis: University of Minnesota, Institute on Community Integration (UAP)]

Larson, S. A., & Lakin, K. C. (1989). Deinstitutionalization of persons with mental retardation: Behavioral outcomes. *Journal of the Association for Persons With Severe Handicaps, 14,* 324-332.

Larson, S. A., & Lakin, K. C. (1991). Parent attitudes about residential placement before and after deinstitutionalization: A research synthesis. *Journal of the Association for Persons With Severe Handicaps, 16,* 25-38.

Larson, S. A., & Lakin, K. C. (1992). Direct-care staff stability in a national sample of small group homes. *Mental Retardation, 30,* 13-22.

Molony, H., & Taplin, J. (1988). Deinstitutionalization of people with developmental disability. *Australia and New Zealand Journal of Developmental Disabilities, 14,* 109-122.

Pagel, S. E., & Whitling, C. A. (1978). Readmissions to a state hospital for mentally retarded persons: Reasons for community placement failure. *Mental Retardation, 16,* 164-166.

Reichle, J. (Ed.). (1990, June). *National working conference on positive approaches to the management of excess behavior: Final report and recommendations.* Minneapolis: University of Minnesota, Research and Training Center on Residential Services and Community Living.

Scheerenberger, R. C. (1981). Deinstitutionalization: Trends and difficulties. In R. H. Bruininks, C. E. Meyer, B. B. Sigford, & K. C. Lakin (Eds.), *Deinstitutionalization and community adjustment of mentally retarded people* (pp. 3-13). Washington, DC: American Association on Mental Deficiency.

White, C. C., Lakin, K. C., Bruininks, R. H., & Li, X. (1991). *Persons with mental retardation and related conditions in state-operated residential facilities: Year ending June 30, 1989, with longitudinal trends from 1950 to 1989.* Minneapolis: University of Minnesota, Center for Residential and Community Services.

Wikoff, R. L. (1989). Review of the Inventory for Client and Agency Planning. In J. C. Conoley & J. J. Kramer (Eds.), *The tenth mental measurements yearbook* (pp. 385-387). Lincoln, NE: Buros Institute of Mental Measurements.

3

Epidemiology and Topographic Taxonomy of Self-Injurious Behavior

JOHANNES ROJAHN

Prevalence of SIB

One of the most basic requirements for obtaining reasonably accurate estimates of prevalence of a phenomenon is the capability of the researcher to classify correctly the index cases in a population. With self-injurious behavior (SIB) (and with many other behavioral phenomena for that matter), case classification has been a problem.

Case classification of a behavioral phenomenon is closely related to the behavior definition. Depending on the kind of definition used, one can identify two basic types of epidemiologic studies on self-injurious behavior. The first one classifies different forms of SIB under a global category (*global classification*), whereas the second one distinguishes between specific SIB subtypes (*specific classification*). An example of a global SIB assessment instrument is the Behavior Development Survey (Neuropsychiatric Research Group, 1979), which features only one SIB item, "Does physical violence to self." This single, generic item is expected to capture reliably topographies that are as discrepant as

AUTHOR'S NOTE: Preparation of this manuscript was supported in part by grants awarded from the U.S. Department of Health and Human Services, Administration on Developmental Disabilities (Grant No. 07DD0270/16), and Bureau of Maternal and Child Health and Resources Development, Division of Maternal and Child Health (Grant MCJ #922), to Nisonger Center, a University Affiliated Program at The Ohio State University. I would like to thank Michael G. Aman for his suggestions on earlier versions of the manuscript.

self-banging and self-induced vomiting, to exclude behaviors that typically are not considered SIB although somebody may argue they ought to be (e.g., nicotine consumption), and to provide clarification about behaviors that have proven to be controversial as to whether they do or do not constitute SIB (e.g., pica). Global SIB assessment is based on two unsubstantiated assumptions: (a) it is heuristically and/or clinically unnecessary to distinguish among these different behaviors and (b) global categories reliably classify SIB cases.

The specific approach suggests that a global SIB category is too nonspecific, and that it is prudent until evidence to the contrary has been accumulated to collect data that allow us to make differential statements about specific topographical subtypes of SIB. As I try to show in this chapter, little evidence exists to justify global SIB assessment, because SIB consists of a very heterogeneous group of behaviors (c.f. Schroeder, Mulick, & Rojahn, 1980).

Global SIB data usually are collected in studies that have a much wider scope of interest than just SIB, and they typically are based on relatively large populations and tend to have appropriate sampling procedures. Specific SIB studies, on the other hand, typically employ single-site surveys of selective populations, such as the residents from one developmental center, which yield information of questionable generalizability. Therefore, global SIB assessment studies tend to be more representative than most specific SIB studies. In other words, although studies with global SIB assessment are often superior as far as sampling procedures are concerned, specific SIB studies have an advantage in the greater detail provided for assessment.

Prevalence of Global SIB

As mentioned above, global SIB definitions often appear in studies with a wider focus of inquiry than SIB alone and typically include a host of variables such as complete adaptive behavior instruments encompassing adaptive and maladaptive behaviors, medical, residential, occupational, information, service needs, and so on. The reason for the lack of differentiation in the SIB classification in those studies is often one of economy and necessity to keep the number of items at a manageable size. Three global epidemiology studies from the United States and one from Europe were chosen as examples (see Table 3.1). These studies were selected because (a) they were published after 1980, (b) they featured acceptable sampling procedures, (c) they incorporated the full

Table 3.1 Prevalence (Number of Cases in 100) of Global SIB in
Populations With Mental Retardation

	Prevalence	Number of Cases	Size of Sampling Frame
Borthwick et al. (1981)	6.5	372*	6,202
Jacobson (1982)	8.2	2,632*	32,112
Hill & Bruininks (1984)	16.4*	323*	2,271
Kebbon & Windahl (1985)	4.2	1,198	28,215

*These figures were not made available in the original publications; they were projected by the author
from other published figures.

spectrum of levels of mental retardation and chronological age, and, (d)
as a consequence, they were representative for identifiable populations.

For the first study, Borthwick, Meyers, and Eyman (1981) surveyed
6,202 persons from three western U.S. states (Arizona, California, and
Nevada) who received state-funded developmental disability services
at the time. Data were collected via the above-mentioned Behavior
Development Survey, which has institution and community norms, an
empirically determined factor structure, and acceptable levels of in-
formant agreement. The next set of data came from the New York State
service database, which held more than 30,000 clients at the time
(Jacobson, 1982). Subjects were individuals who had a developmental
disability and/or who were in need of developmental disability services.
Data routinely were collected with the Developmental Disabilities Information Survey (Janicki & Jacobson, 1982). Raters were professional
and paraprofessional staff familiar with the subject being surveyed. A
three-stage sampling procedure was designed to include those who
actually received services as well as those who were eligible but who
did not. The third study was a national survey by Hill and Bruininks
(1984) that involved 2,271 subjects from 236 residential facilities
across the United States. A two-stage probability sampling procedure
was employed to select first facilities and then residents within those
facilities. The fourth global study was conducted by Kebbon and Windahl (1985), who attempted to survey the entire Swedish population
who received mental retardation services at a given time.

Prevalence estimates varied considerably across the three studies,
ranging from 4.2% to 16.4% in the respective populations (see Table
3.1). Of course, this was not surprising, given the differences among

these studies. One decisive difference lies in the different case-classification criteria. Borthwick and colleagues (1981) and Hill and Bruininks (1984), for instance, used quantitative cutoff criteria. The Borthwick and colleagues (1981) data in Table 3.1 reflect only behaviors that were rated as "frequent." Hill and Bruininks (1984) had staff persons describe all maladaptive behaviors of their clients and then rate their frequency on a 5-point scale ranging from once per month to one or more times an hour. The Jacobson (1982) study, on the other hand, included only "self-injurious action" that constituted a behavioral impediment to independent functioning. Kebbon and Windahl (1985) used a generic definition ("Overt motor movement, one body part has to move against another body part or against objects") and lists of behaviors to be included (e.g., head hitting, hitting other parts of the body, hair pulling) and others to be excluded (e.g., pica, vomiting).

It also should be pointed out that all four studies were based on service system databases kept by public MR/DD agencies. Service system databases are intended primarily for reasons other than research and thus adhere to different standards. One concern must be the likelihood of a biased sample. Service system databases typically are biased toward persons with relatively urgent service needs and against those who fulfill criteria without having service needs (Borthwick-Duffy & Eyman, 1990), and against those who were unaware of available services or those who were prevented otherwise from taking advantage of available services.

Prevalence of Specific SIB

For the comparison of specific prevalence estimates of SIB subtypes, six studies were selected (see Table 3.2). Maurice and Trudel (1982) surveyed three Canadian public facilities and found 417 SIB cases among 2,858 adult residents. Griffin, Williams, Stark, Altmeyer, and Mason (1984) screened all residents of 13 Texas state institutions and found 1,352 cases with SIB, 120 of which were described as severe. In 1986, Rojahn (1986) conducted a nationwide survey in West Germany and screened 25,872 people living in the community; 431 SIB cases were found. Oliver, Murphy, and Corbett (1987) examined 616 SIB cases who were found among the population with mental retardation who were receiving health services in one health region in the United Kingdom. Johnson, Day, and Hassanein (1988) reported that 544 SIB cases were identified among 7,335 children and adolescents from 472 special education classrooms from all 61 school districts in Kansas. The most recent study came from the United Kingdom and described 163 SIB cases who were screened out among 525 hospital residents (Emberson & Walker, 1990). A total of 38 different SIB topographies were reported in these six studies, but only nine of them appeared in more than half of the studies. This illustrates that there is no consensus among researchers as to which topographies are considered SIB. It also indicates that SIB prevalence estimates from different studies can be compared only with great caution because of the difference in case classification (besides other significant differences). This suggests a need for a standardized assessment and screening instrument that is founded in an empirically based taxonomy.

Even among the specific studies, different types of definitions can be detected. For instance, whereas Johnson and colleagues (1988) relied on a relatively broad behavioral category for "striking," others chose even smaller units for striking behaviors, distinguishing between the target area (head vs. the rest of the body) and the damage inflictor (body parts vs. objects) (Maurice & Trudel, 1982; Oliver et al., 1987; Rojahn, 1986). Again, the appropriate unit of measurement for epidemiological research ultimately will have to be proven empirically.

Variables Associated With SIB

To investigate in a descriptive fashion the association between SIB and other important clinical or demographic variables has been one of the primary goals of SIB epidemiology studies over the years. For a more comprehensive review of the literature than is possible in this context see Johnson and Day (1992). In the following, the relationship with only the most pertinent variables will be discussed. Reference citations from the literature are exemplary rather than exhaustive.

Level of Mental Retardation

The level of mental retardation has been found consistently to be related to the prevalence of destructive behavior in general (e.g., Borthwick et al., 1981; Eyman & Borthwick, 1980; Eyman & Call, 1977; Hill & Bruininks, 1981, 1984; Jacobson, 1982; Sherman, 1988) and to SIB in particular (e.g., Maurice & Trudel, 1982; Rojahn, 1986; Schroeder, Schroeder, Smith, & Dalldorf, 1978). There are at least two ways to look at this relationship. The first one is to examine the SIB prevalence in a

Table 3.2 Relative Prevalence (Number of Cases in 100 Subjects With at Least One Type of SIB) of 38 Different SIB Topographies

	Studies					
	Maurice & Trudel (1982)	Griffin et al. (1984)	Rojahn (1986)	Oliver et al. (1987)	Johnson et al. (1988)	Emberson & Walker (1990)
1. Head banging with/against body	9	49	45	36	*	39
2. Head banging with objects	9	43	30	28	*	13
3. Body hitting with body part	9	10	31	8	*	—
4. Body hitting with object	8	—	17	10	*	7
5. Striking	*	*	*	*	57	*
6. Biting self	13	32	45	38	42	37
7. Lip chewing	*	*	*	1	*	*
8. Scratching	13	50	42	—	—	28
9. Pinching self	1	—	19	4	—	—
10. Fingers in body cavities	*	*	16	—	*	—
11. Eye gouging	1	8	*	6	—	—
12. Throat gouging	*	2	*	*	—	—
13. Anal poking	*	*	*	2	—	—
14. Objects in body cavities	*	*	4	*	*	—
15. Fingers or objects in orifices	5	13	*	*	*	—
16. Hair pulling	4	8	15	8	—	10

17. Pinch, scratch, poke, pull	*	*	*	*	54	*
18. Pica	5	13	15	—	24	—
19. Ruminative vomiting	0	4	8	—	9	—
20. Pulling out nails, flesh, teeth	5	—	—	—	—	—
21. Nail removal	*	—	—	1	*	—
22. Digging in wounds	4	*	—	—	—	—
23. Introducing sharp objects	1	—	—	—	—	—
24. Rubbing body against own body	4	—	—	—	—	—
25. Teeth grinding	1	—	—	—	—	—
26. Rubbing body part with object	1	—	14	—	—	—
27. Masturbation	3	—	—	—	—	—
28. Burning self	2	—	—	—	—	—
29. Cutting self	2	—	—	2	—	—
30. Self-choking	0	—	—	—	—	—
31. Stopping blood circulation	2	—	—	—	—	—
32. Mouthing	—	13	—	—	—	—
33. Air swallowing	—	—	4	—	—	—
34. Excessive drinking	—	—	11	—	—	—
35. Skin picking	—	—	—	39	—	16
36. Eating feces	*	*	—	—	—	—
37. Tool banging	—	—	—	2	—	—
38. Teeth banging	—	—	—	1	—	—

*Hidden categories: The specific behaviors were not assessed separately, but they were subsumed under another topography of the same study. For instance, in Maurice and Trudel (1982), "eating feces" was a hidden category included under "pica" (p. 88).

Table 3.3a Prevalence of SIB (Number of Cases in 100) as a Function of Different Mental Retardation Levels

| | Mental Retardation | | | |
	Mild	Moderate	Severe	Profound
Schroeder et al. (1978)	2.0	9.0	14.0*	
Jacobson (1982)	2.6	3.4	7.1	16.9
Kebbon & Windahl (1985)	0.2	1.4	7.1	12.7

*No distinction was made between severe and profound mental retardation.

Table 3.3b Prevalence of Mental Retardation Levels in SIB Populations

| | Mental Retardation | | | |
	Mild	Moderate	Severe	Profound
Maurice & Trudel (1982)	10.0	37.0	53.0*	
Griffin et al. (1984)	1.2	9.1	29.1	60.7

*No distinction was made between severe and profound mental retardation.

sample of persons with mental retardation that accurately reflects the true proportions of mental retardation levels of the population in general. Such data are presented in Table 3.3a. The other approach is to examine the proportion of different levels of mental retardation in a sample of persons with SIB (see Table 3.3b). Tables 3.3a and 3.3b both illustrate that the prevalence of SIB strongly increases with a decreasing level of mental retardation.

Residential Setting

The order in which residential settings are arranged in Table 3.4 approximates a continuum of restrictiveness, ranging from relatively restrictive public residential facilities to relatively nonrestrictive, independent living in the community. The data by Borthwick and colleagues (1981), Jacobson (1982), and Hill and Bruininks (1984), along with many others that are not presented here (e.g., Borthwick-Duffy, Eyman, & White, 1987; Eyman & Borthwick, 1980; Eyman & Call, 1977; Hill & Bruininks, 1981; Sherman, 1988), indicate that SIB is more prevalent in public residential institutions than in the community. This, of course, is not surprising, as it corroborates the notion of maladaptive behavior being a prime culprit for unsuccessful community placement and read-

Table 3.4 Percentage of Cases With SIB Among Persons With MR/DD
by Community and Institutional Living Conditions

	Borthwick et al. (1981)	Jacobson (1982)	Hill & Bruininks (1984)
Public residential facilities	15.0	15.3	21.7
Community residential facilities or convalescent hospitals	5.0	5.4	11.1
Board homes/family care	2.0	1.8	—
Living with parents	2.0	2.9	—
Independent living	2.0	1.2	—

mission to public residential facilities (Intagliata & Willer, 1981; Vitello, Atthowe, & Cadwell, 1983). Whether restrictive environments can cause or contribute to the development of challenging behaviors or whether institutionalization is a function of the presence of behavior problems cannot be answered with the existing data. It can be assumed, however, that it can work both ways.

Chronological Age

Earlier cross-sectional studies found an uneven distribution of SIB across age groups, giving rise to the assumption that there is some developmental progression in SIB. For instance, Eyman and Call (1977) reported that the prevalence of SIB was significantly higher in younger individuals (0-12 years) than in older ones (13+ years) among almost 7,000 recipients of mental retardation services in Colorado and Nevada. Similarly, Maurice and Trudel (1982) found that their SIB sample was 12 years younger on the average than the rest of the residents. More recent studies that looked at chronological age more carefully found that it was related to SIB, although not in a linear but a curvilinear function (inverse U-shape): Adolescents and adults have a much higher prevalence of SIB than young children and the elderly (see Figure 3.1).

It must be pointed out, however, that it is conceivable that challenging behaviors in infants and toddlers are underreported, partly because certain behaviors may be in a "cocoon" stage yet and therefore may not appear in the fully developed topography typical for later life. A hypothetical example for this would be the presence of upper-body rocking in a child that develops into head bumping later. It also may be that

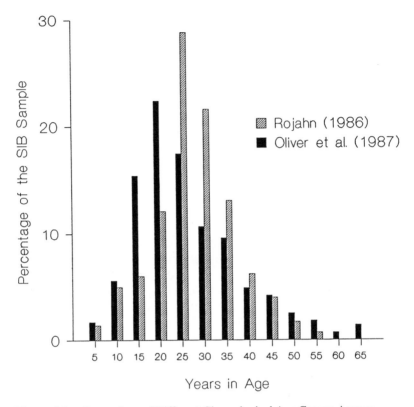

Figure 3.1. Proportions of Different Chronological Age Groups Among Populations With Mental Retardation and SIB From Sweden (Oliver et al. [1987], *n* = 596) and From Germany (Rojahn [1986], *n* = 431)

informants are reluctant to attach as strong a label as SIB for something that may have the same topography (e.g., infantile mouthing fingers) as the counterparts in adolescent/adult life (e.g., finger biting) except for the harmful effect. Therefore, SIB in young children or their behavioral precursors may be underrepresented in surveys such as the ones in Figure 3.1.

Gender

Several authors have reported on the relationship between sex and SIB (e.g., Eyman & Call, 1977; Maurice & Trudel, 1982; Oliver et al., 1987; Schroeder et al., 1978). But with the exception of some relatively rare genetic syndromes such as the X-linked Lesch-Nyhan syndrome, no particularly revealing sex-SIB relationship has been reported. Overall, males are slightly overrepresented among SIB cases (Johnson et al., 1988), but there may be gender preferences for certain topographies, such as scratching among women (Rojahn, Fenzau, & Hauschild, 1985), that may warrant further exploration.

Psychopathology

SIB and Maladaptive Behavior

Self-injury often is portrayed as one of several notorious problem behaviors in persons with mental retardation, such as aggressive outbursts, stereotypies, violent tantrums, and destruction of property. To this date, however, it is uncertain whether these behaviors really are related to one another. This issue has been addressed in instrument development research. For instance, in designing the Aberrant Behavior Checklist (ABC), Aman, Singh, Stewart, and Field (1985) collected lists of maladaptive behaviors from case records and other rating instruments. After several item selection procedures, factor analysis was computed on a data set from almost 1,000 persons with moderate to profound MR/DD. All aggressive behavior items (e.g., "aggressive to other patients and staff," "temper tantrums") and all SIB ("injures self," deliberately hurts him/herself," "does physical violence to self") loaded highly on a factor labeled "*irritability,*" together with some other items. Several subsequent studies of this instrument have obtained a similar clustering of SIB with aggressive and irritable behaviors (Aman, Richmond, Stewart, Bell, & Kissel, 1987; Bihm & Poindexter, 1991; Freund & Reiss, in press; Marshburn & Aman, 1991; Newton & Sturmey, 1988). This finding suggests that aggressive and self-injurious behavior share a common, possibly etiologically relevant component.

However, there also have been divergent results. For instance, using the very same ABC instrument, Rojahn and Helsel (1991) found in a population of hospitalized children and adolescents with MR/DD and a psychiatric diagnosis that SIB and aggression items loaded on separate factors, suggesting their relative independence from one another. And so did Heal, Hill, and Bruininks (1982) in developing a maladaptive behavior scale. More than 2,000 clients constituted a representative national sample from community and public residential facilities. Two orthogonal subscales were derived, which were labeled "*extrapunitive*" and "*intrapunitive.*" Groups that scored high on either one of these subscales had distinctly different characteristics. Those with high intrapunitive scores had lower levels of adaptive behavior, whereas those with high extrapunitive scores were younger, heavier, and on the average more ambulatory, and tended to live in a public facility. These findings are also consistent with a more recent paper by McGrew, Ittenbach, Bruininks, and Hill (1991), who also found that the structure of maladaptive behavior changes over the life span in terms of a proliferation of factors with progressing age.

Whether SIB and aggression should be treated as etiologically related or unrelated phenomena that may or may not require similar treatment has not been determined yet, and further research is needed. One of those approaches would be to look at subtypes of SIB and aggressive behavior in terms of topographical and/or functional characteristics.

SIB and Psychiatric Disorders

It has been debated how and/or to what extent maladaptive behaviors in mental retardation are related to mental illness. It is conceivable (a) that maladaptive behavior is a primary symptom of some underlying psychiatric disorder, which manifests itself differently in persons without mental handicaps (e.g., depression); (b) that mental illness is a risk factor for maladaptive behavior; or (c) that maladaptive behavior and mental illness are independent phenomena that coincide due to independent relationships to an external variable, such as mental retardation, which seems generally to enhance the vulnerability for physical and psychological problems. I am not aware of any empirical research that has focused primarily on the relationship between SIB and psychiatric illness, but at least two studies should be mentioned that shed some light on the issue.

Fraser, Leudar, Gray, and Campbell (1986) conducted a study that involved 160 adults with mild to moderate retardation who had been randomly chosen from three Scottish mental subnormality hospitals. Data were collected through a standardized and factor analyzed psychiatric interview and the Behavior Disturbance Scale, an empirically derived instrument that incorporates items on aggression, conduct problems, and SIB. On the basis of stepwise multiple regression analysis the researchers concluded that behavior disturbances are not expressions of psychiatric disorders and that psychiatric illness and behavior disorders are, therefore, not interchangeable terms.

Table 3.5a "Personal Maladaption" (which includes SIB) as a Function of Dual Diagnosis in Children and Adolescents With Mental Retardation

| | Own Home | | Community Care | |
	DD^a	Control	DD^a	Control
Pervasive developmental disorders	74	86	63	76
Conduct disorder	83	91	75	85
Adjustment disorders	86	90^b	80	84^b

SOURCE: Adapted from Nihira et al. (1988).
a. Groups with a dual diagnosis.
b. Statistically nonsignificant.

Table 3.5b "Personal Maladaption" (which includes SIB) as a Function of Dual Diagnosis in Children and Adolescents With Mental Retardation

| | Independent Living | | Community Care | | State Hospitals | |
	DD*	Control	DD*	Control	DD*	Control
Schizophrenic disorder	86	92	79	87	65	70
Personality disorder	88	93	84	88	71	74

SOURCE: Adapted from Nihira et al. (1988).
* Groups with a dual diagnosis.

Nihira, Price-Williams, and White (1988) surveyed almost 4,000 individuals with dual diagnosis and a matched control group from the California DD state agency. Behavioral data were collected with the Client Development Evaluation Report (CDER, 1978), a factor analyzed instrument with two maladaptive behavior domains of "social maladaptation" (aggression) and "personal maladaptation" (including SIB, stereotypy, and autistic and hyperactive behavior). Clinical psychiatric diagnoses achieved higher scores on the "personal maladaption" subscale (which includes SIB) than did the control subjects without psychiatric diagnosis (see Tables 3.5a and 3.5b), which suggests that there was a positive relationship between SIB and psychiatric diagnosis. However, these data do not explain how exactly SIB and psychiatric illness might be related.

In summary, it is uncertain at this point whether and, if so, how SIB might be related to psychiatric illness. One of the main problems with the existing data, in addition to the before-mentioned questions about global SIB assessment, is the uncertainty concerning the applicability of traditional psychiatric categories to this population and the reliability of those categories particularly among lower functioning individuals.

Topographical Taxonomy of SIB

A review of epidemiological studies on SIB reveals that one of the greatest barriers for the advancement of our knowledge about SIB from an epidemiological perspective has been the lack of reliable and valid assessment and screening instruments, which are more differentiated than global items in general behavior rating scales can afford to be. An instrument is needed that categorizes SIB in specific topographies. Such a tool would assist in making basic decisions about the units of measurement of SIB and about what behaviors should be part of it at all.

The Behavior Problems Inventory (BPI) (Rojahn, 1986) is an empirically developed, specific assessment instrument that was originally designed for SIB and stereotyped behavior surveys and was later expanded to include aggressive behavior as well (Rojahn, Polster, Mulick, & Wisniewski, 1989). One earlier report on the BPI was published a few years ago (Rojahn, 1986). For that paper, dichotomous data (occurrence/nonoccurrence) from 431 individuals with SIB were subjected to cluster analyses, and three SIB clusters emerged. This indicated that different topographies, which often are lumped together carelessly as SIB, may in fact belong to separate SIB subgroups with potentially important theoretical and/or treatment implications. In a reanalysis of that data set, but taking advantage of the 5-point Likert-type rating scales for the frequency at which these behaviors were observed (ranging from "SIB does not occur," "occurs monthly," "occurs weekly," "occurs daily," and "occurs hourly"), principal factor analysis followed by Varimax and Promax rotation was conducted as a cross-method validation of the cluster analysis (see Table 3.6).

A five-factor solution was found (eigenvalue > 1), which explained 52.7% of the variance. The first factor consisted of four different *hitting* behaviors. The second factor contained five behaviors of *inserting* objects into body orifices (stuffing objects into body cavities, poking fingers in body cavities, pica, aerophagia, and excessive drinking). And the third factor included biting, scratching, pinching, and hair pulling.

Table 3.6   Factor Analytic Taxonomy of SIB: Factor Loadings (correlations)
of 15 SIB Topographies on a Five-Factor Solution Generated
by Principal Component Factor Analysis With Varimax and
Promax Rotations

	Factors				
	I	II	III	IV	V
Head hitting with body parts	.76	.01	.14	.21	−.08
Head hitting with objects	.73	.16	−.11	.16	−.03
Body hitting with body parts	.70	−.02	.33	.02	.07
Body hitting with objects	.69	.01	.12	−.09	.01
Objects in cavities	.00	.72	.00	−.19	−.14
Fingers in cavities	.01	.57	.26	.35	−.05
Pica	.07	.68	−.09	−.06	.00
Air swallowing	.01	.35	.13	.34	.20
Excessive drinking	.04	.64	.07	.30	.05
Biting	.15	.25	.46	−.07	−.09
Scratching	−.08	−.07	.65	.12	−.00
Pinching	.25	.03	.74	.06	−.02
Hair pulling	.13	.15	.23	.21	−.68
Teeth grinding	.09	.01	.02	.84	−.02
Vomiting and rumination	.10	.09	.12	.19	.72

The first three factors resemble very closely the previous cluster analytic solution (Rojahn, 1986).

The main difference between the previous cluster-analysis solution and the present factor-analytic one is that factors 1 and 3 were combined in a single cluster. Rumination and teeth grinding were residual topographies that formed their own cluster. Given their infrequent occurrence and the difficulties in reliably assessing them, one may eventually consider excluding them from the SIB screening instrument.

Conclusions

There is consistent evidence that SIB in general is associated with a number of variables with potential explanatory value for its pathogenesis, such as the level of mental retardation, chronological age, and the residential placement. It must not be overlooked, however, that estimates of basic epidemiological parameters are highly variable across studies, which is partly due to the fact that SIB as a heuristic concept is of limited value. Often SIB has been treated as an ambiguous and ill-defined entity, without a strong rationale or empirical evidence for its validity. Therefore, as far as case classification and assessment for future epidemiological studies are concerned, a useful specific assessment instrument with solid psychometric properties is needed, and the Behavior Problem Inventory (BPI) was proposed as a possible solution.

Although it is unquestionable that more work needs to be done on the BPI, this instrument may be a step in the right direction. Regardless of the ultimate value of the BPI as an assessment instrument, it has served already at least one important function, namely, to illustrate that global SIB assessment is of limited scientific merit for epidemiological research. It stands for a heterogeneous group of behaviors with little in common as far as topographical features, motivational[1] characteristics, or treatment implications are concerned. From a factor-analytic perspective it appears that there are several subgroups of SIB, and further research needs to determine what the distinguishing features between these subgroups entail and whether it is warranted from an assessment perspective to treat them as an entity. For future epidemiological research in this area it is recommended to protect the diversity of different SIB subtypes until more is learned about SIB subgroups. Future research also should consider combining topographical and functional information (e.g., Iwata, 1991) to determine the relationship between the two.

Note

1. Functional analysis classification of SIB has not yet played an important role in epidemiological research.

References

Aman, M. G., Richmond, G., Stewart, A. W., Bell, J. C., & Kissel, R. C. (1987). The Aberrant Behavior Checklist: Factor structure and the effect of subject variables in American and New Zealand facilities. *American Journal of Mental Deficiency, 91,* 570-578.

Aman, M. G., Singh, N. N., Stewart, A. W., & Field, C. J. (1985). The Aberrant Behavior Checklist: A behavior rating scale for the assessment of treatment effects. *American Journal of Mental Deficiency, 89,* 485-491.

Bihm, E. M., & Poindexter, A. R. (1991). Cross-validation of the factor structure of the Aberrant Behavior Checklist for Persons With Mental Retardation. *American Journal on Mental Retardation, 96,* 209-211.

Borthwick, S. A., Meyers, C. E., & Eyman, R. K. (1981). Comparative adaptive and maladaptive behavior of mentally retarded clients of five residential settings in three western states. In R. H. Bruininks, C. E. Meyers, B. B. Sigford, & K. C. Lakin (Eds.), *Deinstitutionalization and community adjustment of mentally retarded people* (Monograph No. 4) (pp. 351-359). Washington, DC: American Association of Mental Deficiency (Retardation).

Borthwick-Duffy, S. A., & Eyman, R. K. (1990). Who are the dually diagnosed? *American Journal on Mental Retardation, 94,* 586-595.

Borthwick-Duffy, S. A., Eyman, R. K., & White, J. F. (1987). Client characteristics and residential placement pattern. *American Journal of Mental Deficiency, 92,* 24-30.

CDER. (1978). *Client development evaluation record.* Sacramento: California Department of Developmental Services.

Emberson, J., & Walker, E. (1990). Self-injurious behavior in people with a mental handicap. *Nursing Times, 86,* 43-46.

Eyman, R. K., & Borthwick, S. A. (1980). Patterns of care for mentally retarded persons. *Mental Retardation, 18,* 63-66.

Eyman, R. K., & Call, T. (1977). Maladaptive behavior and community placement of mentally retarded persons. *American Journal of Mental Deficiency, 82,* 137-144.

Fraser, W. I., Leudar, I., Gray, J., & Campbell, I. (1986). Psychiatric and behavior disturbance in mental handicap. *Journal of Mental Deficiency Research, 30,* 49-57.

Freund, L. S., & Reiss, A. L. (in press). Rating psychopathology in mentally retarded outpatients: Use of the Aberrant Behavior Checklist. *Research in Developmental Disabilities.*

Griffin, J. C., Williams, D. E., Stark, M. T., Altmeyer, B. K., & Mason, M. (1984). Self-injurious behavior: A state-wide prevalence survey, assessment of severe cases, and follow-up of aversive programs. In J. C. Griffin, M. T. Stark, D. E. Williams, B. K. Altmeyer, & H. K. Griffin (Eds.), *Advances in the treatment of self-injurious behavior* (pp. 1-25). Austin: Texas Department of Mental Health and Mental Retardation.

Heal, L. W., Hill, B. K., & Bruininks, R. H. (1982). *Maladaptive behavior in a national sample of public and community residential facilities.* Unpublished manuscript.

Hill, B. K., & Bruininks, R. H. (1981). *Physical and behavioral characteristics and maladaptive behavior of mentally retarded people in residential facilities.* Minneapolis: University of Minnesota, Department of Psychoeducational Studies.

Hill, B. K., & Bruininks, R. H. (1984). Maladaptive behavior of mentally retarded individuals in residential facilities. *American Journal of Mental Deficiency, 88,* 380-387.

Intagliata, J., & Willer, B. (1981). Reinstitutionalization of mentally retarded persons successfully placed into family-care and group homes. *American Journal of Mental Deficiency, 87,* 34-39.

Iwata, B. (1991, April 10). *The functional analysis of self-injury.* Paper presented at the Conference on Destructive Behavior in Developmental Disabilities, Minneapolis, MN.

Jacobson, J. (1982). Problem behavior and psychiatric impairment within a developmentally disabled population I: Behavior frequency. *Applied Research in Mental Retardation, 3,* 121-139.

Janicki, M. P., & Jacobson, J. W. (1982). The character of developmental disabilities in New York State: Preliminary observations. *International Journal of Rehabilitation Research, 5,* 191-202.

Johnson, W. L., & Day, R. M. (1992). The incidence and prevalence of self-injurious behavior. In J. K. Luiselli, J. L. Matson, & N. N. Singh (Eds.), *Self-injurious behavior: Analysis, assessment, and treatment* (pp. 21-56). New York: Springer Verlag.

Johnson, W. L., Day, R. M., & Hassanein, R. E. S. (1988, June). *Prevalence of self-injurious behaviors within public school special education programs.* Paper presented at the 112th annual meeting of the Association on Mental Retardation, Washington, DC.

Kebbon, L., & Windahl, S. I. (1985, March 24-28). *Self-injurious behavior: Results of a nation-wide survey among mentally retarded persons in Sweden.* Paper presented at the 7th world congress of the International Association for the Scientific Study of Mental Deficiency, New Delhi.

Marshburn, E., & Aman, M. G. (1991). Factor validity and norms for the Aberrant Behavior Checklist in a community sample of children with mental retardation. *Journal of Autism and Developmental Disorders, 22,* 357-373.

Maurice, P., & Trudel, G. (1982). Self-injurious behavior prevalence and relationships to environmental events. In J. H. Hollis & C. E. Meyers (Eds.), *Life-threatening behavior: Analysis and intervention* (Monograph No. 5) (pp. 81-103). Washington, DC: American Association on Mental Retardation.

McGrew, K. S., Ittenbach, R. F., Bruininks, R. H., & Hill, B. (1991). Factor structure of maladaptive behavior across the lifespan of persons with mental retardation. *Research in Developmental Disabilities, 12,* 181-199.

Neuropsychiatric Research Group. (1979). *Behavior Development Survey: User's manual.* Unpublished manuscript, University of California at Los Angeles, Neuropsychiatric Research Group at Lanterman State Hospital, Pomona, CA.

Newton, J. T., & Sturmey, P. (1988). The Aberrant Behavior Checklist: A British replication and extension of its psychometric properties. *Journal of Mental Deficiency Research, 32,* 87-92.

Nihira, K., Price-Williams, D. R., & White, J. F. (1988). Social competence and maladaptive behavior of people with dual diagnosis. *Journal of the Multihandicapped Person, 1,* 185-199.

Oliver, C., Murphy, G. H., & Corbett, J. A. (1987). Self-injurious behavior in people with mental handicap: A total population study. *Journal of Mental Deficiency Research, 31,* 147-162.

Rojahn, J. (1986). Self-injurious and stereotyped behavior in noninstitutionalized mentally retarded people: Prevalence and classification. *American Journal of Mental Deficiency, 91,* 268-276.

Rojahn, J., Fenzau, B., & Hauschild, D. (1985). Selbstverletzungsverhalten geistig Behinderter [Self-injurious behavior in the mentally retarded]. *Geistige Behinderung,* 183-192.

Rojahn, J., & Helsel, W. J. (1991). The Aberrant Behavior Checklist in children and adolescents with mental retardation and mental illness. *Journal of Autism and Developmental Disorders, 21,* 17-28.

Rojahn, J., Polster, L. M., Mulick, J. A., & Wisniewski, J. J. (1989). Reliability of the Behavior Problem Inventory. *Journal of the Multihandicapped Person, 2,* 283-293.

Schroeder, S. R., Mulick, J. A., & Rojahn, J. (1980). The definition, taxonomy, epidemiology, and ecology of self-injurious behavior. *Journal of Autism and Developmental Disorders, 10,* 417-432.

Schroeder, S. R., Schroeder, C. S., Smith, B., & Dalldorf, J. (1978). Prevalence of self-injurious behavior in a large state facility for the retarded: A three-year follow-up study. *Journal of Autism and Childhood Schizophrenia, 8,* 261-269.

Sherman, B. R. (1988). Predictors of the decision to place developmentally disabled members in residential care. *American Journal on Mental Retardation, 92,* 344-351.

Vitello, S. J., Atthowe, J. M., & Cadwell, J. (1983). Determinants of community placement or institutionalized mentally retarded persons. *American Journal of Mental Deficiency, 87,* 539-545.

4

Developmental Psychopathology of Destructive Behavior

WILLIAM E. MACLEAN, JR.
WENDY L. STONE
WILLIAM H. BROWN

Mental retardation is a social condition defined by significantly sub-average intellectual functioning and attendant deficits in adaptive behavior that are manifest before 18 years of age (Grossman, 1983). People with mental retardation face significant challenges in adaptation to daily life and have an increased risk of behavior problems and psychopathology relative to the general population (Borthwick, Meyers, & Eyman, 1981; Bruininks, Hill, & Morreau, 1988; Jacobson, 1982). People with severe to profound mental retardation are at the greatest risk for the development of severe behavior problems such as aggression, property destruction, and self-injurious behavior (Jacobson, 1982). Prevalence rates among the severely mentally retarded are 5.4% for property destructive behavior, 7.1% for self-injurious behavior, and 13.5% for aggressive behavior (Jacobson, 1982). Comparable values for people with profound mental retardation are 6.1% for property destructive behavior, 16.9% for self-injurious behavior, and 15.4% for aggressive behavior (Jacobson, 1982). Although diverse in form, and presumably function, these behaviors have come to be termed "destructive behavior" in the context of a national debate on the use of aversive behavior management techniques (National Institutes of Health, 1991). Destructive behavior has been defined as "culturally unacceptable behavior that, due to its intensity, or frequency, presents an imminent danger either to the person who exhibits the behavior, to other people, or to property" (Schroeder, Rojahn, & Oldenquist, 1991, p. 126). Destructive behavior is a significant clinical problem. Not only can it lead to undesirable personal and/or social consequences, but also destructive behavior is quite intractable, requiring intensive and specialized behavioral programming. One of the most serious ramifications of destructive behavior is that some of the acts (e.g., eye gouging, severe and repetitive head banging, tissue laceration) produce acute and chronic physical harm and result in the need for immediate and, sometimes, ongoing medical intervention and care (Hyman, Fisher, Mercugliano, & Cataldo, 1990). In addition to causing personal injury, destructive behavior is socially stigmatizing (Isett, Roszkowski, & Spreat, 1983; Jones, Wint, & Ellis, 1990) and has been associated with decreased interaction with caregivers (Schroeder et al., 1991). Moreover, there is evidence that people who exhibit aggression and other conduct problems are at an increased risk for physical abuse from institutional staff members (Rusch, Hall, & Griffin, 1986). Destructive behavior is also a primary reason for placement of persons with mental retardation in highly restrictive residential settings that may or may not have high-quality, active habilitation training (Craig & McCarver, 1984; Vitello, Atthowe, & Cadwell, 1983). In addition, destructive behavior can be a major factor in the termination of persons with mental retardation from community employment and habilitative programs (Greenspan & Shoultz, 1981; Salzberg, Likins, McConaughy, & Lignugaris/Kraft, 1986).

Destructive behavior also has important clinical ramifications. Although intensive behavioral interventions have been shown to be effective in reducing the frequency or intensity of destructive behavior, particularly when it has been possible to isolate environmental factors that set the occasion for the behavior (Cataldo, 1991), such intervention efforts have been largely ineffective in *eliminating* destructive behavior. In many cases the behavior rebounds when intervention efforts are terminated (Cataldo, 1991; Schroeder et al., 1982). Moreover, these interventions usually include labor-intensive programming that often necessitates the use of special protocols and procedures, detailed record keeping, and a multidisciplinary staff (Schroeder et al., 1991). Alternative interventions may include controversial aversive procedures or psychopharmacological agents with undesirable side effects (Schroeder, 1991).

This chapter discusses destructive behavior within the framework of developmental psychopathology. Consistent with this approach, specific attention is paid to the etiology of destructive behavior and its relation to normal development. Although research in this area is scant, examples are drawn from related areas of research where relevant. Implications of a developmental approach for further research on destructive behavior in people with mental retardation also are discussed.

Etiological Perspectives

Despite the clinical significance of destructive behavior; its moderate level of prevalence, especially among severely and profoundly mentally retarded people; and its intractability to pharmacological and behavioral intervention, it is surprising that there is almost no research on the *development* of destructive behavior. This state of affairs is not unique to destructive behavior, as little effort has been directed toward the early identification and development of behavioral disorders generally in young children with mental retardation (Shoemaker, Saylor, & Aikman, 1988). Although not all young children who exhibit behavioral problems continue to have difficulties as adults, Kohlberg, LaCrosse, and Ricks (1972) concluded that early and severe behavioral problems in nonretarded children are "the single most powerful predictor of later adjustment problems" (p. 1249). Moreover, some types of behavioral problems such as aggression are stable and highly predictive of adjustment problems in adulthood (Parker & Asher, 1987).

The importance of examining the developmental roots of different forms of psychopathology has been a major tenet of the paradigm of developmental psychopathology. Developmental psychopathology has been defined as "the study of the origins and course of individual patterns of behavioral maladaptation whatever the age of onset, whatever the causes, whatever the transformations in behavioral manifestation, and however complex the course of the developmental pattern may be" (Sroufe & Rutter, 1984, p. 18).

The developmental psychopathology approach has much to offer the study of destructive behavior in people with mental retardation. Important components of this paradigm are the examination of the continuity and discontinuity of pathology from childhood to adulthood and the relation between disordered behavior and normal development (Garber, 1984; Sroufe & Rutter, 1984). Problem behavior is investigated in light of its precursors, protective factors, situational and environmental influences, developmental sequelae, and changes in symptom expression with maturity (Garber, 1984; Sroufe & Rutter, 1984; Wenar, 1982). Problem behavior also is studied within the context of normal developmental progression, tasks, and milestones.

Despite a paucity of empirical data, there has been considerable speculation regarding the etiology of destructive behavior. Several theories have been proposed in the literature, though no single theory has been able to explain the origin of destructive behavior in every individual. For the purpose of this discussion, the etiological theories pertaining to self-injurious behavior (SIB) and aggression/property destruction are presented separately.

Self-Injurious Behavior

Etiological perspectives on self-injurious behavior can be grouped into five broad categories: organic, psychodynamic, learning, developmental, and homeostatic. The data in support of these perspectives have been reviewed recently (Matson, 1989; Schroeder, 1991) and are not replicated here. However, of relevance to the present chapter is the fact that most theories fail to differentiate adequately between the *origin* of SIB and the factors that *maintain* SIB. For example, according to learning theory, the moment-to-moment expression of a behavior may be influenced greatly by environmental consequences, such as positive reinforcement. However, this does not necessarily mean that the behavior first emerged through the process of learning. Similarly, Romanczyk (1986) proposed that some SIB has the effect of producing arousal stimuli or respondently conditioned emotional states that are reinforcing to the person and that lead to subsequent expression of the behavior. However, this thesis does not explain how the SIB emerged originally. Bearing this distinction in mind, the various theories differ in their ability to explain the *genesis* of the behavior. Two perspectives, the organic and the developmental, do provide some insight into the genesis of particular SIB topographies.

Organic Theories

Given the disproportionate incidence of self-injurious behavior in severely/profoundly mentally retarded people who also are likely to have a biomedical diagnosis as a basis of their mental retardation, it is tempting to conclude that self-injurious behavior has a biological basis. Indeed, genetic conditions such as Lesch-Nyhan, Cornelia de Lange, Riley-Day, Prader-Willi, and Rett syndromes have as associated features both mental retardation and SIB. However, the majority of people with mental retardation and SIB have none of these syndromes (Oliver, Murphy, & Corbett, 1987). Although the biological basis of the SIB in these syndromes has not been fully explained, there has been some study of the destructive behavior in Lesch-Nyhan syndrome. An autopsy study of three patients with Lesch-Nyhan syndrome revealed significantly deficient dopamine pathways in the nigrostriatal bundle (Lloyd et al., 1981). Lloyd and colleagues suggested that given the relation between the dopamine system and motor behavior, the reported structural abnormality and the consequent imbalance among neurotransmitters might be responsible for the self-biting in Lesch-Nyhan patients. An animal model of self-biting provides more direct evidence in support of this conclusion by Lloyd and colleagues. This model includes psychopharmacological alteration of the dopamine pathways in unborn rat pups. Perinatal administration of 6-hydroxydopamine, a substance that selectively destroys dopamine neurons, results in severe self-biting upon administration of a dopamine agonist (Baumeister, Frye, & Schroeder, 1984; Schroeder, Breese, & Mueller, 1990). Conversely, administration of a dopamine antagonist leads to decreased self-biting in the previously treated animals (Schroeder et al., 1990). Further research of this type in other syndromes will yield important knowledge of the role of organic factors in the origin of specific forms of SIB.

Developmental Perspective

Repetitive motor behaviors in early childhood have been a focus of study since the 1940s. A variety of topographies have been described, one of which (head banging) resembles a form of self-injurious behavior exhibited by people with developmental disabilities. Many early reports emphasized that repetitive motor behaviors were common and normal aspects of development (de Lissovoy, 1961; Kravitz & Boehm, 1971; Kravitz, Rosenthal, Teplitz, Murphy, & Lesser, 1960; Lourie, 1949; Sallustro & Atwell, 1978; Wolff, 1967). Later studies confirmed the importance of repetitive motor behaviors in motor development (MacLean & Baumeister, 1982; Thelen, 1979, 1981). For example, Thelen reported that repetitive motor behaviors appear to peak in frequency at transition points in development. Kicking movements are most prevalent just before the onset of locomotion and decrease rapidly following attainment of that milestone. Similarly, rocking on hands and knees appears just before crawling. Of particular interest is the fact that the appearance of these behaviors coincides with motor development in delayed as well as nondelayed populations. Children with developmental delays exhibit the behaviors at much older chronological ages than nondelayed children (Field, Ting, & Shuman, 1979; Kravitz & Boehm, 1971; MacLean, Ellis, Galbreath, Halpern, & Baumeister, 1991).

Head banging has been observed in nondelayed children aged 5 to 17 months (de Lissovoy, 1962; Kravitz & Boehm, 1971; Sallustro & Atwell, 1978; Werry, Carlielle, & Fitzpatrick, 1983). The behavior most often occurs in the hands-and-knees or sitting position at bedtime (de Lissovoy, 1962; Kravitz et al., 1960). Prevalence rates range from 5% to 19% in nonretarded children (Werry et al., 1983). However, these prevalence values may represent an underestimate of the number of children who exhibit the behavior for two reasons. First, the behavior may be exhibited for a very brief period during the course of normal development. Second, it is likely that the behavior is exhibited at times when caregivers are not present (in the child's crib). Although there is a normative component to head banging during the early developmental period, it also has been suggested that this behavior might also serve the function of alleviating pain associated with otitis media (de Lissovoy, 1963) or tooth eruption (Kravitz et al., 1960).

Severely delayed children have very slow motor development and reach a plateau that is difficult to overcome (Molnar, 1978). As a result they may exhibit behavior that is developmentally appropriate but chronologically very aberrant for longer periods than would be expected as compared with nondelayed children. Other factors might then lead to the continued expression of the behavior even after the child has developed beyond that point in motor development. If the head banging results in pain, it is possible that the release of endogenous opiates might sustain the behavior through some addictive process (Sandman et al., 1983). It is also possible that the response of caregivers to the head banging may lead to continued expression of the behavior. Some have suggested that self-injurious behavior is a form of communication, such as signaling a need for attention, and that interventions that include functional communication training produce dramatic decreases in SIB (Carr & Durand, 1985). Given the very limited language abilities of severely retarded young children, this appears to be a plausible explanation for the development of severe self-injury in some people.

Aggression and Property Destruction

There have been several longitudinal studies of the development of behavior problems during childhood (Achenbach & Edelbrock, 1981; Jenkins, Bax, & Hart, 1980; Lapouse & Monk, 1958; MacFarlane, Allen, & Honzik, 1954; Werry & Quay, 1971). From these investigations it is possible to determine the prevalence of particular behaviors as well as their developmental course over time. Taken together, these studies indicate that aggressive behavior such as temper tantrums, fighting, attacking, and property destruction are commonly reported by parents during early childhood. The behaviors peak at approximately 3 years of age and decrease in both frequency and severity during the preschool years, as children learn more mature and more adaptive ways to express anger and frustration, to gain attention, and to solve problems.

Children acquire rule-governed behavior and learn social conventions gradually through interactions with socializing agents such as parents, teachers, and, in later years, peers. In most cases, the long-standing and pervasive nature of parent-child interactions casts parents in the primary role of teaching appropriate social responses. It falls to parents to be aware that behavioral change should occur and to have the skills to bring this change about. Given the importance of parental input, it is plausible that aggression and property destruction in people with mental retardation develop in the same way as does antisocial behavior in nonretarded youth. Certainly the same basic processes such as inadequate parental discipline (i.e., noncontingent use of both positive reinforcement for prosocial behavior and effective punishment for deviant behavior) and inconsistent monitoring may be operating (Patterson, 1982).

At the same time, the stress of raising a developmentally disabled youth must be recognized as a factor that could affect parenting efficacy. For example, the child's excessive activity level or abnormal sleep pattern may present a challenge for parents. Similarly, the slow development of the child in the cognitive, language, and social realms has clear implications for the acquisition of self-control. Borrowing from the work of Campbell (1990) with preschoolers and of Patterson (1982, 1986) with older children, a case could be made that the oppositional behavior characteristic of 18- to 36-month-old nonretarded children may be the genesis of later aggression and property destruction in people with mental retardation.

Implications for Future Research

If one applies a developmental psychopathology perspective to the phenomenon of destructive behavior, several implications for future research are evident.

1. Rather than viewing problem behavior as inherently pathological, the developmental psychopathology perspective is concerned with the degree to which a child's behavior represents a difference or distortion from normative expectations for the child's age, gender, developmental level, and environmental circumstances (Achenbach & Edelbrock, 1979; Garber, 1984). The need for normative data on the prevalence of problem behaviors at different developmental levels, such as those collected by Lapouse and Monk (1958), is critical to the growth of this emerging discipline (Achenbach, 1982).

2. Within the developmental psychopathology framework, normal processes of development are viewed with respect to what they may contribute to the understanding of disordered behavior. We need longitudinal investigations of the early behavioral development of children at risk for developing destructive behavior. Risk factors include particular genetic conditions, severe mental retardation, and sensory impairment. These studies should consider age and gender trends, rate and progression of development, relation to developmental tasks, and the context in which the behavior occurs, and should define deviance according to specific parameters such as form, intensity, frequency, duration, and co-occurrence of behaviors (Garber, 1984).

3. A developmental perspective dictates a new approach to the problems of classification. Global terms such as *self-injurious behavior, property destruction,* and *aggression* may not suffice. For example, property destruction and aggression may fit an already well-understood pattern of oppositional and antisocial behavior. Similarly, we may be approaching the point at which we will need to describe particular forms of self-injurious behavior. Simply stated, self-biting may result from neurochemical abnormalities, whereas head banging may have a developmental basis. Such differentiation may permit construction of a theoretically driven classification system that informs intervention efforts.

4. Increased understanding of the precursors of destructive behavior will aid in designing preventive interventions. Empirical research can provide not only normative expectations that suggest the presence of deviation or disorder but also insight into which preventive intervention efforts would be developmentally appropriate. For example, if SIB has a communicative function, then intensive communication training at an early age for a person who is at risk for developing SIB might prevent the development

of such behavior. Similarly, if noncompliance serves as a precursor to aggression and property destruction in children at risk for destructive behavior, then behavioral parent training in early childhood might prevent the onset of such behavior.

References

Achenbach, T. M. (1982). *Developmental psychopathology* (2nd ed.). New York: John Wiley.

Achenbach, T. M., & Edelbrock, C. S. (1979). The Child Behavior Profile II: Boys aged 12-16 and girls aged 6-11 and 12-16. *Journal of Consulting and Clinical Psychology, 47,* 223-233.

Achenbach, T. M., & Edelbrock, C. S. (1981). Behavioral problems and competencies reported by parents of normal and disturbed children aged four to sixteen. *Monographs of the Society for Research in Child Development, 46* (Serial No. 188).

Baumeister, A. A., Frye, G. R., & Schroeder, S. R. (1984). Neurochemical correlates of self-injurious behavior. In J. A. Mulick & B. L. Mallory (Eds.), *Transitions in mental retardation: Advocacy, technology and science* (pp. 207-228). Norwood, NJ: Ablex.

Borthwick, S. A., Meyers, C. E., & Eyman, R. K. (1981). Comparative adaptive and maladaptive behavior of mentally retarded clients of five residential settings in three Western states. In R. H. Bruininks, C. E. Meyers, B. B. Sigford, & K. C. Lakin (Eds.), *Deinstitutionalization and community adjustment of mentally retarded people* (Monograph No. 4) (pp. 351-359). Washington, DC: American Association on Mental Deficiency.

Bruininks, R. H., Hill, B. K., & Morreau, L. (1988). Prevalence and implications of maladaptive behaviors and dual diagnosis in residential and other service programs. In J. A. Stark, F. J. Menolascino, M. H. Albarelli, & V. C. Gray (Eds.), *Mental retardation and mental health: Classification, diagnosis, treatment, services* (pp. 3-29). New York: Springer Verlag.

Campbell, S. B. (1990). *Behavior problems in preschool children.* New York: Guilford.

Carr, E. G., & Durand, V. M. (1985). Reducing behavior problems through functional communication training. *Journal of Applied Behavior Analysis, 18,* 111-126.

Cataldo, M. F. (1991). The effects of punishment and other behavior reducing procedures on the destructive behaviors of persons with developmental disabilities. In *Treatment of destructive behaviors in persons with developmental disabilities* (NIH Publication No. 91-2410) (pp. 231-341). Washington, DC: Government Printing Office.

Craig, E. M., & McCarver, R. B. (1984). Community placement and adjustment of deinstitutionalized clients: Issues and findings. In N. R. Ellis & N. W. Bray (Eds.), *International review of research in mental retardation* (Vol. 12, pp. 95-122). Orlando, FL: Academic Press.

de Lissovoy, V. (1961). Head banging in early childhood: A study of incidence. *Journal of Pediatrics, 58,* 803-805.

de Lissovoy, V. (1962). Head banging in early childhood. *Child Development, 33,* 43-56.

de Lissovoy, V. (1963). Head banging in early childhood: A suggested cause. *Journal of Genetic Psychology, 102,* 109-114.

Field, T. M., Ting, G., & Shuman, H. H. (1979). The onset of rhythmic activities in normal and high-risk infants. *Developmental Psychobiology, 12,* 97-100.

Garber, J. (1984). Classification of childhood psychopathology: A developmental perspective. *Child Development, 55,* 30-48.

Greenspan, S., & Shoultz, B. (1981). Why mentally retarded adults lose their jobs: Social competence as a factor in work adjustment. *Applied Research in Mental Retardation, 2,* 23-38.

Grossman, H. J. (Ed.). (1983). *Classification in mental retardation.* Washington, DC: American Association on Mental Deficiency.

Hyman, S. L., Fisher, W., Mercugliano, M., & Cataldo, M. F. (1990). Children with self-injurious behavior. *Pediatrics, 85,* 437-441.

Isett, R., Roszkowski, M., & Spreat, S. (1983). Tolerance for deviance: Subjective evaluation of the social validation of the focus of treatment on mental retardation. *American Journal of Mental Deficiency, 87,* 458-461.

Jacobson, J. W. (1982). Problem behavior and psychiatric impairment within a developmentally disabled population I: Behavior frequency. *Applied Research in Mental Retardation, 3,* 121-139.

Jenkins, S., Bax, M., & Hart, H. (1980). Behavior problems in preschool children. *Journal of Child Psychology and Psychiatry, 21,* 5-18.

Jones, R. S., Wint, D., & Ellis, N. C. (1990). The social effects of stereotyped behavior. *Journal of Mental Deficiency Research, 34,* 261-268.

Kohlberg, L., LaCrosse, J., & Ricks, D. (1972). The predictability of adult mental health from childhood behavior. In B. B. Wolman (Ed.), *Manual of child psychopathology.* New York: McGraw-Hill.

Kravitz, H., & Boehm, J. J. (1971). Rhythmic habit patterns in infancy: Their sequence, age of onset, and frequency. *Child Development, 42,* 399-413.

Kravitz, H., Rosenthal, V., Teplitz, Z., Murphy, J., & Lesser, R. (1960). A study of headbanging in infants and children. *Diseases of the Nervous System, 21,* 203-208.

Lapouse, R., & Monk, M. (1958). An epidemiological study of behavior characteristics of children. *American Journal of Public Health, 48,* 1134-1144.

Lloyd, K. G., Hornykiewicz, O., Davidson, L., Shannak, K., Farley, I., Goldstein, M., Shibuya, M., Kelley, W. N., & Fox, I. H. (1981). Biochemical evidence of dysfunction of brain neurotransmitters in the Lesch-Nyhan syndrome. *New England Journal of Medicine, 305,* 1106-1111.

Lourie, R. (1949). The role of rhythmic patterns in childhood. *American Journal of Psychiatry, 105,* 653-660.

MacFarlane, J. W., Allen, L., & Honzik, M. P. (1954). *A developmental study of the behavior problems of normal children between twenty-one months and fourteen years.* Berkeley: University of California Press.

MacLean, W. E., Jr., & Baumeister, A. A. (1982). Effects of vestibular stimulation on motor development and stereotyped behavior of developmentally delayed children. *Journal of Abnormal Child Psychology, 10,* 229-245.

MacLean, W. E., Jr., Ellis, D. N., Galbreath, H. N., Halpern, L. F., & Baumeister, A. A. (1991). Rhythmic motor behavior of preambulatory motor impaired, Down syndrome, and nondisabled children: A comparative analysis. *Journal of Abnormal Child Psychology, 19,* 319-330.

Matson, J. L. (1989). Self-injury and stereotypies. In T. H. Ollendick & M. Hersen (Eds.), *Handbook of child psychopathology* (2nd ed.) (pp. 265-275). New York: Plenum.

Molnar, G. E. (1978). Analysis of motor disorder in retarded infants and young children. *American Journal of Mental Deficiency, 83,* 213-222.

National Institutes of Health. (1991). *Treatment of destructive behaviors in persons with developmental disabilities* (NIH Publication No. 91-2410). Bethesda, MD: U.S. Department of Health and Human Services.

Oliver, C., Murphy, G. H., & Corbett, J. A. (1987). Self-injurious behavior in people with mental handicap: A total population study. *Journal of Mental Deficiency Research, 31,* 147-162.

Parker, J. G., & Asher, S. R. (1987). Peer relations and later adjustment: Are low-accepted children "at risk"? *Psychological Bulletin, 102,* 357-389.

Patterson, G. R. (1982). *Coercive family process.* Eugene, OR: Castalia.

Patterson, G. R. (1986). Performance models for antisocial boys. *American Psychologist, 41,* 432-444.

Romanczyk, R. G. (1986). Self-injurious behavior: Conceptualization, assessment and treatment. In K. Gadow (Ed.), *Advances in learning and behavioral disabilities* (Vol. 5, pp. 29-56). Greenwich, CT: JAI.

Rusch, R. G., Hall, J. C., & Griffin, H. C. (1986). Abuse-provoking characteristics of institutionalized mentally retarded individuals. *American Journal of Mental Deficiency, 90,* 618-624.

Sallustro, F., & Atwell, C. W. (1978). Body rocking, head-banging, and head-rolling in normal children. *Journal of Pediatrics, 93,* 704-708.

Salzberg, C. L., Likins, M., McConaughy, E. K., & Lignugaris/Kraft, B. (1986). Social competence and employment of retarded persons. In N. R. Ellis & N. W. Bray (Eds.), *International review of research in mental retardation* (Vol. 14, pp. 225-257). Orlando, FL: Academic Press.

Sandman, C. A., Datta, P. C., Barron, J., Hoehler, F. K., Williams, C., & Swanson, J. M. (1983). Naloxone attenuates self-abusive behavior in developmentally disabled clients. *Applied Research in Mental Retardation, 4,* 5-11.

Schroeder, S. R. (1991). Self-injury and stereotypy. In J. L. Matson & J. A. Mulick (Eds.), *Handbook of mental retardation* (2nd ed.) (pp. 382-396). New York: Pergamon.

Schroeder, S. R., Breese, G. R., & Mueller, R. A. (1990). Dopaminergic mechanisms in self-injurious behavior. In M. Wolraich & D. K. Routh (Eds.), *Advances in developmental and behavioral pediatrics* (Vol. 9, pp. 181-198). London: Jessica Kingsley.

Schroeder, S. R., Kanoy, R. C., Mulick, J. A., Rojahn, J., Thios, S. J., Stephens, M., & Hawk, B. (1982). Environmental antecedents which affect management and maintenance of programs for self-injurious behavior. *Monographs of the American Association on Mental Deficiency, 5,* 105-159.

Schroeder, S. R., Rojahn, J., & Oldenquist, A. (1991). Treatment of destructive behaviors among people with mental retardation and developmental disabilities: Overview of the problem. In *Treatment of destructive behaviors in persons with developmental disabilities* (NIH Publication No. 91-2410) (pp. 125-171). Bethesda, MD: U.S. Department of Health and Human Services.

Shoemaker, D. S., Saylor, C. F., & Aikman, K. (1988, April). *Assessment of behavior problems in retarded preschoolers: Utility of the Achenbach Scales.* Paper presented at the Southeastern Psychological Association Annual Meeting, New Orleans, LA.

Sroufe, L. A., & Rutter, M. (1984). The domain of developmental psychopathology. *Child Development, 55,* 17-29.

Thelen, E. (1979). Rhythmical stereotypies in normal human infants. *Animal Behaviour, 27,* 699-715.

Thelen, E. (1981). Rhythmical behavior in infancy: An ethological perspective. *Developmental Psychology, 17,* 237-257.

Vitello, S. J., Atthowe, J. M., & Cadwell, J. (1983). Determinants of community placement of institutionalized mentally retarded persons. *American Journal of Mental Deficiency, 87,* 539-545.

Wenar, C. (1982). Developmental psychopathology: Its nature and models. *Journal of Clinical Child Psychology, 11,* 192-201.

Werry, J. S., Carlielle, J., & Fitzpatrick, J. (1983). Rhythmic motor activities (stereotypies) in children under five: Etiology and prevalence. *Journal of the American Academy of Child Psychiatry, 22,* 329-336.

Werry, J. S., & Quay, H. C. (1971). The prevalence of behavior symptoms in younger elementary school children. *American Journal of Orthopsychiatry, 41,* 136-143.

Wolff, P. H. (1967). The role of biological rhythms in early psychological development. *Bulletin of the Menninger Clinic, 31,* 197-218.

PART II

Observational Data Recording Systems for Analyzing Destructive Behavior and Analyzing Results From Multiple Small-Sample Investigations

5

Laptop Computer System for Data Recording and Contextual Analyses

ALAN C. REPP
KATHRYN G. KARSH

The conference on which this book is based addressed destructive behavior in many areas including diagnosis, measurement, developmental perspectives, ethics, epidemiology, evaluation, functional analysis, neurochemical factors, data collection, and intervention. The purpose of this chapter is to discuss one of these, data collection, in the general context of another, intervention.

There are two major intervention strategies used with destructive behavior, and they involve psychopharmacological and environmental manipulations. Each requires a data collection system that is sensitive to the parameters of these independent variables, and the purpose of this chapter is to present such a system. Before discussing the system we have developed, however, we will discuss our approach to intervention, thus putting the data collection system into the context of this book.

A Contextual Approach to Analysis

From our perspective, destructive behavior is either independent of the environment, dependent on the environment, or both independent

AUTHORS' NOTE: This research was supported in part by Grant No. H023C00092-91.

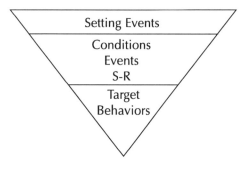

Figure 5.1.   A Model for Correlating (a) Setting Events and (b) Conditions, Events, and Stimulus-Response Interactions With (c) Destructive Behaviors of a Subject

and dependent (i.e., environmental manipulations may reduce the behavior substantially but never totally). The extent to which the behavior is independent of the environment may dictate the treatment of choice. In some cases, that choice may be a psychopharmacological or medical approach (see chapters by Schroeder, Thompson, and Nyhan); in other cases, that choice may be an environmental approach (see chapters by Foxx and Taylor).

Because much of our work has been conducted in schools, we have chosen an environmental approach and have developed a model for changing the context in which destructive behaviors occur. As such, one of our objectives is to design a data collection system that allows us to correlate environments with the problem behaviors. The system requires measurement of both environments and target behaviors so that we can identify the context in which destructive behavior occurs.

Our model, presented in Figure 5.1, requires data collection on three components: (a) setting events; (b) conditions, events, and stimulus-response interactions; and (c) behaviors of the subject. An example of the way we use the model is provided in Table 5.1. The first step involves identifying the target behaviors of interest.

Some examples from a study in progress are presented, and they include self-injurious behaviors (SIBs) (head banging, face slapping, and hand biting), aggression, disruption, stereotypy, other inappropriate behavior, and no inappropriate behavior. The second step involves identifying the conditions, events, and stimulus-response interactions

Table 5.1 Analysis for Environmentally Dependent Behaviors

Step 1: Identify Target Behaviors
    Examples: Self-injury, aggression, disruption, stereotypy, other inappropriate,
    no inappropriate
Step 2: Identify Conditions, Events, Stimulus-Response Interactions
    Examples: Set I: Attention, no attention
    Set II: Demand, no demand
    Set III: Task, no task
Step 3: Identify Setting Events
    Examples: Set I: Teacher 1, Teacher 2
    Set II: Preferred activity, nonprefered activity
    Set III: Apartment, classroom

of interest. In this case, we have chosen three pairs of mutually exclusive environments: (a) Set I: attention and no attention; (b) Set II: demand and no demand; and (c) Set III: task and no task.

The third step involves selecting setting events or those settings that change the correlation between a condition, event, or stimulus-response interaction and behavior. For example, one setting event we have chosen is type of activity because it in turn can determine whether or not an event such as demand will produce destructive behaviors. Other examples of setting events we study include location, staff, schedules of activities, medical complications, and diet.

Hypotheses for Destructive Behavior

Because we are concerned with environmentally based behavior, we need to determine which parts of the environment control behavior. One approach to this task involves correlating environments to the rate or percentage of duration of behavior (e.g., headbanging occurs 1.2 times per minute during a task and 0.006 times per minute when there is no task). Our data collection system, which we use to produce a taxonomy, provides such information.

These data can be better used as a basis for treatment, however, if they are based on the function of these behaviors. Such an approach has been taken by numerous investigators. For example, Durand and Crimmins (1988) have hypothesized three functions of SIB: positive reinforcement through attention or access to materials, negative reinforcement through escape from a condition, and sensory or automatic reinforcement. Iwata, Vollmer, and Zarcone (1990) have also suggested these functions,

Table 5.2 Possible Interventions for Learned Problem Behaviors

---

Negative Reinforcement Hypothesis
1. Use functional equivalence training
2. Alter conditions associated with high rates
3. Use conditions associated with low rates
4. Modify educational curriculum

Positive Reinforcement Hypothesis
1. Use a differential reinforcement procedure that produces the same reinforcer that the problem behavior produces. However, it should be produced more efficiently, on a denser schedule of reinforcement, with greater magnitude, and/or with previously unproduced reinforcers. Examples include:
   a. Differential reinforcement of other behavior
   b. Differential reinforcement of incompatible behavior
   c. Differential reinforcement of alternative responding
   d. Differential reinforcement of low rates of responding
2. Provide a skills acquisition program to garner more reinforcement

Stimulation Hypothesis
1. Program present environment to provide stimulation at a higher rate
2. Intersperse or substitute other conditions that provide stimulation at a higher rate

---

although they noted that automatic reinforcement can be viewed as positive reinforcement (e.g., SIB that provides sensory stimulation) or negative reinforcement (e.g., SIB that attenuates pain).

Our system also addresses three hypotheses: (a) positive reinforcement, (b) negative reinforcement, and (c) arousal induction or stimulation. The latter can be viewed as a positive reinforcement paradigm (i.e., a response that produces stimulation is positively reinforced). However, we separate arousal induction or stimulation from reinforcement in our analysis for several reasons: (a) It can be operationalized very easily as an increase in behavior under environments that do not require motoric responses; (b) it is suited to the study of stereotypy, which is important because individuals who engage in SIB tend to engage in stereotypy; (c) we have data indicating the utility of the construct (Repp & Karsh, 1992; Repp, Karsh, Deitz, & Singh, 1992); and (d) if we conceptualize some environments as requiring too little responding, then treatment is obvious and is based on the function of the behavior.

The latter point is illustrated in Table 5.2, which shows some interventions that might be appropriate given particular functions of behavior. For example, the negative reinforcement hypothesis would suggest that the individual finds the environment aversive and that problem behaviors function to escape or avoid these environments. Interventions, then, should be directed toward reducing the aversiveness of the environment and, as such, would be very different from interventions for behaviors that were being positively reinforced.

Alternative treatments for the negative reinforcement hypothesis could include (a) functional equivalence training (e.g., teaching the individual an appropriate response that would be functionally equivalent to the problem behavior, thus producing a brief escape from the condition) (Steege et al., 1990); (b) altering conditions associated with high rates (e.g., making tasks easier by employing an errorless learning procedure) (Repp & Karsh, 1992; Weeks & Gaylord-Ross, 1981); (c) interspersing conditions associated with low rates of the problem behavior among conditions associated with high rates (Carr, Newsom, & Binkoff, 1976; Winterling, Dunlap, & O'Neill, 1987); and (d) modifying a curriculum (e.g., by changing from repetitive, nonfunctional tasks to functional tasks) (Dunlap, Kern-Dunlap, Clarke, & Robbins, 1991).

If the behavior is being maintained by positive reinforcement rather than by escape from aversive conditions, treatment would focus more on changing consequences than on changing conditions antecedent to the behavior. All the differential reinforcement procedures (DRA, DRI, DRL, DRO)[1] would be suitable, but we believe that key to the success of these procedures is the relationship between the response and the consequence. The appropriate response should produce the same consequence as the inappropriate response has been producing and perhaps a more powerful reinforcer as well. In addition, the appropriate response should produce the reinforcer more efficiently, with less effort, on a denser schedule, and/or with greater magnitude (Carr, 1988; Horner & Day, 1991; Wacker et al., 1990). A related reinforcement program is skills acquisition training (Carr, Robinson, Taylor, & Carlson, 1990), a systematic DRA program in which an individual is taught several skills that efficiently garner multiple reinforcers. Although the program is not discussed in this way, we view it as an application of the matching law in which the problem behavior decreases because it receives less reinforcement than the set of alternative responses (Epling & Pierce, 1990; Herrnstein, 1961, 1970).

If the behavior is maintained because of the stimulation it produces, then interventions associated with negative reinforcement would not be appropriate unless they increased stimulation. Several of the interventions associated with positive reinforcement would be appropriate provided they increased the rate of responding by the individual. However, we find treatment to be more directly obvious if we find problem behaviors to be associated with conditions that do not produce consistent and relatively high rates of motoric responding. In a recent effort, we showed that 8 (of 15) severely disabled students, involved in a teaching program that increased their engaged time by more than a factor of 1.5, decreased their problem behaviors from 51% of the session to 10% (Repp & Karsh, 1992).

Analyzing Behavioral Functions in Their Context

There are numerous ways to analyze functions of aberrant behaviors including interviews, analogue assessments, and naturalistic assessments. The interview format can be found in the work by Durand and Crimmins (1988), which is a 16-item questionnaire that seeks to isolate one of the functions of SIB. The reliability and validity of this instrument have however, been questioned (see Iwata et al., 1990; Newton & Sturmey, 1991; Rourke, Dorsey, Green, Barry, & Kimball, 1990; Zarcone, Rodgers, Iwata, Rourke, & Dorsey, 1991). An alternative has been provided by O'Neill, Horner, Albin, Storey, and Sprague (1990), who developed and field tested a manual for problem behaviors. The interview section is 10 pages long, but even at that length the authors do not intend for it to stand alone. Instead, they combine it with a direct observation format that indicates the times at which the problem behavior occurs, the setting events and discriminative stimuli that occasion it, the consequences, and the perceived functions of the behavior. We have found this assessment program to be valuable, and we use it to isolate setting events, conditions, short-term events, and stimulus-response interactions that may occasion problem behaviors (see Figure 5.1).

An alternative approach has been developed by Iwata and his colleagues (see Iwata, Dorsey, Slifer, Bauman, & Richman, 1982). In this approach, an analogue procedure, conditions are presented in a clinical setting to address possible functions of aberrant behavior. In their original article, four conditions were used: (a) positive reinforcement (attention was contingent on the occurrence of SIB); (b) negative reinforcement (escape from demands was contingent on SIB); (c) stimulation (the subject was placed in a barren room without access to attention or toys); and (d) a control for the three other conditions (no attention for SIB, no demands, toys available, and attention contingent on the absence of SIB). The function of behavior can often, although not always, be found through this assessment procedure, and treatment is based on the identified function (Day, Rea, Schussler, Larsen, & Johnson, 1988; Iwata,

Pace, Kalsher, Cowdery, & Cataldo, 1990; Mason & Iwata, 1990; Steege, Wacker, Berg, Cigrand, & Cooper, 1989).

The latter is a very useful approach for identifying the function of behavior and is particularly suited to severe behavior problems. However, its use in public schools is limited because it requires a condition that will exacerbate the problem. As such, school personnel are often reluctant to approve its use. As a result, we have been developing a procedure in which we analyze behavior in its natural context without setting up artificial conditions and without deliberately increasing the problem behavior. We analyze the naturally occurring conditions within the framework of three functions: (a) positive reinforcement, (b) negative reinforcement, and (c) stimulation.

The problem with analyzing natural environments is that they can (and should) be very complex, with changing tasks, various adults interacting with the subject, different behaviors occurring, and so forth. The advantages of a naturalistic, contextual analysis are that (a) behavior will be occurring at its normal rate; (b) the consequences or antecedents that can be manipulated during intervention will be present during the assessment; (c) there is no need for considerations of generalization from the assessment to the treatment environments; (d) there are no artificial conditions; (e) administrative approval is easy to obtain; and (f) the assessment, which requires no changes from the normal routine, is not intrusive (although data collection may be).

Our objective has been to design a system that can be used in school and work environments that would allow us to determine the function of problem behavior in its natural context. Examples of this system are shown in Figure 5.2, which is a series of hypothesis-based matrixes representing possible interactions between SIB and conditions, events, and stimulus-response relationships found in classrooms. Data are collected and the computer program develops the data for each behavior of interest in the appropriate row-column intersect for any matrix.

The examples in Figure 5.2 have been selected to address the three hypotheses for SIB (i.e., positive reinforcement, negative reinforcement, and stimulation). For each matrix, there is a cell that should have the highest rate or percentage time of SIB if a specific hypothesis is operable.

The key cell for the positive reinforcement matrix in our example is the one representing the intersect of SIB and attention. The rationale is that if one teacher (Teacher 1) is reinforcing SIB with attention while another (Teacher 2) is not, there would be a higher proportion of entries in the SIB/attention cell under the setting events of Teacher 1 than there

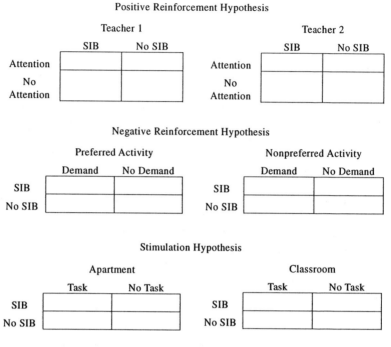

Figure 5.2.   Matrixes for Contextual Analyses in Classrooms

would be in the SIB/attention cell under the setting event of Teacher 2. Treatment might involve shifting attention for Teacher 1 to the no SIB/attention cell; the matching law (Herrnstein, 1961) would predict that SIB would then decrease because its relative rate of reinforcement would decrease substantially.

The key cells in our example for the negative reinforcement hypothesis are represented by the intersect of SIB and activity preference. For example, if the student were given preferred and nonpreferred activities and found the nonpreferred aversive, SIB might be used to escape the nonpreferred activities. In that case, there would be a higher proportion of entries in the demand/SIB cell under the setting event of nonpreferred activity than there would be in the demand/SIB cell under the setting event of preferred activities. The rationale is that if the individual was trying to avoid or escape tasks the most aversive condition would be demands during nonpreferred activities. A less aversive condition would be demand under preferred activity. The condition of no demand/preferred activity would serve as a control, and the proportion of entries should be the lowest in this cell. The key cells for the stimulation hypothesis would be those associated with the absence of tasks. The rationale is that these cells describe environments that are the least stimulating in terms of active responding and human stimulation. The highest rates of SIB should occur in no task/SIB, and the lowest rates of SIB should occur in task/ SIB. If tasks in Setting 1 (apartment) required more gross motor movement than tasks in Setting 2 (classroom), then the lowest rates of SIB should occur in task/SIB in the apartment setting.

Data Collection

In the prior section, we described a taxonomy for the study of problem behaviors in order to discuss the data collection system in the context of this book. We would like to stress the point, however, that the system is independent of both the dependent and independent variables we have discussed. For example, the system was designed to evaluate the transfer of persons from institutions to group homes in Britain (Felce, de Kock, & Repp, 1986; Felce, Thomas, de Kock, Saxby, & Repp, 1985). Since then, we have also used it to study the relationship of staff consequences to the behavior of residents (Felce, Saxby, et al., 1987), the relationship of staff-client ratios to the behavior of residents (Felce, Repp, et al., 1991), the effects of a teaching procedure on adaptive and maladaptive behavior (Karsh & Repp, 1992; Repp & Karsh, 1992), and the effects of various procedures on severe feeding problems of persons with disabilities (O'Brien & Repp, 1991).

Hardware

Generic programs have been written for collecting and analyzing data on MS-DOS laptop computers, although some analyses are faster on a desktop computer. Data may also be collected on Hewlett-Packard palmheld computers. All the computers have a built-in timer, accurate to 1 second, which is used to indicate the time at which each behavior (e.g., head banging) and each environmental condition (e.g., task) begins and ends. Codes are assigned to as many as 45 keys, and press-on tabs with the code abbreviation and keystroke written on them are placed on each key. Keys struck are illuminated on the LCD and remain for the duration of the event.

Software

Software has been written for two functions: data collection and data analysis. The collection programs include *Observe* and *Reliable,* and the analysis programs include *Edit, Combine, Bout, Nesting,* and *Lag.* Each of these will be discussed separately.

Observe. This is the data collection program, and it has three sections: pre–data collection, data collection, and output. Initially, the operator answers two sets of information. One set identifies the situation and asks questions like name of subject(s) and observer, date, session number, and so forth. The other set involves questions relevant to data collection itself, and they include the following:

1. *Engaged keys:* defines operable and inoperable keys. Prevents inoperable keys accidentally hit from entering the data set. Also decreases time required to print session totals.

2. *Event keys:* determines keys of short durations. Used for codes that have a short and relatively constant duration. Operator presses this key once, and the computer assigns a 1-second duration.

3. *Duration keys:* determines keys of varying duration. Operator presses key once for initiation and once for termination, and the computer determines the duration of each episode.

4. *Mutually exclusive and exhaustive codes:* defines sets of exhaustive (i.e., one member of the code must be on at all times) and mutually exclusive codes (i.e., only one key in a set can be on at a time). For example, the cells of each matrix in Figure 5.2 form a set of mutually exclusive and exhaustive codes. When the operator indicates the keys that form a mutually exclusive set, the code that was on will be turned off automatically when another key is depressed, saving a key stroke and making data collection easier. In addition, data analysis from the experimenter's (not the computer's) viewpoint is easier.

5. *Subsessions:* allows operator to observe one subject in a group, then move to another subject, then another, and so forth, while preserving separately the data on each subject. Computer sounds a tone every t seconds, indicating when to move from one subject to another.

These five options need to be indicated only once, and the program saves the decisions from one session to another. The identifier information is provided each session, after which the observer presses a key to begin the session. Keys are pressed according to their occurrence, and nothing additional has to be done to provide the information for the contextual analysis. The observer indicates the occurrence of events, conditions, and behaviors all in the same way. At the end of the session, the disengage key is pressed, and the timer is stopped.

The computer then provides three sets of output data: the identifiers, the sequence in which the codes appeared, and the frequency and duration of each code. Table 5.3 provides an example of a 43-second session. Normally, sessions are 20 to 60 minutes, and the printouts can be quite long; our example is short to save space. One of the advantages of using a computer is evident at this stage. The operator simply has to issue the command, and then all the data will be provided automatically, quickly, and without errors.

Reliability. The second part of the data collection program involves reliability. As usual, two records are compared, with the records arising from two operators simultaneously observing or from one observer recording twice from audiotape or videotape.

Two types of reliability are calculated: one for data presented by the experimenter as rate data and one for data presented as duration data. For the rate data, the experimenter indicates the number of seconds (e.g., 1 or 2) that the two records could differ from each other and still be considered an agreement. The computer then looks at each occurrence on one observer's record and compares with it the other record to determine whether the event appeared within t seconds. The printout then shows the agreements and disagreements for each code for its initiation and termination. An example for the 43-second session is presented in Table 5.3.

For the duration data (usually presented as "percentage of session in which x occurred"), the computer scans both records on a second-by-second basis to determine whether there is agreement on each code for each second. It then automatically calculates the occurrence agreement and nonoccurrence agreement for each code (Hartmann, 1975). An example for the 43-second session is also presented in Table 5.3.

Data Analysis

The following will indicate the five programs involved in data analysis beyond the analyses presented in Table 5.3.

Table 5.3 Examples of the Session and Reliability Printouts Provided by the Collector Program

Data from the OBSERVE program:

TABLE 1: Heading

Date	:	2/2/89
Subject ID	:	ALAN
Instructor	:	KATHY
Serial No.	:	S-1
Observer	:	DALE
Ending Time	:	43 sec.
Location	:	school
Session No.	:	1
Observer No.	:	1

Table 2: Event sequence for session

Beha-vior	Starting second	Finishing second	Dura-tion
1	1	43	42
R	2	13	11
J	2	20	18
W	6	7	1
T	12	16	4
R	15	43	28

NOTES: child ill today

Table 3: Frequency and duration of the events recorded.

Beh = code for event or behavior
\# = number of occurrences of event
RPM = responses per minute
Dur = duration of event
%T = % of session event occurred

Beh	#	RPM	Dur	%T
1	1	1.4	42	98
W	1	1.4	1	2
R	2	2.8	39	91
T	1	1.4	4	9
J	1	1.4	18	42

RELIABILITY DATA

FREQUENCY RELIABILITY

Beh	Start A	D	%	Finish A	D	%
1	1	0	100	1	0	100
W	1	0	100	1	0	100
R	2	0	100	2	0	100
T	1	0	100	0	1	0
J	1	0	100	1	0	100

Agreement on initiation of behavior	100%
Agreement on termination of behavior	83%
Overall Agreement	92%

A = agreement
D = disagreement

DURATION RELIABILITY

Beh	OA	%	NA	D	OT
1	41	95	0	2	0
W	0	0	41	2	95
R	34	85	3	6	33
T	4	13	11	28	28
J	17	94	25	1	96

Total Seconds of agreement on occurrence	96
Total Seconds of agreement on non-occurrence	25
Total seconds of disagreement	39
Occurrence agreement	71 %
Nonoccurrence agreement	87 %
Overall agreement	76 %

OA = occurrence agreement
NA = non-occurrence agreement
D = disagreement
OT = overall total

Edit. This program allows the experimenter to edit data collected through the *Observe* program, and it addresses three concerns:

1. errors: A key depressed in error (and noted by immediately following it with an error code) can be erased from the data set.

Table 5.4 Bout Lengths Tabulated Into Bins to Indicate Durations of the Behavior

Bin Number	1	2	3	4	5	6	7	8	9	10
Bin Start Time	1	3	5	7	9	11	13	15	17	19
Bin End Time	2	4	6	8	10	12	14	16	18	20
A	0	2	0	0	0	0	1	0	1	0
Bin Number	11	12	13	14	15	16	17	18	19	20
Bin Start Time	21	26	31	36	41	46	51	56	61	66
Bin End Time	25	30	35	40	45	50	55	60	65	70
A	1	0	0	0	0	0	0	0	0	0

	Min	Max	Mean	Standard Deviation
A	4	25	12.6	8.96

2. identifiers: Script can be added to the printout to indicate the setting events or any session anomalies (e.g., the subject was ill), thus providing a permanent record with the data printout.

3. combination: The experimenter can combine codes into a class (e.g., headbanging, handbiting, and eye gouging may have been recorded separately but can now be analyzed as one behavior, self-injury).

Combine. Although the computer keyboard has 45 keys that can be used as codes, an occasional study may involve more codes. This program allows the experimenter to combine two data sets gathered simultaneously by two observers on two computers, or by one observer using audiotape or videotape. The output will be just like that in Table 5.3, and data analysis can proceed as if one observer recorded 50 or 60 codes on one computer.

Bout/Interbout. In some experiments, we may be interested in the durations of the episodes of behavior (bouts) and the times between episodes (interbouts). This information can be used in basic research to measure such things as schedule or drug effects. It can also be used in applied research to indicate the interval to be used in a DRO schedule to reduce problem behavior.[2]

This program provides two tables: one for bout and one for interbout. Table 5.4 provides an example for bout lengths that have been tabulated into bins indicating the durations of behavior. In this table, the first 10 bins are for 2 seconds' duration, and the second 10 bins are for 5 seconds' duration. In the table, Event A occurred five times, two times with a duration of 3-4 seconds and one time each with durations of 13-14 seconds, 17-18 seconds, and 21-25 seconds. The same type of table

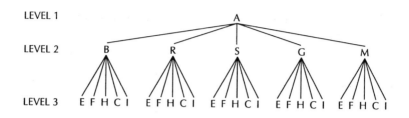

Figure 5.3. Schema of Nesting Program for Three Levels of Analysis

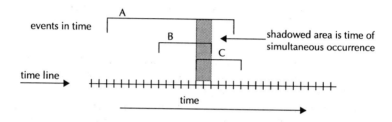

Figure 5.4. An Example of Nesting Analysis to Determine Percentage of Time of Simultaneous Occurrence of A and B and Percentage of Time of Simultaneous Occurrence of A, B, and C

would be provided for interbout lengths. The operator indicates how many seconds the first and second 10 bins should be for bouts and then interbouts; the computer scans the data stream and then prints two tables like the one in Table 5.4.

Nesting. This program provides information on the simultaneous occurrence of different codes. Data are automatically aggregated under the conditions chosen for nesting. The schema for this program appears in Figure 5.3. Nesting allows the experimenter to choose three levels for analysis. The first level has one code (e.g., task), the second level can have five codes,[3] and the third level can have five codes under each of the five codes on the second level. Figure 5.4 indicates the manner in which the computer makes the analysis. Two questions can be asked of this example. The first is at Level 2: In what percentage of the time that A is occurring is B also occurring? The second is at Level 3: In what percentage of the time that both A and B are occurring is C also occurring? The complexity of this analysis when there are multiple occurrences of A, B, and C and when there are multiple codes at each

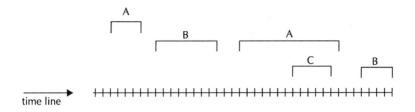

Figure 5.5. A Sequence of Events A, B, and C as the Computer Would Preserve Them in Real Time

level makes one appreciate the computer. The operator indicates the codes at each level and then the computer scans the sequence of codes and prints the analysis.

Lag. This program provides an analysis of the sequence of codes, perhaps of a person (as in a chain of behaviors), or of a didactic interchange, or of target behaviors to consequences, or of antecedents to target behaviors.

Lag can be conceptualized as an if-then statement: If Event A happens, what is the probability that B will then happen? The *then* statement takes two forms. In event lag, the generic question is: If A happens, what is the probability that the next event will be B (instead of C, D, etc.)? This question can be asked for Lag 1 (i.e., the probability that the next event after A will be B) or Lag 2 (i.e., the probability that the event after the one immediately following A will be B), and so forth. The other type of lag, time-based lag, also asks the if-then question. However, the question is based on time: If A happens, what is the probability that B will occur within 5 seconds (or 10, etc.)? So, in one case, the experimenter asks what the probability of a particular sequence is; in the other case, the experimenter asks what the probability of two events (A then B) occurring within a particular time is.

There are many decisions to be made in this program, and we have detailed them elsewhere (Karsh, Repp, & Ludewig, 1989). The most basic questions can be deduced from Figure 5.5, which shows a sequence of events—A, B, and C—as the computer would preserve them (see Table 5.3's printout of the sequence of behavior). The experimenter must decide the basis of the *if* question, that is, "if the onset of A . . . ," "if the offset of A . . . ," or "if while A is occurring . . . ." We have designed these options so that various researchers could use the program even if their experimental questions are quite different from each other's.

Data are statistically analyzed by importing into statistical packages such as SPSS-PC, SASS, or SYSTAT, and we are very grateful to our statistical consultant Roger Bakeman for his guidance in this area. These procedures are detailed elsewhere (Karsh et al., 1989); the basis for the analysis, however, can be seen in Figure 5.2. This is a 2 × 2 analysis of the if-then question, regardless of whether it is in the event-based or time-based format. The program enters the data into each cell and then runs statistical analyses addressing various questions.

Returning to the context of the book and Figure 5.2, the columns are read as the *if* statement, and the rows are read as the *then* statement. The positive reinforcement matrixes then are read as follows: (a) If there is SIB, what is the probability that attention will be present or absent; and (b) if SIB is not occurring, what is the probability that attention will be present or absent? The negative reinforcement matrixes are read as follows: (a) If there is a demand, what is the probability that SIB will be present or absent; and (b) if a demand is not occurring, what is the probability that SIB will be present or absent? Finally, the stimulation matrixes are read as follows: (a) If there is a task, what is the probability that SIB will be present or absent; and (b) if there is no task, what is the probability that SIB will be present or absent?

Summary

In the prior discussions, we have tried to put the computer-based data collection system into the context of problem behaviors. The system, of course, is independent of problem behavior and most of our studies with it have been in other areas. However, we see a number of advantages to using this system with such behavior when researchers are conducting contextual functional analyses, providing behavioral interventions, studying the effects of drugs, or assessing the effects of school, work, or residential placements. These advantages include:

1. Data are in real time and real sequence.
2. There are no inherent sampling errors as in systems using partial interval or momentary time sampling.
3. Analyses can be conducted that would be too complicated and time-consuming to conduct if using hand-collected data or impossible to conduct if using data from partial interval or momentary time sampling.

4. All calculations are correct because there are no numerical data for humans to input to a calculator or computer.
5. We can study more complex environments.
6. We may be able to learn more about the variables controlling human behavior.

The major disadvantage is cost, which is about $1,000 for hardware and software. When large amounts of data are collected, some of that cost can be regained through saving time in summarizing and analyzing data collected by paper and pencil. Many people presume that the time involved in training would be a disadvantage, but this is not so. Time for training is not a function of the computer; rather it is a function of the complexity of the code. If there are five codes, the observer with a computer simply has to learn which codes correlate with which keys; the observer using paper and pencil has to learn which columns on a paper correlate to which codes. In each case, there are some commonsense dictates on how to group codes that tend to occur together, that occur frequently, or that occur infrequently. If there are 30 codes, the training is just as difficult for the observer using a computer as for the observer using paper and pencil. The difference occurs when the observer with a computer scores 30 codes, whereas the observer with paper and pencil scores only 5 codes. But this difference is an experimental one and one that the computer allows us to address with considerable ease.

Notes

1. The differential reinforcement of alternative behavior (DRA), the differential reinforcement of incompatible behavior (DRI), the differential reinforcement of low rates of responding (DRL), and the differential reinforcement of other responding (DRO).
2. DRO is a procedure in which reinforcement is presented if behavior does not occur for a specified interval. The interbout data indicate how long the subject pauses between episodes and thus provide information on the initial interval to use in a DRO.
3. If there are more than 5 codes at Level 2 (which is frequently the case), the operator simply runs the analysis twice (for 6-10 codes), three times (for 11-15 codes), and so on.

References

Carr, E. G. (1988). Functional equivalence as a mechanism of response generalization. In R. H. Horner, G. Dunlap, & R. L. Koegel (Eds.), *Generalization and maintenance: Lifestyle changes in applied settings* (pp. 221-241). Baltimore, MD: Brooks.

Carr, E. G., Newsom, C. D., & Binkoff, J. A. (1976). Stimulus control of self-destructive behavior in a psychotic child. *Journal of Abnormal Child Psychology, 4*, 139-153.

Carr, E. G., Robinson, S., Taylor, J. C., & Carlson, J. L. (1990). *Positive approaches to the treatment of severe behavior problems in persons with developmental disabilities: A review and analysis of reinforcement and stimulus-based procedures* (Monograph of the Association for Persons With Severe Handicaps). Seattle, WA: TASH.

Day, R. M., Rea, J. A., Schussler, N. G., Larsen, S. E., & Johnson, W. L. (1988). A functionally based approach to the treatment of self-injurious behavior. *Behavior Modification, 12*, 565-589.

Dunlap, G., Kern-Dunlap, L., Clarke, S., & Robbins, F. R. (1991). Functional assessment, curricular revision and severe behavior problems. *Journal of Applied Behavior Analysis, 24*, 387-397.

Durand, V. M., & Crimmins, D. B. (1988). Identifying the variables maintaining self-injurious behavior. *Journal of Autism and Developmental Disorders, 18*, 99-117.

Epling, W. F., & Pierce, W. D. (1990). Laboratory to application: An experimental analysis of severe-problem behavior. In A. C. Repp & N. N. Singh (Ed.), *Perspectives on the use of nonaversive and aversive interventions for persons with developmental disabilities* (pp. 451-464). Sycamore, IL: Sycamore.

Felce, D., de Kock, U., & Repp, A. C. (1986). An eco-behavioral analysis of small community-based houses and traditional large hospitals for severely and profoundly mentally handicapped adults. *Applied Research in Mental Retardation, 7*, 393-408.

Felce, D., Repp, A. C., de Kock, U., Thomas, M., Ager, A., & Blunden, R. (1991). Staff/client ratios and their relationship to staff interactions and client behaviors in large and small facilities for severely handicapped adults. *Research in Developmental Disabilities, 12*, 315-331.

Felce, D., Saxby, H., de Kock, U., Repp, A. C., Ager, A., & Blunden, R. (1987). To what behaviors do attending adults respond? A replication. *American Journal of Mental Deficiency, 91*, 496-504.

Felce, D., Thomas, M., de Kock, W., Saxby, H., & Repp, A. C. (1985). An ecological comparison of small community-based houses and traditional institutions-II. *Behaviour Research and Therapy, 23*, 337-348.

Hartmann, D. P. (1975). Considerations on the choice of interobserver reliability estimates. *Journal of Applied Behavior Analysis, 10*, 103-116.

Herrnstein, R. J. (1961). Relative and absolute strength of response as a function of frequency of reinforcement. *Journal of the Experimental Analysis of Behavior, 4*, 267-272.

Herrnstein, R. J. (1970). On the law of effect. *Journal of the Experimental Analysis of Behavior, 13*, 243-266.

Horner, R. H., & Day, M. (1991). The effects of response efficiency on functionally equivalent, competing behaviors. *Journal of Applied Behavior Analysis, 24*, 719-732.

Iwata, B. A., Dorsey, M. F., Slifer, K. J., Bauman, K. E., & Richman, G. S. (1982). Toward a functional analysis of self-injury. *Analysis and Intervention in Developmental Disabilities, 2*, 1-20.

Iwata, B. A., Pace, G. M., Kalsher, M. J., Cowdery, G. E., & Cataldo, M. F. (1990). Experimental analysis and extinction of self-injurious behavior. *Journal of Applied Behavior Analysis, 23*, 11-27.

Iwata, B. A., Vollmer, T. R., & Zarcone, J. H. (1990). The experimental (functional) analysis of behavior disorders: Methodology, application, and limitations. In A. C. Repp

& N. N. Singh (Eds.), *Perspectives on the use of nonaversive and aversive interventions for persons with developmental disabilities* (pp. 301-330). Sycamore, IL: Sycamore.

Karsh, K. G., & Repp, A. C. (1992). The task demonstration model: A concurrent model for teaching groups of persons with severe disabilities. *Exceptional Children, 59,* 54-67.

Karsh, K. G., Repp, A. C., & Ludewig, D. (1989). *Portable computer systems for observational research: A software user's guide.* DeKalb, IL: Communitech.

Mason, S. A., & Iwata, B. A. (1990). Artifactual effects of sensory-integrative therapy on self-injurious behavior. *Journal of Applied Behavior Analysis, 23,* 361-370.

Newton, J. T., & Sturmey, P. (1991). The Motivation Assessment Scale: Inter-rater reliability and internal consistency in a British sample. *Journal of Mental Deficiency Research, 35,* 472-474.

O'Brien, S., & Repp, A. C. (1991). *Feeding problems of children with severe handicaps: Evaluation and treatment in the educational environment.* Paper presented at the meeting of the Association for Behavior Analysis, Atlanta, GA.

O'Neill, R. E., Horner, R. H., Albin, R. W., Storey, K., & Sprague, J. R. (1990). *Functional analysis of problem behavior: A practical assessment guide.* Sycamore, IL: Sycamore.

Repp, A. C., & Karsh, K. G. (1992). An analysis of a group teaching procedure for persons with developmental disabilities. *Journal of Applied Behavior Analysis, 25,* 701-712.

Repp, A. C., Karsh, K. G., Deitz, D. E. D., & Singh, N. N. (1992). A study of the homeostatic level of stereotypy and other motor movements of persons with mental handicaps. *Journal of Intellectual Disability, 36,* 61-75.

Rourke, D. R., Dorsey, M. F., Green, M. A., Barry, G. A., & Kimball, J. W. (1990). *The Motivation Assessment Scale: A failure to replicate.* Paper presented at the annual conference of the Berkshire Association for Behavior Analysis and Therapy.

Steege, M. W., Wacker, D. P., Berg, W. K., Cigrand, K. K., & Cooper, L. J. (1989). The use of behavioral assessment to prescribe and evaluate treatments for severely handicapped children. *Journal of Applied Behavior Analysis, 22,* 23-33.

Steege, M. W., Wacker, D. P., Cigrand, K. C., Berg, W. K., Novak, C. G., Reimers, T. M., Sasso, G. M., & DeRaad, A. (1990). Use of negative reinforcement in the treatment of self-injurious behavior. *Journal of Applied Behavior Analysis, 23,* 459-467.

Wacker, D. P., Steege, M. W., Northup, J., Sasso, G., Berg, W., Reimers, T., Cooper, L., Cigrand, K., & Donn, L. (1990). A component analysis of functional communication training across three topographies of severe behavior problems. *Journal of Applied Behavior Analysis, 23,* 417-429.

Weeks, M., & Gaylord-Ross, R. (1981). Task difficulty and aberrant behavior in severely handicapped students. *Journal of Applied Behavior Analysis, 14,* 449-463.

Winterling, V., Dunlap, G., & O'Neill, R. E. (1987). The influence of task variation on the aberrant behaviors of autistic students. *Education and Treatment of Children, 10,* 105-119.

Zarcone, J. R., Rodgers, T. A., Iwata, B. A., Rourke, D., & Dorsey, M. F. (1991). Reliability analysis of the Motivation Assessment Scale: A failure to replicate. *Research in Developmental Disabilities, 12,* 349-360.

6

Data Collection
With Bar Code Technology

RICHARD R. SAUNDERS
MURIEL D. SAUNDERS
JAY L. SAUNDERS

Recently Repp, Harman, Felce, Van Acker, and Karsh (1989) described a computer software program that permitted complex behavioral assessments with observational data, collected using an Epson HX-20® laptop portable computer as the recording device. In addition to producing tables of the number, rate, and duration of observed events and the percentage of sessions in which responding occurred, the program permitted automated assessments of interobserver agreement and lag-sequential analysis (Sackett, 1978, 1979; Sackett, Holm, Crowley, & Henknins, 1979) of antecedent events and subsequent behaviors, or behaviors and subsequent consequences. Advantages of data collection and data analysis with this combination of software and hardware include the ability to record multiple events concurrently, to track precisely when the events occurred in time and in relation to each other, to conduct assessments on the data in the field with the same equipment that was used to record the data, and a low overall cost (Repp et al., 1989).

Another recent development in data collection technology is the application of bar code symbols and portable optical scanners for behavioral

AUTHORS' NOTE: Preparation of this manuscript was supported in part by National Institute of Child Health and Human Development Grants No. 5-P30HD02528 and 1-P01HD26927 to the Schiefelbusch Institute for Life Span Studies, University of Kansas.

data collection. Eiler, Nelson, Jensen, and Johnson (1989) described the use of hand-held bar code scanners by residential teaching staff in a facility for persons with developmental disabilities. Data sheets were constructed as "menus" of bar codes that included codes for staff names, client names, behaviors, point values (in the residences' behavioral incentive system), and so forth. The staff recorded the responses of their clients by passing the lens of the scanner (a Videx TimeWand®) over the appropriate code for each response. The scanned code was stored in the random access memory (RAM) of the scanner until it could be transferred to a computer for analysis. Eiler et al. (1989) reported benefits derived from this approach in data management, timeliness of processed reports of observations, accuracy and level of measurement, staff management, and staff morale.

Comparing Laptop Computers and Bar Code Scanners

In comparing the systems of Repp et al. (1989) and Eiler et al. (1989), it is clear that the former was developed for the research environment using independent observers and is highly suited to that application; the latter approach was deployed to improve data collection by the treatment provider in the treatment setting. Although the laptop system provides a distinct advantage if one requires immediate, onsite analysis of the just-collected data, the bar code system offers a distinct advantage in portability. A Videx TimeWand® weighs less than 2 ounces, as opposed to several pounds for portable computers, and can be carried in a pocket when not in use. The bar code system also may offer advantages in the accuracy of data entry (Harmon & Adams, 1984).

At the time of the Repp et al. (1989) and the Eiler et al. (1989) reports, we were seeking a new approach to data collection for teachers and other treatment personnel in educational and residential settings for persons with developmental disabilities. In classrooms, for example, data often are collected using paper-and-pencil methods (Alberto & Troutman, 1982; Kerr & Nelson, 1983; Martin & Pear, 1988), augmented with stopwatches for time-based data collection (Bailey, 1977) and hand-held counters (Lindsley, 1968) or pocket calculators (Drash, Ray, & Tudor, 1989) for frequency counts. These methods are inexpensive, do not require the learning of special codes associated with keystroke-entered data, and can be modified easily from day to day. We were particularly interested in determining whether these advantages were inherent in a bar code system.

Our tests not only confirmed these features but also indicated that bar code technology (we also employed Videx equipment) was a highly reliable system electronically and mechanically (see Saunders, Saunders, & Saunders, 1993). The teachers, trainers, and direct care staff of the facilities with which we work have now scanned several million bar codes with few scanning errors or character substitutions (see Eiler et al., 1989, for specific error projections). Moreover, the scanning and communications equipment also has proved to be durable and easy to use. Our test also revealed that bar code systems could be configured to collect data in a format similar to that described by Repp et al. (1989) and could be processed in a similar manner with similar software.

There is a high degree of similarity between the logic behind the operation of a bar code scanner and other electronic methods of data collection, such as that used by Repp et al., that allow the continuous observation and recording of behavior. Both types of systems operate by having the observer enter a code that represents the onset or termination of a behavior and the time that the code was entered. The data are stored in a similar, sequential fashion. Because each scan or key press links an observation with an actual time, both systems can be powerful tools for monitoring human behavior. Both have distinct advantages and disadvantages.

Laptop computers operate by utilizing a computer program during the data collection process; therefore, data collection cannot occur without a predefined computer program. All observations must conform to the computer program, with predefined expectations for the behaviors that occur. Some computer programs are designed to immediately sort the data in a manner different from the original sequence of events and the time when the events occurred, retaining only the results that the program was designed to calculate (potentially destroying raw data before it can be analyzed in other ways). Although there are advantages to having this capability at the site of the observation, using the capability eliminates further observation until the processing is completed. Unfortunately, laptop computers that are ideal for data collection may be relatively slow in processing the data. Data analysis in the field also may be limited by the speed of the internal printer or access to an external printer. An additional problem can be that the processed results of the observation may be in printed form only, requiring key entry of this information into another computer if the information is to be used to create additional tables or graphs across observation sessions.

With laptop systems, different computer programs may be needed for different types of observations and analysis, or the program must be edited if new codes are assigned to behaviors or if the key-code assignment is altered. Usually, the number of different codes that can be employed is limited to twice the number of keys on the laptop keyboard (Shift key down or up), although the advent of touchscreen technology may minimize this limitation. Laptop computers would appear to be particularly well suited to recording a small class of very high rate behaviors. Under these conditions, an experienced observer may not need to look at the keyboard and most of the behaviors should be recorded accurately. With a large number of events to record, however, the full keyboard may be in use and accuracy may not remain as high, because of both the increase in codes to input and the potential need to scan the keyboard for the correct key (thereby missing the occurrence of other behavior).

Bar code scanners seem particularly attractive alternatives to laptop computers because they are very lightweight and portable, yet are quite rugged. In most cases, battery life of bar code scanners is greater than the potential interval between opportunities to recharge without disrupting data collection. The system always stores data in a continuous sequence for subsequent computer manipulation. Only the data-reading program in the scanner is required for data collection and can be adapted to many different observation formats. There also is almost no limit on the number of different codes that can be created.

Whereas a laptop computer may require a different program for different observational situations or research experiments, with bar code scanners only the substitution of different bar code recording sheets may be necessary. This flexibility could make for more rapid shifts in observational strategies within an ongoing research or clinical program. Bar code scanning produces a sequence of data that can be analyzed subsequently in a variety of ways with a variety of different analysis approaches and programs. Because the data are uploaded to a host computer for this analysis, the user can select a computer with a high-speed processor to facilitate interpretation of large amounts of data. Further, the data can be transmitted to the computer by modem, thus releasing the bar code scanner in the field for further data collection without having to return to a central location.

The most obvious disadvantage to using bar code scanners for data collection may be a serious one: The observer must look away from what is being observed and at the bar code on the recording sheet in order to scan the code. The apparent advantage of greater portability also may create a problem: The ability to record events when the subjects are moving between locations, for example, may create moments when one or more of the observers may be unable to see or hear all or part of the target interaction. Although this may happen in static situations, too, the increased likelihood in mobile situations may create a major issue in the interpretation of reliability data.

Evaluation of the TimeWand I® Scanner for Research Data Collection

Nevertheless, based on the particular advantages to bar code systems, we undertook a pilot project to evaluate the suitability of this new technology for use in a research environment with independent observers. Specifically, the pilot research was designed to determine whether spoken and manual prompts from teaching staff serve as antecedent events that affect rates of students' aberrant behaviors. The portable bar code scanner we employed was the TimeWand I® (Videx, Inc.) with 16K (kilobyte) memory (see Saunders et al., 1993, for more detailed description). The TimeWand I® is about the size of a very thick credit card with an infrared light-sensing scanning lens protruding from one corner and a control button mounted in the side. When the button is depressed and the scanner's lens is passed across a bar code, the scanner stores in internal memory several pieces of information: the alphanumeric code indicated by the bars, the date of the scan (year, month, and day), and the time of the scan (hours, minutes, and seconds to the nearest fourth of a minute). The number of codes that can be scanned before transferring (uploading) the data to a personal computer, as described below, depends on the memory capacity of the particular unit purchased. The scanner can be programmed with the operating software to inform the user, with auditory signals, that memory is nearing capacity, that bar codes have been scanned out of the correct sequence, that a "good" scan has been made, and so forth.

We created data sheets similar to the one shown in Figure 6.1, using a Macintosh II® (Apple, Inc.) computer and Superpaint® Version 1.1 (Silicon Beach Software, Inc.) with a bar code font. Bar code fonts are now available in much the same way as fonts for different print styles and different alphabets. Our data sheets were printed with a laser printer to produce a sufficiently high contrast for reliable scanning. We laminated the data sheets to protect the scanning lens of the scanner from abrasion, but transparent tape over the bar codes works as well.

Each observer was equipped with a scanner and carried the plastic-coated data sheets on a clipboard. Each observation session began with the observer entering the codes representing his or her name and the activity being observed. Teacher and student responses that were targeted for observation were recorded as they occurred. In this test, each behavior targeted for each individual in the group had a distinctive code. This approach permitted the recording of an event with a single pass of the scanner as opposed to scanning the name of the individual and the behavior in separate scans. This scanning system permitted the observers to scan a student's or teacher's behavior repeatedly to produce a frequency count. The duration of these behaviors could be measured by adding a stop code for each behavior. Duration measures were not taken, however, in this study.

The data held in the scanner's memory were transferred (uploaded) at the end of the observation day to a microcomputer by inserting each scanner into a receiving slot in a recharging and downloading device that is connected to the computer's communication port by cable. When the scanners were inserted, the operating software transferred the data to a file on the disk in the computer. At the end of this brief operation, the program automatically downloaded program information and the correct date and time to ensure that the scanner was appropriately readied for the next day. It also should be noted that due to the brevity of our codes for names, objectives, and scoring, the 16K version of the Time-Wand that we used could store more than 3,600 scans before it became necessary to upload. The file of data created by the upload process was in the form of an ASCII file formatted according to specifications that we provided via the operating software and transferred to a file that could be read by the database program we wrote for sorting and computation.

A difficulty that we encountered with the TimeWand I® is that the timing mechanism was designed to report times in 16-second intervals (produced by a software "clock"). Thus the time stamped on each data entry may be up to 15 seconds discrepant from the actual time of the event. For nonresearch uses, this level of timing accuracy may pose no serious problems. When the records of two observers are to be compared for reliability, however, the discrepancy in recorded time may be as

Observer

#1

||||||||||||||||||||||
* 1 0 1 *

#2

||||||||||||||||||||||
* 1 0 2 *

#3

||||||||||||||||||||||
* 1 0 3 *

Activity

#1

||||||||||||||||||||||
* 2 0 1 *

#2

||||||||||||||||||||||
* 2 0 2 *

#3

||||||||||||||||||||||
* 2 0 3 *

Teacher

Instruction

||||||||||||||||||||||
* 3 1 1 *

Physical

||||||||||||||||||||||
* 3 1 2 *

Verbal

Reward

||||||||||||||||||||||
* 3 1 3 *

Physical

||||||||||||||||||||||
* 3 1 4 *

Verbal

Intervention

||||||||||||||||||||||
* 3 1 5 *

Physical

||||||||||||||||||||||
* 3 1 6 *

Verbal

Students

#1

||||||||||||||||||||||
* 3 2 1 *

Aggression
to Others

||||||||||||||||||||||
* 3 2 2 *

Aggression
to Objects

||||||||||||||||||||||
* 3 2 3 *

Self-Injury

#2

||||||||||||||||||||||
* 3 3 1 *

Aggression
to Others

||||||||||||||||||||||
* 3 3 3 *

Self-Injury

#3

||||||||||||||||||||||
* 3 4 1 *

Aggression
to Others

||||||||||||||||||||||
* 3 4 2 *

Aggression
to Objects

Figure 6.1. An Example of a Data Sheet With Bar Codes

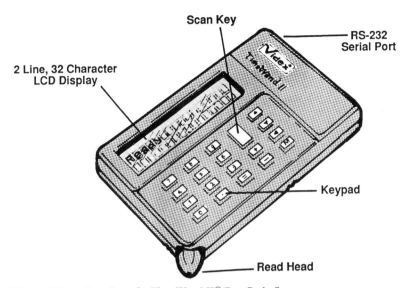

Figure 6.2. A Drawing of a TimeWand II® Bar Code Scanner

much as 32 s (2 × 16 s). The potential temporal discrepancy also limits use of the TimeWand I® as a tool for accurately monitoring the duration of events.

Evaluation of the TimeWand II® Scanner for Research Data Collection

For subsequent research we selected a more advanced bar code scanner, the TimeWand II® (Videx, Inc.). The TimeWand II®, shown in Figure 6.2, is equipped with a timing mechanism that is accurate to about 1 second. The device is about the size of a pocket calculator, is encased in cast metal, and weighs about 6 ounces. The accurate timing mechanism in this version allows for the subsequent computer calculation of interobserver agreement and lag-sequential analysis while retaining the same advantages of portability and no requirement of a predefined recording system.

With the addition of this new equipment, we designed a comprehensive experiment-management software package to facilitate the initiation of experiments with unique recording requirements but similar postrecording analysis requirements. The package permits the user to identify

Title: Tom's Tennis Ball Program   Date: 04/30/92   Time: 9:19:33 a.m.
Session #: 12   Observer: Martha   Session Length: 00:29:29
Teacher Observed: Bill   Activity: Vocational Task

Type	Event	Frequency	Rate	Duration	Avg. Dur.	Percent of Session
DE	Mouthing	2 0	0.678	0	0.0	0.00
DE	Rocking	3 8	1.289	0	0.0	0.00
DE	Object Flipping	3 9	1.323	0	0.0	0.00
DE	Out of Seat	5	0.170	0	0.0	0.00
DE	Bites to Self	0	0.000	0	0.0	0.00
DE	Body Hits	0	0.000	0	0.0	0.00
DE	Aggression	0	0.000	0	0.0	0.00
MED	Working	1 0	0.339	8 5 3	85.3	48.22
MED	Not Working	1 0	0.339	9 1 4	91.4	51.67

Figure 6.3. A Sample of a Report of the Results of One Observation Session of a Student With Various Aberrant Behaviors

NOTE: The frequency, rate per minute, duration, average duration, and percentage of session time are shown, as applicable, for discrete behaviors (DE) and mutually exclusive duration behaviors (MED).

categories of events within an experiment to include setting events (e.g., classroom, teacher, activity, and subactivity), discrete behavioral events (e.g., verbal instruction, physical prompt, or head banging), events with long durations (e.g., body rocking, hand waving, or availability of activity materials), and mutually exclusive events (e.g., sitting versus standing, or peer present or absent). A code and a label are assigned to each event in the category selected. When the experiment is given a number and a title and stored with the selected events, the program automatically creates the database structures necessary to hold the data collected for the experiment. A matching report format also is created that provides the printed reports for each experimental session. An example is shown in Figure 6.3.

The package also provides for the rapid determination of the interobserver reliability for each of the three categories of behavioral events. Reliability for discrete events and for the onset of duration-scored events is calculated similarly to that described by Repp et al. (1989). The experimenter selects an interval of time t (1-60 s) and the record of one observer (the primary observer) is compared to the record of a second observer. If the second observer recorded an event within t s (either side) of the time the first observer recorded the event, an agreement is scored. Further, and perhaps more stringently than in the method used by Repp et al. (1989), the two records then are compared using the second observer as the primary observer. Although the agreements will be unaltered by this second comparison, additional disagreements may

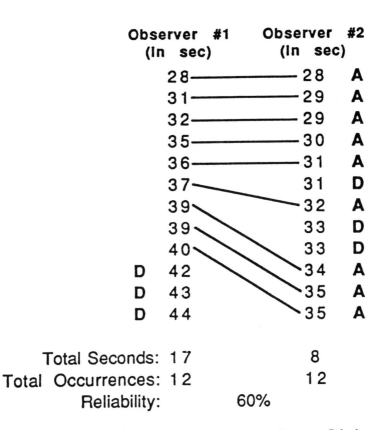

Figure 6.4. A Schematic Showing How the Computer Program Calculates Occurrence Reliability Using a *t* Value of 5 s

NOTE: When Observer 1 is used as the primary observer, the disagreements are identified at seconds 42, 43, and 44 of that observer's record. When Observer 2 is used as the primary observer, additional disagreements are detected at seconds 31, 33, and 33 of that observer's record.

be identified as shown in the schematic in Figure 6.4. The degree of agreement for duration events is the same second-by-second analysis described by Repp et al. (1989). A sample report of reliability scoring is shown in Figure 6.5.

The package also allows the experimenter to select events from the experiment for sorting and combining for exportation to programs that facilitate graphic representation of the results. One format for exportation is simply the arrangement of, for example, the rate per minute of a

Study Code: 117	Title: Tom's Tennis Ball Program	Date: 04/30/92
Time: 9:19:33 a.m.	Session Length: 00:29:29	Session Length 2: 1769 sec
Primary Session #: 12	Primary Observer: Martha	
Reliability Session #: 9	Reliability Observer: Rick	Reliability Interval: 5 sec

Code	Event	Occ. R.	Agrmts.	Disagrmts.	Dur. Occ. R.	Sec. Agr.	Sec. Nonagr.
501	Mouthing	100.0	20	0	0.00	0	0
502	Rocking	78.57	33	9	0.00	0	0
503	Object Flipping	82.93	34	7	0.00	0	0
504	Out of Seat	83.33	5	1	0.00	0	0
505	Bites to Self	100.0	0	0	0.00	0	0
506	Body Hits	100.0	0	0	0.00	0	0
507	Aggression	100.0	0	0	0.00	0	0
601	Working	75.00	9	3	86.61	841	130
602	Not Working	66.67	8	4	86.08	798	129
	Total	81.95	109	24	86.35	1639	259

Figure 6.5. A Sample of a Report of the Results of Reliability Calculations on One Observation Session of a Student With Various Aberrant Behaviors

NOTE: The report shows the reliability for each discrete event, the onset of each duration event, the total session, and second-by-second agreement for each duration event and for the total session.

particular behavior, under some combination of setting events, for a particular series of sessions or dates. This format permits creation of the typical graph of a subject's behavior. The package also permits selecting or combining events from the record of one or more sessions and arraying them into bins or cells defined by a unit of time. One particular method of data analysis that takes advantage of this process is the event map or scatter plot (Touchette, MacDonald, & Langer, 1985). With the current sophistication of computer graphics software, however, the maps can be produced now in three-dimensional format. Figure 6.6 shows an example of this type of graph with the behaviors of a student and his teacher that were collected during one observational session. The result is a display that permits a visual analysis of the degree to which certain behaviors of the student are related temporally with some teacher behaviors. This approach to analysis can be effective when the potential relationship between events is expected to be relatively clear or when the events recorded are not mutually exclusive. Lag-sequential analysis can be conducted only when the events analyzed are mutually exclusive (occur in sequence) or when nonexclusive events (concurrent events) are combined to form mutually exclusive events (Bakeman, 1978).

The most significant problem that we have encountered thus far in our use of the TimeWand II® system has been the anticipated problem of obtaining reliability at levels that appear acceptable. One problem,

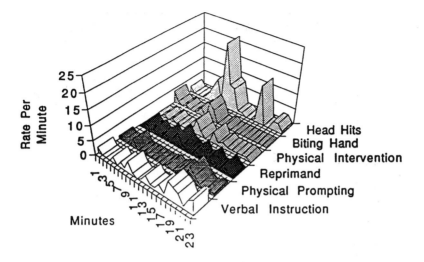

Figure 6.6. A Three-Dimensional Graph Depicting Data From a 23-Minute Observation of a Period of Interaction Between a Teacher and a Student With Aberrant Behavior

NOTE: The height of the "mountains" indicates the rate of the observed behavior for each minute of observation.

of course, is that there are no clear standards for reliability computed on continuously collected data. Because of statistical problems with calculating reliability by applying an arbitrary overlay interval, the Repp et al. (1989) approach, or some variation, seems the most appropriate one at the moment. The choice of the value for the t used to calculate reliability will have a substantial effect on the percentages obtained. Further, the t value acceptable for laptop-collected data may be substantially different from that for bar-code-collected data. For example, we have noted that our observers scan codes at different rates but ultimately record the same or nearly the same number of events. Even when the actual number of events recorded is the same and is accurate (as verified from videotape), the reliability percentages can vary from 40% to 100% depending on the value of t selected.

In terms of the sequence of events, the variation in scanning speed is not particularly troublesome when the rate of events is low, if all of the data for a session are obtained from the primary observer, and if the primary observer is the same across sessions. When rates of observable events increase, however, a slower scanner will be more likely to miss

114   Bar Code Technology

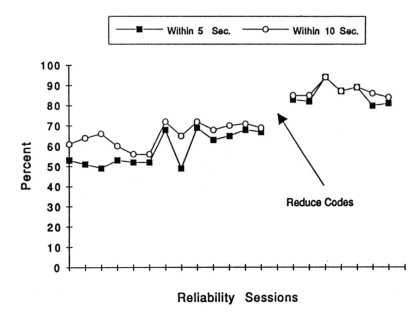

Figure 6.7. A Comparison of Reliability Calculated With a *t* Value of 5 s and a
t value of 10 s

NOTE: The graph shows the effect on degree of reliability before and after the number of observation codes was decreased from 13 to 7.

events than a more rapid scanner. A more troublesome problem arises when one observer is used to record the behavior of one subject (e.g., a student) and a second observer records the behavior of another subject (e.g., the teacher). If the two observers scan at differing rates, although every event may be recorded, the behaviors of the teacher will appear in a different location in the temporal stream than the behaviors of the student.

As many other investigators have found with other forms of data collection, one of the most efficient ways of improving recording accuracy and, therefore, interobserver reliability is to decrease the number of events to be observed. As shown in Figure 6.7, when we decreased the number of events observed in a particular experiment from 13 to 7, reliability improved. Figure 6.7 also indicates that the observers compared during these sessions did not have substantially different rates of scanning because the degree of reliability varied little under *t* values of 5 s and 10 s.

The Importance of Appropriate Software

In our pilot projects, we learned that one of the most important steps in creating a bar code data collection system is the selection of a database or programming language that will be used to analyze data and to produce reports. Experienced programmers can develop data interpreting programs with languages such as C, Pascal, and FORTRAN. These languages can be used to create powerful and fast programs but much of the development time will involve re-creating functions and abilities found in commercially available database packages. The length of time necessary for producing a flexible and comprehensive analysis tool most likely would be prohibitive for many projects.

If a commercially available database software package is selected for interpreting bar code data, it is important to choose a program with programming capability and a complete library of commands and functions. Database packages including dBASE IV® (Borland International, Inc.), Paradox® (Borland International, Inc.), FoxBase® and FoxPro® (Fox Software, Inc.), and 4th Dimension® (Acius, Inc.) are relatively complete. For MS-DOS users, a database generator program called Clipper® (Nantucket, Inc.) is a potentially powerful development tool.

Regardless of which software package is selected, some degree of programming will be required. A program for data analysis and a set of databases for interpreting bar code meaning also will be required. Additional programming for editing databases, exporting data to graphing packages, and additional analysis will be required if any persons using the software do not have a comprehensive understanding of the database software and the functioning of the bar code system. Software development will require an experienced programmer for a considerable time depending on the user friendliness, complexity, and flexibility of the desired program.

Nevertheless, the power and flexibility of bar code data collection warrant efforts to incorporate it into overall research plans. The data produced for straightforward visual analysis combined with the transitional probability methods of analysis (cf. Repp et al., 1989; Sackett, 1978, 1979; Sackett et al., 1979; Vyse & Mulick, 1988; Vyse, Mulick, & Thayer, 1984) have significant potential for improving our ability to identify causal relationships among the behaviors of two or more persons. Applications in research on aberrant behaviors in persons with developmental disabilities are clear.

References

Alberto, P. A., & Troutman, A. C. (1982). *Applied behavior analysis for teachers.* Columbus, OH: Charles E. Merrill.

Bailey, J. S. (1977). *A handbook of research methods in applied behavior analysis.* Tallahassee: Florida State University.

Bakeman, R. (1978). Untangling streams of behavior. In G. P. Sackett (Ed.), *Observing behavior: Data collection and analysis methods* (Vol. 2, pp. 63-78). Baltimore, MD: University Park.

Drash, P. W., Ray, R. P., & Tudor, R. M. (1989). An inexpensive event recorder. *Journal of Applied Behavior Analysis, 22,* 453.

Eiler, J. M., Nelson, W. W., Jensen, C. C., & Johnson, S. P. (1989). Automated data collection using bar code. *Behavior Research Methods, Instruments, & Computers, 21,* 53-58.

Harmon, C. K., & Adams, R. (1984). *Reading between the lines: An introduction to bar code technology.* Peterborough, NH: Helmers.

Kerr, M. M., & Nelson, C. M. (1983). *Strategies for managing behavior problems in classrooms.* Columbus, OH: Charles E. Merrill.

Lindsley, O. (1968). Technical note: A reliable wrist counter for recording behavior rates. *Journal of Applied Behavior Analysis, 1,* 77-78.

Martin, G., & Pear, J. (1988). *Behavior modification: What it is and how to do it.* Englewood Cliffs, NJ: Prentice Hall.

Repp, A. C., Harman, M. L., Felce, D., Van Acker, R., & Karsh, K. G. (1989). Conducting behavioral assessments on computer collected data. *Behavioral Assessment, 11,* 249-268.

Sackett, G. P. (1978). Measurement in observational research. In G. P. Sackett (Ed.), *Observing behavior: Data collection and analysis methods* (Vol. 2, pp. 25-43). Baltimore, MD: University Park.

Sackett, G. P. (1979). The lag sequential analysis of contingency and cyclicity in behavioral interaction research. In J. D. Osofsky (Ed.), *Handbook of infant development* (pp. 623-649). New York: John Wiley.

Sackett, G. P., Holm, R., Crowley, C., & Henknins, A. (1979). A FORTRAN program for lag sequential analysis of contingency and cyclically in behavioral interaction data. *Behavior Research Methods and Instrumentation, 11,* 366-378.

Saunders, M. D., Saunders, J. L., & Saunders, R. R. (1993). A program evaluation of classroom data collection with bar codes. *Research in Developmental Disabilities, 14,* 1-18.

Touchette, P. E., MacDonald, R. F., & Langer, S. N. (1985). A scatter plot for identifying stimulus control of problem behavior. *Journal of Applied Behavior Analysis, 18,* 343-351.

Vyse, S. A., & Mulick, J. A. (1988). Ecobehavioral assessment of a special education classroom: Teacher-student behavioral covariation. *Journal of the Multihandicapped Person, 1,* 201-216.

Vyse, S., Mulick, J. A., & Thayer, B. M. (1984). An ecobehavioral assessment of a special education classroom. *Applied Research in Mental Retardation, 5,* 395-408.

7

Aggregating Results From Multiple Studies

LYNNE K. EDWARDS
AMY N. SPIEGEL

Studies on destructive behaviors typically are based on single-subject designs. In some cases, there is only one subject being examined; in others, there may be two or three, using multiple baselines. In either situation, classical statistical procedures that are based on large sample sizes are at odds with the single-subject design. And yet, in this field, destructive behavior is not something for which large control and experimental groups can be found. Necessarily we must deal with these studies for which only small sample sizes are available.

Typically, federal grants on destructive behaviors are reviewed by methodologists who are trained in traditional statistics based on large samples. The proposals with extremely small sample sizes may appear inadequate for establishing any significance of intervention effects. Furthermore, the frequency of destructive behaviors is relatively small, unless intensive behavioral observations are made. Lack of power associated with small samples and the often infrequent target behavior make it doubly difficult to document any intervention effects. Faced with this dilemma, researchers on destructive behaviors have been seeking some guidance in this area, but help is not readily forthcoming. In this chapter we discuss existing statistical or heuristic single-subject data analysis methods. First, we present an overview of each analysis method at the single study level. Then, we discuss issues with aggregating results across multiple subjects within a single study, and across different subjects in different studies. Our hope is not to propose an authoritative guide-line in dealing with aggregation problems in single-subject designs but rather to discuss pros and cons among the several tools currently available. The goal of this chapter is to stimulate discussion on methodology in documenting treatment effects in small sample studies.

Methods for Interpreting Single-Subject Designs

A variety of methods are currently available for interpreting single-subject design studies (e.g., Kazdin, 1982; Kratochwill, 1978; Suen & Ary, 1989). A recent overview of major methods can be found in Janosky (1991). Among the currently available methods, one class of methods attempts to describe the underlying phenomenon. Another attempts to provide statistical significance or quantitative summary. Yet another focuses on a design that allows for logically strong arguments in establishing the treatment effectiveness. We present an overview of selected interpretation methods frequently used with single-subject designs and discuss some of the advantages and limitations associated with these methods. Then, we discuss issues of aggregating results.

Descriptive Procedures

Visualization

Visual representation of raw data in a graphic form is widely used in single-subject studies. Easy to comprehend, a plot of time against frequency of behavior can be a practical and simple way to monitor and evaluate treatment effects (Campbell, 1988). Through visual inspection of base and treatment time periods displayed in the graph, a judgment regarding the effectiveness of the treatment can be made. Parsonson and Baer (1978) argue that the relative insensitivity of graphic interpretation (i.e., only large effects can be detected by "eyeballing") compared to statistical analyses can be advantageous in that it assures the therapist or researcher that the intervention effects detected via visualization are real and substantial.

However, graphs can be misleading because of distortion in perspective, context, or proportion (Tufte, 1983), and, more significantly, visual inspection results in highly inconsistent interpretation among experts (Kazdin, 1982). Ottenbacher (1986) found that in two of five artificial data sets, virtually split decisions were drawn by the practitioners.

Although specifying a priori decision criteria, such as the critical changes in trend, level, and slope, may improve agreement in the interpretation of graphs, this method of evaluation, despite its long history and widespread use, remains a subjective and intuitive means of interpreting data. Most researchers agree that visual inspection can play a role in interpreting data but recommend that visualization should be accompanied by more formal statistical analyses (Campbell, 1988; Dattilo & Nelson, 1986).

Exploratory Data Analysis: Smoothing

Tukey's exploratory data analytic (EDA) technique of smoothing time-sequenced raw data is conceptually similar to regression (Tukey, 1977). Similar to the general notion of "data = fit + residual," the smoothing process leads to "data = smooth + rough," and attempts to capture the underlying pattern of the data. This is accomplished by reducing the random variation or noises in the series of data points through the use of running medians, a running weighted average, or other location statistics. Each data point is re-expressed to become more similar to nearby data points, and thus the changes are smoothed from abrupt to gradual variation. This smoothed curve is then interpreted just as in the visualization of raw data. The reasoning behind the smoothing is that it clarifies a pattern for processes that occur over time (Tukey, 1977; Velleman & Hoaglin, 1981). Therefore, it is particularly applicable to single-subject research designs.

As is the case with any nonparametric technique, the sequential smoothing is not restricted by the assumptions of independence of errors or normal distribution that are necessary for t and F tests. Of the EDA techniques, smoothing is considered the most appropriate for detecting trends in data (Tukey, 1977; Velleman & Hoaglin, 1981). However, the criticisms raised for visualization are also applicable here, as well as some other difficulties. For example, if the exact numerical values of the smoothed data points are needed, they have to be visually approximated from the graph.

Statistical Methods

ANOVA

More conventional statistical tests typically used with between group designs, such as analysis of variance (ANOVA) or t tests, also are used to evaluate single-subject data. However, because all the data in single-subject designs are measured repeatedly, the errors or residuals associated with the data points are correlated. Thus the results, which are based on the assumption of independent samples, produce biased interpretations (Weiner & Eisen, 1985). Although typical repeated-measures designs do demand multiple subjects in order to estimate the experimental error variance, this is not always possible in single-subject designs. Replacing this error variance with the intrasubject variance violates the assumption of independent errors and also results in the underestimation of the variance. Rosner (1982) proposed a correction factor when there is an intraclass correlation; however, his correction is applicable only when there are multiple subjects.

In addition to ANOVA, which is used for continuous dependent measures, it is tempting to use traditional statistical procedures for rates and proportions. In many of the destructive behavior studies, the response variable is often in the form of a proportion. When $N = 1$, there will be a series of correlated proportions all obtained from the same subject. As in the case of ANOVA for correlated observations, Rosner's correction assumes proportions are derived from multiple subjects rather than from multiple observations of a single subject (Le, 1988). Therefore, neither the traditional correlated proportions test (Fleiss, 1981) nor the intraclass correlation correction (Rosner, 1982) is applicable.

Regression

Fitting a least squares regression line to a series of data points collected over time is a simple and widely used method. By fitting one line to the base data and another to the treatment data, the differences in slope, intercept, and level are calculated and tested for significance (Mood, 1963). Gottman, McFall, and Barnett (1969) point out two potential problems with using a regression model for single-subject data. First, assuming a linear relationship among the observations may be inappropriate. This may be overcome by calculating higher-order trends. Second, assuming the repeated observations are independent samples also may lead to inappropriate interpretation of the data. This weakness can be circumvented by using a time series model and correcting the degrees of freedom. However, the problem of estimating the error variance as discussed in ANOVA also is applicable in regression. Consequently, testing is expected to be more troublesome whereas estimation, such as a curve-fitting method, may produce a reasonable approximation of the trend in the data.

Time Series

Time-series analyses, in contrast to an independent t test and ordinary regression analyses, provide an appropriate statistical model that accommodates observations obtained repeatedly over time from a single entity. Typically, in interrupted time-series analyses (ITSA), an autoregressive (AR) or autoregressive integrated average (ARIMA) model is adopted. This method can detect whether a reliable change in the slope or level of the behavior was due to the intervention. Although time-series analysis is a useful method that can detect small effects, the recommended number of observations per experimental phase is 50 to 100 (Hartmann et al., 1980). This can be costly and time-consuming and is an unreasonable demand on persons with behavioral problems. Although ARIMA is a recommended method for single-subject designs (Suen & Ary, 1989), its utility is quite limited because single-subject studies typically contain only 3 to 5 data points per phase. Furthermore, the typical assumption in ITSA of stable variance across time may not hold. Variances within and across individuals do not tend to be very stable. Trying to estimate variances and correlations based on this fallible assumption may be too restrictive and may bias the results (Edwards, 1991).

C-Statistic

Tryon (1982) illustrated the use of the C-statistic (Young, 1941) as a simpler alternative to ARIMA. Requiring fewer data points per phase (8 instead of 50 to 100) and simplified calculations, the C-statistic follows the same logic as visual analysis and evaluates change in slope from one phase to the next. Criticisms of the C-statistic pointed out by Blumberg (1984) include the lack of sensitivity of this method in certain cases, the possible compounding of errors due to its insensitivity, and the small number of observations allowed in each phase. An example of its insensitivity is in its inability to detect a difference in intercepts between the baseline phase and the treatment phase when they share a common slope. Tryon (1984) concedes that under some circumstances the C-statistic may be entirely a function of the number of observations. As such, caution must be used when employing this method.

Meta-Analysis

Meta-analysis is one means of aggregating data from several studies to draw conclusions about the effectiveness of a treatment method. Although used extensively in various research fields, it only recently has been applied to single-subject designs. Using effect size generally is considered the most appropriate meta-analytic technique for single-subject research design (Busk & Serlin, 1991; Hedges & Olkin, 1985). It allows researchers to compare and combine results of single-subject designs quantitatively rather than qualitatively, as most reviews are typically done. The effect size in a single-subject design takes the form of the mean difference between the treatment phase and the baseline over the standardized intraindividual variation obtained either during the control phase alone or from both the control and the experimental phases. The effect size can be computed for each individual or for the group. Subsequently, such a quantity can be compared across different studies. However, as described by Busk and Serlin (1991), to have generalizability of the results, certain stringent assumptions with regard to the distribution and homogeneity of variance must be met. Inability to meet these assumptions necessarily limits one to a descriptive review rather than a systematic examination of treatment effects.

Typically, meta-analyses do not meet the necessary criteria to be useful and the results generalizable. Sacks, Berrier, Beitman, Ancona-Berk, and Chalmers (1987) reported after examining 86 meta-analyses of randomized clinical trials that the quality of the studies tended to be low in the areas they selected. The factors they used, such as study design, combinability, control of bias, statistical analysis, sensitivity analysis, and application of results, are all important yardsticks of meta-analytic studies. Although these types of critical assessments of meta-analytic procedures are appearing in various fields, the focus of many single-subject designs is, unfortunately, still on formulating various individual effect sizes, which may not be appropriate in most cases.

Nonparametric Randomization

Randomization test procedures have been advocated as a valid means of evaluating the effectiveness of randomized clinical trials (Edgington, 1980; Levin, Marascuilo, & Hubert, 1978; Wampold & Worsham, 1986). A randomization model is distinct from a population model in that the former asks whether the observed phenomenon could have been obtained by chance from the random assignment of treatment phases to each subject. Significance is calculated by computing the probability of obtaining the sample data at hand or more extreme cases over the total permutation of the sample data. This model, which can be used with a variety of designs, answers the question of how likely it is that the difference obtained between the baseline and treatment would be as large as it is (Edgington, 1980).

This statistical method is gaining increasing visibility and use. However, the computations can be tedious and time-consuming, though less so now with the use of computers, and the design of the study must be developed with this analysis in mind. The assumption of random assignment of treatment phases in single-subject design must be met (Edgington, 1980). However, even for systematic, rather than randomized, clinical trials, a randomization-model-based statistic will be a good approximation (Levin et al., 1978). A real limitation is that a relatively large number of observations (i.e., time points) are required to reach a significance level of .05.

Among the available statistical procedures, randomization is the most versatile and the least dependent on assumptions. We use a simple ABA design to illustrate this method. Suppose we are studying self-abuse and attempting an intervention of functional communication training. The behavior we will record is the number of self-abusive acts occurring during a specified period. When treatment will begin and when treatment will end are the aspects of the design that are randomly determined; however, the sequence of the phases, ABA, has not been randomized. We will use 20 observation periods and restrict the implementation of the intervention to allow at least four observation periods of A at the beginning and four of A at the end. Also, we will need at least five observation periods of B. This allows the treatment to begin randomly between observation period 4 and observation period 13, and end, depending on implementation time, between periods 9 and 17. There are 36 possibilities. If treatment were randomly selected to begin with observation period 7, the data might look something like Table 7.1. Although the frequency of self-abusive behavior is reported with an assumption that exactly the same number of observational sessions were employed at each period, using the proportion of such behavior would have worked as well.

In a one-tailed test, we want to test whether the observed self-abusive behaviors are reduced during the treatment phase. The test statistic we will use is $M_A - M_B$, the mean of the A measurements minus the mean of the B measurements. The 36 data divisions we will use are the 36

Table 7.1 Hypothetical Data for ABA Treatment Design Illustrating Randomization Tests

	Observation Period																			
	1	2	3	4	5	6	7	8	9	10	11	12	13	14	15	16	17	18	19	20
Treatments phase	A	A	A	A	A	A	B	B	B	B	B	B	B	B	B	B	A	A	A	A	A
Observation measure	9	7	10	7	9	8	2	6	4	6	5	4	7	5	4	7	8	10	7	8

possible ways for the ABA design to be implemented over the 20 periods. The observed test statistic value for the actual difference between A and B phases is $90/11 - 46/9 = 8.18 - 5.11 = 3.07$. Of the 35 remaining possible divisions to compare this to, one arrangement is the mean of the first 4 and last 11 observation periods (A phases) minus the mean of the remaining 5 (B phase). This equals $104/15 - 32/5 = 6.93 - 6.4 = .53$. A second possible division is the mean of the first 4 and last 10 observation periods (A phases) minus the mean of the remaining 6 (B phase). This equals $98/14 - 38/6 = 7 - 6.33 = .67$. Calculating all other possible divisions shows that the observed value is the largest of all possible arrangements using this design and thus achieves a significance of 1/36, or .028. If another division had achieved an equally high or higher statistic, the significance would have been 2/36, or .056, not achieving significance at the .05 level.

Logically Strong Design

Another approach to analyzing single-subject studies is through the use of a logically strong design. Because of the small sample sizes used in this area of research, it is impractical to seek credibility of study results by a powerful test based on large sample sizes. It may be more important and more practical to establish a logically strong result. For example, the effectiveness of an intervention will be more credible if it is accomplished by satisfying the tenets of a causal argument. First, the temporal order, that the intervention was implemented before the improved behavior was observed, is trivially satisfied. Second, sufficiency also must be established by showing that the target intervention is followed by the reduction in destructive behavior. In addition, the internal validities—that all other variables were controlled and that the intervention alone produced the effect—should be demonstrated. Third, necessity must be satisfied. We have to show that the target intervention, and no other intervention, produced the reduction in destructive behavior; without this intervention the behavior will not be reduced. One way to show this is to adopt a reversal design such as the ABA design to show that the destructive behavior increases during the second baseline phase. Another is to show that an alternative intervention is not effective in reducing behavior (see, e.g., Carr, Newsom, & Binkoff, 1976). Yet another is to show that a treatment that "deprives" the key ingredient of the target intervention actually increases the problem behavior. Unlike the ABA design where the "absence" of B is presented in the second A phase, a design ABB*, where B* is the "anti" B, is applied here. Although the demonstration of increased problem behavior in the B* phase over the baseline will strengthen the understanding of the cause of the problem behavior, some ethical issues may be raised. Indeed, though most studies show that increasing reinforcers increase positive behavior responses, few studies also show that decreasing reinforcers (below the baseline) result in decreases in positive behavior (Carr & Durand, 1985). We are not recommending that researchers in this area ignore such ethical issues but that they recognize that it may be more important to seek consistent results through rigorous designs than to seek power by increased sample sizes.

Aggregating Results

Because of the small number of subjects per study, it is tempting to aggregate results within a single study with multiple subjects or across studies. We now examine how and the conditions under which it is appropriate to do so.

Aggregating Subjects Within the Same Study

Many single-subject designs include two or three subjects in the same environment using multiple baselines, in which the designs for the subjects are varied slightly. This variation may be in the length of the baseline phase, in the length of the treatment phase, or in some aspect of the treatment delivery (cf. Repp, Barton, & Brulle, 1983). With these variations, we question whether it is valid to aggregate the results across subjects within the same study. A summary statistic such as a group mean at each observation period may hide the individual changes. Trends may be examined, however, if a smoothing was applied to each subject in each period and a consistent pattern was found across subjects. This provides a qualitative aggregation of treatment effects.

As for the quantitative aggregation, the group-level summary information cannot be ascertained unless the individual meta-analysis is applied. If a large number of time points are available, time-series analysis based on multiple subjects is possible but the nonequivalent observation points across subjects make it difficult to interpret the results. Similarly, smoothing across different subjects with different numbers of data points or baselines can produce an ambiguous interpretation. With the design variations typically found in single-subject studies with two or three subjects, quantitative aggregation is not recommended.

Aggregating Results Across Different Studies

The difficulties faced in aggregating subjects within a single study are compounded when aggregating results across different studies. With potentially different treatments, experimenters, and environments, it is rare to have the exact replication of the same study. Furthermore, in behavioral sciences, even a conceptual replication in which a slightly different operationalization is employed is rarely attempted. The discrepancies in experimental conditions across different studies and the reluctance among the researchers to conduct any form of replications make it nearly impossible to compute a valid summary effect size for meta-analysis.

A logical classification table is possible as a qualitative means of combining and summarizing the results from different studies. Each cell of the table could represent the relationship between a particular destructive behavior and a particular intervention. For example, one cell may contain three studies: one on head-banging behavior using giving attention as an intervention, another on property destruction using withholding praise as an intervention, and the third on self-biting using teaching alternative communication as an intervention. Head banging, property destruction, and self-hitting fit into a larger category of destructive behavior; attention, praise, and instruction can be classified into a larger concept of interaction with an authority figure. Clearly, the more specific the classification, the more useful the information. For example, self-abusive behavior (e.g., self-biting and head banging), or head-banging behavior alone, would provide more specific information about effective intervention than the larger classification of destructive behavior. By identifying which conditions are filled with more than one study with positive outcome, one can be more sure of the relationship between a specific behavior and the intervention. Similar to all scientific inquiry in which different studies with their various conditions may point to the same solution, single-subject studies in destructive behaviors may be examined as a whole to see what trends, if any, can be found.

Concluding Remarks

Several existing methods for interpreting results from single-subject designs are examined in this chapter. Of these, nonparametric randomization and Tukey's EDA seem most practical and useful for single-subject designs. If both necessity and sufficiency can be established within one study, it presents a stronger form of inference than sufficiency alone. The ABA design, better than the AB design, incorporates sufficiency and a weak form of necessity in that the absence of intervention increases problem behaviors.

Aggregation, even within the same study, typically is plagued by lack of consistency in data points per phase and other inconsistencies. Therefore, quantitative aggregation, in hopes of increasing sample sizes, should be discouraged. Across different studies, these problems of replications are compounded because of the nonexacting experimental conditions. Although meta-analysis may be a potentially useful tool for aggregating results in single-subject designs, its stringent assumptions limit its usefulness.

Given these overview results, a logical summary rather than a statistical summary should be sought. Currently, methods specific to single-subject studies are useful but they do not provide the power of test that classical statisticians typically seek. Although improved methods will surely become available in the future, these methodological refinements must be examined to ascertain their adequacy and usefulness. In the meantime, it is important to recognize that statistical measurements based on large samples are not appropriate for single-subject designs, and this must be accepted and understood among those who review studies on destructive behaviors.

References

Blumberg, C. J. (1984). Comments on "A simplified time-series analysis for evaluating treatment interventions." *Journal of Applied Behavior Analysis, 17,* 539-542.

Busk, P. L., & Serlin, R. C. (1991, April). *Meta-analysis for single-subject research.* Paper presented at the meeting of the American Educational Research Association, Chicago, IL.

Campbell, P. H. (1988). Using single-subject research design to evaluate the effectiveness of treatment. *American Journal of Occupational Therapy, 42,* 732-738.

Carr, E. G., & Durand, V. M. (1985). Reducing behavior problems through functional communication training. *Journal of Applied Behavior Analysis, 18,* 111-126.

Carr, E. G., Newsom, C. D., & Binkoff, J. A. (1976). Stimulus control of self-destructive behavior in a psychotic child. *Journal of Abnormal Child Psychology, 4,* 139-153.

Dattilo, J., & Nelson, G. D. (1986). Single-subject evaluation in health education. *Health Education Quarterly, 13,* 249-259.

Edgington, E. S. (1980). Validity of randomization tests for one-subject experiments. *Journal of Educational Statistics, 5,* 235-251.

Edwards, L. K. (1991). Fitting a serial correlation pattern to repeated observations. *Journal of Educational Statistics, 16,* 52-76.

Fleiss, J. L. (1981). *Statistical methods for rates and proportions* (2nd ed.). New York: John Wiley.

Gottman, J. M., McFall, R. M., & Barnett, J. T. (1969). Design and analysis of research using time series. *Psychological Bulletin, 72,* 299-306.

Hartmann, D. P., Gottman, J. M., Jones, R. R., Gardner, W., Kazdin, A. E., & Vaught, R. S. (1980). Interrupted time-series analysis and its application to behavioral data. *Journal of Applied Behavior Analysis, 13,* 543-559.

Hedges, L. V., & Olkin, I. (1985). Statistical methods for meta-analysis. Orlando, FL: Academic Press.

Janosky, J. E. (1991, April). *An overview of the analysis of a single-subject design with recommendations.* Paper presented at the meeting of the American Educational Research Association, Chicago, IL.

Kazdin, A. E. (1982). *Single-case research designs: Methods for clinical and applied settings.* New York: Oxford University Press.

Kratochwill, T. R. (Ed.). (1978). *Single subject research: Strategies for evaluating change.* New York: Academic Press.

Le, C. T. (1988). Testing for linear trends in proportions using correlated otolaryngology or ophthalmology data. *Biometrics, 44,* 299-303.

Levin, J. R., Marascuilo, L. A., & Hubert, L. J. (1978). N = Nonparametric randomization tests. In T. R. Kratochwill (Ed.), *Single subject research: Strategies for evaluating change* (pp. 167-196). New York: Academic Press.

Mood, A. F. (1963). *Introduction to the theory of statistics* (2nd ed.). New York: McGraw-Hill.

Ottenbacher, K. J. (1986). Reliability and accuracy of visually analyzing graphed data from single-subject designs. *The American Journal of Occupational Therapy, 40,* 464-469.

Parsonson, B. S., & Baer, D. M. (1978). The analysis and presentation of graphic data. In T. R. Kratochwill (Ed.), *Single subject research: Strategies for evaluating change* (pp. 101-165). New York: Academic Press.

Repp, A. C., Barton, L. E., & Brulle, A. R. (1983). A comparison of two procedures for programming the differential reinforcement of other behaviors. *Journal of Applied Behavior Analysis, 16,* 435-445.

Rosner, B. (1982). Statistical methods in ophthalmology: An adjustment of the intraclass correlation between eyes. *Biometrics, 38,* 105-114.

Sacks, H. S., Berrier, J., Beitman, D., Ancona-Berk, V. A., & Chalmers, T. C. (1987). Meta-analysis of randomized controlled trials. *New England Journal of Medicine, 316,* 450-454.

Suen, H. K., & Ary, D. (1989). *Analyzing quantitative behavioral observation data.* Hillsdale, NJ: Lawrence Erlbaum.

Tryon, W. W. (1982). A simplified time-series for evaluating treatment interventions. *Journal of Applied Behavior Analysis, 15,* 423-429.

Tryon, W. W. (1984). A simplified time-series analysis for evaluating treatment interventions: A rejoinder to Blumberg. *Journal of Applied Behavior Analysis, 17,* 543-544.

Tufte, E. R. (1983). *The visual display of quantitative information.* Cheshire, CT: Graphics Press.

Tukey, J. W. (1977). *Exploratory Data Analysis.* Reading, MA: Addison-Wesley Publishing Company.

Velleman, R. F., & Hoaglin, D. C. (1981). *Applications, basics, and computing of exploratory data analysis.* Belmont, CA: Duxbury Press.

Wampold, B. E., & Worsham, N. L. (1986). Randomization tests for multiple-baseline designs. *Behavioral Assessment, 8,* 135-143.

Weiner, I. S., & Eisen, R. G. (1985). Clinical research: The case study and single-subject designs. *Journal of Allied Health, 14,* 191-201.

Young, C. L. (1941). On randomness in ordered sequences. *Annals of Mathematical Statistics, 12,* 293-300.

PART III

Biological Interventions for Destructive Behavior

8

Neurobehavioral Mechanisms of Drug Action in Developmental Disabilities

TRAVIS THOMPSON
MARK EGLI
FRANK SYMONS
DAWN DELANEY

Background

Destructive Behavior in Developmental Disabilities

In his *Treatise on Madness,* first published in 1758, William Battie wrote:

> Madness has . . . shared the fate common to many other distempers of not being precisely defined. . . . No wonder therefore, it is, whilst several disorders . . . are thus blended together in our bewildered imagination, that a treatment, rationally indicated by any of those disorders, should be injudiciously directed against Madness itself, whether attended with such symptoms or not. (1758/1969, p. 3)

In our efforts to understand the destructive behavior of people with mental retardation and related disabilities we find ourselves continuing to struggle with the lesson Battie taught his medical students more than two centuries ago. We are confronted with individuals presenting a complex array of symptoms of multiple origins. Our definitions have been imprecise, lending themselves to the blending together of conditions that share little but superficial appearances.

133

Today, most people with mental retardation and related disabilities develop the necessary skills to participate in integrated educational, vocational, residential, and recreational settings. But a significant minority of people with developmental disabilities are self-destructive, harmful toward others, or damage property, which causes them to lead restricted lives. Destructive behavior continues to limit integration of people with developmental disabilities into community settings and is a major factor in reinstitutionalization (Intagliata & Willer, 1981; Vitello, Atthowe, & Cadwell, 1983). Community integration is largely devoid of practical meaning for many who live in isolated settings or in highly specialized treatment centers and are subjected to chemical or mechanical restraints to control their disturbed behavior.

The most common forms of destructive behavior include assault, self-injury, and property destruction. Self-injury includes head banging (with hands or against objects); self-biting; striking other parts of the body with hands or fists; self-scratching; gouging with fingernails in eyes, ears, mouth, throat, nose, or rectum; striking body parts with knees (e.g., chest, face, head); kicking with knees, shins, toes, heels, or balls of feet against hard surfaces; and swallowing harmful substances. Some destructive behavior is of special concern because of its pervasiveness and high frequency (e.g., repetitive skin picking), whereas other behavior's salience is due to harm caused by even a few instances (e.g., assault, severe self-biting). Consequences of such behavior problems can include extensive disfigurement and a life in restraints (e.g., self-mutilation in Lesch-Nyhan syndrome).

Schroeder, Rojahn, and Oldenquist (1991) found that the prevalence of aggressive behavior in people with mental retardation and developmental disabilities ranged from 8.9% to 23.4%, and property destruction was reported in 4.3% to 14.4% of this population. Early investigations, such as that by Schroeder, Schroeder, Smith, and Dalldorf (1978), assessed prevalence of self-injurious behavior (SIB) in a large state residential facility for people with mental retardation. The assessment initially was conducted in 1973 and was repeated during 1975 and 1976 to determine changes in SIB in individuals across time. Each survey resulted in a prevalence of about 10%, 23% of which required medical treatment for SIB. Maisto, Baumeister, and Maisto (1978) found that 14% of an institutional sample exhibited SIB. More recent surveys reveal similar, if not higher, prevalence rates. To say we face a serious problem when one quarter to one half of people with mental retardation display significant behavior disorders is a significant understatement.

Treatment Alternatives: Costs and Benefits

Costs associated with providing educational, residential, and health-care services to people with destructive behavior are staggering. Recent conservative estimates place the total governmental expenditure in 1988 for institutional and community residential care of people with mental retardation and destructive behaviors at $3.537 billion (National Institutes of Health [NIH], 1991). The suffering of affected individuals, the anguish of family members and other care providers, as well as the enormous financial implications make the development of effective interventions for severe behavior problems in developmental disabilities a national priority.

Commonly used treatments for severe destructive behaviors are intrusive punishment procedures such as farradic skin shock, manual overcorrection, squirts in the face with a water mist, and other physically aversive interventions. Despite their effectiveness in producing rapid reductions in severely disturbed behavior (Cataldo, 1991), these treatments are also the least socially acceptable and have been the object of extensive debate. Positive intervention procedures have been designed to reduce behavior problems in persons with developmental disabilities by teaching individuals the skills to gain control over events in their surroundings using more socially acceptable methods (Horner et al., 1990). These involve reducing difficult task demands (Weeks & Gaylord-Ross, 1981), increasing skills in alternative means of communicating needs or wishes (Carr & Durand, 1985a), and increasing reinforcement frequency contingent on displaying adaptive skills (Tarpley & Schroeder, 1979). Often, however, these interventions have been implemented less rigorously and without the same degree of involvement of professionally trained staff as in studies employing intrusive methods; thus the results have been less dramatic (Carr, Taylor, Carlson, & Robinson, 1991).

Finally, numerous studies have been published over the past two decades reporting effects of psychotropic drugs on behavior problems in mental retardation (Aman & Singh, 1988; Lipman, 1970; Sprague & Werry, 1971). Pharmacological interventions are intended to permit a more typical range of environmental events to occasion adaptive behavior, making maladaptive behavior unnecessary and improbable. Such interventions may make it possible for the individual to adjust successfully in a wider range of normalized environments that do not provide environmental prostheses. Little attention has been paid to differentiating factors distinguishing persons who respond favorably to a particular intervention from those who do not benefit. In recent years, more promising psychotropic drug research has begun to emerge, but due to the small number of investigators working in this area, limited funding, and numerous procedural impediments involved in the consent procedures, progress has been slow (NIH, 1991).

The most widely studied interventions recently have been critically reviewed as part of an NIH Consensus Development Conference on Destructive Behavior in Developmental Disabilities (NIH, 1991). This report suggested that many behavior problems are multifaceted, involving both biological and environmental components. Several of the treatments reviewed produce temporary reductions in problem behavior, although in many cases the destructive behavior resumes after the treatment is stopped. Interventions have been designed primarily based on the assumption of a single basic controlling mechanism (usually either neurochemical or environmental, but rarely both). It appears increasingly that many of these most difficult to treat behavior problems are both neurochemically and environmentally regulated, suggesting that interventions focusing on only one mechanism would be expected to produce evanescent effects.

Theories of Destructive Behavior

Since the mid-1960s, scores of articles have appeared in scientific periodicals and in edited volumes on this topic. Theories of environmental and biological mechanisms regulating behavior problems in people with developmental disabilities have been proposed, but increasingly it appears that multiple causation is likely in many cases. Moreover, confusion reigns in the literature because writers conflate theories concerning the etiology of destructive behavior with the current conditions maintaining the problem, which may be very different. The primary environmental theories hypothesize that disturbed behavior is a learned response class inadvertently positively reinforced (e.g., by parent or staff attention contingent on disturbed behavior [Lovaas, Freitag, Gold, & Kassorla, 1965]) or negatively reinforced (e.g., by termination of a demand contingent on self-injury [Carr, Newsom, & Binkoff, 1976]). Other environmental theories hypothesize homeostatic processes and sensory reinforcement theories. One homeostatic theory emphasizes the limited ability of some people with developmental disabilities (especially people with autism) to interpret multiple sources of sensory input (Berkson & Mason, 1964; Green, 1967). According to this view, stereotyped and disturbed behaviors are seen as homeostatic responses to bring the overwhelming sensory input under some degree of control. A related theory proposes that when environmental stimulation is too low, some individuals engage in SIB or stereotypic behavior as a means of increasing stimulation (Repp, Karsh, & Van Acker, 1987). The sensory reinforcement theory (Rincover, Cook, Peoples, & Packard, 1979) is based on the observation that some repetitive movements do not seem to be maintained by any extrinsic consequence and supposes that sensory feedback from repeated motor patterns is intrinsically reinforcing.

Three main neurochemical theories of disturbed behavior of people with developmental disabilities have been proposed: (a) dopaminergic theory, (b) opioid theory, and (c) serotonergic theory. The dopaminergic (D1) receptor theory grew out of the observation that patients with Lesch-Nyhan syndrome who exhibit very severe self-mutilation exhibit markedly lower levels of dopamine and its metabolites in the central nervous system than persons without the syndrome (Lloyd et al., 1981). It has been suggested that the self-injury exhibited by these individuals may result from dopaminergic supersensitivity, particularly involving the D1 dopamine receptor (Goldstein et al., 1986). The opioid receptor theory grows out of the observation that pain causes release of the endogenous opioid ligand, β-endorphin (Willer, Dehen, & Cambier, 1981), which binds to the opiate receptors. Either via modulation of normal pain sensation or due to the rewarding effects of the opioid ligand binding to opiate receptors (Cataldo & Harris, 1982; Stein & Belluzzi, 1989), the behavior producing self-inflicted pain becomes repetitive. The serotonergic theory is based on several observations. First, about one third of children with autism display elevated blood serotonin levels (Ritvo et al., 1970). Moreover, there is a relation between serotonin levels and the amount of disturbed behavior exhibited by patients with autism (Campbell et al., 1975; Coleman & Gillberg, 1985; Schain & Freedman, 1961). Another line of evidence indicates that antidepressants binding to serotonin receptors often are effective in treating obsessive-compulsive disorder in nondevelopmentally disabled individuals (Thoren, Asberg, Cronholm, Jörnestedt, & Träskman, 1980). Finally, serotonin agonists reduce aggression in nonhuman models (Miczek, Mos, & Olivier, 1989; White, Kucharik, & Moyer, 1991) as well as in humans. For example, impulsive aggression manifested in primary DSM-III personality disorder was reduced by the serotonin agonist buspirone (Coccaro, Gabriel, & Siever, 1990). Some view self-injury as self-directed aggression and, as we review in a later section, serotonin agonists have been used to treat SIB.

Individual Differences and Predictors of Treatment Outcome

The search for predictors of treatment outcome is beginning to be seriously engaged. Putative neurochemical abnormalities underlying destructive behavior, and their neurochemical markers or correlated physiological measures, are being sought. Many other investigators believe the best predictors of treatment outcome are to be found in the interactions of the person displaying the problem behavior with his or her social environment. Both approaches emphasize the need to base treatment decisions on the function (either neurochemical or social) served by the behavior. A functional approach seeks to determine the factors regulating the person's destructive behavior by examining proximal controlling variables and setting conditions (Carr, 1977; Donnellan, Mirenda, Mesaros, & Fassbender, 1984; Iwata, Dorsey, Bauman, & Richman, 1982; O'Neill, Horner, Albin, Storey, & Sprague, 1989; Repp & Karsh, 1990). These factors typically include events that immediately precede or follow the target behavior. For destructive behavior that occurs regularly or at a high rate, events following the behavior and that maintain its recurrence are referred to as reinforcers. Antecedent events (e.g., task demands) also gain control over the destructive behavior. In this way, behavior comes under control of both antecedent and consequent events, and environmentally based treatments are designed to change one or both. Knowing the function of a problem behavior may be important for practitioners designing habilitative or educational programs to promote alternative adaptive behaviors while reducing the disturbing behavior (Carr et al., 1976; Gaylord-Ross, Weeks, & Lipner, 1980; Iwata et al., 1982; Repp, Felce, & Barton, 1988; Weeks & Gaylord-Ross, 1981).

Neurobehavioral Pharmacology of Destructive Behavior

Behavioral Mechanisms of Drug Action

Choosing a treatment on the basis of a functional assessment of the conditions setting the occasions for and maintaining problem behaviors has been the standard when investigating the effectiveness of behavioral interventions. This procedure is less common in studies designed to assess the effectiveness of pharmacotherapies (Cerutti & Thompson, 1990). An understanding of environmental conditions giving rise to the behavior at hand, as well as how various drugs modulate the effects of those conditions, is necessary. This strategy has been described as an analysis of *behavioral mechanisms of drug action* (Thompson, 1984; Thompson & Schuster, 1968). Prescribing drugs that alter the manner in which environmental (including social) conditions give rise to and maintain the maladaptive behavior of people with retardation has been neglected. This may be due to unreasonable expectations for immediate change, and limited resources for obtaining necessary information as a basis for drawing conclusions regarding the proximal factors contributing to the behavior. Until recently, these limitations may have been compounded by a lack of theory regarding the etiology of destructive behavior, as well as a lack of awareness of behavioral mechanisms of drug action.

In using a functional approach to diagnosis, the goal is to integrate diagnostic entities by their putative behavioral and neurochemical mechanisms, not by their appearance. The same form of behavior may be regulated by different neurochemical mechanisms. Although pain-elicited and dopaminergically driven self-injury outwardly may appear the same, the neurochemical (as well as behavioral) mechanisms regulating each case may be very different. Similarly, behavior that leads to positive reinforcement (e.g., attention from staff) or negative reinforcement (e.g., removal of an aversive task demand) may respond differentially to a pharmacological intervention.

Therapeutic drugs change the status of a person's health by moderating the operation of normal or pathological physiological or chemical processes. According to this fundamental pharmacological tenet, the body's natural physiological processes regulating an aspect of that person's functioning following perturbation are moderated by drugs. For example, a person's blood pressure may increase to dangerous levels when he or she walks rapidly up a flight of stairs. A blood pressure medication, such as Clonidine, reduces the magnitude of blood pressure increase when the person takes the stairs two steps at a time by increasing the diameter of peripheral blood vessels.

By contrast, when we consider the way in which psychotropic drugs alter the behavior of people with developmental disabilities, we find that the foregoing reasoning is seldom followed in prescribing such behaviorally active medicinal agents. Part of the reason has been the unreasonable expectation that drugs should make an immediate improvement in the affected person's condition, which is rarely possible. Psychotropic drugs contribute to managing behavior problems; they do not cure them. More important, the problem stems from a common theoretical misconception, namely that *brain chemical or physiological processes cause behavior to change, independent of the environmental circumstances within which the person functions.* Brain chemical and physiological events set the parameter values at which these external environmental processes operate. Arriving at a more adequate understanding of the *neurobehavioral mechanisms of action* of psychotropic drugs in developmental disabilities requires that we better understand the individual's history as well as the current circumstances moderating his or her behavior. These factors create the substrates upon which drugs act to produce their behavioral outcome.

Much as we choose an environmental treatment on the basis of a functional assessment of the conditions setting the occasion for and maintaining destructive behavior, a similar approach is required to rationally select the most appropriate pharmacotherapy. Few physicians would think of pharmacologically treating a throat infection without obtaining an accurate measure of body temperature, making an otoscopic examination of the eardrum, palpating the neck for signs of enlarged and tender lymph glands, obtaining a throat culture, and taking an appropriate history. Yet physicians often are expected to prescribe medication to treat a behavior disorder of a person with a developmental disability without the comparable information required for an adequate functional diagnosis. Not only is this often misunderstood, but also the implications often are resisted due to limited resources. Personnel costs are involved in obtaining the essential information that can establish an informed basis for pharmacotherapy. The alternative is treatment in the dark, which euphemistically has been called "treating empirically."

In adopting a functional diagnostic approach, one identifies environmental moderating factors with which a medication may interact to improve the person's ability to function more adaptively and reduce his or her destructive responses to environmental events. The goal is to arrive at a functional diagnosis making it possible to treat the underlying behavioral and neurochemical mechanisms, not their appearance. What appear to be very similar forms of behavior (e.g., hitting a caregiver with a fist and shoving another client so he or she falls down) may be regulated by very different neurochemical and behavioral mechanisms. One may be in response to an attempt by the staff to restrain the person during a panic attack, whereas the second may be a learned operant response to increase social distance from a fellow client. The term *aggression* does not do justice to the variety of causes involved in these cases either environmentally or neurochemically.

Type of Consequence

Positive and Negative Reinforcement

Behavior that is maintained or suppressed by different types of consequences can be differentially affected by the same drug. Positive reinforcers include attention from others (Carr & Durand, 1985b; Lovaas et al., 1965) and tangible reinforcers such as access to a preferred toy, food, or playground equipment (Durand & Crimmins, 1988; Edelson, Taubman, & Lovaas, 1983). Treatment in these cases typically entails teaching the person more acceptable ways of gaining attention or requesting desired items. Among the negative reinforcers that maintain some forms of destructive behavior are removal or avoidance of instructional demands (Carr et al., 1976; Carr, Newsom, & Binkoff, 1980) and cessation or attenuation of the level of ongoing painful stimulation, as in the case of an ear infection (de Lissovoy, 1963). Treatment might involve decreasing the aversiveness of instructional demands in the first example and reducing the discomfort of the painful ear infection in the second by appropriate antibiotic and analgesic treatment.

Sensory changes arising from the behavior itself (such as visual, tactile, or vestibular feedback) also may strengthen and maintain destructive behaviors (Carr, 1977; Favell, McGimsey, & Schell, 1982; Iwata et al., 1982; Rincover & Devaney, 1982). A rational treatment approach for problem behaviors controlled by this mechanism involves teaching the individual alternative ways of producing similar sensory experiences (e.g., playing video games).

Neuroleptic Effects on Behavior Maintained by Positive Reinforcers and Self-Injurious Avoidance Behavior

Neuroleptics most commonly are administered for treating schizophrenia, though they also are widely used in treating behavior problems of people with mental retardation, some of whom have symptoms of schizophrenia; however, neuroleptics most commonly are administered to people with mental retardation in an attempt to reduce aggression and self-injury without regard to presence or absence of schizophrenic symptoms. Although neuroleptics may decrease destructive behavior, the mechanisms by which this effect is produced are more likely due to nonspecific sedation than to ameliorating specific underlying biochemical disturbance (Aman & Singh, 1988; McConahey, Thompson, & Zimmerman, 1977; Thompson, Schaal, & Hackenberg, 1991). Neuroleptics reduce a wide array of learned performances maintained by positive reinforcement in pigeons, rats, monkeys, and other organisms. These decrements may result from a general weakening of reinforcer effectiveness produced by neuroleptics (Wise, 1982). Pimozide administration increases the magnitude of intercranial stimulation required to maintain lever pressing by rats (Zarevics & Setler, 1979), suggesting a dopaminergically mediated reduction in reinforcement efficacy. Heyman (1983) reinforced rats' lever pressing under a positive multiple reinforcement schedule where each component was associated with different reinforcement rates and corresponding response rates. Pimozide and chlorpromazine reduced lever pressing under the lower reinforcement rates more than lever pressing maintained under richer reinforcement conditions. This has been interpreted as an anhedonic effect (Heyman & Monaghan, 1987). As neuroleptic dose increased, asymptotic lever-press rates under the high reinforcement density conditions decreased, which is said to occur when motor behavior is impaired. Staff, parents, and other caregivers often inadvertently teach people with mental retardation to display aggressive or self-injurious behavior by providing access to preferred commodities following outbursts. Such coercive behavior may be weakened by neuroleptics by reducing the effectiveness of positive reinforcement as well as reducing motoric capacity nonspecifically.

Neuroleptics weaken avoidance behavior at doses having little or no effect on escape behavior. For example, following chlorpromazine administration, rats trained to climb a pole when a tone is followed with a series of foot shocks (i.e., the tone is a conditioned negative reinforcer) will be less likely to avoid the impending shock. Once the shock begins, however, the rats will readily climb the pole to escape the shock (Cook & Weidley, 1957). Increasing preshock warning intervals facilitated avoidance responding (Posluns, 1962). This suggests that neuroleptics reduce avoidance by reducing the tendency to initiate an avoidance response. Furthermore, neuroleptic-induced reductions in avoidance are apparently not a product of motor incapacitation, as once avoidance responding is initiated, it proceeds at its usual nondrug rate. Neuroleptics' selective weakening of avoidance but not escape behavior has been demonstrated repeatedly (Cook & Catania, 1964; Cook & Sepinwall,

1975) and has been used as a means of distinguishing neuroleptics from other drug classes (Davidson & Weidley, 1976). These laboratory findings with rats have been replicated with human subjects. Fischman and Schuster (1979) trained human volunteers under a Sidman avoidance schedule where lever pressing postponed shock delivery or loss of points exchangeable for money. Subjects were administered pentobarbital (a barbiturate) and chlorpromazine (a neuroleptic). Chlorpromazine decreased avoidance responding at doses minimally affecting motor performance, whereas pentobarbital only affected avoidance responses at doses that also disrupted motor performance.

Reductions in self-injury and aggression in response to neuroleptic treatment cannot reasonably be attributed to any single mechanism. From the literature discussed above, destructive behavior maintained by positive reinforcement (e.g., attention from staff or access to preferred commodities) or negative reinforcement (e.g., removal or delay of aversive task demands) would be expected to decrease following neuroleptic treatment in some individuals. Behavioral reduction would not be expected to be specific to aggression, however, as other adaptive behaviors are likely to be impaired as well.

Reducing Self-Injury Maintained by Endogenous Opiate Self-Administration

Recently several clinical studies have evaluated the extent to which self-injury is reduced by the opiate antagonists naloxone and naltrexone (Bernstein, Hughes, Mitchell, & Thompson, 1987; Sandman et al., 1983). Self-injury may begin for a variety of reasons (e.g., through inadvertent social reinforcement from direct care providers or due to a D1 receptor supersensitivity). Over time a child with severe handicaps may repeatedly injure himself or herself with sufficient intensity and frequency to trigger endogenous opioid release. These endogenous opioids (endorphins/enkephalins) are produced naturally in the body in response to painful stimulation, binding to the same neuronal receptor sites as exogenous opiates such as heroin. Endogenous opioids not only attenuate pain (Loh, Tseng, Wie, & Li, 1976; Tseng, Loh, & Li, 1976) but also function as effective reinforcing stimuli, substituting for self-injections of morphine but not for other nonopiate agents in self-administration laboratory procedures with nonhumans (Woods, Herling, & Young, 1981). Physical dependence can also result, similar to that seen with repeated administration of heroin or morphine (Wei & Loh, 1976), as evidenced by acute withdrawal symptoms triggered by administering opiate antagonists.

Some forms of self-injury may be described as "addictive" behavior maintained in part by the contingent relation between the self-injurious response, the subsequent endogenous opioid release, and the occupation of the opiate receptor. Some evidence suggests that some people with autism have abnormal endorphin levels (cf. Gillberg, Terenius, & Lonnerhold, 1985; Herman et al., 1989; Weizman et al., 1984), although the present analysis does not require this assumption because the early stages of self-injury may be maintained concomitantly by a variety of environmental factors (e.g., attention from parents and/or teachers). However, with the passage of time, self-injury may come progressively under the control of opioid mechanisms. It is at this point that the self-injurious individual becomes dependent on opioid self-administration, much as a heroin addict becomes dependent on exogenously administered opiates.

Cronin, Wiepkema, and van Ree (1985), in a semi-naturalistic study of opiate antagonist effects with partially restrained sows, found that repetitive, stereotyped movements (some of which could be considered self-injurious) were reduced by intramuscularly administered naloxone. Under conditions of restraint, sows (and other animals) frequently develop repetitive, stereotyped movements. In this case, the sows repeatedly rubbed up against restraints until severe lesions developed. Naloxone reduced stereotyped movements, but adaptive behavior (i.e., feeding, grooming, exploring) was unaffected.

Several single, clinical case studies have evaluated the effectiveness of opiate antagonists in reducing self-injurious behavior in persons with severe mental handicaps. Sandman and colleagues (1983) reported that naloxone reduced self-injury by approximately 50% in one subject and eliminated it in the other. For both subjects the naloxone effects were evident within the first 10 minutes following injection; however, the effects of the drug began to diminish after 70-80 minutes, presumably due to naloxone's short half-life. In addition, both subjects displayed increases in SIB when given sedative-hypnotic drugs. Beckwith, Couk, and Schumacher (1986) studied effects of naloxone on self-injury in two persons with long self-abuse histories. Using a double-blind, crossover design, the effects of three doses of naloxone (0.1, 0.2, and 0.4 mg/day) or placebo were examined. No systematic effects of naloxone on self-injury for either subject were reported. However, Sandyk (1985), using a similar double-blind arrangement, reported a favorable response to naloxone (1.2 mg/day), but Davidson, Kleene, Carroll, and Rockowitz (1983) reported conflicting results. Although the overall frequency of head banging remained constant across dose levels of naloxone, staff members indicated that the intensity of the problem behavior was lower. Richardson and Zaleski (1983) reported that naloxone (1.0 and 2.0 mg/day) reduced self-injury by a single subject from 77% during placebo to 25% under 2.0 mg of the opiate antagonist. In a comparison of the effectiveness of naloxone and naltrexone, Barrett, Feinstein, and Hole (1989) reported on a single subject with extremely high rates of self-injury (more than 400/hour). It was found that naltrexone (an orally effective opiate antagonist with a much longer duration of action) was superior to naloxone, with reductions in self-injury of approximately 92% from predrug baseline levels. Bernstein and colleagues (1987) also have reported on the effects of opiate antagonists on self-injury. Results of a clinical trial with a single subject having a long history of self-injury suggest that naloxone reduced self-injury (hand-to-head hits) by approximately half (from 20-25/hour to 10-12/hour) on three separate occasions (twice under 0.5 mg/day and once under 1.0 mg/day). Bernstein and colleagues (1987) replicated the effect with the same subject using naltrexone within a double-blind, placebo-controlled design. Self-injury was reported to have decreased in a dose-dependent fashion under 25 mg/day and 50 mg/day of naltrexone. A 33% reduction in self-injury from drug-free baseline conditions was evident under the highest dose of naltrexone.

Recently, Thompson, Hackenberg, Cerutti, Baker, and Axtell (in press) administered naltrexone alone and in combination with Clonidine to four men and four women (mean age = 34.6 years) with severe to profound retardation and extensive histories of self-injurious behavior. Three self-injury forms were monitored for each participant at four intensity levels. Self-injury episodes were observed randomly out of every hour from 8:00 a.m. through 3:00 p.m., Monday through Friday, for four two-week phases (baseline, placebo, 50 mg, and 100 mg of naltrexone daily). The frequency distribution of self-injury was constructed for all phases of the study, and comparisons were made of changes in proportion of low frequency and high frequency self-injury days during baseline and at each naltrexone dose. Percentage of days on which head banging and self-biting were frequent was lower ($p < .05$) when treated with naltrexone than baseline. Days on which blows to the head or self-biting were infrequent or did not occur at all were greater ($p < .05$) during naltrexone than baseline. Other self-injury forms or

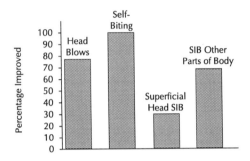

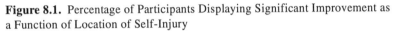

Figure 8.1. Percentage of Participants Displaying Significant Improvement as a Function of Location of Self-Injury

NOTE: Improvement is shown by more days with low frequency of self-injury, fewer days with high frequency of self-injury. Both head blows and self-biting were significantly reduced by naltrexone, whereas superficial self-injury, including superficial scratching, poking, and so on, was not reliably reduced. Self-injury involving other parts of the body were variably affected by naltrexone (Thompson et al., in press).

body locations (scratching, self-pinching, thrusting fingers in nose) were not predictably influenced by naltrexone. These results are summarized in Figure 8.1. Self-injurious participants slept an average of 1.38 hours less per night, which was unaffected by naltrexone. Clonidine had no reliable effect on self-injury or sleep.

Antisuppressive Effects of Benzodiazepines

Self-injurious behavior often is reinforced by terminating or preventing aversive or demand situations. For example, a person may be asked to perform a difficult or unfamiliar task. Failure to comply with similar demands in the past may have resulted in reprimands or removal of privileges by caregivers, which can establish the verbal demand or request as a conditioned negative reinforcer. Removing verbal requests can maintain the behavior leading to their termination. A direct care staff teaching a child with severe mental retardation may discontinue language training whenever the pupil becomes frustrated and hits himself; if the training task is aversive to the student, the self-hitting may be reinforced by avoiding the beginning of the task or escaping from it (Carr et al., 1976). Eventually, the child may continue to hit himself to terminate stimuli preceding such training sessions, thereby successfully avoiding the task in its entirety.

Some studies revealed decreased continuous shock avoidance behavior and increased shock frequency when chlordiazepoxide was administered at doses not affecting positively reinforced behavior (Cook
& Catania, 1964). Other studies (Cook & Catania, 1964; Heise & Boff,
1962; Randall, Schallek, Heise, Keith, & Bagdon, 1960) report increases
in shock frequency with no change in overall lever-press rates under
chlordiazepoxide. Some individuals who self-injure display violent bouts
of self-injury following administration of benzodiazepines and other
sedative hypnotics (Barron & Sandman, 1983, 1985). These drugs counter-
act suppressive effects of aversive consequences in laboratory studies
with rats and squirrel monkeys (Sepinwall & Cook, 1978). Jeffery and
Barrett (1979) established identical overall operant response rates by
pigeons under a multiple reinforcement schedule, in which one component included purely positive reinforcement, whereas in the other a
conflict condition was in effect (i.e., positively reinforced responses
periodically produced aversive consequences as well). Chlordiazepoxide
increased responding in both components; however, far larger increases
in responding were obtained in the component that was suppressed by
the aversive consequence, suggesting that chlordiazepoxide selectively
reduced the suppressing effects of punishment. Carlton, Siegel, Murphree,
and Cook (1981) demonstrated that performance of a laboratory task by
human volunteers, which was suppressed by monetary loss, increased
following diazepam administration. Increases in assaultive, aggressive,
and hostile behaviors have been documented following one-week administration of chlordiazepoxide in adults functioning in a normative cognitive range (DiMascio, Shader, & Harmatz, 1967; Salzman, DiMascio,
Shader, & Harmatz, 1969). Similarly, Gardos (1980) describes a case of
a woman whose depressive symptoms did not respond to tricyclic
antidepressants. Diazepam was prescribed for symptoms of anxiety.
Over the course of several weeks, the patient began experiencing sexual
and aggressive impulses. In response, the patient increased her consumption of diazepam, which resulted in acting out aggressively. Aggressive behaviors included property destruction, verbal and physical
assault of family and therapist, and head banging. These behaviors
diminished following termination of benzodiazepine treatment.

   If the usual consequence for the person with retardation who engages
in self-injury is the painful feedback consequent to that action, one
would assume that such painful stimulation functions, at least in part,
as a suppressive punisher. Caregivers often verbally reprimand or restrain
a person immediately following a self-injurious act, which also may

have suppressive effects in some cases. The fact that benzodiazepines and other sedative hypnotics reduce the suppressive effects of these typical consequences for SIB is not really "paradoxical," because it is consistent with a large laboratory research literature indicating these drugs reduce the suppressive effects of punishment. The notion that "paradoxical" increases in aggression produced by benzodiazepines result from antisuppressive effects is supported by ethopharmacological studies (Olivier, Mos, & Miczek, 1991) demonstrating that aggression-enhancing effects are particularly exacerbated when aggression is suppressed by internal or external events.

Serotonin Agonists

Studies with nonhuman primates have tied serotonin (5-hydroxytryptamine [5-HT]) levels to self-injury (Kraemer & Clarke, 1990) and aggression (Soubrie, 1986). Serotonergic agonists reduce isolation-induced aggression by rats (White, Kucharik, et al., 1991); the degree to which these agents reduce aggression in this assay correlates with 5-HT$_{1A}$ receptor affinity (McMillen, DaVanzo, Scott, & Song, 1988). Serotonergic drugs have been used recently to reduce aggression and SIB of people with developmental disabilities. Markowitz (1992) administered the 5-HT reuptake inhibitor fluoxetine (20-40 mg/day) to 21 people with severe or profound mental retardation who displayed SIB. Moderate to marked reduction in destructive behaviors was observed in 17 of the patients. Cook, Rowlett, Jaselskis, and Beventhal (1992) examined effects of fluoxetine (20-80 mg/day) on obsessive-compulsive behaviors, impulsive behaviors, aggression, and SIB in children and adults with autism and mental retardation. Of the 8 patients presenting SIB, 2 were said to be "less aggressive" following fluoxetine treatment and SIB was reduced or eliminated in 3. The 5-HT$_{1A}$ receptor agonist buspirone, which has both anxiolytic and anti-aggressive properties, has been used to treat aggressive outbursts and self-injury by a woman with moderate mental retardation (Gedye, 1991). Outbursts were decreased (by 65%-67%) when buspirone was given and decreased even further when a high serotonin diet was introduced concomitantly. Ratey, Sovner, Parks, and Rogentine (1991) examined effects of buspirone in 6 people with mental retardation, anxiety, and aggressive behavior including SIB. Buspirone reduced measures of anxiety and aggression.

Elevated aggression and self-injury correlated with reductions in central 5-HT activity may reflect a reduced efficacy of the naturally occurring punishers that normally would suppress such behavior. If this interpretation is correct, elevations in an experimental aggression baseline following 5-HT antagonist administration would be predicted in addition to the decreases in aggression following 5-HT agonist administration discussed above. Observed increases in muricidal aggression (mouse killing; Katz, 1980; Waldbillig, 1979) and shock-induced fighting (Kantak, Hegstrand, & Eichelman, 1981; Sewell, Gallus, Gault, & Cleary, 1982) in response to neurotoxins leading to 5-HT depletion are consistent with this prediction. 5-HT may serve multiple functions in regulating aggressive behavior or self-injury; it may determine their frequency and intensity by modulating punishment suppression and determine reactivity of neurochemical systems to antecedent aversive stimuli.

Reinforcer Presentation Schedule

Intermittent Schedules

Since the 1950s it has been known that the strength of behavior is related to the pattern of consequences maintaining the behavior in question. Over a 40-year period it became a truism in laboratory research in behavioral pharmacology that the effects of drugs on performance depend critically on the schedule of presentation of positive reinforcers, negative reinforcers, or punishers (Dews, 1955; Thompson & Schuster, 1968). A given dose of a specific drug (e.g., pentobarbital or methamphetamine) may increase or decrease rate of performance, depending on the schedule of presenting consequences maintaining the behavior of interest. Though there have been a modest number of studies exploring this generalization in human laboratory settings, few investigations have been done in clinical or educational settings to evaluate this notion. This is somewhat surprising, as it is widely known that the amount of adaptive or maladaptive behavior in schools (Martens, Lockner, & Kelly, 1992) and other settings (McDowell, 1982) is directly related to the relative distribution of reinforcement (often in the form of attention). Of what relevance is this idea to evaluating effects of drugs on destructive behavior of people with developmental disabilities? It is widely recognized that parents, teachers, and other caregivers attend to aggressive, self-injurious, or other destructive behavior intermittently, sometimes necessarily. The reinforcing effects of caregiver attention for destructive behavior are well known (Picker, Poling, & Parker, 1979).

We also know that behavior that is reinforced more frequently (Heyman, 1983) is more resistant to effects of some of the drugs most commonly used to treat behavior problems in mental retardation (neuroleptics). It is possible the same dose of the same drug (e.g., a neuroleptic) might have very different effects on the aggressive or self-injurious behavior of a person with mental retardation, depending on the frequency with which that problem behavior receives attention from caregivers. On a day that staff are not overworked and are more likely to respond quickly to a client's outburst, the behavior persists at a high rate, though the individual is receiving 8 mg of haloperidol. Two weeks later when there has been a change in the staffing, and the individual receives very little attention, even though he has repeated outbursts, the overall frequency of outbursts may gradually decline. Variability in response to psycho-tropic medications, such as neuroleptics, may depend critically on the type and pattern of reinforcement that is maintaining the behavior in question. In such a situation, the staff likely would report that "nothing had changed" in the way they were treating the client, while, in fact, the effect observed was due to an interaction between the dose of medica-tion and the schedule of social reinforcement contingent on outbursts.

Concurrent Schedules

Nettie, a woman with moderate mental retardation who lives in a community group home, intermittently strikes out at people around her in the vocational setting where she is employed. Observational measures of the frequency with which Nettie receives attention for work-related activities, and for aggression and other disturbed behavior, reveal that she receives twice as much attention per unit time for her various forms of inappropriate behavior than for her vocationally relevant activities. The staff in Nettie's group home take her to the doctor, who prescribes thioridazine for her outbursts, but the staff members soon discover that, although her outbursts decrease by 25%, her vocationally relevant activities nearly stop. Such an effect should have been predictable from an examination of the research literature on *concurrent reinforcement schedules*.

A concurrent reinforcement schedule is one in which two operants (i.e., responses) are available at the same time, and each is maintained by an independent reinforcement schedule (Catania, 1963; Ferster & Skinner, 1957; Thompson & Grabowski, 1972). Concurrent reinforcement schedules provide a procedure for studying the distribution of behavior among several available activities and their associated reinforcement alternatives. Herrnstein (1961) described the relation between relative rates of alternative behaviors and relative reinforcement rates contingent on those responses by the Matching Law, which states that relative behavior rates are proportional to relative rates of reinforcement. Choice among alternative responses is viewed as a continuous process in which an individual "allocates" his or her activities among various options. In the above example, because the rate of reinforcement for disturbed behavior is twice as high per unit time, it is not surprising that the maladaptive behavior is far more resistant to the effects of the neuroleptic drug than the adaptive, vocational performance, which seldom was reinforced.

There are several interpretations of differential performance under concurrent reinforcement schedules. In both experimental and applied settings, multiple stimuli exert control over behavior. In laboratory situations with concurrent reinforcement schedules, consideration must be given to alternative reinforcement sources, variables that bias responding, and conditions affecting sensitivity to the operating contingencies (Pierce & Epling, 1983). The pharmacological properties of drugs may affect sensitivity to concurrent environmental contingencies. For example, Galizio and Allen (1991) used concurrent reinforcement schedules to study the effects of d-amphetamine and morphine on behavior maintained under different types of negative reinforcement. Rats were trained under variable-ratio and variable-interval concurrent schedules to press one lever to avoid a shock and press the other lever to produce periods of freedom from avoidance (timeout). Behavior maintained by timeout was reduced by morphine at doses that increased or had no effect on avoidance responding. In contrast, large increases in timeout responding were produced by d-amphetamine at doses that had minimal effect on avoidance responding. Higgins and Stitzer (1988) demonstrated differential effects of d-amphetamine on the way people distributed responding under concurrent schedules. Relative response rate was measured for two exclusive options (socializing vs. monetary reinforcement) in two nondisabled humans under controlled laboratory conditions. Relative reinforcement rate was manipulated until subjects divided their time equally between the activities leading to socializing or the monetary reinforcement. For both subjects, amphetamine increased the percentage of time allocated to the social option, though such a behavioral change resulted in a loss of monetary reinforcement. The results suggest amphetamine increases relative reinforcing effects of social interaction.

These laboratory findings may have important implications for clients with severe destructive behaviors in complex natural environments. For example, classroom and workshop settings are environments providing alternative, and concurrently available, sources of reinforcement. At any given moment, students engage in a variety of activities, some of which are socially appropriate and others that are socially inappropriate (Mace & Shea, 1990). Their behavior may be allocated among response alternatives in proportion to obtained reinforcement. Martens and colleagues (1992) used Herrnstein's matching equation to account for an average of 51% of the variance in the on-task behaviors of a 6-year-old boy during naturally occurring classroom routines (e.g., math and language arts activities). Earlier, McDowell (1982) showed that the Matching Law could describe the relation between high rates of self-injury and parental verbal reprimands for a 10-year-old boy. In most cases the student or client is likely to engage in the option that produces the highest reinforcement rate. When high reinforcement rates favor destructive behavior, we would expect higher frequencies of observed problem behavior and fewer appropriate responses. Interventions that interrupt only the response-reinforcer contingency for problem behavior may be ineffective to the extent that increasing the relative reinforcement rate for appropriate behavior is ignored. This suggests that studies reporting medication or behavioral intervention failures may not have taken into account alternative response classes and their relative reinforcement rates (Stanford & Nettlebeck, 1982). Differential responding also may be influenced by interactions between positive and negative reinforcement contingencies, reinforcers differing in value, and uncontrolled reinforcement histories. Furthermore, the ability to discriminate between alternative sources of reinforcement may be weak or absent (Pierce & Epling, 1983). Sprague and Horner (1992) experimentally examined the effects of physical blocking and reprimanding versus instructional-based interventions (teaching positive, socially acceptable behaviors or providing additional teacher assistance) on the reduction of multiple problem behaviors exhibited by two school-age students with severe intellectual impairments. Positive and negative collateral behavioral changes within a response class varied with the treatment. Such analyses suggest that to document the effects of pharmacological treatments, careful attention must be given to the maintaining contingencies. Variables that may affect or influence the observed reallocation of problem behaviors to members of the response class's "appropriate behavior" may include, but are not limited to, the value of the competing reinforcers, the dimensions of the competing reinforcement schedules, the physical effort of the competing responses, and the comparative time delay between the environmental prompt and the reinforcer. Presumably, the effects of pharmacological interventions for individuals with developmental disabilities would be moderated by these and other variables.

Multiple Schedules

All psychoactive drugs will terminate destructive behavior at some dosage. However, these doses frequently are associated with untoward changes in other nondestructive behavior such as general sedative effects (Ortiz & Gershon, 1986) and impairments in learning. Self-injury and aggression are complex behavior classes having many determinants. Damage to self or others may lead to desired attention or concrete commodities, or destructive behavior may reduce prevailing aversive conditions (Feshbach, 1964; Valzelli, 1981). Destructive behavior may be suppressed by social punishers from staff or, in more extreme cases, retaliation by the victim of an aggressive outburst. When attempting to evaluate behavioral mechanisms of drug effects on destructive behavior, the ways positive reinforcement, negative reinforcement, or punishment regulates behavior are analyzed.

To demonstrate that a drug effect is specific to a given behavior class, experimenters often examine more than one behavior in a multiple schedule (Ferster & Skinner, 1957). Multiple schedules consist of two or more independent controlling conditions presented successively, each in the presence of a distinctive cue (Ferster & Skinner, 1957; Thompson & Grabowski, 1972). For example, in a residential investigation, McConahey and colleagues (1977) examined effects of chlorpromazine on adaptive and maladaptive behavior of women with mental retardation under a multiple schedule in which adaptive behavior was reinforced in one component (e.g., during a morning training period) but unreinforced during the second component (e.g., during an afternoon unstructured period). In the laboratory, lever pressing could be maintained by a food reinforcement schedule when a specific color of light is present, and maintained by avoidance when the light is extinguished, during a single experimental session. If drug administration alters avoidance behavior in the absence of concomitant changes in responding under the positive reinforcement baseline, the drug's effects could be said to be specific to negative reinforcement. To examine drug effects on behavior suppressed by negative consequences, it is necessary to create a baseline performance. The typical way of accomplishing this is to use a conflict procedure (Geller & Seifter, 1960). In this procedure, food-reinforced lever pressing by animals is concomitantly followed by occasional aversive stimuli (e.g., foot shocks). Increases in lever pressing following treatment with chlordiazepoxide or pentobarbital in a conflict situation decreases the efficacy of the punisher. By using a conflict schedule as a component of a multiple schedule in which the other component contains the same positive reinforcement contingency without aversive consequences, the antipunishment interpretation can be strengthened. Drugs that increase suppressed responding and decrease responding maintained by negative reinforcement are said to reduce anxiety (e.g., benzodiazepines).

Recurring Evocative Stimuli

Excessive behaviors can be evoked by a periodic schedule of intermittent positive reinforcement but are not tied directly to the reinforcement contingency. Such behavior is said to be adjunctive or schedule induced (Falk, 1971; Thompson & Lubinski, 1986). Rats given free access to water while lever pressing for food pellets under interval schedules consumed up to 10 times their normal daily water intake (Falk, 1961). The magnitude of excessive behaviors (e.g., polydipsia) evoked by concurrent intermittent reinforcement depends on the reinforcer's physical characteristics as well as on the temporal properties of the reinforcer's presentation. People displaying very low frequencies and intensities of destructive behavior may escalate their problem behavior when placed in situations where powerful positive reinforcers are given only periodically. Wiesler, Hanson, Chamberlain, and Thompson (1988) found that the frequency of noninjurious stereotypic behaviors increased as the fixed-interval (FI) schedule value of concurrent positive reinforcement of a table-top task increased. Emerson and Howard (1992) also found evidence for schedule-induced stereotypy. Stereotypy increased when reinforcement for performing simple experimental tasks was available at FI or differential reinforcement of low response rate (DRL) schedules. No changes in stereotypy were observed if the same number of reinforcers were given all at once, however.

Studies using nonhuman subjects have examined drug effects on emergence of schedule-induced behaviors. Pellon and Blackman (1992) examined the effects of d-amphetamine or diazepam on schedule-induced polydipsia generated by an intermittent food presentation schedule in rats. Although the overall rate of drinking was unaffected by drug administration, the temporal distribution of licking was shifted somewhat by d-amphetamine. The effects of the common neuroleptic drug haloperidol (a D_1 and D_2 receptor antagonist) and SCH3390 (a D_1 antagonist) on schedule-induced polydipsia in rats have been compared (Todd, Beck, & Martin-Iverson, 1992). Each drug increasingly reduced the volume of water consumed and the percentage of time spent drinking as dose increased. As drinking declined, the amount of time spent chewing increased, suggesting that reductions in schedule-induced polydipsia cannot be attributed to sedative effects of the drugs. The opiate antagonist naloxone was given to rats with previous exposure to an intermittent food-presentation schedule and rats with no such pre-exposure (Geter, Kautz, Wetherington, & Riley, 1991). Subsequent schedule-induced polydipsia was reduced by naloxone in both groups, although the reduction was greater in the group having no prior exposure to the generator schedule. This suggests that naloxone may have a specific effect on the emergence of schedule-induced behaviors.

Presenting food pellets to hungry laboratory animals on a time-based schedule escalates a variety of concurrent behaviors; the type of behavior escalated does not depend on form. For example, gnawing or drinking by rodents, preening and nonfood-directed pecking by birds, and aggressive behavior in a variety of species frequently occur under such circumstances. It appears that the periodic nature of the food presentation schedule boosts the reinforcing value of events maintaining behaviors present in the experimental environment. Rats given access to a cocaine solution and water primarily drink the water (Falk, in press; Falk, Vigorito, Tang, & Lau, 1990). Introducing an FI 1-minute food pellet presentation schedule markedly increased cocaine consumption to the extent that it became the consistently preferred solution.

Falk (1986) hypothesized that schedule-induced behavior involves conflicting response dispositions, in this case, the tendency to remain in close proximity to a food source and the tendency to leave the previously available food source as the time since last food delivery increases. If low probability behaviors present in this situation are strengthened, the organism will more likely remain in the situation and will be more likely to consume subsequent food sources. The function of adjunctive behaviors, therefore, is to prevent the animal from leaving the environment prematurely. This interpretation is supported by laboratory evidence showing that schedule-induced behaviors do not occur if reinforcer

presentation intervals are very short, in which case the rich food availability sustains the animal's presence in the situation. If reinforcer
presentations are spaced too far apart, adjunctive behaviors also are not
evoked, perhaps because, in nature, remaining in such a situation would
be futile.

It is likely that the frequency and variety of positive reinforcers impact-
ing on the behavior of people with severe disabilities are restricted.
Introducing effective positive reinforcement programs for such people
would be expected to occur in the context of an otherwise lean reinforcement milieu. As such the programmed reinforcement conditions not
only increase adaptive target behaviors but also may enhance the reinforcing capacity of events maintaining self-stimulation or self-injury. Administering drugs that seem to alter reinforcer effectiveness, such as
neuroleptics, would be expected to reduce evocative power of the
generator schedule. Drugs that affect the temporal pattern of responding,
such as stimulants, might be expected to influence the temporal relation
between food deliveries and responding, thereby shifting schedule-
induced responding. Blocking endogenous opiates, which may be involved in the acquisition of adjunctive behavior, may not only reduce
behaviors maintained by endogenous opiate release but also impair
escalation of the reinforcing properties of events maintaining adjunctive behavior.

Discriminative and Contextual Control

Aggression or self-injury may be occasioned by demands placed on
the individual (Carr et al., 1980), crowding (Boe, 1977; McAfee, 1987),
staff change (Touchette, MacDonald, & Langer, 1985), task repetition
(Winterling, Dunlap, & O'Neill, 1987), and even certain items of clothing (Rojahn, Mulick, McCoy, & Schroeder, 1978). Carr and colleagues
(1991) suggest that dissimilar stimuli can function as a single functional
category (such as aversive stimulation). It has been suggested that, in
addition to identifying the environmental variables that immediately
precede and follow a targeted behavior, a rigorous assessment should
include global environmental setting factors such as the physical and
social contexts in which the behavior occurs, as well as the intrapersonal
behavior of the afflicted individual (Schroeder et al., 1991). These may
include factors such as physical discomfort (e.g., menstrual cramping or
a middle ear infection), time since last meal, or the presence of a
particular staff member. Conducting this type of assessment should

provide useful information in evaluating the appropriateness of specific medications.

Exteroceptive Stimuli and Attention

Neurochemical mediators interact with environmental factors to alter the degree of control environmental stimuli have over the behavior. The behavior of an individual with an attentional problem is poorly controlled by environmental stimuli (e.g., teacher's verbal instructions) that typically lead most children to respond to those features. In some cases, the threshold for such stimulus control can be regulated downward by administering a central nervous system (CNS) stimulant such as methylphenidate or methamphetamine. The therapeutic outcome is improved compliance with requests, though the mechanism by which this occurs may be a lowered threshold for stimulus control by environmental cues. Similarly, the person who is exceedingly anxious responds to a wide array of environmental cues as though they were frightening warning signals. When such a person is treated with a benzodiazepine, the threshold for such avoidance behavior is elevated and the person tends not to display avoidance as frequently and/or with such vigor. The person may appear less agitated and irrationally fearful, while the mechanism may be an elevated threshold for avoidance mediated by a GABA receptor process. There is a large behavioral pharmacology research literature addressing such an analytic approach. In general, behavior under weak stimulus control is more easily disrupted by drugs than behavior under strong stimulus control. Moreover, a smaller dose of a given drug produces a disruption in performance when the behavior is weakly controlled as opposed to when it is under greater stimulus control (Laties & Weiss, 1966).

Attention is a form of stimulus control in which some aspect of a cue sets the occasion for responding to another stimulus. A teacher shows a student with moderate mental retardation where the knife, fork, and spoon are placed on the table's placemat and then removes them and asks the student to reproduce the same place-setting. The student is unable to do so correctly, and the teacher says, "You weren't paying attention." The implication of this statement is that the student was not orienting her eyes toward the table and was not listening during the teacher's demonstration, so that correct responding could be accomplished later. People with attentional problems frequently fail to "pay attention" to relevant aspects of a stimulus complex, so they are unable to respond correctly later. People must be taught that orienting toward a source of information is often associated with a higher rate of reinforcement than not doing so. The opportunity to see a particularly colorful bird is enhanced by orienting one's eyes toward the same tree at which several other viewers are looking. Children with retardation often have difficulty learning that attending is associated with a higher rate of reinforcement than not attending.

CNS stimulant drugs, such as amphetamine and methylphenidate, often improve stimulus control, including improved attending. Although neurophysiological and neurochemical mechanisms underlying attention are not fully understood, at a behavioral level it appears that increasing the reward value of stimulus feedback seems to be an integral component of that process. Hill (1970) and later Robbins (1982) hypothesized that such aminergic compounds enhance the efficacy of the stimulus feedback controlling behavior (i.e., as occurs for looking at objects). Robbins and colleagues (Lyon & Robbins, 1975; Robbins, 1978) argued that aminergic compounds reduce the variability in response categories while increasing the frequency of the fewer categories that persist, thereby increasing stereotypies.

Interoceptive Stimulus Control: Rage, Anxiety, and Panic Attacks

Provocative and demanding environmental conditions often elicit internal autonomically mediated responses that produce discriminative changes in the way a person feels. Some may be discriminated as "anger" or "rage" and are terminated following an aggressive outburst (Berry & Pennebaker, 1993; Sinha, Lovallo, & Parsons, 1992) and, thus, may function as a negative reinforcer. People with developmental disabilities may have difficulty learning to behave in socially acceptable ways in the face of these internal emotional cues (e.g., communicating their feelings "I'm angry!" counting to 10, walking out of the room, etc.). Nevertheless, if the magnitude of these interoceptive reactions can be decreased pharmacologically, the frequency and intensity of explosive outbursts may decline as a result, even though exteroceptive antecedent conditions are unchanged.

Propranolol, a nonselective β-adrenergic receptor antagonist, has been used in treating destructive behaviors of psychiatric patients (Lader, 1988) and persons with mental retardation (Ruedrich, Grush, & Wilson, 1990). Most reports of propranolol's efficacy in reducing explosive behavioral outbursts have been case studies lacking placebo controls, and double-blind drug administration. A double-blind crossover study using placebo control conditions (Greendyke, Kanter, Schuster, Verstreate, & Wooton, 1986) showed that daily propranolol administration reduced assaultive behavior in patients with organic brain damage. It is not yet clear whether propranolol's anti-aggressive effects are mediated peripherally, or if CNS 5-HT blockade (Middlemiss, 1986) occurring when propranolol crosses the blood-brain barrier is required. Nadolol, a β-adrenergic antagonist that does not readily penetrate the brain, has been shown to reduce aggressive outbursts in psychiatric inpatients (Ratey et al., 1992). Further, propranolol does not ameliorate punishment-suppressed behavior in a conflict procedure (Sepinwall, Grodsky, Sullivan, & Cook, 1973), suggesting beta blockers' anti-aggressive effects may be mediated peripherally.

There are no validated ways of diagnosing panic attack or obsessive-compulsive disorder in people with severe to profound mental retardation. Some of the manifestations of such problems may take very different forms in people with mental retardation than with typically developing people. Typically developing people hyperventilate, become diaphoretic, display pupilary dilatation, and pull at the clothing around their neck when having a panic attack. When someone attempts to comfort them, they typically push others away. A person with severe mental retardation may exhibit similar physiological signs but may tear his or her clothing and, if touched, strike out violently toward caregivers. This may be misinterpreted as a rage outburst, rather than severe anxiety, and it is likely such individuals would be treated with neuroleptics in many settings. Although serotonin reuptake blockers are the treatments of choice for obsessive-compulsive and panic attack disorder in typically developing populations (Insel & Zohar, 1987; Rickels & Schweizer, 1987), there has been no systematic study of these problems in people with mental retardation, though some evidence indicates heterocyclic antidepressants may be effective in reducing some problem behavior, at least in a subset of people with mental retardation (Langee & Conlon, 1992).

Effects of Prior Exposure to Medication and Experience

Some forms of psychotherapy are based on the assumption that assisting clients in reconstructing their own history can be helpful in better understanding the reasons individuals respond to current environmental stressors and social conditions the way they do. The importance of an individual's history was studied experimentally by Harold Weiner, who conducted a series of studies that showed a human subject's response to a current reinforcement contingency (e.g., a fixed-interval schedule) depended on his or her experience with other reinforcement schedules (Weiner, 1964, 1969). In these studies human subjects (some were people with schizophrenia, others nonmentally ill adult volunteers) were exposed to reinforcement histories under low-rate (DRL) or high-rate (FR) schedules prior to exposure to the same fixed-interval schedule. The rate and pattern of responding under the FI schedule depended on the subject's specific schedule histories. In other studies, subjects who were first taught to respond at lower rates through use of response cost (i.e., punishment) procedures responded differently to FI schedules than those who had not had such histories.

Operant behavioral studies with nonhuman subjects have suggested that drug effects on behavior can be modified by variables that may not be apparent under the current experimental circumstances (Barrett, 1985). Sources of unseen moderation include behavioral history, drug treatment history, and environmental context. If a drug is given that often increases activity level (e.g., d-amphetamine), one might assume that giving that medication to a group of subjects sharing a common set of environmental conditions would lead to a similar change in responding. A study examining effects of d-amphetamine on rats' lever pressing under an FI schedule of reinforcement suggests otherwise. Half of the rats had histories of lever pressing under a fixed-ratio (FR) food reinforcement schedule, whereas the other half had histories of low lever-pressing rates under a DRL schedule. Effects of amphetamine depended on the history each subject brought to the current environment, with rats having low-rate histories increasing lever pressing under d-amphetamine and those with high-rate histories decreasing lever pressing under d-amphetamine (Urbain, Poling, Millam, & Thompson, 1978). Barrett (1977) examined the effects of d-amphetamine administration on food-reinforced lever pressing of squirrel monkeys that was suppressed by a concomitant shock-suppression condition. Shock-suppressed lever pressing decreased in response to d-amphetamine admini- stration prior to 2 weeks of exposure to an interpolated shock-avoidance schedule, whereas comparably suppressed behavior was *increased* by d-amphetamine after a history of shock avoidance. Subsequent studies have examined the effects of a prior positive reinforcement schedule in determining drug effects on operant baselines (Nader & Thompson, 1987). Prior exposure to certain drugs can alter subsequent effects of other drugs on behavior. Pentobarbital increased lever pressing by squirrel monkeys under a shock-escape schedule, but only in monkeys that had not previously received morphine injections when working under the same schedule (Glowa & Barrett, 1983). When drug effects on a behavioral baseline are examined in the context of conditions maintaining behavior other than the baseline (e.g., concurrent schedules, multiple schedules), the contextual variables can influence the direction and degree of the drug's effect. Barrett and Stanley (1980) found that the size of an FR schedule in a multiple schedule influenced the effect of ethanol on key pecking by pigeons on a constant FI food-reinforcement schedule. As FR increased, ethanol-induced response-rate reductions under the fixed-interval component decreased. Further, drug administration may differentially reduce control by one source of control in complex reinforcement schedules, bringing behavior under control of alternative sources that are minimally operative under nondrug conditions (Egli & Thompson, 1989).

Neurobehavioral Mechanisms of Drug Action: Three Hypothetical Case Studies

In this section we discuss three hypothetical cases to illustrate the way a functional analysis of variables regulating behavior can be informative in predicting the likely effects of behaviorally active medications on self-injury, aggression, and other disturbed behavior. Our purpose is not to recommend treatments, but to outline the decision process that underlies a treatment based on an understanding of the behavioral mechanisms of drug action.

Juan

Juan is a 26-year-old man with a history of self-injury dating from around 2 years of age, with occasional violent, aggressive outbursts. He functions in the low-severe range of mental retardation, displaying no spoken language and limited skills of daily living. Juan has surprisingly good fine motor skills for his level of retardation and he seems to periodically understand far more that is spoken by caregivers than might be expected. He has been diagnosed as having autism, intermittent explosive disorder, and undersocialized conduct disorder, at various times. Staff in his group home say he frequently rocks and bangs his head against walls, bites his hand and wrist, and strikes the bridge of

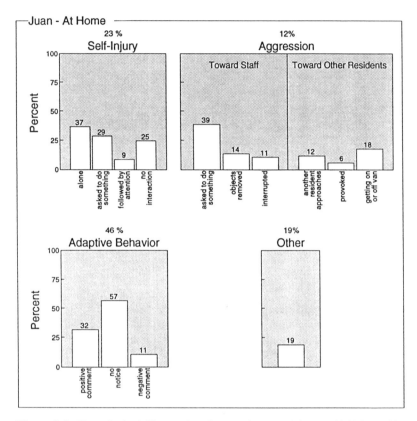

Figure 8.2. Hypothetical Observational Data of Juan, a 26-Year-Old Man With Severe Mental Retardation, Who Displays Self-Injury and Aggressive Behavior

NOTE: The data presented here are based on a hypothetical random observation schedule of 5 minutes out of every hour for 7 hours per afternoon and evening for 10 days in Juan's residence. The percentage of the total observations that include self-injury (23%), aggression (12%), adaptive behavior (46%), and other behavior (19%) is shown above the labels of each behavior type. Within each graph are shown the percentages of each behavior category as a function of social circumstances (e.g., when alone, when asked to do something, when followed by attention from staff, and when there has been no interaction, though others are present).

his nose with his fist until it bleeds. When he is excited he makes "running in place" movements and waves and flaps his arms and hands, emitting a screeching sound.

Behavioral observations are made at home between 3:30 and 10:30 p.m. for 10 evenings. During each hour, one 5-minute period was randomly observed. Instances of adaptive behavior, self-injury, aggression, and "other" behavior (i.e., rocking, staring, flicking his fingers in front of his face) were recorded. The data shown in Figure 8.2 resulted. Juan's doctor is concerned about his self-injury and aggression. The physician is weighing various alternative psychoactive medications after hearing the pattern of complaints about Juan's behavior and perusing the above data. Based on the functional analysis conducted over the preceding 10 days, it should be possible to make certain predictions about the effects of alternative medications on the four forms of behavior analyzed.

It appears most of Juan's self-injury occurs when he is alone or when no social interactions occur either before or after SIB. Moreover, very little of his self-injury seems to be followed by staff attention, which suggests it is not being maintained by a generalized positive reinforcer. This suggests his self-injury is either dopaminergically driven or maintained by endogenous opioid self-administration or both. The fact that he displays little stereotypy and he self-injures with high frequency suggests that an opioid mechanism is more likely. Absence of a family history of schizophrenia strengthens the case for an opioid, as opposed to a dopaminergic, mechanism.

Sixty-four percent of Juan's aggression is directed toward staff, primarily when he is asked to do something he apparently does not want to do, or when material objects are taken away from him or if he is interrupted while doing a preferred activity. Aggression seems to be an avoidance response. Similarly, aggressive behavior toward other clients, though less often, occurs when other clients are too close to him or perhaps bump into him (e.g., getting into or out of the van). It is possible Juan's threshold for aggression may vary with a serotonergic receptor mechanism associated with anxiety.

Though Juan's adaptive behavior (e.g., household chores, self-grooming) occurred in nearly half of the observed intervals, in more than half of those instances his adaptive behavior produced no positive social consequences, and it occasionally was punished (11%), such as when Juan attempts to help with meal preparation and the staff tell him, "No, don't touch the spoon." If we conceive of his adaptive behavior as a performance maintained under a concurrent reinforcement schedule, it is weakly maintained by comparison with the aggressive behavior and self-injury, which are reinforced most of the time.

Finally, Juan's "other" behavior, which includes a variety of stereotyped movements, consumes a small amount of his time (19%). He displays a variety of "time-filling" nonfunctional activities commonly displayed by people with autism when they are not provided with anything else to do. Some of these movements may be learned adaptations to the absence of anything to do.

If Juan is given a *neuroleptic* medication, self-injury may be reduced somewhat, as the behavior serves some avoidance function. Juan's aggression appears to be largely avoidance-motivated and also may be reduced somewhat by a dopamine antagonist. Regrettably, because Juan's everyday living skills are infrequently positively reinforced, those performances will be disproportionately weakened by a dopamine antagonist, and his adaptive skills would be expected to drop sharply. Finally, Juan's stereotyped rocking and finger flicking may be reduced by a neuroleptic, but when he is unoccupied he also may be drowsy and fall asleep due to the medication's sedative side effects.

A *beta blocker* such as propranolol or an *alpha adrenergic agonist* such as clonidine will be likely to have fewer effects on Juan's behavior than a neuroleptic. There is no reason to believe such a medication would affect opioid-regulated self-injury. A beta blocker may elevate Juan's threshold for violently reacting to having his personal space violated or striking out when he is frightened or alarmed. This would be particularly true if the activity is something he finds anxiety-provoking (e.g., going to a place that is frightening). Such medications would have little effect on the value of positive reinforcers and therefore have no effect on adaptive behavior. Finally, propranolol may reduce Juan's agitation and thereby reduce his rocking and finger flicking when he is excited or apprehensive about an upcoming activity or event (e.g., a visit by his parents) but would be unlikely to have an effect otherwise (e.g., when he is simply bored and has nothing to do).

The *opiate antagonist, naltrexone,* is likely to have the most specific effect in reducing Juan's self-injury and little other effect. Naltrexone probably would reduce self-biting and head hitting, but not necessarily other superficial forms of SIB (Thompson et al., in press). Further analysis would be required to determine whether those superficial forms of SIB account for most of the instances in which SIB seems to serve an avoidance function (29% of SIB).

Finally, a *serotonin reuptake blocker,* such as *clomipramine,* might have favorable effects on aggression and possibly reduce stereotyped behavior but would be less likely to affect self-injury. As self-injury seems to be associated with periods of being alone or when there is no social antecedent or consequence, SIB does not seem to fall into the category of self-directed aggression. Serotonin reuptake medications seem to have specific effects on repetitive avoidance responses (e.g., obsessive-compulsive rituals) and on the threshold for aggression. It is possible clomipramine would elevate the threshold for aggression sufficiently that situations in which other clients crowd around Juan would no longer provoke aggressive outbursts. If Juan's "other" behavior includes skin picking, hair pulling, and other compulsive rituals, it may be reduced. However, it is unlikely that clomipramine would have any effect on rocking and hand flapping.

It is important to bear in mind that the four groups of responses outlined above may involve overlapping classes, and effects on one may influence the outcome seen with others: Some self-injury and aggression may actually belong in the same class, because they serve the same function (social and task avoidance). A treatment that reduces avoidance-motivated self-injury also may reduce avoidance-motivated aggression. A second factor that needs to be borne in mind is that, if a behavioral treatment is directed toward one behavior problem (e.g., aggression), other members of that same class that go untreated may worsen. For example, if a timeout procedure were implemented for instances of aggression, self-injury that was maintained by the same consequence may increase. If a medication were simultaneously administered (e.g., naltrexone), one might erroneously conclude the medication had no effect, when in fact the absence of a decrease in self-injury really reflected a behavioral contrast phenomenon in response to the suppression of aggression that was also maintained by avoidance.

Elaine

Elaine is a 24-year-old woman currently displaying aggression toward others and toward herself. Her problems with hurting others date from around 12 years of age; self-injury has become a problem in the past 3 or 4 years. She functions in the moderate range of mental retardation and has functional expressive and receptive communication skills. She resides in a small group home and works in a vocational training program during the day, five days per week. Staff in the home and in the training facility indicate that when she harms others, the episode is brief and usually consists of a strong shove or a single blow directed toward staff or other clients. During the day at the training facility, Elaine works putting address labels on envelopes, assembling hotel toiletry kits, and sorting cans for recycling. She earns tokens that are exchangeable for snacks and privileges as well as money. The staff state that she usually works well, but that some days when she arrives they can tell from her appearance that it is going to be "a bad day." During these bad days, according to the staff, they are careful not to "cross her path" and try to keep other clients away from her when possible. The group home staff recently have become concerned about Elaine's aggression and have called in a psychiatric consultant. She has targeted another resident for her attacks and they have been occurring daily. When asked whether the other resident provoked these attacks, a staff member replied in the negative, stating that "Elaine just seems to enjoy being mean." Over a 10-day period, the observations shown in Figure 8.3 were taken at home and at the vocational training service facility.

When comparing the observations in the two settings, a number of conclusions emerge. Self-injury occurred exclusively in the training facility, and on most of these occasions it followed a request from the staff. Aggression in this setting was directed primarily toward staff making a demand. A likely hypothesis is that self-injury and aggression in this setting are maintained primarily by negative reinforcement. Generally, Elaine spends time engaging in adaptive behavior, which suggests that the demands and/or the tasks are aversive only under some circumstances. If the tasks were inherently aversive, we might expect more time to be spent engaging in "other" behavior, such as self-stimulating. Because these episodes result in attention from staff, it is possible some of these behaviors are maintained by positive reinforcement; however, the rich reinforcement for behaving appropriately in this setting suggests this is not a major source of control.

Data collected at home reveal a different picture. There were no instances of SIB in this setting. Aggression was directed primarily toward another resident, and was not preceded by provocation. Attention from staff following such outbursts occurred frequently and immediately. We may conjecture that these attacks are positively reinforced by staff attention. This conclusion is further supported by the extensive adaptive behavior that occurs without notice by the staff at home. Further, the earlier report by the staff that "Elaine enjoys being mean" and the fact that the same person is the target of these unprovoked attacks are consistent with this interpretation.

This example illustrates the importance of examining data from the several contexts in which behavior problems occur. The rich reinforcement schedule in the work setting may make effects of the relative lack of attention at home for adaptive behavior more pronounced (i.e., behavioral contrast). Elaine may be more likely to act aggressively at

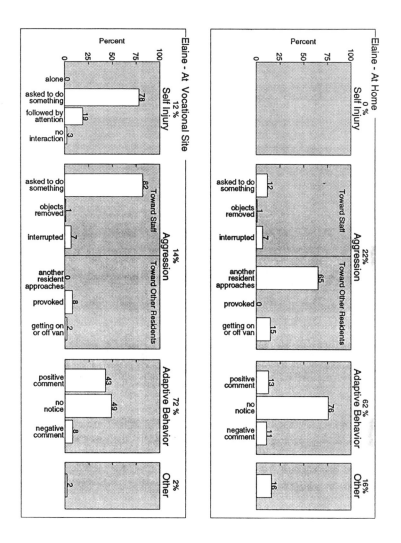

Figure 8.3. Hypothetical Observational Data for Elaine, a 24-Year-Old Woman With Moderate Mental Retardation, Who Displays Aggressive Behavior Toward Staff and Other Residents as Well as Self-Injury

NOTE: The data presented here are based on a hypothetical random observation schedule at Elaine's residence (right set of graphs) as well as at her vocational site (left set of graphs). The percentage of the total observations that include self-injury, aggression, adaptive behavior, and other behavior is shown above the labels of each behavior type. Within each graph are shown the percentages of each behavior category as a function of social circumstances (e.g., when asked to do something, when objects are removed, when interrupted).

home to receive the same level of attention at home as she does at work. It also becomes clear that if we were to treat behavior pharmacologically, based on information from one setting, incidents of destructive behavior may not only remain unchanged but also actually escalate.

For example, if a *serotonin agonist* (e.g., buspirone) were administered based on the hypothesis that her behavior was maintained by negative reinforcement, we may see improvement in aggression at the work setting because the aversiveness of task demands would be expected to decrease. Aggression at home, which is reinforced by staff attention, would not be expected to respond to this treatment and may become more persistent as effects of punishment by staff may be weakened when the drug is given. Because there is reason to believe that the work tasks are not aversive in general, this treatment may not produce the desired effect.

Neuroleptics may reduce aggression and self-injury somewhat in both settings because they reduce the efficacy of both positive and negative reinforcement. Such a treatment, however, likely would be found unsatisfactory by the staff at the training facility, as it would disrupt positively reinforced work behavior. Adaptive behavior at home would be even more vulnerable because most of it (69%) occurs without any attention from staff. Further, because SIB was not observed when Elaine was alone there is no reason to suspect a dopaminergic mechanism. By this reasoning, *naltrexone* would not be expected to be effective in either setting.

A *beta blocker* (e.g., propranolol) may have some effect on outbursts in the vocational setting. If being asked to work upsets Elaine, causing her to become physically aggressive, propranolol might reduce autonomic responses and associated interoceptive cues following such requests, therefore decreasing the likelihood of aggression. Propranolol would not be expected to interfere with positively reinforced adaptive behavior in either setting; however, it also would have minimal effects on aggression occurring at home.

If it were confirmed that the "bad days" observed by the vocational training staff were associated with Elaine's menses, it is possible that treating Elaine for menstrual pain, in conjunction with propranolol administration, would effectively raise the threshold for aggression following requests, thereby reducing SIB and aggression in the vocational setting and producing reductions in aggression at home as well. Although positively reinforced aggression at home would not be expected to respond to this pharmacotherapy, introducing positive reinforcement at home for behavioral alternatives to aggression (e.g., verbal requests) may effectively reduce aggressive behavior entirely.

Russell

Russell attends a public high school where he is enrolled in a supported employment/transitions program for students with learning disabilities. He spends his mornings in the classroom receiving instruction in daily living skills (e.g., money management) and his afternoons working at a nearby restaurant. Russell has mild to borderline mental retardation, has well-developed interpersonal skills, and a few good friends at school with whom he socializes. He competently fulfills his work duties, which include assembling pizza boxes and janitorial activities. Periodically Russell displays brief, intense outbursts of aggression during which time he violently hits staff or peers or destroys property. On occasion, such outbursts have produced significant injury. Indeed, staff describe Russell as having a "short fuse" and an uncontrollable temper. His outbursts seem to occur when somebody "sets him off." When asked about his outbursts, Russell states that "When people tease me it feels like my head's going to blow up." Given the severity of the episodes and the possible risk of injury and subsequent litigation, both the school principal and Russell's employer are considering suspending him.

Based on two weeks of systematic daily observations in both the school and the work setting, the data shown in Figure 8.4 were obtained.

Our observations reveal that aggressive episodes are reliably preceded by provocation (taunting and teasing) from peers in school and co-workers at the restaurant. (Few aggressive episodes were reported to occur in the home.) Aggressive episodes are successful in terminating peer teasing. However, the vast majority of Russell's day is spent either actively engaged with appropriate instructional materials at school or working with minimal supervision at his work site. No relation was noted between teacher or staff demands and aggression, nor was Russell observed to engage in aggression to solicit attention. Although it was observed that staff attention followed aggression on most instances, this would be expected given the intensity of the assaults.

Neuroleptic medication might be expected to reduce his outbursts; however, it would most certainly disrupt his school performance as well as other adaptive behaviors. Russell's aggressive outbursts seem to function as avoidance responses, terminating teasing by other clients. It is important that Russell learn more adaptive ways of responding to

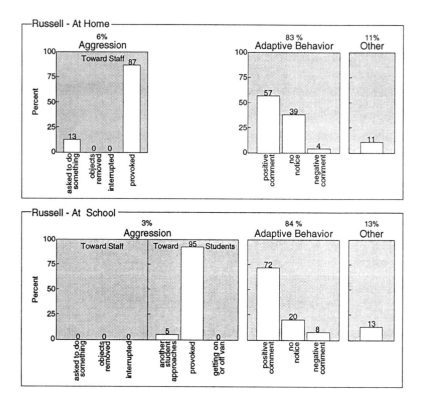

Figure 8.4. Hypothetical Observational Data for Russell, a High School Student With Mild Mental Retardation, Who Displays Aggressive Behavior Toward Staff and Other Students

NOTE: The data presented here are based on a hypothetical random observation schedule at Russell's home (upper set of graphs) and school (lower set of graphs). The percentage of the total observations that include aggression, adaptive behavior, and other behavior is shown above the labels of each behavior type. Within each graph are shown the percentages of each behavior category as a function of social circumstances (e.g., when asked to do something, when objects are removed, when interrupted, when provoked, etc.).

taunts (such as leaving the area, verbally objecting to the taunt, or seeking assistance from a supervisor). It is likely a neuroleptic would reduce Russell's effectiveness in displaying these more adaptive reactions to teasing and would, therefore, be counterproductive.

Serotonin agonists would be expected to raise the threshold for aggression in response to taunts and thereby reduce the probability that provocative peer comments would end in aggression. If the interval between onset of taunting and Russell's anger and explosive reaction were prolonged by serotonergic agents, it may facilitate his ability to learn more appropriate responses such as leaving the situation or talking to a supervisor.

Environmental stresses such as peer teasing may elicit internal autonomically mediated responses that produce internal discriminative changes in the way Russell feels. Russell's statement that when he is angry in these provocative situations he feels like his head is "going to blow up" may reflect elevated heart rate and blood pressure. Reducing the intensity of these autonomic responses by using a nonselective β-adrenergic receptor antagonist (e.g., propranolol) may reduce both the frequency and the intensity of the violent outbursts. Unlike the serotonergic agents, beta blockers would not be expected to affect adaptive behaviors controlled by punishment and negative reinforcement.

Conclusion

All are agreed that we must do a far better job of identifying which people will profit most from specific treatments and at what cost. Battie's (1758/1969) plea for a more adequate approach to diagnosis is as apt today as it was 236 years ago. We believe, as Mayr (1982) has argued, that meaningful classification of biological phenomena, including destructive behavior, is unlike classification of library books or rocks. Meaningful classification arises from an understanding of the origins and processes responsible for the current status of the system in question. Clinical behavioral pharmacologists are striving to understand the conditions under which pharmacological treatments change destructive and adaptive behavior of people with developmental disabilities (Thompson, 1986). In this chapter we proposed that arriving at a more appropriate system of classification and diagnosis may be achieved most effectively through combining principles and techniques from behavioral pharmacology, and advances in neurochemistry and neuropharmacology, with the technologies permitting a refined functional analysis of environmental variables regulating destructive and adaptive behavior of people with retardation in natural settings. The resulting taxonomy will be based on an analysis of neurobehavioral mechanisms of drug action. We concluded by providing three hypothetical examples of people with developmental disabilities who displayed serious behavior problems, and suggested ways in which it may be possible to predict responses to pharmacological intervention, which may be a useful step in arriving at a differential diagnosis.

References

Aman, M. G., & Singh, N. N. (1988). *Psychopharmacology of the developmental disabilities.* New York: Springer Verlag.

Barrett, J. E. (1977). Behavioral history as a determinant of the effects of *d*-amphetamine on punished behavior. *Science, 198,* 67-69.

Barrett, J. E. (1985). Modification of the behavioral effects of drugs by environmental variables. In L. S. Seiden & R. L. Balster (Eds.), *Behavioral pharmacology: The current status* (pp. 7-22). New York: Alan R. Liss.

Barrett, J. E., & Stanley, J. A. (1980). Effects of ethanol on multiple fixed-interval fixed-ratio schedule performances: Dynamic interactions at different fixed-ratio values. *Journal of the Experimental Analysis of Behavior, 34,* 185-198.

Barrett, R. P., Feinstein, C., & Hole, W. T. (1989). Effects of naloxone and naltrexone on self-injury: A double-blind placebo controlled analysis. *American Journal on Mental Retardation, 93,* 644-651.

Barron, J., & Sandman, C. (1983). Relationship of sedative-hypnotic response to self-injurious behavior and stereotypy for mentally retarded clients. *American Journal of Mental Deficiency, 88,* 177-186.

Barron, J., & Sandman, C. A. (1985). Paradoxical excitement to sedative-hypnotics in mentally retarded clients. *American Journal of Mental Deficiency, 90,* 124-129.

Battie, W. (1969). *A treatise on madness.* New York: Brunner/Mazel. (Original work published 1758)

Beckwith, B. E., Couk, D. I., & Schumacher, K. (1986). Failure of naloxone to reduce self-injurious behavior in two developmentally disabled females. *Applied Research in Mental Retardation, 7,* 183-188.

Berkson, G., & Mason, W. A. (1964). Stereotyped movements of mental defectives III: Situational effects. *Perceptual and Motor Skills, 19,* 635-652.

Bernstein, G. A., Hughes, J. R., Mitchell, J. E., & Thompson, T. (1987). Effects of narcotic antagonists on self-injurious behavior: A single case study. *Journal of the American Academy of Child and Adolescent Psychiatry, 26,* 886-889.

Berry, D. S., & Pennebaker, J. W. (1993). Nonverbal and verbal emotional expression and health. *Psychotherapy and Psychosomatics, 59,* 11-19.

Boe, R. B. (1977). Economical procedures for the reduction of aggression in a residential setting. *Mental Retardation, 15,* 25-28.

Campbell, M., Friedman, E., Green, W. H., Collins, P. J., Small, A. M., & Breuer, H. (1975). Blood serotonin in schizophrenic children: A preliminary study. *International Pharmacopsychiatry, 10,* 213-221.

Carlton, P. L., Siegel, J. L., Murphree, H. B., & Cook, L. (1981). Effects of diazepam on operant behavior in man. *Psychopharmacology, 73,* 314-317.

Carr, E. G. (1977). The motivation of self-injurious behavior: A review of some hypotheses. *Psychological Bulletin, 84,* 800-816.

Carr, E. G., & Durand, V. M. (1985a). Reducing behavior problems through functional communication training. *Journal of Applied Behavior Analysis, 18,* 111-126.

Carr, E. G., & Durand, V. M. (1985b). The social-communicative basis of severe behavior problems in children. In S. Reiss & R. Bootzin (Eds.), *Theoretical issues in behavior therapy* (pp. 219-254). New York: Academic Press.

Carr, E. G., Newsom, C. D., & Binkoff, J. A. (1976). Stimulus control of self-destructive behavior in a psychotic child. *Journal of Abnormal Child Psychology, 4*, 139-153.

Carr, E. G., Newsom, C. D., & Binkoff, J. A. (1980). Escape as a factor in the aggressive behavior of two retarded children. *Journal of Applied Behavior Analysis, 13*, 101-117.

Carr, E. G., Taylor, J. C., Carlson, J. I., & Robinson, S. (1991). Reinforcement and stimulus-based treatments for severe behavior problems in developmental disabilities. In *Treatment of destructive behaviors in persons with developmental disabilities* (NIH Publication No. 91-2410) (pp. 73-230). Bethesda, MD: Department of Health and Human Services.

Cataldo, M. (1991). The effects of punishment and other behavior reducing procedures on the destructive behaviors of persons with developmental disabilities. In *Treatment of destructive behaviors in persons with developmental disabilities* (NIH Publication No. 91-2410) (pp. 231-341). Bethesda, MD: Department of Health and Human Services.

Cataldo, M., & Harris, J. (1982). The biological basis for self-injury in the mentally retarded. *Analysis and Intervention in Developmental Disabilities, 2*, 21-39.

Catania, A. C. (1963). Concurrent performances: Reinforcement interaction and response independence. *Journal of the Experimental Analysis of Behavior, 6*, 253-263.

Cerutti, D., & Thompson, T. (1990). "Artificial hibernation" evolved: Drug therapy in mental retardation [Review of M. Aman & N. H. Singh's *Psychopharmacology of the Developmental Disabilities*]. *Contemporary Psychology, 35*, 1148-1150.

Coccaro, E. F., Gabriel, S., & Siever, L. J. (1990). Buspirone challenge: Preliminary evidence for a role for central 5-HT 1a receptor function in impulsive aggressive behavior in humans. *Psychopharmacology Bulletin, 26*, 393-405.

Coleman, M., & Gillberg, C. (1985). *The biology of the autistic syndromes*. New York: Praeger.

Cook, E. H., Rowlett, R., Jaselskis, D. O., & Beventhal, B. L. (1992). Fluoxetine treatment of children and adults with autistic disorder and mental retardation. *Journal of the American Academy of Child and Adolescent Psychiatry, 31*, 739-745.

Cook, L., & Catania, A. C. (1964). Effects of drugs on avoidance and escape behavior. *Federation Proceedings, 23*, 818-835.

Cook, L., & Sepinwall, J. (1975). Psychopharmacological parameters of emotion. In L. Levi (Ed.), *Emotions: Their parameters and measurement* (pp. 379-404). New York: Raven.

Cook, L., & Weidley, E. (1957). Behavioral effects of some psychopharmacological agents. *Annals of the New York Academy of Sciences, 66*, 740-752.

Cronin, G. M., Wiepkema, P. R., & van Ree, J. M. (1985). Endogenous opioids are involved in abnormal stereotyped behavior of tethered sows. *Neuropeptides, 6*, 527-530.

Davidson, A. B., & Weidley, E. (1976). Differential effects of neuroleptics and other psychotropic agents on acquisition of avoidance in rats. *Life Science, 18*, 1279-1284.

Davidson, P. W., Kleene, B. M., Carroll, M., & Rockowitz, R. J. (1983). Effects of naloxone on self-injurious behavior: A case study. *Applied Research in Mental Retardation, 4*, 1-4.

de Lissovoy, V. (1963). Head banging in early childhood: A suggested cause. *Journal of Genetic Psychology, 102*, 109-114.

Dews, P. B. (1955). Studies on behavior: I. Differential sensitivity to pentobarbital of pecking performance in pigeons depending on the schedule of reward. *Journal of Pharmacology and Experimental Therapeutics, 113*, 393-401.

DiMascio, A., Shader, R. I., & Harmatz, J. (1967). Psychotropic drugs and induced hostility. *Psychosomatics, 10,* 46-47.

Donnellan, A. M., Mirenda, P. L., Mesaros, R. A., & Fassbender, L. L. (1984). Analyzing the communicative functions of aberrant behavior. *Journal of the Association of Persons With Severe Handicaps, 9*(3), 201-212.

Durand, V. M., & Crimmins, D. B. (1988). Identifying the variables maintaining self-injurious behavior. *Journal of Autism and Developmental Disorders, 18,* 99-117.

Edelson, S. M., Taubman, M. T., & Lovaas, I. O. (1983). Some social contexts of self-destructive behavior. *Journal of Abnormal Child Psychology, 11,* 299-312.

Egli, M., & Thompson, T. (1989). Effects of methadone on alternative fixed-ratio fixed-interval performance: Latent influences on schedule-controlled responding. *Journal of the Experimental Analysis of Behavior, 52,* 141-153.

Emerson, E., & Howard, D. (1992). Schedule-induced stereotypy. *Research in Developmental Disabilities, 13,* 335-361.

Falk, J. L. (1961). Production of polydipsia in normal rats by an intermittent food schedule. *Science, 133,* 195-196.

Falk, J. L. (1971). The nature and determinants of adjunctive behavior. *Physiology and Behavior, 6,* 577-588.

Falk, J. L. (1986). The formation and function of ritual behavior. In T. Thompson & M. Zeiler (Eds.), *Analysis and integration of behavioral units* (pp. 335-355). Hillsdale, NJ: Lawrence Erlbaum.

Falk, J. L. (in press). Schedule-induced drug self-administration. In F. van Haaren (Ed.), *Methods in behavioral pharmacology.* Amsterdam and New York: Elsevier.

Falk, J. L., Vigorito, M., Tang, M., & Lau, C. E. (1990). Schedule-induced cocaine drinking: Choice between cocaine and vehicle. *Pharmacology Biochemistry & Behavior, 35,* 187-193.

Favell, J. E., McGimsey, J. F., & Schell, R. M. (1982). Treatment of self-injury by providing alternate sensory activities. *Analysis and Intervention in Developmental Disabilities, 2,* 83-104.

Ferster, C. B., & Skinner, B. F. (1957). *Schedules of reinforcement.* New York: Appleton-Century-Crofts.

Feshbach, S. (1964). The function of aggression and the regulation of aggressive drive. *Psychological Review, 71,* 257-272.

Fischman, M. W., & Schuster, C. R. (1979). The effects of chlorpromazine and pentobarbital on behavior maintained by electric shock or point loss avoidance in humans. *Psychopharmacology, 66,* 3-11.

Galizio, M., & Allen, A. R. (1991). Variable-ratio schedules of timeout from avoidance: Effects of *d*-amphetamine and morphine. *Journal of the Experimental Analysis of Behavior, 56,* 193-203.

Gardos, G. (1980). Disinhibition of behavior by antianxiety drugs. *Psychosomatics, 21,* 1025-1026.

Gaylord-Ross, R. J., Weeks, M., & Lipner, C. (1980). An analysis of antecedent, response, and consequence events in the treatment of self-injurious behavior. *Education and Training of the Mentally Retarded, 15,* 35-42.

Gedye, A. (1991). Buspirone alone or with serotonergic diet reduced aggression in a developmentally disabled adult. *Biological Psychiatry, 30,* 88-91.

Geller, I., & Seifter, J. (1960). The effects of meprobamate, barbiturates, *d*-amphetamine and promazine on experimentally induced conflict in the rat. *Psychopharmacologia, 1,* 482-492.

Geter, B., Kautz, M. A., Wetherington, C. L., & Riley, A. L. (1991). The effects of food schedule adaptation on the ability of naloxone to suppress the acquisition of schedule-induced polydipsia. *Pharmacology Biochemistry & Behavior, 38,* 85-92.

Gillberg, C., Terenius, L., & Lonnerhold, G. (1985). Endorphin activity in childhood psychosis: Spinal fluid levels in 24 cases. *Archives of General Psychiatry, 42,* 780-783.

Glowa, J. L., & Barrett, J. E. (1983). Drug history modifies behavioral effects of pentobarbital. *Science, 220,* 333-335.

Goldstein, M., Kuga, S., Kusano, N., Meller, E., Dancis, J., & Schwartz, R. (1986). Dopamine agonist induced self-mutilative biting behavior in monkeys with unilateral ventromedial tegmental lesions of the brainstem: Possible pharmacological model for Lesch-Nyhan syndrome. *Brain Research, 367,* 114-119.

Green, A. (1967). Self-mutilation in schizophrenic children. *Archives of General Psychiatry, 17,* 234-244.

Greendyke, R. M., Kanter, D. R., Schuster, D. B., Verstreate, S., & Wooton, J. (1986). Propranolol treatment of assaultive patients with organic brain disease. *Journal of Nervous and Mental Disease, 174,* 290-294.

Heise, G. A., & Boff, E. (1962). Continuous avoidance as a base-line for measuring behavioral effects of drugs. *Psychopharmacologia, 3,* 264-282.

Herman, B. H., Hammock, M. K., Egan, J., Arthur-Smith, A., Chatoor, I., & Werner, A. (1989). Role for opioid peptides in self-injurious behavior: Dissociation from autonomic nervous system functioning. *Developmental Pharmacology and Therapeutics, 12,* 81-89.

Herrnstein, R. J. (1961). Relative and absolute strength of response as a function of frequency of reinforcement. *Journal of the Experimental Analysis of Behavior, 13,* 267-272.

Heyman, G. M. (1983). A parametric evaluation of the hedonic and motor effects of drugs: Pimozide and amphetamine. *Journal of the Experimental Analysis of Behavior, 40,* 154-161.

Heyman, G. M., & Monaghan, M. M. (1987). Effects of changes in response requirement and deprivation on the parameters of the Matching Law equation: New data and review. *Journal of Experimental Psychology: Animal Behavior Processes, 13,* 384-394.

Higgins, S. T., & Stitzer, M. L. (1988). Time allocation in a concurrent schedule of social interaction and monetary reinforcement: Effects of *d*-amphetamine. *Pharmacology, Biochemistry, and Behavior, 31,* 227-231.

Hill, R. T. (1970). Facilitation of conditioned-reinforcement as a mechanism of psychomotor stimulation. In E. Costa & S. Garattini (Eds.), *Amphetamines and related compounds* (pp. 781-795). New York: Raven.

Horner, R. H., Dunlap, G., Koegel, R. L., Carr, E. G., Sailor, W., Anderson, J., Albin, R. W., & O'Neill, R. E. (1990). Toward a technology of "nonaversive" behavioral support. *Journal of the Association for Persons With Severe Handicaps, 15,* 125-132.

Insel, T. R., & Zohar, J. (1987). Psychopharmacologic approaches to obsessive-compulsive disorder. In H. Y. Meltzer (Ed.), *Psychopharmacology: The third generation of progress* (pp. 1205-1210). New York: Raven.

Intagliata, J., & Willer, B. (1981). Reinstitutionalization of mentally retarded persons successfully placed into family-care and group homes. *American Journal of Mental Deficiency, 87,* 34-39.

176   Neurobehavioral Mechanisms of Drug Action

Iwata, B. A., Dorsey, M. F., Bauman, K. E., & Richman, G. S. (1982). Towards a functional analysis of self-injury. *Analysis and Intervention in Developmental Disabilities, 2,* 3-20.

Jeffery, D. R., & Barrett, J. E. (1979). Effects of chlordiazepoxide on comparable rates of punished and unpunished responding. *Psychopharmacology, 64,* 9-11.

Kantak, K. M., Hegstrand, L. R., & Eichelman, B. (1981). Facilitation of shock-induced fighting following intraventricular 5, 7-dihydroxytryptamine and 6-hydroxy DOPA. *Psychopharmacology, 74,* 157-160.

Katz, R. J. (1980). Role of serotonergic mechanisms in animal models of predation. *Progress in Neuro-Psychopharmacology, 4,* 219-231.

Kraemer, G. W., & Clarke, A. S. (1990). The behavioral neurobiology of self-injurious behavior in rhesus monkeys. *Progress in Neuro-Psychopharmacology and Biological Psychiatry, 14,* S141-S168.

Lader, M. (1988). β-adrenergic antagonists in neuropsychology: An update. *Journal of Clinical Psychiatry, 49,* 213-223.

Langee, H. R., & Conlon, M. (1992). Predictors of response to antidepressant medications. *American Journal on Mental Retardation, 97,* 65-70.

Laties, V. G., & Weiss, B. (1966). Influence of drugs on behavior controlled by internal and external stimuli. *Journal of Pharmacology and Experimental Therapeutics, 152,* 388-396.

Lipman, R. S. (1970). The use of psychopharmacological agents in residential facilities for the retarded. In F. J. Menolacin (Ed.), *Psychiatric approaches to mental retardation* (pp. 387-398). New York: Basic Books.

Lloyd, K. G., Hornykiewicz, O., Davidson, L., Shannak, K., Farley, I., Goldstein, M., Shibuya, M., Kelley, W. N., & Fox, I. H. (1981). Biomedical evidence of dysfunction of brain neurotransmitters in the Lesch-Nyhan Syndrome. *New England Journal of Medicine, 305,* 1106-1111.

Loh, H. H., Tseng, L. F., Wie, E., & Li, C. H. (1976). β-endorphin is a potent analgesic agent. *Proceedings of the National Academy of Science, 73,* 3308-3310.

Lovaas, O. I., Freitag, G., Gold, V. J., & Kassorla, I. C. (1965). Experimental studies in childhood schizophrenia: Analysis of self-destructive behavior. *Journal of Experimental Child Psychology, 2,* 67-84.

Lyon, M., & Robbins, T. (1975). The action of central nervous system stimulant drugs: A general theory concerning amphetamine effects. In W. B. Essman & L. Valzelli (Eds.), *Current developments in psychopharmacology* (Vol. 2, pp. 80-163). Laurel, MD: Spectrum Publications.

Mace, F. C., & Shea, M. C. (1990). New directions in behavior analysis for the treatment of severe behavior disorders. In S. L. Harris & J. S. Handleman (Eds.), *Aversive and non-aversive interventions: Controlling life threatening behavior by the developmentally disabled* (pp. 57-79). New York: Springer.

Maisto, C. R., Baumeister, A. A., & Maisto, A. A. (1978). An analysis of variables related to self-injurious behavior among institutionalized retarded persons. *Journal of Mental Deficiency Research, 22,* 27-36.

Markowitz, P. I. (1992). Effect of fluoxetine on self-injurious behavior in the developmentally disabled: A preliminary study. *Journal of Clinical Psychopharmacology, 12,* 27-31.

Martens, B. K., Lockner, D. G., & Kelly, S. Q. (1992). The effects of variable-interval reinforcement on academic engagement: A demonstration of matching theory. *Journal of Applied Behavior Analysis, 25,* 143-151.

Mayr, E. (1982). *The growth of biological thought*. Cambridge, MA: Belknap.

McAfee, J. K. (1987). Classroom density and the aggressive behavior of handicapped children. *Education and Treatment of Children, 10*, 134-145.

McConahey, O. L., Thompson, T., & Zimmerman, R. (1977). A token system for retarded women: Behavior therapy, drug administration, and their combination. In T. Thompson & J. Grabowski (Eds.), *Behavior modification of the mentally retarded* (2nd ed.) (pp. 167-234). New York: Oxford University Press.

McDowell, J. J. (1982). The importance of Herrnstein's mathematical statement of the law of effect for behavior therapy. *American Psychologist, 37*, 771-779.

McMillen, B. A., DaVanzo, E. A., Scott, S. M., & Song, A. H. (1988). N-alkyl-substituted aryl-piperazine drugs: Relationship between affinity for serotonin receptors and inhibition of aggression. *Drug Development Research, 12*, 53-62.

Miczek, K. A., Mos, J., & Olivier, B. (1989). Serotonin, aggression, and self-destructive behavior. *Psychopharmacology Bulletin, 25*, 399-403.

Middlemiss, D. N. (1986). Blockade of the central 5-HT autoreceptor by β-adrenoceptor antagonists. *European Journal of Pharmacology, 120*, 51-56.

Nader, M. A., & Thompson, T. (1987). Interaction of methadone, reinforcement history, and variable-interval performance. *Journal of the Experimental Analysis of Behavior, 48*, 303-315.

National Institutes of Health. (1991). *Treatment of destructive behaviors in persons with developmental disabilities* (NIH Publication No. 91-2410). Bethesda, MD: Department of Health and Human Services.

Olivier, B., Mos, J., & Miczek, K. A. (1991). Ethopharmacological studies of anxiolytics and aggression. *European Neuropsychopharmacology, 1*, 97-100.

O'Neill, R. E., Homer, R. H., Albin, R. W., Storey, R., & Sprague, J. R. (1989). *Functional analysis: A practical assessment guide*. Eugene: University of Oregon.

Ortiz, A., & Gershon, S. (1986). The future of neuroleptic psychopharmacology. *Journal of Clinical Psychiatry, 47*, 3-11.

Pellon, R., & Blackman, D. E. (1992). Effects of drugs on the temporal distribution of schedule-induced polydipsia in rats. *Pharmacology Biochemistry & Behavior, 43*, 689-695.

Picker, M., Poling, A., & Parker, A. (1979). A review of children's self-injurious behavior. *The Psychological Record, 29*, 435-452.

Pierce, W. D., & Epling, W. F. (1983). Choice, matching, and human behavior: A review of the literature. *The Behavior Analyst, 6*, 57-76.

Posluns, D. (1962). An analysis of chlorpromazine-induced suppression of the avoidance response. *Psychopharmacologia, 3*, 361-373.

Randall, L. O., Schallek, W., Heise, G. A., Keith, E. F., & Bagdon, R. E. (1960). The psychosedative properties of methaminodiazepoxide. *Journal of Pharmacology and Experimental Therapeutics, 129*, 163-171.

Ratey, J. J., Sorgi, P., O'Driscoll, G. A., Sands, S., Daehler, M. L., Fletcher, J. R., Kadish, K. J., Spuiell, G., Polakoff, S., Lindem, K. J., Bemporad, J. R., Richardson, L., & Rosenfeld, B. (1992). Nadolol to treat aggression and psychiatric symptomatology in chronic psychiatric inpatients: A double-blind placebo-controlled study. *Journal of Clinical Psychiatry, 53*, 41-46.

Ratey, J. J., Sovner, R., Parks, A., & Rogentine, K. (1991). Buspirone treatment of aggression and anxiety in mentally retarded: A multiple-baseline, placebo lead-in study. *Journal of Clinical Psychiatry, 52*, 159-162.

Repp, A. C., Felce, D., & Barton, L. E. (1988). Basing the treatment of stereotypic and self-injurious behavior on hypotheses of their causes. *Journal of Applied Behavior Analysis, 21,* 281-289.

Repp, A. C., & Karsh, K. G. (1990). A taxonomic approach to the nonaversive treatment of maladaptive behavior of persons with developmental disabilities. In A. C. Repp & N. N. Singh (Eds.), *Perspectives on the use of nonaversive and aversive interventions for persons with developmental disabilities* (pp. 331-348). Sycamore, IL: Sycamore.

Repp, A. C., Karsh, K., & Van Acker, R. (1987). *Arousal states: The relationship between stereotypy and activity level.* Paper presented at the annual meeting of the Association for Persons With Severe Handicaps, Chicago.

Richardson, J. S., & Zaleski, W. A. (1983). Naloxone and self-mutilation. *Biological Psychiatry, 18,* 99-101.

Rickels, K., & Schweizer, E. E. (1987). Current pharmacotherapy of anxiety and panic. In H. Y. Meltzer (Ed.), *Psychopharmacology: The third generation of progress* (pp. 1193-1203). New York: Raven.

Rincover, A., Cook, R., Peoples, A., & Packard, D. (1979). Sensory extinction and sensory reinforcement principles for programming multiple adaptive behavior change. *Journal of Applied Behavior Analysis, 12,* 221-233.

Rincover, A., & Devaney, J. (1982). The application of sensory extinction procedures to self-injury. *Analysis and Intervention in Developmental Disabilities, 2,* 67-81.

Ritvo, E. R., Yuwiler, A., Geller, E., Ornitz, E. M., Saeger, K., & Plotkin, S. (1970). Increased blood serotonin and platelets in infantile autism. *Archives of General Psychiatry, 23,* 566-572.

Robbins, T. W. (1978). The acquisition of responding with conditioned-reinforcement: Effects of pipradrol, methylphenidate, *d*-amphetamine and nomifensive. *Psychopharmacology, 58,* 79-87.

Robbins, T. W. (1982). Stereotypies: Addictions or fragmented actions? *The British Psychological Society, 35,* 297-300.

Rojahn, J., Mulick, J. A., McCoy, D., & Schroeder, S. R. (1978). Setting effects, adaptive clothing, and the modification of head-banging and self-restraint in two profoundly retarded adults. *Behavioral Analysis and Modification, 2,* 185-196.

Ruedrich, S. L., Grush, L., & Wilson, J. (1990). Beta adrenergic blocking medications for aggressive or self-injurious mentally retarded persons. *American Journal on Mental Retardation, 95,* 110-119.

Salzman, C., DiMascio, A., Shader, R. I., & Harmatz, J. S. (1969). Chlordiazepoxide, expectation and hostility. *Psychopharmacologia, 14,* 38-45.

Sandman, C. A., Datta, P. C., Barron, J., Hoehler, F. K., Williams, C., & Swanson, J. M. (1983). Naloxone attenuates self-abusive behavior in developmentally disabled clients. *Applied Research in Mental Retardation, 4,* 5-11.

Sandyk, R. (1985). Naloxone abolishes self-injuring in a mentally retarded child [Letter]. *American Journal of Psychiatry, 17,* 520.

Schain, R., & Freedman, D. (1961). Studies of 5-hydroxindol metabolism in autistic and other mentally retarded children. *Journal of Pediatrics, 58,* 315-320.

Schroeder, S. R., Rojahn, J., & Oldenquist, A. (1991). Treatment of destructive behaviors among people with mental retardation and developmental disabilities: An overview of the problem. In *Treatment of destructive behaviors in persons with developmental disabilities* (NIH Publication No. 91-2410) (pp. 125-172). Bethesda, MD: Department of Health and Human Services.

Schroeder, S. R., Schroeder, C. S., Smith, B., & Dalldorf, J. (1978). Prevalence of self-injurious behaviors in a large state facility for the retarded: A three-year follow-up study. *Journal of Autism and Childhood Schizophrenia, 8,* 261-269.

Sepinwall, J., & Cook, L. (1978). Behavioral pharmacology of antianxiety drugs. In L. L. Iversen, S. D. Iversen, & S. H. Snyder (Eds.), *Handbook of psychopharmacology* (Vol. 13, pp. 345-393). New York: Plenum.

Sepinwall, J., Grodsky, F. S., Sullivan, J. W., & Cook, L. (1973). Effects of propranolol and chlordiazepoxide on conflict behavior in rats. *Psychopharmacologia, 31,* 375-382.

Sewell, R. G., Gallus, J. A., Gault, F. P., & Cleary, J. P. (1982). P-chlorophenylalanine effects on shock-induced attack and pressing responses in rats. *Pharmacology Biochemistry & Behavior, 17,* 945-950.

Sinha, R., Lovallo, W. R., & Parsons, O. A. (1992). Cardiovascular differentiation of emotions. *Psychosomatic Medicine, 54,* 422-435.

Soubrie, P. (1986). Reconciling the role of central serotonin neurons in human and animal behavior. *Behavioral and Brain Sciences, 9,* 319-364.

Sprague, J. R., & Horner, R. H. (1992). Covariation within functional response classes: Implications for treatment of severe problem behavior. *Journal of Applied Behavior Analysis, 25,* 735-746.

Sprague, R. L., & Werry, J. S. (1971). Methodology of psychopharmacological studies with the retarded. In N. R. Ellis (Ed.), *International review of research in mental retardation* (Vol. 5, pp. 147-219). New York: Academic Press.

Stanford, D., & Nettlebeck, T. (1982). Medication and reinforcement within a token program for disturbed mentally retarded residents. *Applied Research in Mental Retardation, 3,* 21-36.

Stein, L., & Belluzzi, J. D. (1989). Cellular investigations of behavioral reinforcement. *Neuroscience and Biobehavioral Reviews, 13,* 69-80.

Tarpley, H. D., & Schroeder, S. R. (1979). Comparison of DRO and DRI on rate of suppression of self-injurious behavior. *American Journal of Mental Deficiency, 84,* 188-194.

Thompson, T. (1984). Behavioral mechanisms of drug dependence. In T. Thompson, P. B. Dews, & J. E. Barrett (Eds.), *Advances in behavioral pharmacology* (Vol. 4, pp. 2-45). Orlando, FL: Academic Press.

Thompson, T. (1986). Developmental behavioral pharmacology. In N. A. Krasnegor, D. B. Gray, & T. Thompson (Eds.), *Advances in behavioral pharmacology: Vol. 8. Developmental behavioral pharmacology* (pp. 3-20). Hillsdale, NJ: Lawrence Erlbaum.

Thompson, T., & Grabowski, J. G. (1972). *Reinforcement schedules and multioperant analysis.* New York: Appleton-Century-Crofts.

Thompson, T., Hackenberg, T., Cerutti, D., Baker, D., & Axtell, S. (in press). Opioid antagonist effects on self-injury in adults with mental retardation: Response form and location as determinants of medication effects. *American Journal on Mental Retardation.*

Thompson, T., & Lubinski, D. (1986). Units of analysis and kinetic structure of behavioral repertoires. *Journal of the Experimental Analysis of Behavior, 46,* 219-242.

Thompson, T., Schaal, D. W., & Hackenberg, T. D. (1991). Pharmacological treatments for behavior problems in developmental disabilities. In D. B. Gray & T. Thompson (Eds.), *Treatment of destructive behaviors in persons with developmental disabilities* (NIH Publication No. 91-2410) (pp. 343-440). Bethesda, MD: Department of Health and Human Services.

Thompson, T., & Schuster, C. R. (1968). *Behavioral pharmacology.* Englewood Cliffs, NJ: Prentice Hall.

Thoren, P., Asberg, M., Cronholm, B., Jörnestedt, L., & Träskman, L. (1980). Clomipramine treatment of obsessive compulsive disorder: A controlled clinical trial. *Archives of General Psychiatry, 37,* 1281-1285.

Todd, K. G., Beck, C. H., & Martin-Iverson, M. T. (1992). Effects of D1 and D2 dopamine antagonists on behavior of polydipsic rats. *Pharmacology Biochemistry & Behavior, 42,* 381-388.

Touchette, P. E., MacDonald, R. F., & Langer, S. N. (1985). A scatter plot for identifying stimulus control of problem behavior. *Journal of Applied Behavior Analysis, 18,* 343-351.

Tseng, L., Loh, H. H., & Li, C. H. (1976). β-endorphin as a potent analgesic by intravenous injection. *Nature, 263,* 239-240.

Urbain, C., Poling, A., Millam, J., & Thompson, T. (1978). *d*-Amphetamine and fixed-interval performance: Effects of operant history. *Journal of the Experimental Analysis of Behavior, 29,* 385-392.

Valzelli, L. (1981). *Psychobiology of aggression and violence.* New York: Raven.

Vitello, S. J., Atthowe, J. M., & Cadwell, J. (1983). Determinants of community placement of institutionalized mentally retarded persons. *American Journal of Mental Deficiency, 87,* 539-545.

Waldbillig, R. J. (1979). The role of the dorsal and medial raphe in the inhibition of muricide. *Brain Research, 160,* 341-346.

Weeks, M., & Gaylord-Ross, R. (1981). Task difficulty and aberrant behavior in severely handicapped students. *Journal of Applied Behavior Analysis, 14,* 449-463.

Wei, E., & Loh, H. (1976). Physical dependence on opiate-like peptides. *Science, 193,* 1262-1263.

Weiner, H. (1964). Conditioning history and human fixed-interval performance. *Journal of the Experimental Analysis of Behavior, 7,* 383-385.

Weiner, H. (1969). Controlling human fixed-interval performance. *Journal of the Experimental Analysis of Behavior, 12,* 349-373.

Weizman, R., Weizman, A., Tyano, S., Szekely, G., Weissman, B. A., & Same, Y. (1984). Humoral-endorphin blood levels in autistic, schizophrenic, and healthy subjects. *Psychopharmacology, 82,* 368-370.

White, S. M., Kucharik, R. F., & Moyer, J. A. (1991). Effects of serotonergic agents on isolation-induced aggression. *Pharmacology Biochemistry & Behavior, 39,* 729-736.

Wiesler, N. A., Hanson, R. H., Chamberlain, T. P., & Thompson, T. (1988). Stereotypic behavior of mentally retarded adults adjunctive to a positive reinforcement schedule. *Research in Developmental Disabilities, 9,* 393-403.

Willer, J. C., Dehen, H., & Cambier, J. (1981). Stress-induced analgesia in humans. *Science, 212,* 680-691.

Winterling, V., Dunlap, G., & O'Neill, R. E. (1987). The influence of task variation on the aberrant behaviors of autistic students. *Education and Treatment of Children, 10,* 105-119.

Wise, R. A. (1982). Neuroleptics and operant behavior: The anhedonia hypothesis. *Behavioral and Brain Sciences, 5,* 39-53.

Woods, J. H., Herling, S., & Young, A. M. (1981). Comparison of discriminative and reinforcing stimulus characteristics of morphine-like opioids and two met-enkephalin analogues. *Neuropeptides, 1,* 409-419.

Zarevics, P. H., & Setler, P. E. (1979). Simultaneous rate-independent assessment of intracranial self-stimulation: Evidence for direct involvement of dopamine in brain reinforcement mechanisms. *Brain Research, 169,* 499-512.

9

The Lesch-Nyhan Disease

WILLIAM L. NYHAN

It is appropriate to consider the biological bases of self-injurious behavior because it is implicit that, if it were possible to understand any kind of destructive behavior at its most fundamental molecular level, it would permit the design of highly specific measures for its control, and insights learned likely would be generalizable to other forms of abnormal behavior and their therapeutic management. The Lesch-Nyhan disease (Lesch & Nyhan, 1964) is in essence a pure culture of self-injurious behavior. It exemplifies the most ferocious type of self-injurious behavior, and it is associated with impressive loss of tissue. It is extraordinarily resistant to the usual measures of management. Aversive methods of conditioning, for example, have been documented to make the behavior worse. At the same time, it is tantalizing in the sense that the molecular nature of the abnormality is known in intimate detail. This has led to the conviction that there is an underlying chemical cause of the behavior and that the cause is linked somehow to the basic chemical abnormality. Further, it is likely that if the link could be fully understood that it would lead to rational approaches to treatment. It also could lead us to understandings of self-injurious behavior in general.

AUTHOR'S NOTE: This chapter was aided by U.S. Public Health Service HD23042 from the National Institute of Child Health and Human Development and No. RR00817 of General Clinical Research Centers Program, Division of Research Resources, National Institutes of Health, Bethesda, Maryland.

Clinical Features

The clinical phenotype of the patient with the Lesch-Nyhan disease includes neurological features, behavioral characteristics, and clinical consequences of uric acid excess. The neurological phenotype consists of abnormal motor development, spastic cerebral palsy, and involuntary movements. The severity of the motor defect is such that no patient with this disease can walk or stand unaided. The usual appearance of a patient with this disease is in a narrow, form-fitting wheelchair, supported by a seatbelt and a belt about the chest, which permits the individual to participate in the world about him or her (Figure 9.1).

In England a majority of these patients are seen at Harrow, where each receives the individual attention of a seat maker who makes an individually molded plastic seat with places for the appropriate straps and material for wheelchair mounting. Attention to getting the patient properly seated makes a considerable difference in the lifestyle of the patient. Properly secured in the upright, he or she can be part of the action; placed in a wheelchair the individual can be mobile.

On the other hand, in Japan there is much less emphasis in everyone's life on furniture. The nonambulatory patient in an institution is freely mobile, scooting about on a well-padded floor (Figure 9.2). The discrepancy between motor defect and intelligence is illustrated by an ability to play with a video game.

Most patients display considerably more cognitive ability than the motor defect would imply. Most speak, and a few have tested normally on IQ testing. At least one has mastered a normal school curriculum. In fact, the testing of intelligence is so complicated by the behavior that most testing is doubtless inaccurate. A patient presented with images or written words for testing who cannot resist an inner urge to tear up the book or throw it on the floor or at the examiner is difficult to test accurately.

Muscle tone is markedly hypertonic. The muscle pull is so strong that most patients ultimately dislocate both hips. Furthermore, for many of those in whom surgical correction has been undertaken the attempt has failed, because the muscle pull has ripped out the hardware, sometimes with resultant disfigurement. Scissoring of the lower extremities is frequently seen. Deep tendon reflexes are exaggerated. Positive Babinski responses are common. Opisthotonos is frequent, even in infancy. Later it becomes periodic, often a sudden arching, which may become incorporated into the behavior, providing a method for injuring the patient

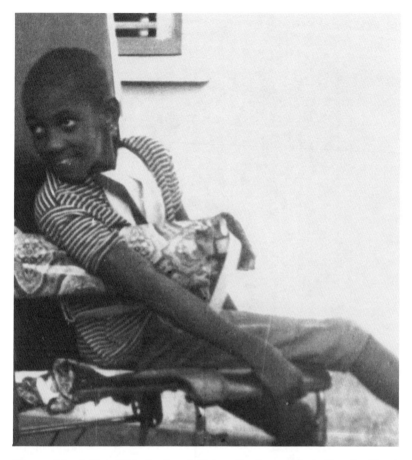

Figure 9.1. A Boy With the Lesch-Nyhan Syndrome Illustrating the Usual Seated Appearance and Choreoathetoid Posturing

NOTE: This boy also typifies a certain joie de vivre of the patient when not worried about self-mutilation.

or someone else, as the suddenly thrown back head finds a hard surface or the face of a caretaker. Involuntary movements have been seen in all of our patients. They are quite characteristic but may take choreic, athetoid, or dystonic form. They are increased by intention or by emotion. Speech is dysarthric. Swallowing is inefficient.

The behavioral phenotype is also an absolutely uniform feature of the disease (Christie et al., 1982). Its best-known manifestation is self-injurious biting, and most patients display this behavior, but not all do.

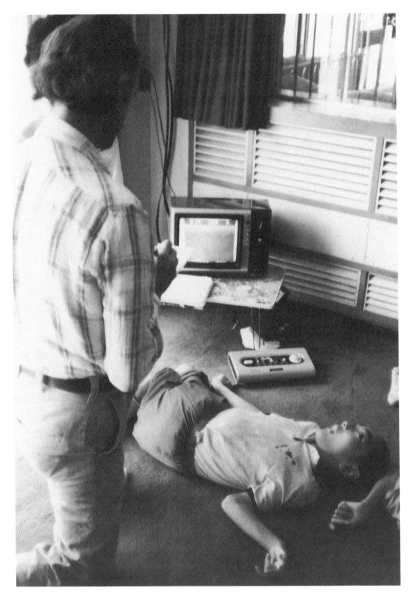

Figure 9.2. A Japanese Patient With Advanced Contractures in Spastic, Athetoid Position, Nevertheless an Expert at Controlling the Video Game

However, those who do not bite indulge in some other self-injurious behavior such as head banging or bruising the chin on a hard surface. Loss of tissue through biting, especially of the lips or fingers, is the hallmark feature by which the disorder is often recognized. Partial amputations occur of the fingers or tongue. Sensation is normal and patients scream in pain when they injure themselves. They even scream in fright when in danger of injuring themselves. This often leads to sleepless nights for the entire family until methods of secure protection are developed. Aggressive behavior also is directed against others. Eyeglasses are a frequent target. If he or she is successful in hurting another, the patient is often as remorseful as if the behavior is self-targeted. With time the patient learns to use speech and situations aggressively.

Most of these patients vomit. This interferes with nutrition. It may lead to esophagitis, ulcers, anemia from chronic blood loss, or acute hemorrhage. It also may be incorporated into the behavior as a form of aggression against others.

Aside from the behavior the patients generally are friendly, loving, and loveable. Many live at home. On the other hand, the behavior may lead some to aggression against the patient, especially in an institution. We have seen at least two patients with femoral fractures, one bilateral, but on different occasions.

The differential diagnosis of self-injurious behavior is not very extensive. The majority of self-injuring individuals have nonspecific diagnoses of mental retardation, autism, or both. They tend not to be referred for diagnosis to a tertiary referral center. Many are in institutions, and the behavior is often self-stimulatory, or stereotypic. The consequences of the behavior are usually very different from what is seen in patients with Lesch-Nyhan disease. The damage to tissue tends to be low-grade and chronic and more often results in hypertrophy of the target area rather than loss of tissue, such as a cauliflower ear.

One of the first things that comes to mind in trying to explain self-mutilative behavior is a patient with something wrong with sensation. Patients with congenital sensory neuropathy are seen very rarely. They do not appreciate pain. These patients do not usually self-mutilate. Their problems are accidental injuries, and the patient looks like a pugilist. Burns are common in such patients, as are unrecognized fractures.

A variation on this theme is the patient with dysautonomia. Patients with dysautonomia have abnormalities in sensation, but they also have behavioral abnormalities. They may have self-mutilative consequences such as the loss of the alar region of the nose, which would be indistinguishable from lesions that have been encountered in Lesch-Nyhan patients.

We have reported (Bryson, Sakati, Nyhan, & Fish, 1971; Shear, Nyhan, Kirman, & Stern, 1971) self-mutilative behavior in patients with the multiple malformation syndrome first described by Cornelia de Lange. These patients have characteristic facies and usually some skeletal abnormalities. We also have reported (Johnson, Ekman, Friesen, Nyhan, & Shear, 1976; Nyhan, 1972) that these patients have an abnormal behavioral phenotype as well as their unusual phenotype of abnormal morphogenesis. One of the features, not an invariable one, is self-mutilation. The acutely bitten lip of the patient in Figure 9.3 could easily pass for that of a Lesch-Nyhan patient. The difference is in responsiveness to management. The biting behavior of the boy illustrated responded successfully to a brief period of operant conditioning, whereas the Lesch-Nyhan behavior is characteristically resistant, worsening with aversive approaches to behavioral modification. Self-mutilative behavior also has been reported in a 13-month-old girl with atypical 3-methylglutaconic aciduria (Knoll, Mienie, & Erasmus, 1990).

The hyperuricemia phenotype usually is manifest first by the presence of what appears to be orange sand in the diaper. The usual concentration of uric acid in plasma ranges from 9 to 12 mg/dl, approximating the limits of solubility of urate in plasma. Higher concentrations indicate some degree of acute or chronic glomerular insufficiency. A few patients are so efficient at excreting urate that values are lower. They are rarely in the normal range, but laboratories that report normals obtained in series of adult males do report them as normal. The excretion of large amounts of uric acid in the urine is invariable. Twenty-four-hour values range from 600 to 1,000 mg. Expressed as a function of creatinine (Kaufman, Greene, & Seegmiller, 1968) excretion, throughout childhood, patients excrete 3 to 4 mg of uric acid/mg of creatinine; in control individuals of more than 1 year of age the value is less than 1. We have been presented with patients in whom a normal urinary excretion of urate has been recorded yet we found the definitive enzyme defect. This is likely a consequence of the fact that bacterial contamination of specimens can lead to rapid consumption of purines. False-positive urate to creatinine ratios also have been recorded in spot samples and attributed to diurnal variation (Wortman & Fox, 1980).

The clinical consequences of accumulation of uric acid are those classically described for gout. They include hematuria, painful crystalluria, urinary tract stone disease, calculi, and urinary tract infections.

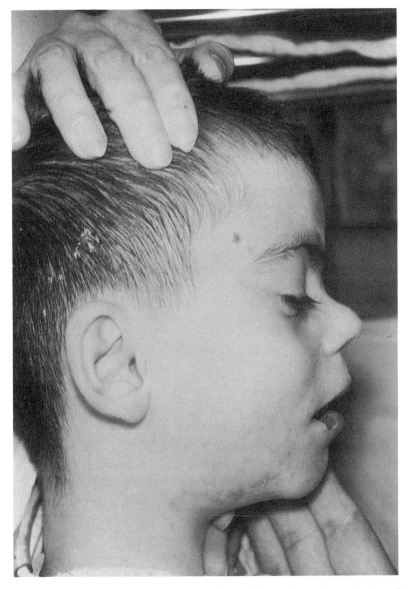

Figure 9.3. A Boy With the DeLange Syndrome Illustrating an Acute Lesion of the Lip That Resulted From Biting Himself

NOTE: He also bit his fingers.

In the absence of treatment urate nephropathy leads to death from renal failure, usually before 10 years of age. Tophi develop in cartilage of the ears and the joints, and gouty arthritis occurs usually in adolescent or adult patients. The acute arthritic symptoms respond to colchicine.

Biochemical Features

The accumulation of uric acid is a function of markedly increased synthesis of purine de novo (Nyhan, 1968). In studies of the incorporation of labeled glycine into urinary urate the overproduction of purines approximated 20 times the normal value. Adults with gout seldom exceed twice the normal value. Among purines other than uric acid hypoxanthine accumulates. In the cerebrospinal fluid the level is four times that of control subjects (Sweetman, 1968). Concentrations of uric acid are not elevated in the spinal fluid of patients with this disease.

The defective enzyme that is the fundamental abnormality in Lesch-Nyhan disease is hypoxanthine-guanine phosphoribosyl transferase (HPRT) (Seegmiller, Rosenbloom, & Kelley, 1967). This enzyme catalyzes the formation of the nucleotides, inosinic and guanylic acids from hypoxanthine or guanine, and phosphoribosyl pyrophosphate (PRPP). The enzyme is guanine and phosphoribosyl pyrophosphate. The enzyme is readily measured in erythrocyte hemolysates, and in Lesch-Nyhan disease the activity of the enzyme approximates zero.

The establishment of the enzyme defect led promptly to the recognition that there were individuals with a certain amount of residual enzyme activity who displayed only the hyperuricemia phenotype and presented with gout or renal disease (Kelley, Greene, Rosenbloom, Henderson, & Seegmiller, 1969). Thus there appeared to be two populations of patients with HPRT deficiency (Table 9.1). More recent patients have been reported (Bakay, Nissinen, Sweetman, Francke, & Nyhan, 1979) in whom the neurological phenotype appeared identical to that of the classic Lesch-Nyhan patient but intelligence was normal, as was behavior. In these patients the erythrocyte assay revealed no enzyme activity, and some of those with the pure hyperuricemia phenotype also could not be distinguished from Lesch-Nyhan by enzyme assay of erythrocyte lysates. Accordingly, a sensitive, more physiological method for the assay of the enzyme was developed utilizing intact cultured fibroblasts and assessing the conversion of labeled hypoxanthine to all of the purine nucleotide products isolated by high-performance liquid

Table 9.1 Populations of Patients With Deficiency of HPRT

	HPRT Activity	Clinical Features
Lesch-Nyhan syndrome	0	Mental retardation, spasticity, choreo-athetosis, self-mutilation, hyperuricemia, nephropathy, stones, arthritis, tophi
Partial defects	1-50%	Hyperuricemia, arthritis, nephropathy, stones, tophi

Table 9.2 Enlarging Spectrum of Deficiency of HPRT

	Whole Cell HPRT Activity (% of control)	Clinical Features
LN variant	0.0-1.2	Lesch-Nyhan syndrome
Neurological variants	1.6-8.0	Spasticity, choreoathetosis, normal behavior and mental function, hyperuricemic manifestations
Partial	8.0-60.0	Hyperuricemic consequences

chromatography. Patients with Lesch-Nyhan disease have activity that is less than 1.2% of normal (Page, Bakay, Nissinen, & Nyhan, 1981). Patients with other phenotypes can be readily distinguished because they display considerably more activity. Most have enough activity in intact cells to permit studies of the kinetic properties of the variant enzyme.

These observations permitted the consideration of an enlarging spectrum of patients with deficient activity of HPRT (Table 9.2). The whole cell assay permits reasonable correlation between the amount of enzymatic activity and the mildness or severity of the clinical manifestations (Page, Bakay, & Nyhan, 1982b).

The enzyme is normally active in amniocytes and chorionic villus cells. A number of prenatal diagnoses have been made (Bakay, Francke, Nyhan, & Seegmiller, 1977). The gene for the enzyme is on the long arm of the X chromosome. Its deficiency is a fully recessive trait. In fact, in heterozygous carriers most tissues assayed have normal activity. Heterozygote detection can be carried out by the assay of the enzyme in hair follicles, which are largely clonal (Page, Bakay, & Nyhan, 1982a). Restriction fragment length polymorphism (RFLP) also may be used for prenatal diagnosis and carrier detection (Gibbs et al., 1984; Nussbaum, Crowder, Nyhan, & Caskey, 1983).

Molecular Biology of the HPRT Gene

The gene for human HPRT has been cloned and sequenced (Jolly et al., 1983). The coding sequence contains 654 nucleotides in 9 exons that correspond to a 218 amino acid protein sequence. Southern analysis using labeled cDNA probes and restriction endonucleases have yielded evidence of a few deletions and rearrangements (Yang et al., 1984), but in more than 85% of patients there was no gross alteration in the DNA, and the mRNA was normal in size and amount.

The polymerase chain reaction has permitted the precise identification of alterations in the sequences of bases resulting from point mutation. In this way a number of mutations have been identified (Sege-Peterson, Nyhan, & Page, 1993). In general, each family studied has represented a different mutation.

Sequences that specify a stop codon and lead to a truncated protein molecule, as well as large deletions that might lead to no mRNA product, are seen in patients with Lesch-Nyhan syndrome. Patients with variant, milder phenotypes have had mutations that specify a single amino acid substitution. Such alterations in sequence in a Lesch-Nyhan patient suggest that they are in more important parts of the molecule. It is of interest that the milder variant mutations have clustered in the amino terminal end of the gene. A similar observation has been made in the case of deficiency of glucose-6-phosphate dehydrogenase (Beutler, 1991).

Neuropathogenesis

Substantial evidence indicates that the abnormality in purine metabolism in some way influences the balance of neurotransmitters in the central nervous system and in this way causes the neurological and behavioral characteristics of the classic disease. The best evidence for altered dopaminergic function came from postmortem studies of the brains of three patients with Lesch-Nyhan disease (Lloyd et al., 1981). As in previously autopsied patients, there were no morphological alterations in any of these brains. Studies of discrete neurotransmitter biochemistry in regions of the brain indicated that dopamine neuronal function in the caudate nucleus, putamen, nucleus accumbens, and external pallidum was significantly lower in the patients than in controls. The values ranged from 10% to 30% of the control values. These included levels of dopamine itself, homovanillic acid (HVA), DOPA decarboxylase, and tyrosine hydroxylase. These were all low in the nigra, too, although not significantly, but with this small number of specimens available for study, it is quite surprising that there were so many statistically significant values. The level of dihydroxyphenylacetic acid was low only in the putamen, and this was not a significant difference. These deficits in dopamine function were not as severe as those seen in Parkinson's disease, but they represent appreciable loss. The data are consistent with functional loss rather than cell loss as in Parkinson's disease.

Data on norepinephrine and serotonin function were not significantly different in the brains of the patients. Two of the three had low norepinephrine levels in the accumbens. The activity of dopamine beta-hydroxylase was not decreased in the hypothalamus. Alterations previously had been reported in plasma for this enzyme.

Serotonin levels were slightly increased, statistically significantly so in the putamen; 5-hydroxyindoleacetic acid was appreciably elevated there and in the pallidum. These data highlight the specificity of the depression in dopaminergic function.

Data on monoamine oxidase and catechol-o-methyltransferase indicated that with tyrosine or dopamine as substrates, monoamine oxidase was significantly elevated in the patients. The elevations were not statistically significant with the other substrates, serotonin and phenylethylamine. This provides an interesting contrast to data previously reported on HPRT-deficient cells in culture in which monoamine oxidase activity was depressed. Catechol-o-methyltransferase activity, on the other hand, was significantly depressed in the patients.

GABA synthesizing ability as judged by glutamic acid decarboxylase activity was lower in patients, but not significantly so. In terms of the synthesis of acetylcholine, choline acetyl transferase activity was significantly lower in the putamen in the patients. Guanylate cyclase activity was not different in patients and controls, providing a control enzyme.

The data must be interpreted in the light of the nutritionally depleted condition of the patients who died of the disease, but it is hard to see why that would be so specific for dopamine and not serotonin. It is tempting to think that these observations may explain the extrapyramidal dysfunction of this syndrome. We have reported low levels of HVA in the cerebral spinal fluid (CSF) in Lesch-Nyhan syndrome (Castells et al., 1979).

Silverstein, Johnston, Hutchinson, and Edwards (1985) provided evidence for altered dopaminergic function in the central nervous system in patients with Lesch-Nyhan syndrome who had lower than normal concentrations of homovanillic acid (HVA) in the CSF. Serial measurements were made of CSF HVA in four patients over a 5-year period with a range in ages from 1.5 to 17 years. They covered a considerable age span. There were 94 controls. HVA and 5-hydroxyindoleacetic acid (HIAA) concentrations undergo age-related change in which they fall rapidly during the first 3 years of life and then more gradually through adolescence. The values for the Lesch-Nyhan patients were lower than the mean for age in 18 of 19 samples, and 10 samples fell below the control range. In the same study all but one of the HIAA levels were within the normal range, and about as many fell above as below the mean.

The dopaminergic hypothesis for self-injurious behavior received strong support from the development of a rat model by Breese and colleagues (1984). They were studying the effect of 6-hydroxydopamine (6-OHDA), which destroys catecholamine-containing neurons in the brain, and discovered a major difference in adult and neonatally treated rats. Treatment of adult animals makes them sensitive to a number of behaviors on the administration of DOPA or an agonist, but never to self-injurious behavior, whereas neonatal animals so treated regularly exhibit self-injurious behavior. The effect can be shown much later, even in adulthood, by giving DOPA as long as the 6-OHDA was given neonatally. Dose response data were obtained.

It has been postulated that the lesion makes dopamine receptors supersensitive to dopaminergic stimulation. Pharmacological approaches for its extinction in the neonatal rat model showed some effect of haloperidol and flupentixol, respectively, a D2 and a mixed D1, 2 antagonist, whereas there was virtually complete inhibition with the D1 antagonist Sch-23390. In contrast there was no effect of the pure D2 antagonist, Ly-171555.

With regard to serotonin, the urinary excretion of 5-hydroxyindoleacetic acid, its end product, is actually significantly increased in Lesch-Nyhan patients (Sweetman, Borden, Kulovich, Kaufman, & Nyhan, 1977). Nevertheless, treatment designed to increase cerebral levels of serotonin, by the administration of 5-hydroxytryptophan and carbidopa, usually along with imipramine, was followed by a cessation of the self-mutilative behavior (Nyhan, Johnson, Kaufman, & Jones, 1980). Unfortunately this effect was temporary, lasting only a few weeks at most.

Therapeutic Implications

The hyperuricemic component of the syndrome can be effectively controlled by treatment with allopurinol. Control of the accumulation of uric acid prevents arthritis, nephropathy and other renal complications, and tophi. It has no effect on the neurological or behavioral features of the disorder.

The dopaminergic hypothesis has been explored by treatment with fluphenazine, which is a combined D1 and D2 antagonist (Goldstein, Anderson, Reuben, & Dancis, 1985). It was reported that self-injurious behavior was improved in a 20-month-old boy in whom the behavior had begun 2 months earlier. Furthermore, when the drug was stopped there was an appreciable worsening of the behavior. On the other hand, a 15-year-old with a stable pattern of self-injurious behavior did not improve when treated with fluphenazine. It was reported that biting behavior increased when the drug was withdrawn.

In our experience (Table 9.3) fluphenazine was without obvious effect in two patients 6 and 21 years of age. Trials of clonazepam, naltrexone, and fluoxetine also were without effect (Table 9.3). A trial of aminoimidazole carboxamide riboside (AICAR) provided evidence that the compound is not absorbed after oral administrations. In an uncontrolled outpatient experience one boy's behavior was judged to be improved by his family after treatment was initiated with dantrolene in an attempt to improve his muscle stiffness and hypertonicity.

Table 9.3 Therapeutic Trials in Attempt to Modify Cerebral Effects

						Outcome		
Patient	Years	Drug	mg/kg	Treatment	Medications	Neurological	Behavioral	Other
J. B.	8 10/12	Naltrexone	2.13	2	Diazepam Allopurinol	No change	No change	Daily videotaping for 30 min.
			4.26	24 (3 in hosp.)	Same	No change	No change	
M. S.	16 5/12	AICAR	30	4	Diazepam Allopurinol Docusate-Na Donnatal Ranitidine	No change	No change	P.O. absorptic inadequate IND prepared for IV use Videotaping for 30 min. each day
			78	1	Same	No change	No change	
			100	2	Same	No change	No change	
C. W.	21 9/12	Fluphenazine (Prolixin)	.12	6	Allopurinol Diazepam	No change	No change	Videotaping for 20 min. after each cycle
			.19	6	Same			
G. V.	6 7/12	Placebo	—	5	Allopurinol	No change	No change	Videotaping after each cycle for 30 min. Double-blind study

		Drug	Dose	Duration	Concurrent			
		Fluphenazine	.124	4	Same	No change	No change	
		Clonazepan	.023	3	Same	No change	No change	
G. V.	8 11/12	Fluoxetine	1.0	3	Allopurinol	No change	No change	Videotaping for 30 min. each day Double-blind study
		Placebo	—	3	Same	No change	No change	
G. V.	9 2/12	Dantrolene	1-2	2 years	Allopurinol Rivotril Clonezapan	Improved tone	Slight improvement	

195

References

Bakay, B., Francke, U., Nyhan, W. L., & Seegmiller, J. E. (1977). Experience with detection of heterozygous carriers and prenatal diagnosis of Lesch-Nyhan disease. In M. M. Muller, E. Kaiser, & J. E. Seegmiller (Eds.), *Purine metabolism in man II: Regulation of pathways and enzyme defects* (pp. 351-358). New York: Plenum.

Bakay, B., Nissinen, E., Sweetman, L., Francke, U., & Nyhan, W. L. (1979). Utilization of purines by an HPRT variant in an intelligent, nonmutilative patient with features of the Lesch-Nyhan syndrome. *Pediatric Research, 13,* 1365.

Beutler, E. (1991). Glucose-6-phosphate dehydrogenase deficiency. *New England Journal of Medicine, 324,* 169.

Breese, G. R., Baumeister, A. A., McCown, T. J., Emerick, S., Frye, G. D., Crotty, K., & Mueller, R. A. (1984). Behavioral differences between neonatal- and adult- 6-hydroxydopamine-treated rats to dopamine agonists: Relevance to neurological symptoms in clinical syndromes with reduced brain dopamine. *Journal of Pharmacology and Experimental Therapeutics, 231,* 343.

Bryson, Y., Sakati, N., Nyhan, W. L., & Fish, C. H. (1971). Self-mutilative behavior in the Cornelia de Lange syndrome. *American Journal of Mental Deficiency, 76,* 319-324.

Castells, S., Chakrabarti, C., Winsberg, B. G., Hurwic, M., Perel, J. M., & Nyhan, W. L. (1979). Effects of L-5-hydroxytryptophan on monoamine and amino acids turnover in the Lesch-Nyhan syndrome. *Journal of Autism and Developmental Disorders, 9,* 95.

Christie, R., Bay, C., Kaufman, I. A., Bakay, B., Borden, M., & Nyhan, W. L. (1982). Lesch-Nyhan disease: Clinical experience with nineteen patients. *Developmental Medicine and Child Neurology, 24,* 293.

Gibbs, D. A., McFadyen, I. R., Crawford, M. A., de Muinck-Keizer, E. E., Headhouse-Benson, C. M., Wilson, T.M., & Farrant, P. H. (1984). First trimester prenatal diagnosis of Lesch-Nyhan syndrome. *Lancet, 2,* 1180.

Goldstein, M., Anderson, L. T., Reuben, R., & Dancis, J. (1985). Self-mutilation in Lesch-Nyhan disease is caused by dopaminergic denervation. *Lancet, 1,* 338.

Johnson, H. G., Ekman, P., Friesen, W., Nyhan, W. L., & Shear, C. (1976). A behavioral phenotype in the de Lange syndrome. *Pediatric Research, 10,* 843-850.

Jolly, D. J., Okayama, H., Berg, P., Esty, A. C., Filpula, D., Bohlen, G. G., Johnson, J. E., Shively, T. H., & Friedmann, T. (1983). Isolation and characterization of a full length, expressible cDNA for human hypoxanthine guanine phosphoribosyl transferase. *Proceedings of the National Academy of Science, 80,* 477.

Kaufman, J. M., Greene, M. L., & Seegmiller, J. E. (1968). Urine uric acid to creatinine ratio: Screening test for disorders of purine metabolism. *Journal of Pediatrics, 73,* 583.

Kelley, W. N., Greene, M. L., Rosenbloom, F. M., Henderson, J. F., & Seegmiller, J. E. (1969). Hypoxanthine-guanine phosphoribosyltransferase deficiency in gout: A review. *Annals of Internal Medicine, 7,* 155.

Knoll, D. P., Mienie, L. J., & Erasmus, E. (1990, June). *Treatment of an atypical 3-methylglutaconic aciduria type I.* Paper presented at the Fourth International Congress on Inborn Errors of Metabolism, Pacific Grove, CA.

Lesch, M., & Nyhan, W. L. (1964). A familial disorder of uric acid metabolism and central nervous system function. *American Journal of Medicine, 36,* 561.

Lloyd, K. G., Hornykewicz, O., Davidson, L., Shannak, K., Farley, I., Goldstein, M., Shibuya, M., Kelley, W. N., & Fox, I. H. (1981). Biochemical evidence of dysfunction of brain neurotransmitters in the Lesch-Nyhan syndrome. *New England Journal of Medicine, 305,* 1106.

Nussbaum, R. L., Crowder, W. E., Nyhan, W. L., & Caskey, C. T. (1983). A three-allele restriction-fragment-length polymorphism at the hypoxanthine phosphoribosyl-transferase locus in man. *Proceedings of the National Academy of Science, 80,* 4035.

Nyhan, W. L. (1968). Introduction—Clinical features. In J. H. Bland (Ed.), Seminars on the Lesch-Nyhan syndrome [Special issue]. *Federation Proceedings, 27,* 1027.

Nyhan, W. L. (1972). Behavioral phenotypes in organic genetic disease (Presidential address to the Society for Pediatric Research, May 1, 1971). *Pediatric Research, 6,* 1-9.

Nyhan, W. L., Johnson, H. G., Kaufman, I. A., & Jones, K. L. (1980). Serotonergic approaches to the modification of behavior in the Lesch-Nyhan syndrome. *Applied Research in Mental Retardation, 1,* 25.

Page, T., Bakay, B., Nissinen, R., & Nyhan, W. L. (1981). Hypoxanthine guanine phosphoribosyl transferase variants: Correlation of clinical phenotype with enzyme activity. *Journal of Inherited Metabolic Disease, 4,* 203.

Page, T., Bakay, B., & Nyhan, W. L. (1982a). An improved procedure for the detection of hypoxanthine-guanine phosphoribosyl transferase heterozygotes. *Clinical Chemistry, 28,* 1181.

Page, T., Bakay, B., & Nyhan, W. L. (1982b). Kinetic studies of normal and variant hypoxanthine phosphoribosyltransferases in intact fibroblasts. *Analytical Biochemistry, 122,* 144.

Seegmiller, J. E., Rosenbloom, F. M., & Kelley, W. N. (1967). Enzyme defect associated with a sex-linked human neurological disorder and excessive purine synthesis. *Science, 155,* 1682.

Sege-Peterson, K., Nyhan, W. L., & Page, T. (1993). Lesch-Nyhan disease and HPRT deficiency. In R. N. Rosenberg, S. B. Prusiner, S. DiMauro, R. L. Barchi, & L. M. Kunkel (Eds.), *The molecular and genetic basis of neurological disease* (pp. 241-260). London and Boston: Butterworth.

Shear, C. S., Nyhan, W. L., Kirman, B. H., & Stern, J. (1971). Self-mutilative behavior as a feature of the de Lange syndrome. *Journal of Pediatrics, 78,* 827-834.

Silverstein, F. S., Johnston, M. V., Hutchinson, R. J., & Edwards, N. L. (1985). Lesch-Nyhan syndrome: CSF neurotransmitter abnormalities. *Neurology, 35,* 907.

Sweetman, L. (1968). Urinary and cerebrospinal oxypurine levels allopurinol metabolism in the Lesch-Nyhan syndrome. *Federation Proceedings, 27,* 1055.

Sweetman, L., Borden, M., Kulovich, S., Kaufman, I., & Nyhan, W. L. (1977). Altered excretion of 5-hydroxyindoleacetic acid and glycine in patients with the Lesch-Nyhan syndrome. In M. M. Muller, E. Kaiser, & J. E. Seegmiller (Eds.), *Purine metabolism in man: Vol. 2. Regulation of pathways and enzyme defects* (pp. 398-404). New York: Plenum.

Wortman, R. L., & Fox, I. H. (1980). Limited value of uric acid to creatinine ratios in estimating uric acid excretion. *Annals of Internal Medicine, 93,* 822.

Yang, T. P., Patel, P. I., Chinault, A. C., Stout, J. T., Jackson, L. G., Hildebrand, B. M., & Caskey C. T. (1984). Molecular evidence for new mutation at the HPRT locus in Lesch-Nyhan patients. *Nature, 310,* 412.

10

Dopaminergic and Serotonergic Mechanisms in Self-Injury and Aggression

STEPHEN R. SCHROEDER
RICHARD TESSEL

In 1982 Schroeder and colleagues published an extensive review and analysis of the development and management of self-injurious behavior (SIB) among people with mental retardation and developmental disabilities. We predicted an increased emphasis in research on the antecedents of SIB from both the behavioral and the biological perspectives (Schroeder, Schroeder, Rojahn, & Mulick, 1982). From many of the chapters in this volume, there is ample evidence that this shift in emphasis has occurred for behavioral research in the past decade.

On the biological side Cataldo and Harris (1982) published an analytical review of several potential biological antecedents of self-injury, and we are happy to say that research in this area has truly taken off. In a review by Baumeister, Frye, and Schroeder (1984), three major neurochemical hypotheses were identified as likely strong biological precursors of SIB: (a) a central nervous system (CNS) deficiency in the nigrostriatal dopamine system, (b) a malfunction of the opioid peptide system, and (c) a CNS dysfunction in the serotonergic system. These are not necessarily competing hypotheses. They all may be complementary systems

AUTHORS' NOTE: We wish to acknowledge NICHD Grants No. HD 02528 and HD 26927 as well as MCH Grant No. MCJ 944 and ADD Grant No. 07DD0365 for financial assistance during the writing of this chapter.

whose malfunction leads to an imbalance in regulation in brain catecholamines and serotonin related to the development of SIB, as Nyhan, Johnson, Kaufman, and Jones (1980) have suggested. Since Nyhan's chapter discusses Lesch-Nyhan syndrome and the chapter by Thompson and colleagues discusses the opioid peptide system, the present chapter touches on these topics only briefly. Comments are restricted to several lines of research that suggest that dopaminergic supersensitivity and serotonin dysfunction play a central role in the development of SIB and aggression.

The evidence implicating dopamine in SIB in humans comes from the study of organic syndromes with CNS deficits in dopamine function and theoretically based neuropharmacological treatments of SIB. In rats and monkeys evidence comes from experimental lesion studies, isolate rearing studies, and direct pharmacological induction of SIB with drugs.

Evidence From Human Studies

Dopamine and SIB in Lesch-Nyhan Syndrome

Recent reviews on the biological bases of SIB (Baumeister et al., 1984; Cataldo & Harris, 1982; Schroeder, 1984; Schroeder, Bickel, & Richmond, 1986; Schroeder, Breese, & Mueller, 1990) agree that Lesch-Nyhan syndrome might provide a neurobiological model for conceptualizing a biochemical mechanism responsible for some forms of SIB. Lesch-Nyhan syndrome is a sex-linked disorder of purine metabolism in which the child demonstrates a wide array of symptoms among which are spasticity, choreoathetosis, possible mental retardation, elevated uric acid, self-mutilation, and aggressive behaviors (Lesch & Nyhan, 1964). Self-mutilation, especially biting of the oral structures and fingers, is most common. Patients can cause such severe self-mutilation that the mouth orifice is totally deformed or the fingers lost. Lesch-Nyhan syndrome represents one of the first conditions with a demonstrated biochemical defect in which a high prevalence of very specific self-injurious behaviors are described. However, the genetic and neurochemical mechanisms relating the metabolic defect to the behavior still are not well understood. This is currently an area of great interest for researchers of animal models of the disease. Breese, Criswell, Duncan, and Mueller (1989) and Nyhan and colleagues (1980) conceptualize self-biting in Lesch-Nyhan patients as the result of imbalance in serotonergic, dopaminergic, and noradrenergic mechanisms in the brain. In a double-blind crossover study nine patients were treated with 5-hydroxytryptophan (5-HTP), a precursor of serotonin, in combination with a peripheral decarboxylase inhibitor, carbidopa, and with imipramine to prevent its rapid excretion. Most patients had a dramatic decrease in self-biting in which they could be left free of restraints for several hours for the first time in years. However, within 1 to 3 months each patient developed tolerance to the drug and the pharmacological effect could not be produced again even a year later. The effect apparently was not due to a serotonin deficiency that may have been corrected by 5-HTP but to the temporary restoration of balance among these interacting neurotransmitter systems. That the problem is not shortage of serotonin also was suggested by findings (Sweetman, Borden, Kulovich, Kaufman, & Nyhan, 1977) that urinary excretion of 5-hydroxyindoleacetic acid (HIAA), the metabolite of serotonin, is significantly *greater* in patients with Lesch-Nyhan disease than in controls. Unless the defect was an inability to store serotonin, thus facilitating its metabolism to 5-HIAA, one would have expected a *shortage* of serotonin to be reflected as decreased 5-HIAA excretion.

In postmortem patient studies, Lloyd and colleagues (1981) observed, in fact, an increase in striatal serotonin and a decrease in striatal dopamine content. In this dramatic demonstration, Lloyd and colleagues (1981), in postmortem examination of the brains of three patients with Lesch-Nyhan syndrome, found profound alterations in basal ganglia dopamine content in several brain regions. All indices of dopamine function in the brain regions were decreased, indicating an estimated 65% to 90% functional loss of dopamine terminals. Thus the correlated disregulation of serotonin and dopamine in Lesch-Nyhan syndrome is consistent with Nyhan's hypothesis.

Evidence From Neuroleptic Drug Studies in SIB Patients

Even though neuroleptic drugs such as thioridazine (Mellaril), chlorpromazine (Thorazine), and haloperidol (Haldol) block dopamine release, they have not proven systematically effective with SIB (Singh & Millichamp, 1985). Why? We think this is due to the fact that there are several dopamine receptor subtypes, including the "classical" D1 and D2 receptors. These drugs block D2 receptors primarily, but according to our animal studies, it appears that it is primarily D1 receptors that mediate SIB.

Two populations of dopamine receptors have been characterized in the mammalian brain on the basis of in vitro studies. D1 receptors are positively associated with adenylate cyclase activity and bind in vitro to neuroleptic thioxanthine ligands, such as 3H-piflutixol or 3H-flupentixol. D2 receptors are negatively related to adenylate cyclase and bind to butyrophenone ligands, such as 3H-spiroperidol or 3H-haloperidol. The estimation of the role of each type of receptor has been complicated because of the tendency of most ligands to bind at least to some extent to both D1 and D2 receptors. The identification of the experimental drug, Sch-23390, as a specific D1 receptor antagonist and ligand has aided in these assessments. There currently is no pure D1 receptor antagonist available for clinical use in the United States.

Imaging of dopamine receptors by positron emission tomography (PET) (Wong et al., 1984) was carried out in a 22-year-old patient with Lesch-Nyhan syndrome. Appreciable dopamine receptor binding was demonstrated. Imaging using 11C-Sch-23390 was well within the normal range, and the ratio of D1 to D2 receptor binding was substantially increased. These observations are consistent with the hypothesis that there is a dopaminergic abnormality in Lesch-Nyhan syndrome.

An important study was published in *Lancet* by Goldstein, Anderson, Reuben, and Dancis (1985) in which a brief double-blind crossover study of fluphenazine with two Lesch-Nyhan cases was reported. Fluphenazine had a dramatic effect in a 20-month-old child, but much less of an effect in a 15-year-old child presumably because of the deeply ingrained habits that had been reinforced by caregivers over the years. Haloperidol had no effects. These results are interesting because fluphenazine blocks both D1 and D2 dopamine receptors, whereas haloperidol preferentially blocks D2 receptors.

As a result of this study we began placebo-controlled trials of low doses of fluphenazine with a wide variety of SIB patients who do not have Lesch-Nyhan syndrome (Gualtieri & Schroeder, 1989). Positive effects were obtained in 10 of 15 cases. These results also are consistent with dopamine contributing to SIB. *Therefore, it is important to discover whether dopamine depletion is discernible among a range of self-injurious clients or whether it is true only of Lesch-Nyhan patients as a distinct class of self-biters* (Kelley & Wyngaarden, 1983).

Fluphenazine at low doses blocks both D1 and D2 dopamine receptors, but tends to induce the development of extrapyramidal side effects, especially akathisia, in some patients. Therefore it is a drug of last resort. We think this is less likely with another drug, Clozapine. Clozapine is a D1 and D2 blocker, but mostly a D1 blocker at low dose in rats (Criswell, Mueller, & Breese, 1989). The drug has been used to treat adult schizophrenic patients, but has not been used before for SIB in people who have mental retardation. We have received FDA approval and all of the necessary human subjects approvals to use this drug, and controlled clinical trials currently are underway.

Evidence From Studies of Serotonergic Drugs in SIB and Aggressive Patients

Studies of violent aggression and/or suicide among people who are not developmentally disabled have revealed a relationship between impulsive violent behavior and lowered 5-hydroxyindoleacetic acid (5-HIAA) levels, a major metabolite of serotonin, in cerebrospinal fluid (Brown et al., 1982; Roy & Linnoila, 1988). A number of studies based on this finding have attempted to modulate serotonin levels of aggressive and/or self-injurious clients who are mentally retarded. Many of these studies were single-case, nonblind studies without proper controls. Interpretation often is complicated by the fact that there are at least six different types of serotonin receptors and the drugs used may have multiple effects on other neurotransmitters besides affecting serotonin receptors. Nevertheless, a number of these drugs warrant closer controlled study because of the positive effects found. Among them are buspirone (Ratey, Sovner, Mikkelsen, & Chmielinski, 1989; Realmuto, August, & Garfinkel, 1989), trazodone (O'Neil, Page, Adkins, & Eichelman, 1986; Patterson & Srisopark, 1989), and fluoxetine (Cook, Terry, Heller, & Leventhal, 1990; Markowitz, 1990).

Evidence From Rat Lesion Studies

Age Dependence of Dopamine Lesion on Symptoms and SIB Susceptibility

Parkinson's disease and Huntington's chorea are interesting comparison groups with Lesch-Nyhan syndrome in terms of their motor symptoms (Schroeder et al., 1990). In patients with Parkinson's disease dopamine-containing neurons are largely destroyed, but these patients do not display self-mutilation or the same motor dysfunction seen in Lesch-Nyhan syndrome. One obvious difference in the pathogenesis of these syndromes is the age of neuronal loss and the age of onset of the symptoms in adulthood. Based on these observations, Breese and colleagues (1984a, 1984b) proposed that *reduction of dopamine-containing fibers in the perinatal period is responsible for the subsequent SIB observed in patients with Lesch-Nyhan syndrome and that destruction of dopaminergic neurons during adulthood does not result in this behavioral symptom.* We have labeled this hypothesis the neonatal dopamine depletion hypothesis.

Breese and colleagues (1984a, 1984b) have been able to induce severe self-biting by challenging rats with L-DOPA after they have been lesioned neonatally with 6-hydroxydopamine. This suggests that susceptibility to self-biting may be a developmental phenomenon depending on the age at which dopamine depletion occurs. Furthermore, Breese and colleagues (1984a, 1984b) have been able to completely block self-biting in neonatal-6-OHDA-treated rats challenged with L-DOPA by treating rats with a specific D1 dopamine antagonist (Sch-23390). This suggests that this may be a central nervous system model specifically related to the susceptibility to depletion of brain dopamine for biting behavior of patients with Lesch-Nyhan syndrome and other patients who are self-biters. If this is the case, the SIB could be *prevented* pharmacologically or through behavioral interventions aimed specifically at modulating dopamine release.

Developmental Implications of the Neonatal
Dopamine Depletion Studies

Behavioral epidemiological studies of the incidence of SIB in early development remain a high priority. Prevalence studies of SIB (Baumeister & Rollings, 1976; Maisto, Baumeister, & Maisto, 1978; Schroeder, Schroeder, Smith, & Daildorf, 1978) in adults have suggested that severe neuronal loss correlates with more severe SIB. The chapters by Rojahn and by Borthwick-Duffy in this volume are consistent with this view. However, data on the development of SIB come mostly from hospital records in which identification of early onset and patient histories are generally poor. There has never been an adequate study of the ways symptoms of SIB develop during early infancy and childhood.

Another developmental question of interest is this: Is there a particular age range at which pathological SIB in humans develops? Studies of crib banging among normal infants suggest that it usually stops by 12-18 months (Kravitz & Boehm, 1971) and is very rare beyond 5 years (de Lissovoy, 1961). The behavior of infants with Lesch-Nyhan syndrome is usually not classified as abnormal until about 8 months of age, when choreiform movements and spasticity begin to occur. Their SIB begins at about 12-18 months, about the time the teeth erupt. In early life these symptoms correspond to the period of ontogenesis of terminal regions of nigrostriatal dopamine neurons (Kelley & Wyngaarden, 1983). Retrospective studies of SIB (Schroeder, Mulick, & Rojahn, 1980) suggest it is very difficult to trace SIB before 3 years of age. A developmental study would be very important in identifying age of onset and possible risk factors such as severe developmental disability, seizures, and abnormal extrapyramidal movements related to dopamine depletion. Recent studies of the development of stereotyped SIB among infants with severe retardation suggest that the movements are qualitatively different from those of normal infants (Berkson & Gallagher, 1984).

Another area of interest is early intervention with SIB. Can early behavioral and pharmacological intervention attenuate SIB in later life? With this question in mind, we have recently reviewed the literature (Schroeder et al., 1986). One possible set of behavioral procedures involves the induction of chemotherapeutic effects resulting from mild stress (Antelman & Caggiula, 1977) such as physical exercise. Recently Kern, Koegel, Dyer, Blew, and Fenton (1982); Ohlsen (1978); Tomporowski and Ellis (1984, 1985); and Watters and Watters (1980) showed that stereotyped and disruptive behavior could be decreased by engaging adult clients with severe and profound mental retardation in physical exercise. It has been known for years that exercise influences dopamine turnover. Baumeister and MacLean (1984) and Lancioni, Smeets, Ceccarani, and Capodaglio (1984) have shown dose-effect relationships between noncontingent exercise and decreased SIB. A controlled longitudinal study using active engagement exercises alone and in combination with appropriate behavioral intervention for children exhibiting SIB would allow us to ask several questions: (a) Can early intervention modulate dopamine levels in children exhibiting SIB? (b) Will stimulation that was initiated at earlier ages have a stronger effect than stimulation begun at a later age? (c) Will the effect be different for organic deficits more related to dopamine depletion during adulthood, such as Parkinsonian disorders, extrapyramidal effects, and so on? At present the answer to these questions is unknown.

A second line of evidence for early intervention comes from studies of rearing animals in isolation, which we discuss in the next section.

Evidence From Nonhuman Primate Isolate Rearing

There is overwhelming evidence that SIB can develop in social nonhuman primate species, both in the absence of preexisting brain damage and in the absence of drug treatment. Kraemer and Clarke (1990) recently reviewed more than 25 years of research, mainly at the Harlow laboratories at the University of Wisconsin, on the effects of isolation rearing of otherwise biologically competent rhesus monkeys. Rearing rhesus monkeys without their mothers or other peer-aged monkeys produces many abnormal behaviors, one of which is SIB in nearly 100% of the monkeys (Cross & Harlow, 1965; Harlow, Harlow, & Suomi, 1971). The behavior change emerges at 3 to 4 months in conjunction with teething and persists into adulthood up to 35% of the time during waking hours unless isolation is stopped and rehabilitative intervention is performed. Topographies range from occasional nontraumatic biting and head banging to persistent traumatic self-attack with subsequent loss of digits, lacerations of arms and legs, and eye gouging. Lewis, Gluck, Beauchamp, Keresztury, and Mailman (1990) recently followed such a cohort who had been isolated for the first 9 months of life and later returned to normal group living. As adults they showed long-term alterations in dopamine receptor sensitivity in response to a dopamine challenge with apomorphine. Thus the timing and duration of early social deprivation alter the incidence and severity of SIB in rhesus monkeys.

The study of isolate-reared rhesus monkeys is important to SIB research for several reasons. First, the effect seems to be relatively species-specific, in that other species of monkeys do not show the effect so dramatically. Thus it appears that early isolation rearing results in an abnormal set of somatosensory stimuli and motor responses that mimic the normal developmental patterns of socially aggressive and sexual behaviors that usually occur in monkeys playing with social partners. Deprivation of such socially aggressive opportunities apparently leads to "self-aggression." Thus a developmental link between SIB and aggression seems logical.

Such a rationale may have striking implications for human infants and young children who are already born with severe handicaps that place them at risk for less social developmental opportunities. Failure to provide such interventions may lead to long-term changes in later life related to SIB and aggression. But by this stage they are very difficult to sort out and reverse because the child is permanently biologically different. However, it should be remembered that most SIB cases are not raised under conditions of social deprivation, yet they still perform SIB.

Second, Kraemer, Ebert, Lake, and McKinney (1984) showed that *d*-amphetamine treatment of isolate-reared preadolescent rhesus monkeys produced lethal aggression. Studies of their cerebrospinal fluid (CSF) showed abnormally high norepinephrine (NE) levels, but no change in the concentration of serotonin or dopamine metabolites. This is odd because there is a wealth of literature showing the interaction of NE and serotonin systems. Kraemer and colleagues hypothesized that early social deprivation may have decoupled the NE and serotonin systems, such that the effects of *d*-amphetamine on NE could no longer be modulated. This disruption in modulation of balance between the serotonergic and catecholamine systems is strikingly similar to the hypothesis by Nyhan and colleagues (1980) for serotonergic malfunction in Lesch-Nyhan syndrome. The major difference is that, in Kraemer's monkeys, serotonergic function was lower than normal, but in Lesch-Nyhan cases it was higher than normal. The reasons for these differences are unclear at present. They may be due to the fact that Kraemer's monkeys were initially biologically intact, whereas Lesch-Nyhan cases are born genetically deficient; or it could be that SIB is primarily a D1 dopamine-mediated phenomenon, whereas aggression is a related but primarily serotonergically mediated phenomenon. Several other hypotheses are feasible. In any case, the hypothesis that early social deprivation permanently uncouples these systems is a very important one.

Evidence From Combined Lesion and Isolate Rearing in Rats

An important line of experimentation is to compare different animal models, one aimed at early dopamine depletion and one aimed at early serotonin depletion. Such experiments are currently being conducted by comparing three rat models by Tessel and his colleagues at the University of Kansas: (a) a genetic model, the spontaneously hypertensive rat (SHR); (b) a mental retardation model using methylazoxymethanol (MAM)-induced microcephalic rats; and (c) the Breese neonatal dopamine depletion model in rats. Socially isolate-reared and group-housed rats in each model will be compared in their responses to a learning task of repeated acquisition of stimulus chains and in their topographic response to electric foot shock. Thus far the socially isolated SHRs showed significantly greater shock-induced aggressive biting than group-housed SHRs, but the socially isolated MAM or group-housed MAM or SHR rats did not. No SIB was observed in any of the four groups. As yet we have not run the neonatally dopamine-depleted animals in this paradigm. Nevertheless, the effects of social isolation and mental retardation on shock-induced aggression have been demonstrated. So this may be a very useful methodological strategy for studying developmental organic and environmental risk factors for SIB and aggression and their neurochemical substrates.

Summary and Conclusions

Research on the biological bases of SIB, especially its neurochemical substrates, has been growing at an exponential rate during the past decade. A growing number of epidemiological studies are exploring risk factors for SIB. There are a number of genetic disorders in which SIB has been observed (Gualtieri, 1991), such as Lesch-Nyhan syndrome, Cornelia de Lange syndrome, Rett syndrome, Fragile X syndrome, and Tourette's syndrome. There are a number of neuropharmacologically based treatments recommended for SIB. In fact a special issue of the *Psychopharmacology Bulletin* ("Neurochemistry and Psychopharmacology," 1989) was recently dedicated to the neurochemistry and psychopharmacology of self-injurious behavior.

There are now several animal models using different methods to investigate SIB: (a) lesion models that mimic brain damage related to SIB, (b) direct neurochemical stimulation models that produce SIB, and (c) behavioral developmental models that induce neurochemical changes in the brain related to SIB. At this point it seems that our knowledge of the neurobiological bases of SIB has the potential to grow at an even more rapid pace, helping us to understand other disorders also, such as aggression toward others, stereotyped behavior, and suicidal behavior. Just as Lesch-Nyhan syndrome, a rare disorder of purine metabolism discovered in 1964, has served as a neurobiological window on our understanding of SIB, so the neonatal dopamine depletion model developed by Breese and colleagues may be a window for our understanding of other developmental disorders, such as Parkinson's disease, certain aspects of autism, and developmental psychopathology in general. This research has come of age. It makes an account of SIB based solely on behavioral results inadequate and incomplete.

References

Antelman, S., & Caggiula, A. R. (1977). Stress induced behavior: Chemotherapy without drugs. In I. Hanin & E. Usdin (Eds.), *Animal models in psychiatry and neurology* (pp. 65-104). Oxford: Pergamon.

Baumeister, A. A., Frye, G. R., & Schroeder, S. R. (1984). Neurochemical correlates of self-injurious behavior. In J. A. Mulick & B. L. Mallory (Eds.), *Transitions in mental retardation: Advocacy, technology and science* (pp. 207-228). Norwood, NJ: Ablex.

Baumeister, A. A., & MacLean, W. E., Jr. (1984). Deceleration of self-injurious and stereotypic responding by exercise. *Applied Research in Mental Retardation, 5,* 385-394.

Baumeister, A. A., & Rollings, P. (1976). Self-injurious behavior. In N. R. Ellis (Ed.), *International review of research in mental retardation* (Vol. 9, pp. 1-33). New York: Academic Press.

Berkson, G., & Gallagher, R. J. (1984, September). *Control of feedback from abnormal stereotyped behaviors.* Paper presented at the National Institute of Health and Human Development conference, Bethesda, MD.

Breese, G. R., Baumeister, A. A., McCowan, T. J., Emerick, S., Frye, G. D., Crotty, K., & Mueller, R. A. (1984a). Behavioral differences between neonatal- and adult-6-hydroxydopamine-treated rats to dopamine agonists: Relevance to neurological symptoms in clinical syndromes with reduced brain dopamine. *Journal of Pharmacology and Experimental Therapeutics, 231,* 343-354.

Breese, G. R., Baumeister, A. A., McCowan, T. J., Emerick, S., Frye, G. D., & Mueller, R. A. (1984b). Neonatal-6-hydroxydopamine treatment: Model of susceptibility for self-mutilation in the Lesch-Nyhan syndrome. *Pharmacology Biochemistry and Behavior, 21,* 459-461.

Breese, G. R., Criswell, H. E., Duncan, G. E., & Mueller, R. A. (1989). Dopamine deficiency in self-injurious behavior. *Psychopharmacology Bulletin, 25,* 353-357.

Brown, G. L., Ebert, M. H., Goyer, P. F., Jimerson, D. C., Klein, W. J., Bunney, W. E., & Goodwin, F. K. (1982). Aggression, suicide, and serotonin: Relationships to CSF amine metabolites. *American Journal of Psychiatry, 139,* 741-746.

Cataldo, M. F., & Harris, J. (1982). The biological basis for self-injury in the mentally retarded. *Analysis and Intervention in Developmental Disorders, 2,* 21-39.

Cook, E. H., Terry, E. J., Heller, W., & Leventhal, B. L. (1990). Fluoxetine treatment of borderline mentally retarded adults with obsessive-compulsive disorder. *Journal of Clinical Psychopharmacology, 10,* 228-229.

Criswell, H. E., Mueller, R. A., & Breese, G. R. (1989). Clozapine antagonism of D-1 and D-2 dopamine receptor-mediated behaviors. *European Journal of Pharmacology, 159,* 141-147.

Cross, H. A., & Harlow, H. F. (1965). Prolonged and progressive effects of partial isolation on the behavior of macaque monkeys. *Journal of Experimental Personality Research, 1,* 39-49.

de Lissovoy, V. (1961). Head-banging in early childhood. *Journal of Pediatrics, 58,* 803-805.

Goldstein, M., Anderson, L. T., Reuben, R., & Dancis, J. (1985). Self-mutilation in Lesch-Nyhan disease is caused by dopaminergic denervation. *Lancet, 1,* 338-339.

Gualtieri, C. T. (1991). *Neuropsychiatry and behavioral pharmacology.* New York: Springer Verlag.

Gualtieri, C. T., & Schroeder, S. R. (1989). Pharmacotherapy of self-injurious behavior: Preliminary tests of the D-1 hypothesis. *Psychopharmacology Bulletin, 25,* 364-371.

Harlow, H. F., Harlow, M. K., & Suomi, S. J. (1971). From thought to therapy: Lessons from a primate laboratory. *American Scientist, 59,* 538-549.

Kelley, W. N., & Wyngaarden, J. B. (1983). Clinical syndromes associated with hypoxanthine-guanine phosphoribosyltransferase deficiency. In J. B. Stanbury, J. B. Wyngaarden, D. S. Fredrickson, J. L. Goldstein, & M. S. Brown (Eds.), *The metabolic basis of inherited disease* (5th ed.) (pp. 1115-1143). New York: McGraw-Hill.

Kern, L., Koegel, R. L., Dyer, K., Blew, P. A., & Fenton, L. R. (1982). The effects of physical exercise on self-stimulation and appropriate responding in autistic children. *Journal of Autism and Developmental Disorders, 12,* 399-419.

Kraemer, G. W., & Clarke, H. S. (1990). The behavioral neurobiology of self-injurious behavior in rhesus monkeys. *Progress in Neuropsychopharmacology and Biological Psychiatry, 14,* 141-168.

Kraemer, G. W., Ebert, M. H., Lake, C. R., & McKinney, W. T. (1984). Hypersensitivity to d-amphetamine several years after early social deprivation in rhesus monkeys. *Psychopharmacology, 82,* 266-276.

Kravitz, H., & Boehm, J. (1971). Rhythmic habit patterns in infancy: Their sequence, age of onset and frequency. *Child Development, 42,* 399-413.

Lancioni, G. E., Smeets, P. M., Ceccarani, P. S., & Capodaglio, L. (1984). Effects of gross motor activities on the severe self-injurious tantrums of multihandicapped individuals. *Applied Research in Mental Retardation, 5,* 471-482.

Lesch, M., & Nyhan, W. L. (1964). A familial disorder of uric acid metabolism and central nervous system function. *American Journal of Medicine, 36,* 561-570.

Lewis, M. H., Gluck, J. P., Beauchamp, A. J., Keresztury, M. F., & Mailman, R. B. (1990). Long-term effects of early social isolation in Mucaca mulatta: Changes in dopamine receptor function following apomorphine challenge. *Brain Research, 513,* 67-73.

Lloyd, K. C., Hornykiewicz, O., Davidson, L., Shannak, K., Farley, I., Goldstein, M., Shibuya, M., Kelley, W., & Fox, I. H. (1981). Biochemical evidence of dysfunction of brain neurotransmitters in the Lesch-Nyhan Syndrome. *The New England Journal of Medicine, 305,* 1106-1111.

Maisto, C. R., Baumeister, A. A., & Maisto, A. A. (1978). An analysis of variables related to self-injurious behavior among institutionalized retarded persons. *Journal of Mental Deficiency Research, 22,* 27-36.

Markowitz, P. I. (1990). Fluoxetine treatment and self-injurious behavior in mentally retarded patients. *Journal of Clinical Psychopharmacology, 10,* 299-300.

Neurochemistry and psychopharmacology in self-injurious behavior [Special issue]. (1989). *Psychopharmacology Bulletin, 25*(3).

Nyhan, W. L., Johnson, H., Kaufman, I., & Jones, K. (1980). Serotonergic approaches to modification of behavior in the Lesch-Nyhan syndrome. *Applied Research in Mental Retardation, 1,* 25-40.

Ohlsen, R. L. (1978). Control of body rocking in the blind through the use of vigorous exercise. *Journal of Instructional Psychology, 5,* 19-22.

O'Neil, M., Page, N., Adkins, W. N., & Eichelman, B. (1986). Tryptophantrazodone treatment of aggressive behavior. *Lancet, ii,* 859-860.

Patterson, B. D., & Srisopark, M. M. (1989). Severe anorexia and possible psychosis or hypomania after trazodone-tryptophan treatment of aggression. *Lancet, i,* 1017.

Ratey, J. J., Sovner, R., Mikkelsen, E., & Chmielinski, H. E. (1989). Buspirone therapy for maladaptive behavior and anxiety in developmentally disabled persons. *Journal of Clinical Psychiatry, 50,* 382-384.

210   Dopaminergic and Serotonergic Mechanisms

Realmuto, G. M., August, G. J., & Garfinkel, B. D. (1989). Clinical effect of buspirone in autistic children. *Journal of Clinical Psychopharmacology, 9*, 122-125.

Roy, A., & Linnoila, M. (1988). Suicidal behavior, impulsivity, and serotonin. *Acta Psychiatrica Scandinavica, 78*, 529-535.

Schroeder, S. R. (1984). Neurochemical and behavioral interactions with SIB. In J. C. Griffin, M. T. Stark, D. E. Williams, B. K. Altmeyer, & H. K. Griffin (Eds.), *Advances in the treatment of self-injurious behavior* (pp. 61-88). Austin, TX: Texas Planning Council for Developmental Disabilities.

Schroeder, S. R., Bickel, W. K., & Richmond, G. (1986). Primary and secondary prevention of self-injurious behavior. In K. Gadow & I. Bialer (Eds.), *Advances in learning and behavioral disabilities* (Vol. 5, pp. 65-67). Greenwich, CT: JAI.

Schroeder, S. R., Breese, G. R., & Mueller, R. A. (1990). Dopaminergic mechanisms in self-injury. In D. K. Routh & M. Wolraich (Eds.), *Advances in developmental and behavioral pediatrics* (pp. 181-198). London: Jessica Kingsley.

Schroeder, S. R., Mulick, J. A., & Rojahn, J. (1980). The definition, taxonomy, epidemiology, and ecology of self-injurious behavior. *Journal of Autism and Developmental Disorders, 10*, 417-432.

Schroeder, S. R., Schroeder, C. S., Rojahn, J., & Mulick, J. A. (1982). Self-injurious behavior: An analysis of behavior management techniques. In J. L. Matson & J. R. McCartney (Eds.), *Handbook of behavior modification for the mentally retarded* (pp. 61-115). New York: Plenum.

Schroeder, S. R., Schroeder, C. S., Smith, B., & Dalldorf, J. (1978). Prevalence of self-injurious behavior in a large state facility for the retarded: A three year follow-up study. *Journal of Autism and Childhood Schizophrenia, 8*(3), 261-269.

Singh, H. N., & Millichamp, C. J. (1985). Pharmacological treatment of self-injurious behavior in mentally retarded persons. *Journal of Autism and Developmental Disorders, 15*, 257-267.

Sweetman, L., Borden, M., Kulovich, S., Kaufman, I., & Nyhan, W. L. (1977). Altered excretion of 5-hydroxyindoleacetic and the glycine in patients with the Lesch-Nyhan disease. In M. M. Mueller, E. Kaiser, & E. Seegmiller (Eds.), *Purine metabolism in man II: Regulation of pathways and enzyme defects* (pp. 398ff). New York: Plenum.

Tomporowski, P. D., & Ellis, N. R. (1984). Effects of exercise on the physical fitness, intelligence, and adaptive behavior of institutionalized mentally retarded adults. *Applied Research in Mental Retardation, 5*, 329-337.

Tomporowski, P. D., & Ellis, N. R. (1985). The effects of exercise on the health, intelligence, and adaptive behavior of institutionalized severely and profoundly mentally retarded adults: A systematic replication. *Applied Research in Mental Retardation, 6*, 465-473.

Watters, R. G., & Watters, W. E. (1980). Decreasing self-stimulatory behavior with physical exercise in a group of autistic boys. *Journal of Autism and Developmental Disorders, 10*, 379-387.

Wong, D. F., Wagner, H. N., Dannals, R. F., Links, J. M., Frost, J. J., Ravert, H. T., Wilson, A. A., Rosenbaum, A. E., Gjedde, A., Douglass, K. H., Petronic, J. D., Folstein, M. F., Toung, J. K. T., Burns, H. D., & Kuhar, M. J. (1984). Effects of age on dopamine and serotonin receptors measured by positron tomography in the living human brain. *Science, 226*, 1393-1396.

PART IV

Environmental Interventions for Destructive Behavior

11

Covariation Within Functional Response Classes

Implications for Treatment of Severe Problem Behavior

JEFFREY R. SPRAGUE
ROBERT H. HORNER

Behavior change occurs within a complex ecology. At any point different responses compete, and across time change in the probability of one response affects the probability of other responses (Davison & McCarthy, 1988; Sajwaj, Twardosz, & Burke, 1972; Scotti, Evans, Meyer, & DiBendetto, 1991). Our continued understanding of human behavior must include analysis of such complex, interacting behavioral relationships. The foundation for this analysis is available in the applied (Baer, 1982; Mace et al., 1988; Mace, McCurdy, & Quigley, 1990; Wahler & Fox, 1981) and infrahuman (Dunham & Grantmyre, 1982; Epling & Pierce, 1990; Herrnstein, 1970; McDowell, 1982, 1988) literature. Recently, applied researchers have adopted a more complex perspective in the study of response covariation focused on severe problem behaviors.

AUTHORS' NOTE: Preparation of this manuscript was supported in part by the U.S. Department of Education, Cooperative Agreement No. G0087C023488. However, the opinions expressed herein do not necessarily reflect the position or policy of the U.S. Department of Education, and no official endorsement by the department should be inferred. The authors extend appreciation to Dr. Richard Albin, Dr. Robert O'Neill, Brigid Flannery, Janice Ramsden, Dr. Robert Koegel, Dr. Edward Carr, Dr. Glen Dunlap, Dr. Wayne Sailor, Dr. Jackie Anderson, Dr. Hill Walker, and Dr. John Reid.

Three different but compatible lines of response covariation research warrant acknowledgment. The first relates to the application of functional equivalence training as a procedure for decreasing severe problem behaviors (Carr, 1988; Durand, 1990). This technology draws from early operant recommendations to conduct a functional analysis assessment of a problem behavior that results in documentation of the antecedent variables that predict the behavior and the consequence variables that maintain the behavior (Baer, Wolf, & Risley, 1968; Bijou & Baer, 1961; Bijou, Peterson, & Ault, 1968). A new, socially acceptable response that results in the same consequence is then taught with the expectation that this new skill will compete successfully against the problem behavior, and the probability of the problem behavior will decrease. Empirical support for the predicted covariation associated with functional equivalence training is impressive (Carr & Durand, 1985; Carr, Robinson, Taylor, & Carlson, 1990; Durand, 1984; Durand & Carr, 1987; Durand & Crimmins, 1987; Horner & Budd, 1985; Horner, Sprague, O'Brien, & Heathfield, 1990; Iwata, Dorsey, Slifer, Bauman, & Richman, 1982; Repp, Felce, Barton, & Lyle, 1988; Wacker et al., 1990).

A second line of research has addressed the covariation of multiple positive and negative behaviors emphasizing a model of behavioral allocation. Whereas functional equivalence training operates on a model in which behaviors compete relative to specific outcomes, an allocation model acknowledges that regardless of the consequences of a behavior, there is a limit to the number of responses a person can emit during a specified period, and that the increase in the time spent performing one behavior results in a decrease in the time available to perform other behaviors (Cataldo, Ward, Russo, Riordan, & Bennett, 1986; Fisher, Piazza, Cataldo, & Harrell, 1990; Parrish, Cataldo, Kolko, Neef, & Egel, 1986). This line of research has emphasized that many different factors may affect the covariation of responses. It is possible, for example, that the development of a new, positive behavior could result in a decrease in the opportunity to perform many other behaviors (positive and negative).

The third contribution to our understanding of complex response covariation in applied settings lies in recent application of the matching law (Davison & McCarthy, 1988; Herrnstein, 1970). The matching law predicts the relative probability of multiple responses based on the level of reinforcement associated with each of those responses. The matching law provides a mathematical model for predicting the covariation of responses and has received attention for the implications it holds for clinical treatment of complex problem behaviors (Epling & Pierce, 1990; Epstein, 1983; Fuqua, 1984; Mace et al., 1990; McDowell, 1988; Myerson & Hale, 1984). Recent applications of the matching law in applied contexts have emphasized the need to assess both the comparative level of reinforcement available for different responses *and* the requirements (e.g., efficiency) of the different responses (Horner & Day, 1991; Mace et al., 1990).

The present chapter extends the analysis of variables affecting response covariation. Our specific focus was on the covariation of different responses within a functional response class. A response class is a set of topographically different behaviors that produce the same functional effect and are maintained by the same consequence (Johnston & Pennypacker, 1980; Millenson & Leslie, 1979). The concept of response class analysis is consistent with each of the three lines of covariation research presented above. Members of a response class are predicted to covary as consequences associated with the response class change. Further, response generalization (either positive or negative covariation) is predicted when a new member of the response class is added. Our particular interest was in the feasibility of interventions that not only decrease one undesirable behavior in a response class but also reduce all negative members of a predefined response class. Three studies are presented. In each study a functional analysis is provided to document (a) that a class of negative responses existed and (b) that a reasonable hypothesis can be made as to a consequence that was maintaining the response class. In each of the three studies, a mild punisher was delivered following one member of the defined response class, and the effect of punishment on that response was compared with the effect on other members in the response class. The three studies differ in the alternative instructional strategies they offer to using punishment. Study 1 involved functional equivalence training, Study 2 involved antecedent prompts, and Study 3 involved elevated levels of praise as alternative strategies for decreasing *all* negative members of the targeted response class.

General Methodology

The three studies shared basic methodological characteristics. The shared methods are presented here, and the procedures unique to each study are presented in separate sections below.

Participants

Two young men and one young woman ranging in age from 12 to 16 years participated in the study. A summary of their characteristics is provided in Table 11.1.

Alan was a 15-year-old boy with mild athetoid cerebral palsy. He lived at home with his father and younger brother. His school records indicated that he was functioning in the moderate range of mental retardation. His performance on the Test of Nonverbal Intelligence fell at the .2 percentile. His performance on the American Association on Mental Deficiency adaptive behavior scale, school version, fell within the moderate range of mental retardation, and he could use simple one- and two-word utterances.

The behaviors of concern for Alan were described as tantrums. The tantrums occurred zero to five times per day at school and less often at home. The tantrums included hitting out (in air), head/body shaking, hitting objects, hands to face, hitting others, and screaming. Alan had grown to be taller than some of the classroom staff and some of his tantrums resulted in injury to staff and others.

Barbara was 12 years old, lived with her parents, and carried diagnoses of autism and severe mental retardation. She spoke in simple one- to two-word sentences and often was difficult to understand. Her performance on the PPVT-R indicated a scale score equivalent of < 40 and an age equivalent of 3 to 5 years. Her composite score on the Vineland Adaptive Behavior Scale was 40. Barbara experienced chronic sinus infections and colds that were believed to be associated with her problem behavior.

Behaviors of concern for Barbara included putting her head on the table, screaming, putting her fingers in her ears/mouth, hitting/kicking objects, hitting herself, flapping her hands, hitting/kicking others, and pulling up her shirt. Her behaviors were judged to be so severe that she was temporarily removed from her school program prior to the study.

Dale was a 16-year-old young man who did not speak or use other formal communication strategies. He had lived in a state institution for 6 years before moving to the community to live in a group home with three other young adults with disabilities. His school records indicated that he was functioning in the severe to profound range of mental retardation. His performance on the Wechsler Adult Intelligence Scale-Revised placed him at the .2 percentile for both verbal and performance abilities. Dale experienced generalized tonic-clonic seizures from 0 to

Table 11.1 Participant Characteristics

Participant Age & Gender	IQ	Clinical Diagnoses	Problem Behaviors	Current Placement	Medication During Study	Training Tasks
Alan 15 years Male	IQ < 50	Moderate mental retardation Cerebral palsy	Hitting out Head/body shaking Hitting objects Hands to face Hitting others with fists and head Screaming	Self-contained classroom, regular public middle school Lived at home with father and brother	None	Counting coins Table washing Using "next dollar" strategy Collating and stapling the school newsletter
Barbara 12 years Female	IQ < 50	Severe mental retardation Autism Chronic sinus infections	Putting head on table Putting fingers in ears/mouth Hitting/kicking objects Hitting others Screaming/crying Pulling up shirt Hitting self Flapping hands	Self-contained classroom, regular public middle school Lived at home with mother and father	None	Counting coin values Counting dollars Calculator math (shopping simulation)
Dale 16 years Male	IQ < 25	Profound mental retardation Autism Severe seizures	Stereotypic spitting, flicking, chewing Aggression Pushing objects	Self-contained classroom, regular public middle school Lived in intensive	DepaKote, 1750 mg Phenobarbital, 90 mg	Table washing Picture labeling Use of tape player Shelving books

Table 11.1 Continued

Participant Age & Gender	IQ	Clinical Diagnoses	Problem Behaviors	Current Placement	Medication During Study	Training Tasks
			Hitting objects Hitting self Knee to head Screaming Biting hand Pinching others Hitting others	training group home with 3 other people	Tegretol, 1600 mg	

10 times per day. He was receiving 1750 mg of DepaKote, 90 mg of phenobarbital, and 1600 mg of Tegretol daily to assist in seizure control. Dale also was diagnosed as having farsightedness (20/40-20/200 in the best eye). Glasses were prescribed but he did not wear them very often. He usually removed the glasses to chew on them or flick them in front of his eyes.

Behaviors of concern for Dale included pinching and scratching others, hitting/slapping others, hitting himself, biting his hand, hitting his head with his knee, throwing objects, pushing/grabbing objects, screaming, and spitting. Staff reported extreme difficulty in supporting Dale while he was participating in community activities or moving from class to class in school as he would frequently hit himself, scream, and pinch the staff.

Settings

Observation, training, and probe sessions were conducted in the classrooms and other learning environments where the participants attended school. These included classrooms and adjacent areas such as cafeterias and gymnasiums in the three regular public schools where the study was conducted.

Functional Analysis Assessment

Following the recommendations and procedures described by O'Neill, Horner, Albin, Storey, and Sprague (1990), a functional assessment interview was conducted with the teacher(s) of each student to determine the specific problem behaviors and the events that appeared to predict and maintain those behaviors. In addition, the senior author spent 6 to 10 hours in direct observation with each student to confirm the information obtained from the initial interviews. The information obtained from this assessment affected selection of the behaviors that were monitored and the specific format of the interventions that were applied.

Measurement

Each of the three studies assessed different participant behaviors. Across the three studies, however, a common measurement protocol was used. A videotape was made during each of the 15- to 20-minute training sessions that were conducted 3 to 4 times per week. Observers reviewed each tape using Toshiba 1000 microcomputers and observation software developed by Repp, Harman, Felce, Van Acker, and Karsh (1989). This software allowed documentation of the rate of each behavior, the duration of some behaviors, and the interrelations of each behavior in real time. Three classes of behaviors were monitored.

Problem Behaviors

Observers monitored the rate per minute of each of the problem behaviors identified in Table 11.1 for each participant.

Desirable Behaviors

Alan and Barbara had desirable behaviors, such as use of picture communication symbols and use of verbal requesting, that were monitored as appropriate for them. Dale had no formal communication system at the time of the study. In addition, the percentage of trials correct without assistance per session was monitored for each participant.

Teacher Variables

To control for potential confounds the observers monitored the rate of teacher behaviors that inadvertently could have affected the results. The following teacher behaviors were monitored for each student: (a) reprimands, (b) praise, (c) instruction to perform an "easy" task, (d) instruction to perform a "difficult" task, (e) physical blocks of student behavior, and (f) antecedent prompts.

Three graduate students in special education served as observers throughout the three studies. Each observer had a minimum of 5 years of experience in the field of special education and prior experience in research and observation procedures. Observers received 2 to 5 hours of instruction from the senior author on the observation protocol and behavior definitions. Specific definitions of all observed responses are available from the authors.

Interobserver Agreement

Two observers rated the videotapes during 38% of the sessions in Study 1, 33% of the sessions in Study 2, and 37% of the sessions in Study 3. Interobserver agreement was computed for each measurement variable using the "Reliable" program developed by Repp and colleagues (1989) with a window of ±3 s. The interobserver agreement for each variable reported for each student reached 85% or higher. Tables listing the interobserver agreement mean and range for each variable for each phase for each student are available from the authors.

Study 1: Effects of Blocking and Functional Equivalence Training on Intra-Response Class Covariation

The first study was done with Alan and involved the tasks and behaviors indicated in Table 11.1. The initial functional analysis interview and observations indicated that Alan was most likely to engage in problem behaviors when presented with tasks that were difficult for him to complete without teacher assistance. Further, the analysis led to the hypothesis that problem behaviors were maintained by access to teacher assistance during training.

Procedures and Design

The procedures for Study 1 were designed to provide three distinct analyses. The first four phases of the study provide an ABAB pattern designed to confirm the functional analysis information obtained through the interview and observations. In addition, these first four phases allowed documentation of the covariation of multiple problem behaviors (e.g., documentation of a response class).

Phases 4-6 of the study provided a BCB reversal designed to assess the effects of mild punishment on one response, compared to the other, nonpunished members of the response classes. A third subanalysis included phases 6-10 and assessed the effects of functional equivalence training on all members of the targeted response class. The full study resulted in an ABABCBDB'DE design with the following procedures for each phase.

Easy (A)

The easy phases involved training with a set of tasks that were perceived as easy for Alan to perform (e.g., counting coins, counting whole dollars, computer learning activities, and collating and stapling). "Easy" tasks were recommended by Alan's teacher and operationally defined as tasks that Alan could complete correctly at least 75% of the trials within a session. Training occurred in Alan's classroom with one to five other students present during regular instructional periods. The trainer presented a task with the request to initiate completion. If Alan performed any of the identified problem behaviors additional trainer assistance was provided in the form of verbal and gestural prompts and modeling. If Alan initiated the task or completed the task successfully he received verbal praise. If Alan asked for help (e.g., said "help" or "please help") the teacher provided the same additional assistance that followed performance of problem behaviors.

If Alan's problem behaviors escalated to an extremely disruptive or agitated level the session was terminated. No sessions were terminated during easy phases.

Difficult (B/B')

The difficult phases replicated the procedures in the easy phases with the exception that the tasks presented during difficult phases were preselected by the teacher as being difficult for Alan to complete without assistance. A task was operationally defined as difficult if Alan performed no more than 33% of the trials correctly without assistance during a session.

The difficult' (B') phase was slightly different because Alan had received training to ask for help. If he requested help during this phase he was told, "Do the best you can." All other procedures replicated those of the difficult phase.

Three sessions were terminated during difficult phases due to the perception of the trainer that Alan's problem behaviors were escalating to an unreasonable level. Each of these sessions lasted more than 10 minutes and the data were included in the analysis.

Difficult Plus Reprimand and Blocking

The procedures for this phase replicated those of the difficult (B) phases except that when Alan "hit out" (without hitting a person or object) the teacher would (a) physically block his response, (b) deliver a mild verbal reprimand (e.g., "stop that"), and (c) redirect him back to the task. If Alan verbally requested help, the teacher provided assistance.

Functional Equivalence Training (D)

During this phase the functional equivalence procedures recommended by Carr (1988) and Durand (1990) were applied. An alternative, socially acceptable behavior (verbally asking for help) was taught. Alan already had the ability to say "help." Training involved four 10-minute sessions (a total of 80 trials) during which the word "help" or "help please" was prompted when Alan arrived at a step in the task that previously had been difficult. When Alan performed with 90% accuracy without prompting across two sessions, the procedures for regular training sessions were reintroduced.

Functional Equivalence Follow-Up (E)

Two months after the last functional equivalence session (#36), Alan received three follow-up sessions. These sessions replicated the procedures in the functional equivalence phases except no training took place. Alan, however, was told to ask for help if he needed it at the beginning of the first session.

Results

The results for Study 1 are provided in Table 11.2 and Figures 11.1 and 11.2. Figure 11.1 presents the rate per minute for all problem behaviors in the defined response class. Figure 11.2 presents the rate per minute only for the punished response (hitting out), and Table 11.2 presents the rates per minute per phase for each of the other members of the response class and the rate at which Alan verbally asked for help. Graphs for each of these variables are available from the authors.

Functional Analysis Assessment

The first four phases of the study provide an ABAB reversal with easy and difficult phases. Data presented in Figure 11.1 support the hypotheses developed during the informal assessment. Alan engaged in problem behaviors very infrequently ($M = .02$/min.) across the two easy phases, with immediate and dramatic increases in problem behavior when he was presented with difficult tasks ($M = 9.6$/min. across the two difficult phases).

A second consideration for this ABAB analysis was the extent to which the six problem behaviors identified in the functional analysis interview were a response class (e.g., covary across phases). The results provided in Table 11.2 indicate that for five of the six responses the expected pattern (low rates during easy phases, high rates during difficult phases) occurred. Only hands to face (which was never observed) failed to document an increased response rate during difficult phases.

Table 11.2 Average Rate per Minute of Alan's Problem and Requesting Behaviors per Phase

	Easy	Diff.	Easy	Diff.	Block/ Reprimand	Diff.	F.E.	Diff.'	F.E.	Follow-up
Problem Behaviors										
Hitting out/swinging	0.00	2.90	0.00	1.70	0.50	1.20	0.14	1.96	0.00	0.00
Head/body shaking	0.00	0.76	0.00	0.20	2.30	1.90	0.10	0.43	0.00	0.00
Hitting object	0.03	4.40	0.00	1.60	2.90	0.33	0.00	0.70	0.00	0.00
Putting hands to face	0.00	0.00	0.00	0.00	0.30	0.03	0.00	0.13	0.00	0.00
Hitting others	0.00	1.00	0.00	0.17	0.00	0.00	0.00	0.13	0.00	0.00
Screaming	0.00	6.67	0.00	0.17	1.20	0.03	0.00	0.00	0.00	0.00
Requesting Behavior										
Asking for help	0.00	0.00	0.00	0.00	0.00	0.00	0.76	0.03	1.28	1.40

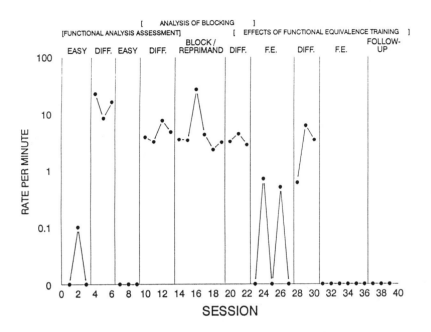

Figure 11.1. Total Problem Behaviors for Alan

Alan did not request help verbally during any session across the first four phases.

Analysis of Mild Punishment

Phases 4-6 of the study provide an opportunity to assess the impact of verbal reprimand plus blocking following the response of "hitting out." The results across all problem behaviors are displayed in Figure 11.1 and indicate no functional effect. With the exception of one atypical peak in problem behavior during Session 16 the response rates across the three phases are very similar.

A micro-analysis of the block/reprimand intervention is provided in Figure 11.2 and Table 11.2. The results in Figure 11.2 indicate that punishment was effective at reducing the targeted response (hitting out).

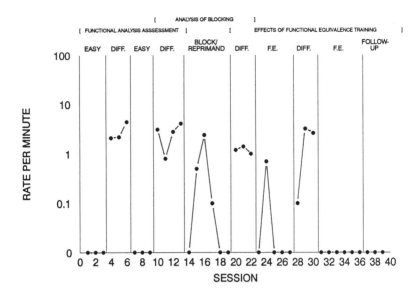

Figure 11.2. The Rate of Hitting Out Across Phases for Alan

Even including the exceptional data in Session 16, the three phases document a clear BCB reversal pattern (*M* rates = 2.3/min., 0.5/min., 1.2/min., respectively). Hitting out was less likely to occur when it was followed by a block and verbal reprimand.

The results in Table 11.2 provide an opportunity to assess the hypothesis that if the rate of a single response class member is reduced, some or all of the remaining members will increase (Green & Streifel, 1988; Schroeder & MacLean, 1987). The data support this hypothesis. Four responses in the response class (head/body shake, hit objects, hands to face, and scream) increased in rate during the block/reprimand phase and decreased when block/reprimand was discontinued. Hit others was performed at zero or near zero levels across the three phases and did not show a change when the block/reprimand intervention was introduced. Alan also continued his pattern of not using any verbal requests for help across the three phases.

Analysis of Functional Equivalence

After training, Alan used "help" regularly throughout the remaining functional equivalence and follow-up phases at a rate of approximately

1 per minute. Phases 6-10 provide a reversal design assessing the effect of using "help" on problem behaviors. The results indicate that problem behaviors were much less likely when the "help" response was used than during the difficult phases when "help" was not used or was ignored. It is important to note that during the first difficult phase in this analysis Alan was not using a "help" request. To assess if rewarding "help" with teacher assistance was the effective component of this intervention the difficult' phase included a change in protocol. If Alan asked for help he was told "do the best you can." In essence this phase involved removal of the assistance that was believed to be the functional reinforcer for saying "help." When saying "help" did not lead to assistance, and problem behavior did lead to assistance, there was an immediate and dramatic increase in the rate of problem behaviors. With reintroduction of the functional equivalence procedures Alan completely stopped performing problem behaviors. This pattern maintained during the three follow-up sessions conducted two months later.

The data in Figure 11.2 and Table 11.2 document that the dramatic reduction of problem behaviors following equivalence training, and increases in problem behavior during difficult', were consistent across all problem behaviors except screaming (which was not observed during any session in Phases 6-10). Functional equivalence training was functionally related to a reduction in all observed problem behaviors in the targeted response class.

Teacher/Control Variables

Independent variable control data are provided in Table 11.3. Teacher praise was delivered at similar levels across all phases. Teacher prompts were delivered at similar levels across all phases, and the percentage of trials correct per session were consistent with the criteria for sessions being easy or difficult with one exception. The reprimand/block phase recorded percentage correct data of 37% rather than 33%.

Study 2: Analysis of Blocking and Antecedent Assistance Training on Intra-Response Class Covariation

Study 2 describes the functional analysis assessment and intervention procedures implemented with Barbara. The initial functional analysis interview and observation process revealed that Barbara used problem

Table 11.3 Teacher/Control Variables for Study 1 (Alan)

	Easy Phases	Difficult Phases	Block/ Reprimand	Functional Equivalence
Teacher praise	3.4/min.	3.2/min.	2.0/min.	4.2/min.
Teacher prompt	7.7/min.	7.6/min.	7.4/min.	7.3/min.
Percentage trials correct w/o assistance	95	33	37	25

behaviors to achieve a variety of behavioral functions including escape from task demands, access to attention, and expressing discomfort or pain. The teaching staff and her parents also reported that she used problem behaviors in an attempt to gain additional assistance from her trainers during instruction. Using problem behaviors to get additional assistance became the focus of the investigation.

Procedures and Design

An initial ABA reversal was conducted to document the existence of a response class and to confirm the interview hypothesis that contingent access to teacher assistance is a maintaining reinforcer for members of the response class. A CBC analysis then was conducted to assess the effects of mild punishment on members of the response class. The full study resulted in an ABACBCA reversal design. The procedures for each phase are described below.

Antecedent Assistance (A)

Barbara was presented with a series of "difficult" coin and money counting tasks. Task difficulty was defined in the same manner as that used in Study 1. Antecedent assistance was defined as a trainer model of the correct response immediately following the presentation of the target task cue. For example, the trainer would present four one-dollar bills to Barbara and say "count the dollars." Immediately following the initial cue the trainer would model the correct response by saying, "Watch me. One, two, three, four. Now you do it!" Barbara would then attempt to complete the task. If she failed to complete the task, the modeled assistance would be repeated. Verbal and physical praise (tickles) were delivered for correct responses and also for attempts to respond. Problem behaviors performed during this phase were ignored. If Barbara asked for help, the modeling assistance was provided immediately.

Contingent Assistance (B)

This condition presented the same "difficult" instructional tasks as the antecedent assistance phase. Antecedent assistance was not provided, however. The contingent assistance condition stipulated that Barbara perform either a targeted problem behavior or a formal request for assistance in order to gain access to the trainer model. For example, the trainer would present four one-dollar bills to Barbara and say "count the dollars." No modeling or assistance would follow this cue. The trainer would wait 5 seconds and repeat the cue if no response was made. If no response was made within another 5 seconds, the cue would be delivered a third time. If still no response was made at this point, the trainer would present the next instructional task. If Barbara performed a problem behavior or asked for help the trainer would immediately deliver the modeling assistance. Praise for correct responding and response attempts was delivered exactly as in the antecedent assistance phase.

Contingent Assistance Plus Blocking (C)

This phase replicated the procedures in the contingent assistance phase except that "head to table" was physically blocked and followed by the author stating "don't do that," or "stop that," in a flat tone of voice. If Barbara verbally requested help, the trainer provided assistance.

Results

Study 2 results are illustrated in Figures 11.3 and 11.4 and in Table 11.4. Figure 11.3 presents the rate per minute for all problem behaviors in the identified response class. Figure 11.4 presents the rate per minute only for the punished response (head to table). Table 11.4 presents the rates per minute per phase for each of the members of the response class, including requests for help.

Functional Analysis Assessment

The results from the functional analysis assessment follow a typical ABA reversal pattern. The rate of the targeted problem response-class

Table 11.4 Average Rate of Barbara's Problem and Adaptive Behaviors per Phase

	Antecedent Assistance	Contingent Assistance	Antecedent Assistance	Contingent Assistance w/Block	Contingent Assistance	Contingent Assistance w/Block	Antecedent Assistance
Problem Behaviors							
Putting head on table	0.00	0.37	0.12	0.02	0.43	0.10	0.05
Putting fingers in ears/mouth	0.10	0.15	0.00	0.28	0.16	0.30	0.00
Hitting/kicking objects	0.03	0.20	0.00	0.33	0.53	0.50	0.17
Hitting others	0.00	0.00	0.00	0.10	0.03	0.60	0.00
Screaming/crying	0.00	0.78	0.00	0.55	0.53	0.03	0.00
Pulling up shirt	0.00	0.00	0.00	0.00	0.03	0.03	0.00
Hitting self	0.00	0.08	0.15	0.075	0.00	0.06	0.01
Flapping hands	0.00	0.97	0.00	0.10	0.33	0.13	0.00
Adaptive Behaviors							
Task-related verbalization	5.20	3.40	6.32	6.50	3.80	3.30	6.65
Request for help	0.06	0.12	0.00	0.18	0.23	0.03	0.00

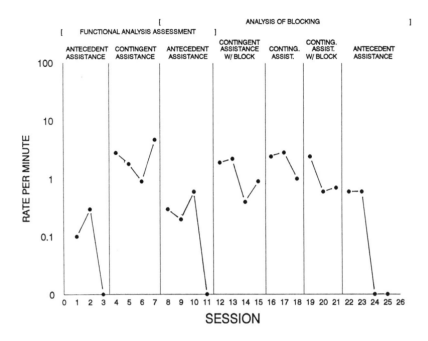

Figure 11.3. Total Problem Behaviors for Barbara

members remained relatively low or nonexistent under the two antecedent assistance conditions ($M = .13$/min. and $.27$/min., respectively). When access to assistance was made contingent on the performance of a problem behavior or request for help, an immediate increase in the rate of problem behaviors was observed ($M = 2.55$/min.).

The rate of occurrence of individual problem and adaptive behaviors was monitored to document which behaviors functioned as members of the response class, "gain access to assistance." The anticipated ABA pattern was observed for putting head on table, hitting/kicking objects, screaming/crying, putting fingers in ears/mouth, and flapping hands. Hitting self did not decrease during the second antecedent assistance phase and kicking/hitting others and pulling up shirt were not observed across the three phases. Barbara requested assistance at a slightly higher rate during "contingent assistance" ($M = .12$/min.), and requests for help also appeared to display a positive covariation with the rate of problem behaviors.

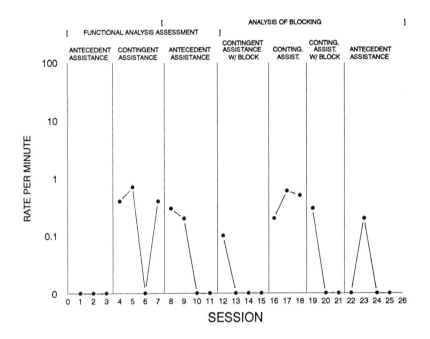

Figure 11.4. Rate of Head on Table for Barbara

Analysis of Mild Punishment

The effects of mild punishment on the response "putting head on table" are presented in Figure 11.4. The effect of mild punishment on all problem behaviors is presented in Figure 11.3 and Table 11.4. When putting head on table was followed by a verbal reprimand and physical block the rate of the behavior was much lower than when reprimand and blocking were not used (block, $M = .02$/min.; no block, $M = .43$/min.; block, $M = .10$/min.). Although the mild punishment was effective at reducing the targeted problem behavior "putting head on table," the effect was less clear when assessing the full class of problem behaviors. The results for all problem behaviors in Figure 11.3 show no reduction in problem behavior rates when blocking and reprimands were used. A

Table 11.5 Teacher/Control Variables for Study 2 (Barbara), Average
Rate per Experimental Condition

	Antecedent Phases	Contingent Assist Phases	Contingent Assist Plus Block
Teacher praise	3.50	2.15	2.45
Teacher request	4.62	5.00	4.68

comparison of the results in Table 11.4 indicates that although putting
head on table rates decreased when punishment was applied other
responses in the class increased.

Rate of task-related verbalizations decreased slowly over the CBC
reversal from an average of 6.5 per minute in the first "block" phase,
3.8 per minute in "contingent assist," and 3.3 per minute in the "block"
replication. Requests for help were observed at an average of .18 per
minute in the first "block" phase, .23 per minute in the return to
"contingent assistance," and .03 per minute in the "block" replication.
The final phase of the study was a return to antecedent assistance. This
manipulation resulted in rapid reduction of all problem behaviors except hitting/kicking objects, which gradually declined to a zero level
over three sessions.

Teacher/Control Variables

Independent variable control data are provided in Table 11.5. Teacher
praise and verbal requests occurred at similar levels across phases.

Study 3: Analysis of Blocking and Differential Rates of Praise on Intra-Response Class Covariation

Study 3 describes the functional analysis assessment and intervention
procedures implemented with Dale. The initial functional analysis interview and observation process revealed that Dale used problem behaviors
to achieve a variety of behavioral functions including escaping from
task demands, maintaining access to stereotypy, and gaining social
attention. Staff were especially concerned with the high rates of stereotypy
that Dale engaged in. The stereotypical behaviors seriously interfered

with attempts to teach Dale. He often would become aggressive toward staff when they attempted to interrupt the stereotypy. An assessment of the variables controlling stereotypy and aggressive behavior became the focus of the investigation.

Procedures and Design

The procedures for Study 3 were designed to provide two distinct analyses. First, an ABA reversal was conducted to replicate the findings from the blocking intervention in Studies 1 and 2 and to document response class membership. Second, an ACAC reversal was conducted to document that a high rate of praise would result in reductions of both stereotypy and aggressive behavior. This series compared instruction with a high rate of praise with low-praise instruction. The full study resulted in an ABACAC design with the following procedures for each phase.

Low Praise (A)

The stimulus conditions for this phase required providing instruction with a low rate of teacher praise (verbal or physical praise delivered less than once/minute). Instructional tasks were varied randomly across sessions.

Low Praise Plus Block (B)

The block condition presented low rates of teacher praise and added blocking of two behaviors: "flicking objects/fingers" and "chewing objects/fingers." The blocking procedure was implemented in the same manner as in Studies 1 and 2. If Dale flicked or chewed he was physically blocked, told "don't do that," and redirected to the task. The exception was if Dale engaged in any aggressive behaviors. Following an aggressive response, Dale was able to engage in flicking/chewing behavior for 10 seconds before being verbally redirected to the task. Task difficulty and rate of praise were maintained at the same level as low praise.

High Praise (C)

The high praise condition was exactly the same as the low praise condition except that the trainer delivered verbal and physical praise at a rate of 4 or more events per minute.

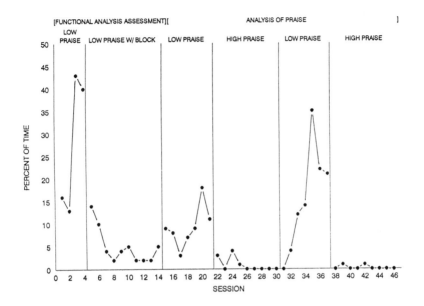

Figure 11.5. Percentage of Time Performing Flick/Chew Behaviors for Dale

Results

Results from Study 3 are presented in Figures 11.5 and 11.6 and in Table 11.6. The hypotheses going into this study were (a) that flicking, chewing, and spitting were a stereotypic response class maintained by automatic reinforcement (Iwata, Vollmer, & Zarcone, 1990); (b) that the eight aggressive behaviors were a response class maintained in part by access to performing stereotypic responses; (c) that blocking some members of the stereotypic responses would lead to two effects, first, an increase in the rate of nonblocked members of the response class and, second, an increase in the rate of aggressive behaviors; and (d) that high levels of teacher praise would be associated with reduction in both stereotypic behaviors and aggressive behaviors.

Effects of Blocking

An assessment of blocking stereotypic behavior is available from the first three phases of the study (low praise, low praise plus blocking, low praise). Because flicking and chewing typically occurred in concert they

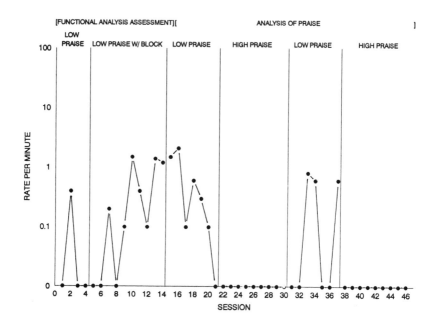

Figure 11.6. Total Aggressive Behaviors for Dale

both were blocked during the blocking phase. The results in Figure 11.5 document an ABA reversal pattern for the amount of time spent in flicking/ chewing responses when blocking was implemented. Data from the same phases are reported in Table 11.6 and document reductions in the average rate of both flicking and chewing when blocking was initiated. Both responses returned to initial levels gradually during the second low praise phase.

Spitting also was viewed as a member of the stereotypic response class. Dale did not spit at people but spit as part of a mouthing routine. When flicking and chewing were blocked there was a threefold increase in the rate of spitting. This rate decreased gradually when blocking was withdrawn.

Aggressive behaviors increased when flicking and chewing were blocked (low praise plus block). The results in Figure 11.6 document an increasing trend up to 1.5 aggressive responses per minute when blocking was instituted. When the use of blocking was terminated there was a gradual reduction in the rate of aggression. The results in Table

Table 11.6 Average Rate per Minute of Dale's Problem Behaviors per Phase

	Low Praise	Low Praise Plus Block	Low Praise	High Praise	Low Praise	High Praise
Stereotypic Behaviors						
Spitting	0.48	1.62	1.43	0.30	0.91	0.31
Flicking fingers/ objects	1.63	1.49	0.91	0.07	0.67	0.11
Chewing objects/ fingers	0.82	0.65	0.89	0.27	1.69	0.04
Aggressive Behaviors						
Pushing objects	0.58	0.09	0.01	0.00	0.02	0.00
Hitting objects	0.00	0.05	0.07	0.06	0.24	0.00
Hitting self	0.42	0.15	0.18	0.00	0.10	0.10
Knee to head	0.00	0.01	0.03	0.00	0.10	0.03
Screaming	0.28	0.36	1.37	0.13	0.45	0.27
Biting hand	0.00	0.07	0.23	0.08	0.09	0.00
Pinching others	0.05	0.40	0.67	0.00	0.28	0.00
Hitting others	0.05	0.10	0.00	0.00	0.00	0.00

11.6 document that the increases in aggression observed during low praise plus block in Figure 11.6 related primarily to changes in the rates of pinching others, hitting others, and screaming. The other five aggressive behaviors either decreased in rate or remained stable during the low praise plus blocking phase. When blocking was terminated there was gradual decrease in aggressive behaviors (the gradual decrease resulted in comparatively high rates for the whole phase).

Effects of High Praise

The last four phases of the study provide an ABAB reversal design examining the effects of high rates of teacher praise versus low rates of teacher praise on stereotypic and aggressive behaviors. Results in Figure 11.5 and Table 11.6 document that when the rate of teacher praise increased from 1 per minute to 4 per minute there was a dramatic reduction in both the rate and the duration of flicking/chewing responses. Unlike the use of blocking, however, the reduction in flicking/chewing responses was not associated with an increase in spitting or an increase in aggressive behaviors (cf. Figure 11.6). In fact both spitting and aggression decreased. When low praise procedures were reinstituted flicking/chewing increased to a level averaging 1.69 responses per minute, the rate of aggressive responses became more variable (increases in three of the seven sessions), and the rate of spitting tripled to .91 per minute. When high-praise procedures were put in place for a second time the effects were replicated. Flicking/chewing and spitting rates dropped to a third of their low-praise levels, and aggressive behaviors were nearly nonexistent.

Teacher/Control Variables

Independent variable control data are provided in Table 11.7. Trainer verbal cues were presented at similar rates during all phases. Trainer praise statements were delivered less often during low praise and low praise plus block. Finally, trainer blocks were delivered only during low praise plus block.

Discussion

The three studies provide an integrated analysis of the manner in which individual behaviors in a response class covary when a subset of the response class is manipulated. Each of the studies documents the existence of a response class and the effect of blocking one member of that class. In each case the blocking of a problem behavior resulted in a decrease in the rate (or duration) of that problem behavior and an increase in other problem behaviors that were members of the same response class. Generalized reduction of all problem behaviors in a response class occurred only when instructional strategies were implemented. In Study 1 (Alan) the effects of teaching a new, functionally equivalent member of a response class on the occurrence of other response-class members were examined. Study 2 (Barbara) examined the effects of eliminating the discriminative stimulus for the problem behaviors. Study 3 (Dale) assessed the effects of increasing the level of praise for desired behavior. Each of these instructional strategies was effective in reducing all problem behaviors in the targeted response class. The key was linking the intervention approach to the function of the class of problem behaviors, as defined through a functional assessment protocol (O'Neill et al., 1990; Repp et al., 1988).

Table 11.7 Teacher/Control Variables for Study 3 (Dale)

	Low Praise	High Praise	Low Praise Plus Block
Teacher praise	0.41	7.25	0.38
Teacher instructions	7.18	8.90	6.53

The major thesis of this chapter is that great caution should be taken when building behavioral interventions for individual problem behaviors. Our experience is that many problem behaviors occur in the context of complex response classes, and that interventions should be targeted toward the response class rather than an individual response. Effective programming for an identified problem behavior involves functional assessment that defines (a) the class of responses that include the targeted problem behavior, (b) the setting events and antecedent stimuli that are predictive of the problem behavior (predictive of both occurrence and nonoccurrence), and (c) the consequences that are hypothesized to maintain the targeted response class (Durand, 1990; Iwata et al., 1990; O'Neill et al., 1990; Pyles & Bailey, 1990; Repp & Karsh, 1990; Wacker et al., 1990). Behavioral programming for problem behaviors should be designed to address the full complement of problem behaviors within a response class.

It is beyond the scope of this chapter, and the research designs that we employed, to define the specific features of each intervention that were uniquely associated with success. It is possible, however, that multiple principles of response covariation are responsible for the observed data patterns. In Studies 1 and 3 competing behaviors were developed that were either within the targeted response class (e.g., asking for help resulted in the same consequences as the problem behaviors) or outside the targeted response class (e.g., performing the task resulted in reinforcers that were different from those available following the problem responses). In these studies, variables such as (a) the value of the competing reinforcers, (b) the dimensions of the competing reinforcement schedules, (c) the physical effort of the competing responses, and (d) the comparative time delay between the discriminative stimulus (Sd) and reinforcement (Sr+) may have influenced the observed change from problem behavior to adaptive behavior (Epling & Pierce, 1990; Horner & Day, 1991; Mace et al., 1990; Newson, Favell, & Rincover, 1983). It also is possible that the antecedent delivery of teacher assistance in Study 2 and the increased praise in Study 3 changed the behavioral economics associated with allocation of time to problem versus appropriate responses (Cataldo et al., 1986).

Our hope is that the data presented in these studies will foster increased interest in the variables that affect response covariation in applied settings. At this time there appear to be a number of applied and theoretical developments that share important implications for our understanding of human behavior and our ability to develop effective, efficient, and minimally intrusive behavioral interventions.

References

Baer, D. M. (1982). The imposition of structure on behavior and the demolition of behavioral structures. In D. J. Bernstein (Ed.), *Response structure and organization* (pp. 217-254). Lincoln and London: University of Nebraska Press.

Baer, D. M., Wolf, M. M., & Risley, T. R. (1968). Some current dimensions of applied behavior analysis. *Journal of Applied Behavior Analysis, 1,* 91-97.

Bijou, S., & Baer, D. M. (1961). *Child development: Vol. 1. A systematic and empirical theory.* New York: Appleton-Century-Crofts.

Bijou, S. W., Peterson, R. F., & Ault, M. H. (1968). A method to integrate descriptive and experimental field studies at the level of data and empirical concepts. *Journal of Applied Behavior Analysis, 1,* 175-191.

Carr, E. G. (1988). Functional equivalence as a mechanism of response generalization. In R. H. Horner, G. Dunlap, & R. L. Koegel (Eds.), *Generalization and maintenance: Lifestyle changes in applied settings* (pp. 221-241). Baltimore, MD: Paul H. Brookes.

Carr, E. G., & Durand, V. M. (1985). Reducing behavior problems through functional communication training. *Journal of Applied Behavior Analysis, 18,* 111-126.

Carr, E. G., Robinson, S., Taylor, J. C., & Carlson, J. I. (1990). *Positive approaches to the treatment of severe behavior problems in persons with developmental disabilities: A review and analysis of reinforcement and stimulus-based procedures* (TASH Monograph No. 4). Seattle, WA: Association for Persons With Severe Handicaps.

Cataldo, M. F., Ward, E. M., Russo, D. C., Riordan, M., & Bennett, D. (1986). Compliance and correlated problem behavior in children: Effects of contingent and non-contingent reinforcement. *Analysis and Intervention in Developmental Disabilities, 6,* 265-282.

Davison, M., & McCarthy, D. (1988). *The matching law: A research review.* Hillsdale, NJ: Lawrence Erlbaum.

Dunham, P. J., & Grantmyre, T. (1982). Changes in a multiple response repertoire during response contingent punishment and response restriction. *Journal of the Experimental Analysis of Behavior, 37,* 123-133.

Durand, V. M. (1984). *Attention getting problem behavior: Analysis and intervention.* Unpublished doctoral dissertation, State University of New York at Stony Brook.

Durand, V. M. (1990). *Severe behavior problems: A functional communication training approach.* New York: Guilford.

Durand, V. M., & Carr, E. G. (1987). Social influences on self-stimulatory behavior: Analysis and treatment application. *Journal of Applied Behavior Analysis, 20,* 119-132.

Durand, V. M., & Crimmins, D. B. (1987). Assessment and treatment of psychotic speech in an autistic child. *Journal of Autism and Developmental Disorders, 17,* 17-28.

Epling, W. F., & Pierce, W. D. (1990). Laboratory to application: An experimental analysis of severe-problem behavior. In A. Repp & N. Singh (Eds.), *Perspectives on the use of nonaversive and aversive interventions for persons with developmental disabilities* (pp. 451-464). Sycamore, IL: Sycamore.

Epstein, R. (1983). Extinction-induced resurgence: Preliminary investigations and possible applications. *The Psychological Record, 35,* 143-153.

Fisher, W. W., Piazza, C. C., Cataldo, M. F., & Harrell, R. (1990, May). *The effects of nonverbal communication training, communication and punishment in the treatment of self-injury and other aberrant behavior.* Paper presented at the 16th Annual International Convention of the Association for Behavior Analysis, Nashville, TN.

Fuqua, R. W. (1984). Comments on the applied relevance of the matching law. *Journal of Applied Behavior Analysis, 17,* 381-386.

Green, G., & Streifel, S. (1988). Response restriction and substitution with autistic children. *Journal of the Experimental Analysis of Behavior, 50*(1), 21-32.

Herrnstein, R. J. (1970). On the law of effect. *Journal of the Experimental Analysis of Behavior, 13,* 243-266.

Horner, R. H., & Budd, C. M. (1985). Acquisition of manual sign use: Collateral reduction of maladaptive behavior, and factors limiting generalization. *Education and Training of the Mentally Retarded, 20,* 39-47.

Horner, R. H., & Day, M. (1991). *The effects of response efficiency on functionally equivalent, competing behaviors.* Manuscript submitted for publication.

Horner, R. H., Sprague, J. R., O'Brien, M. M., & Heathfield, T. L. (1990). The role of response efficiency in the reduction of problem behaviors through functional equivalence training: A case study. *Journal of the Association for Persons With Severe Handicaps, 15*(2), 91-97.

Iwata, B. A., Dorsey, M. F., Slifer, K. J., Bauman, K. E., & Richman, G. S. (1982). Toward a functional analysis of self injury. *Analysis and Intervention in Developmental Disabilities, 2,* 3-20.

Iwata, B. A., Vollmer, T. R., & Zarcone, J. R. (1990). The experimental (functional) analysis of behavior disorders: Methodology, applications and limitations. In A. C. Repp & N. N. Singh (Eds.), *Perspectives on the use of nonaversive and aversive interventions for persons with developmental disabilities* (pp. 301-330). Sycamore, IL: Sycamore.

Johnston, J. M., & Pennypacker, H. S. (1980). *Strategies and tactics of human behavioral research.* Hillsdale, NJ: Lawrence Erlbaum.

Mace, F. C., Hock, M. L., Lalli, J. S., West, B. J., Belfiore, P., Pinter, E., & Brown, D. K. (1988). Behavioral momentum in the treatment of noncompliance. *Journal of Applied Behavior Analysis, 21*(2), 123-141.

Mace, F. C., McCurdy, B., & Quigley, E. A. (1990). A collateral effect of reward predicted by matching theory. *Journal of Applied Behavior Analysis, 23*(2), 197-205.

McDowell, J. J. (1982). The importance of Herrnstein's mathematical statement of the law of effect for behavior therapy. *American Psychologist, 37,* 771-779.

McDowell, J. J. (1988). Matching theory in natural human environments. *The Behavior Analyst, 11,* 95-109.

Millenson, J. R., & Leslie, J. C. (1979). *Principles of behavioral analysis* (2nd ed.). New York: Macmillan.

Myerson, J., & Hale, S. (1984). Practical implications of the matching law. *Journal of Applied Behavior Analysis, 17,* 367-380.

Newson, C., Favell, J. E., & Rincover, A. (1983). The side effects of punishment. In S. Axelrod & J. Apsche (Eds.), *The effects of punishment on human behavior* (pp. 285-315). New York: Academic Press.

O'Neill, R. E., Horner, R. H., Albin, R. A., Storey, K. S., & Sprague, J. R. (1990). *Functional analysis: A practical assessment guide.* Chicago: Sycamore.

Parrish, J. M., Cataldo, M. F., Kolko, D. J., Neef, N. A., & Egel, A. L. (1986). Experimental analysis of response covariation among compliant and inappropriate behaviors. *Journal of Applied Behavior Analysis, 19,* 241-254.

Pyles, D. A., & Bailey, J. S. (1990). Diagnosing severe behavior problems. In A. Repp & N. Singh (Eds.), *Perspectives on the use of nonaversive and aversive interventions for persons with developmental disabilities* (pp. 381-401). Sycamore, IL: Sycamore.

Repp, A. C., Felce, D., Barton, L. E., & Lyle, E. (1988). Basing the treatment of stereotypic and self-injurious behaviors on hypotheses of their causes. *Journal of Applied Behavior Analysis, 21,* 281-290.

Repp, A. C., Harman, M. L., Felce, D., Van Acker, R., & Karsh, K. L. (1989). Conducting behavioral assessments on computer collected data. *Behavioral Assessment, 2,* 249-268.

Repp, A. C., & Karsh, K. G. (1990). A taxonomic approach to the nonaversive treatment of maladaptive behavior of persons with developmental disabilities. In A. Repp & N. Singh (Eds.), *Perspectives on the use of nonaversive and aversive interventions for persons with developmental disabilities* (pp. 331-347). Sycamore, IL: Sycamore.

Sajwaj, T., Twardosz, S., & Burke, M. (1972). Side effects of extinction procedures in a remedial preschool. *Journal of Applied Behavior Analysis, 5,* 163-175.

Schroeder, S. R., & MacLean, W. (1987). If it isn't one thing, it's another: Experimental analysis of covariation in behavior management data of severe behavior disturbances. In S. Landesman & P. Vietze (Eds.), *Living environments and mental retardation* (pp. 315-337). Washington, DC: American Association on Mental Retardation.

Scotti, J. R., Evans, I., Meyer, L., & DiBendetto, A. (1991). Individual repertoires as behavioral systems: Implications for program design and evaluation. In B. Remington (Ed.), *The challenge of severe learning disability* (pp. 139-163). London: John Wiley.

Wacker, D. P., Steege, M. W., Northrup, J., Sasso, G., Berg, W., Reimers, T., Cooper, L., Cigrand, K., & Dunn, L. (1990). A component analysis of functional communication training across three topographies of severe behavior problems. *Journal of Applied Behavior Analysis, 23*(4), 417-430.

Wahler, R. G., & Fox, J. J. (1981). Setting events in applied behavior analysis: Toward a conceptual and methodological expansion. *Journal of Applied Behavior Analysis, 14,* 327-338.

12

Intensive and Long-Term Treatments for Clients With Destructive Behaviors

O. IVAR LOVAAS
TRISTRAM SMITH

In this chapter we contend that understanding and treating destructive behaviors effectively may require a more comprehensive investigation and intervention than many people now anticipate. We use examples from our own research with autistic children to support our contention.

When we began working with autistic children in the early 1960s, we focused on language rather than destructive behaviors. We thought that if we could teach autistic children to speak and communicate, we might observe a concurrent improvement in other areas of functioning as well. In cognitive terminology, our reasoning was that the strengthening of appropriate language may facilitate clients' understanding of the world around them, increase problem solving, and consequently lessen the intensity of their psychopathology. In behavioral terminology, we expected response generalization, meaning that changes in one behavior (language) would produce concurrent changes in other behaviors not specifically targeted for intervention. Itard (1894/1962), as well as psycholinguists such as Sapir (1921) and Whorf (1956), had held similar views

AUTHORS' NOTE: Work on this chapter was supported by Grant H133G801103 from the U.S. Office of Education. Essentials of the chapter were presented as a keynote address at a conference sponsored by the National Institute of Child Health and Human Development in Minneapolis, MN, April 10-12, 1991. Correspondence should be addressed to either author at the Department of Psychology, University of California, Los Angeles, CA 90024.

about the effects of teaching language. This view led us to hope that we would not need to treat destructive behaviors directly because the acquisition of communicative speech automatically would lead to increases in other appropriate behaviors, effectively replacing destructive ones.

This hope was quickly extinguished. Our clients made major gains in language skills with the programs we employed (Lovaas, 1977), but much to our surprise, they often remained assaultive or self-injurious. In other words, response generalization often failed to occur.

Because of this finding, we deviated from our intent to focus mainly on language, and out of clinical concerns for the clients, we decided to study self-injury and assaultive behaviors. Except for our first study involving a single subject (Lovaas, Freitag, Gold, & Kassorla, 1965), we carried out all studies on self-injury in medical settings, at the request of and under the supervision of physicians, who included some of the best-known authorities in the field of mental retardation at that time. Our research was supported by the National Institute of Mental Health and was peer reviewed by the University of California at Los Angeles (UCLA). The research/treatment setting in which we conducted research was open at all times to other professionals and the mass media.

Our first client, Beth, illustrates many of the problems and strategies involved in trying to understand self-injurious behavior. A more detailed presentation of this case is offered in Lovaas and colleagues (1965). Beth was a 9-year-old retarded child whose behaviors were consistent with a diagnosis of autism. Her self-injury dated back to her third year of life and included head banging, scratching the skin of her face and hands, setting her hair on fire by placing it in a wall heater, and so on. Her scalp was covered with scar tissue and her face frequently bled. She had received extensive prior treatment, including a year of inpatient psychiatric care, without change in her clinical status.

We began our behavioral treatment of Beth by teaching socially appropriate behaviors such as language, early academic skills, and recreational activities. During a 6-month period of 5 hours a day of one-to-one treatment we observed a gradual and clinically meaningful increase in the targeted behaviors. However, Beth remained highly self-injurious, particularly outside the clinical setting. Therefore, it was necessary to investigate how better to treat her self-injury. The more salient features of this investigation are now described. Figure 12.1 shows the frequency of Beth's self-destructive behavior over 10-minute observation sessions. The first 15 sessions, distributed over 3 weeks, show considerable session-to-session variation in her self-injury but no signs of improving or worsening over time. In an attempt to decrease her self-injury, we introduced a psychoanalytic treatment procedure, which was then considered the treatment of choice. The procedure was based on the hypothesis that clients such as Beth needed emotional support to help them overcome their feelings of guilt, anxiety, and lowered self-worth. Such support was believed to be particularly important at times when clients were self-injurious, because this was a sign or symptom of just this underlying pathology. Coincidentally, Griffith and Ritvo (1967) have written a detailed presentation of this theory as applied to Beth, who had been in their care.

In short, when Beth did engage in self-injury, we sought to assure and support her with affection and comments such as "I don't think you are bad." As can be seen in Figure 12.1, when we introduced this treatment in sessions 16-19, 20, 24-26, 33, and 38 (all marked by the open circles), there was a noticeable increase in her self-injury. Thus the "treatment of choice" was apparently destructive. Of course, many questions were left unanswered, and we return to some of these later.

Psychoanalytic theory predicted that a worsening of her self-injury would occur if we withdrew our "emotional support," such as by suddenly not smiling or showing affection to her. Surprisingly, when we so intervened in sessions 30-32 and 34-37 (marked by solid triangles) this did not happen. In fact, this major change in her environment left her rate of self-injury unaltered. What did have a dramatic effect was changing to new songs (leaving everything else the same). This relatively minor physical change put an immediate stop to Beth's self-injury.

We attempted to account for these findings by inferring that the new songs, unlike the old songs, were not discriminative for self-injury because they did not have a history of reinforcement withdrawal. In everyday language, the new songs were not associated with frustration. By contrast, the removal of noncontingent "emotional support" turned out to be a neutral or nonfunctional stimulus, so far as self-injury was concerned.

The introduction of new songs was such a minor change that a casual observer probably would have failed to notice it. However, because we deliberately introduced this change and monitored its effects with a sensitive recording procedure, we were able to identify factors controlling Beth's self-injury. We discuss the implications of this research design later in this chapter.

Another interesting result from our work with Beth was that, although we failed to eliminate her self-injurious behaviors despite teaching her

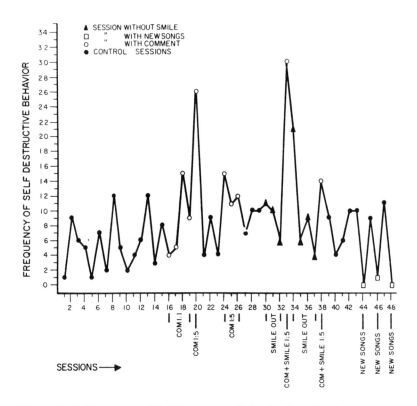

Figure 12.1. Frequency of Self-Destructive Behavior Over Sessions

NOTE: Self-destructive behavior when experimenters commented (O) upon that behavior (16-19, 20, 24-26, 33, 38), when experimenters withdrew smiles and attention (▲) from entire sessions (30-38), and when new songs were introduced (□) (44, 46, 48). All other sessions were controlled sessions (●).

a large array of appropriate behaviors, we did find a connection between these two types of behaviors. In particular, there was an inverse relationship between her rate of self-injury and her rate of alternate appropriate behaviors: "On days when self-destructive behavior was high, appropriate musical behavior was low, and vice versa" (Lovaas et al., 1965, p. 71). The musical behaviors were complex, including singing and dancing, smiling, and laughing, in appropriate and ongoing interaction with the teachers. This finding suggested that, in addition to targeting self-injury, it also would be important to build appropriate and rich behavioral repertoires that could replace self-injury, a point that we address below in a section on treatment implications.

Two more sets of data will help provide background information. These data are presented in more detail in Lovaas and Simmons (1969). We needed to know whether Beth was a unique client, obeying her own laws of behavior, or whether other clients would show similar results. To check this possibility, we replicated one aspect of Beth's treatment with another client, Gregg. Gregg was referred to us because of particularly intense self-injurious behaviors that had not decreased with available treatments. He was 11 years old, had been hospitalized since 3.5 years of age, and had spent the preceding 2 years tied to a bed in full arm and leg restraints to prevent self-injury. He had become unable to walk, apparently as a result of the shortening of his tendons that accompanied the disuse of his legs.

Gregg's self-injurious behavior is presented in cumulative response curves, a more sensitive recording than the session averages presented for Beth. Sessions 1 and 2, each of 10-minute duration, are shown in Figure 12.2 and serve as pretreatment evaluations. As can be seen by the almost flat or horizontal direction of the curves, his rate of self-injury is very low in these recordings (about 10 hits in the beginning of session 1, none in session 2). In session 3 we delivered the same kind of treatment to Gregg as we had to Beth. That is, we provided sympathetic attentions contingent on his self-injury. These interventions are marked by the upward moving hatchmarks in Figure 12.2. As can be seen, the intervention was accompanied by a rapid rise in his rate of self-injury. When we withheld the intervention in session 4, the rate of self-injury decreased. Introduction of sympathetic comments in session 5 again was accompanied by a dramatic rise in self-injury, to about 180 hits in 10 minutes. Again Gregg recovered from the intervention in sessions 6 and 7, when this kind of treatment was withdrawn. We may well have killed him, had we continued with this dangerous use of love.

By this time, we had some inkling that self-injury may be an instance of learned behavior, in particular, learned behavior that is under social reinforcement control. If so, the most effective intervention would involve withholding reinforcement, as would be done to extinguish other forms of learned behaviors. The therapeutic effects of that operation can be observed in the case of our next client, John, an 8-year-old retarded boy who was referred to us on the same basis as Gregg. When admitted to UCLA he had multiple scars all over his head and face, and he was extremely frightened, with a heart rate exceeding 200. After two days of hospitalization his heart rate returned to a normal level, and he seemed less agitated.

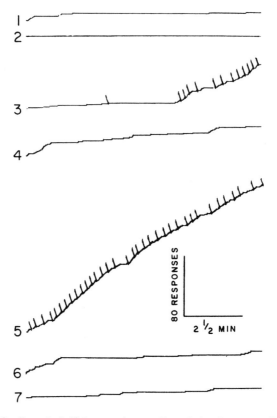

Figure 12.2. Gregg's Self-Destruction, as Cumulative Response Curves, Over Successive Sessions (1-7)

NOTE: The upward moving harchmarks in sessions 3 and 5 mark delivery of sympathetic comments, play, and so on, contingent on self-destruction.

During extinction, John's customary leg and arm restraints were removed from his bed, where he was left free to hit himself. The attending adults refrained from responding to his self-injury. As can be seen in Figure 12.3, John started session 1 with the high rate of about 2,750 self-destructive acts in the first 1.5 hours of extinction (approximately 30 hits per minute). He slowly decreased to zero by session 10. He hit himself 9,000 times before he stopped, a vivid example of how difficult it was for John to overcome the ill effects of the interventions he had previously received, however well meaning these had been.

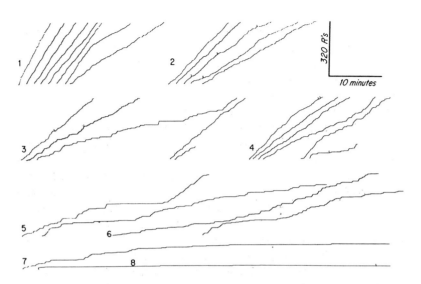

Figure 12.3. Extinction of John's Self-Destructive Behavior, Over 8 Daily, 90-Minute Sessions

NOTE: The self-destructive behavior was recorded as cumulative response curves. Session 7 shows a high of some 2,700 hits, gradually fallling over subsequent sessions to zero rate in session 8.

Subsequent studies have identified additional sources of complexity. Carr, Newsom, and Binkoff (1980) found instances of self-injury that were maintained by escape from or avoidance of demanding situations (i.e., negative reinforcement). Such avoidance/escape learning is another example of the control exerted by social variables over self-injury, because it is other people who manipulate the demands. Later, Favell, McGimsey, and Schell (1982) showed that self-injury sometimes can be an instance of self-stimulatory behavior—that is, behavior maintained by the sensory or perceptual feedback it gives the client, rather than by social events such as presentation of sympathy or removal of demands. Thus self-injury may serve a variety of different functions, depending on the client or the situation he or she is experiencing at the time.

We later discuss the implications of these findings for further research on self-injury, but let us first note some of the complexity inherent in these findings. Timeout (placing a client in relative isolation for brief intervals contingent on a behavior) often is proposed as a treatment for self-injury. Timeout may serve to decrease self-injury based on positive, social reinforcement. However, the same procedure is likely to *increase* self-injury when the behavior is based on negative reinforcement (escape-avoidance learning) and leave it unaltered when it is based on self-stimulation (sensory or perceptual reinforcement). Extinction (ignoring the behavior) would yield decreased rate of self-injury if the behavior is based on social consequences, but leave it unaltered if it is based on sensory reinforcers.

If self-injury is triggered by frustrating situations, as it seemed to be with Beth, one would need to know what kind of reinforcers a particular child values, in order to prevent their loss and avoid the situation that triggers the aggressive outbursts. Given the highly idiosyncratic nature of such reinforcers, this may be easier said than done. Some children show an obsession on small pieces of lint floating in a beam of light and react with fury when the light is not there; others prefer perfectly shaped Cheerios cereal and scream at the sight of irregularity; one may drink only from pink, semitransparent, plastic cups and tantrum if given fluids in other containers; another may demand to be driven forward and may self-injure if the father or mother happens to back the car up (forcing the parent to build a circular driveway); and so on. These are unique preferences, not easily identified. And they may not remain static; old ones may drop off and new ones emerge.

Another intervention often proposed as a treatment for self-injury is to teach clients to communicate their needs verbally (for example, saying "I need help" or "I want juice"). This intervention is intended to help clients use words rather than aggression to get what they need from others. As shown in the case of Beth, teaching communication skills or other appropriate behaviors may be highly beneficial. On the other hand, one may anticipate some difficulties: First, teaching communication skills to developmentally disabled clients is a painstaking process requiring considerable skill and usually taking place over months. Like Beth, many clients will continue to engage in self-injury while they are being taught new communication skills. Therefore, it will be necessary to have a plan for handling self-injury as well as for teaching communication skills. Second, we have seen that any number of situational factors could have a significant influence on the rate of self-injury. Consequently, replacing self-injury with verbal communication in one setting may have no influence on the rate of self-injury in other settings. Third, it will be difficult to teach clients to verbalize what their wants are if those wants are idiosyncratic and not known to the teacher. Finally, we have noted that, in some instances, self-injury does not serve a communicative or other social function; rather it serves to obtain sensory or perceptual stimulation from the environment. In these instances, the acquisition of communication skills probably will have little effect on self-injury.

Although several studies have reported success in reducing self-injury or other destructive behaviors by teaching communication skills, the problems that we have identified appear to remain. For example, Durand and Carr (1991) found that teaching communication skills greatly reduced self-injury in three clients and that these reductions persisted 18 to 24 months following treatment, during which time clients moved from one class to another within the same school. However, all three clients received extinction for self-injury in addition to training in communication skills; one client required "booster" sessions to maintain his reduction in self-injury; and none were tested to see whether reductions in self-injury occurred outside the school in which treatment took place.

The studies we have described all concern the immediate effects of behavioral interventions on rates of self-injury across a few clients. Very little data exist on the long-term effects of behavioral interventions on self-injury. Nor do we know much about the effects of comprehensive behavioral interventions on the overall functioning of autistic children, including self-injury. However, we did conduct one such follow-up on autistic children we treated in the late 1960s, many of whom also displayed self-injurious and destructive behaviors (Lovaas, Koegel, Simmons, & Long, 1973). We provided 40 hours a week of one-to-one behavioral treatment to 20 autistic children in a hospital setting for approximately 1 year. The bulk of the treatment was devoted to developing adaptive behaviors such as language, which increased appreciably. Destructive or inappropriate behaviors also were targeted for intervention and decreased with treatment. Overall, the results of the treatment were mixed. On the positive side, the treatment clearly helped the children develop complex behaviors such as language, and it clearly reduced inappropriate behaviors such as aggression. Moreover, despite large individual differences, all clients showed these improvements. On the negative side, consistent with our earlier self-injury studies, we found little evidence of response generalization. Further, the treatment gains were often specific to the situation in which treatment had taken place and many clients relapsed after treatment ended. Although Lovaas and colleagues did not present data on destructive behaviors (these data are presently being gathered), informal observations indicated that these behaviors resumed when clients relapsed.

This study shows that autistic children may return to destructive behaviors even after a treatment that combines direct attempts to eliminate destructive behaviors and extremely intense efforts to establish adaptive behaviors that could serve as alternatives to such behaviors. The return of destructive behaviors occurred in the study by Lovaas and colleagues despite the provision of more intensive reinforcement of alternative behaviors (DRA) than in any current treatment program that we are familiar with.

The shortcomings in our earlier studies raised the question of how to achieve permanent, clinically meaningful reductions in self-injury with autistic children. The 1973 follow-up study offered several clues: First, the younger children (in their preschool years) did better than older children. Their destructive behaviors had not become as extreme or dangerous as those of the older children. By intervening early, we may have been able to prevent later and more severe manifestations. Also, younger children seemed more receptive to teaching efforts so that they might be able to catch up to "normal" peers more readily and to begin to learn from them. Second, children were most likely to maintain treatment gains over time if their families had learned to provide the treatment and could continue it at home after the children left our program. By contrast, children who left our program and went to an institutional setting such as a state hospital invariably relapsed. Thus it appeared that treatment had to be provided by significant persons in children's everyday settings, rather than only by professionals in clinical settings. Third, it was necessary to treat all significant behavior problems displayed by a child, rather than a handful of "pivotal" behaviors (behaviors that, if acquired, would produce extensive response generalization). Finally, the treatment needed to normalize children's motivations (reinforcement hierarchies) by helping them acquire new, more typical reinforcers, such as the approval of "normal" peers, parents, and teachers. The acquisition of such reinforcers would make the children less likely to be controlled by idiosyncratic reinforcers, such as lint floating in beams of light. It also would curb destructive behaviors by helping us predict what situations would trigger destructive behaviors. In short, to achieve permanent reductions in self-injury and to obtain other clinically significant improvements, we found that we needed to intervene early, involve significant persons in the children's everyday environments, treat as many as possible of the problems that the children presented, and attempt to normalize the children's reinforcement hierarchies.

Lovaas (1987) reported on a treatment that incorporated all of these refinements. An intensively treated experimental group of 19 young autistic children (mean age 32 months at intake) received 2 years or more of one-to-one treatment for 40 hours a week in their homes and communities from a treatment team that included families, normal peers, and teachers of normal classes, as well as staff from UCLA. By the age of 7 years, 9 of the 19 children had achieved IQ scores within the normal range and were being passed from grade to grade in normal classes in the public schools without any intervention from us. Seven of the children were in classes for language delayed, and 2 were placed in classes for retarded and autistic children. In contrast, none of the 19 children in a similarly constituted (alternate treatment) control group achieved normal levels of functioning. About half were in classes for language delayed, and the other half in classes for autistic and retarded. The experimental group gained an average of 20 IQ points; the control group lost 5 IQ points.

A follow-up, conducted when the children had reached an average age of 13, indicated that the children in the experimental group had maintained their gains. The 9 best-outcome children scored within the normal range on a broad range of well-normal tests of intellectual, social, and emotional behaviors. In contrast, control-group children continued to perform poorly (McEachin, Smith, & Lovaas, 1993). Our preliminary data show that all but 2 of the intensively treated experimental subjects in the 1987 study are free of clinically significant problems associated with destructive behaviors. In contrast, the majority of the control group subjects are medicated and living in institutional settings, where their self-injurious and assaultive behaviors present major management problems. Should these initial observations be substantiated in further follow-ups, it may mean that permanent reductions in destructive behaviors displayed by autistic children may come only from intensive home- and community-based intervention, with a comprehensive focus, administered while the children are still in their preschool years. The remainder of this chapter discusses certain implications for research and treatment, as well as ethical or moral issues, of our findings to date.

Implications for Research Methodology

Destructive behaviors are an age-old problem. Perhaps the main reason that behaviorally oriented investigators have made progress against this problem lies in the use of an appropriate research methodology. Four aspects of our methodology seem especially noteworthy:

1. *Sensitive measures.* Figure 12.1 illustrates the importance of using sensitive and objective measures of self-injurious behavior—the dependent variable. In the case of Beth, the effect of the independent or treatment variable is subtle and superimposed on considerable day-to-day variability. Thus sensitive measures were required in order to discern patterns. Accurate, online recording also was required to detect the therapeutic effects of extinction in Figure 12.3. Because of the recording, we had some assurance, already after 10-20 minutes, that John's rate of self-injury was falling. Had the treatment been terminated after 20 minutes (as might have been done without the assurance provided by the recording that the intervention was working), we accidentally may have reinforced him on a very thin schedule and accelerated his self-injury, consistent with the kinds of treatment he probably had received in the past. Studying the effects of our interventions on the rate of self-injury led to much faster progress than we would have made by studying the effects of our interventions on "autism" (e.g., whether it made clients less autistic). "Degree of autism" is a remote, approximate, and unreliable measure of treatment effectiveness (Lovaas & Smith, 1989).

2. *The use of experimental designs.* Replication of the treatment variable is essential to reach agreement on its effect. Going back to Figures 12.1 and 12.2, we would not have been able to ascertain whether it was the intervention we provided that produced the increase in self-injury had we not replicated this intervention. The increase in self-injury could equally well have been caused by some other concurrently operating variable, such as mistreatment by others, medical complications, and so on. Replication of the treatment variable, with similar results, makes the data more believable.

3. *Analysis of individual differences.* We used single-subject designs rather than between-group designs. The use of single-subject designs was a major advance because it allowed for easier identification of individual differences. To study groups of children who had received the same diagnostic label such as "autism" or "retardation" would have obscured the results. In all probability, we were faced with a very heterogeneous group of clients. For example, as noted before, self-injurious behavior is maintained by positive social reinforcement for one subgroup of clients, negative reinforcement for a second subgroup, and sensory reinforcement for a third subgroup. Therefore, across a group of clients the effects of any intervention such as timeout may well be insignificant because the first subgroup of clients would improve, the second subgroup worsen, and the remaining subgroup stay the same.

4. *Stay inductive longer.* We have remained inductive and skeptical about theoretical propositions, as we believe this is still an early stage in our information-gathering phase about developmentally disabled persons. We have tried to stay as flexible as possible, being open for accidental discoveries (serendipity). This inductive strategy has served us well. For

example, had we been primarily interested in testing theoretical models of language, we might not have identified the importance of also treating self-injury. Had we been primarily interested in testing a particular treatment paradigm, we might not have identified the ways to improve treatment that emerged from our 1973 study. By contrast, the theoretical models that have been constructed to date have yet to demonstrate that they promote effective treatment. In fact, some have produced harmful or destructive treatments, and when this occurs, it is often the client who bears the brunt. For example, the ill effects of treatment derived from psychodynamic theories are well illustrated in Figures 12.1 and 12.2 as well as by other findings (Rutter, 1978). Yet such theories formed the basic foundation for the treatment of autism for several decades, and in many countries of the world they still do. Thus old theoretical models are difficult to replace. New ones accumulate faster than old ones winnow out. Theoretical systems are very seductive, and many psychologists and educators are fond of inventing new ones, attracting their own groups of admirers. Once or twice a year, during the past 30 years, we have read of someone discovering the cause of autism, and one such individual has discovered it on more than one occasion. The effective pursuit of discovery requires a weakening of this kind of audience control. The truth is not discovered by a show of hands.

Treatment Implications

One can characterize the intricacies that behavioral research has found by saying that there is a finely tuned match between specific environmental manipulations, a particular person's nervous system, and resultant changes in specific behaviors (Lovaas & Smith, 1989). This implies that research directed at identifying effective psychological and educational treatments for any one individual will be a painstaking procedure. Certain subtle events may have major effects whereas seemingly large environmental manipulations turn out to be nonfunctional. For example, in Figure 12.1 we saw that a seemingly trivial change in the environment (such as changing songs) may have a major impact whereas major environmental changes (such as withdrawing affection and attention) may result in no change. Out of 20 guesses about which variable caused what effects, research would show us to have been wrong on 19.

Seemingly trivial environmental changes may continue to cause mischief even after an appropriate treatment is in place. A child may have had 5 to 15 years of reinforcement for self-injury and hence may resume the behavior with the slightest encouragement. For example, just a one-second glance by the parents contingent on the child's self-injury may be sufficient to wash out any effects of an attempted extinction run. Moreover, such inadvertent reinforcement may be hard to stop because the child's parents may have had an equally long history of being reinforced for attending to the child when he or she was self-injuring. The behavior demands attention and sympathy, and only the coldest of adults would fail to spontaneously provide comfort, particularly because the comfort may temporarily put a stop to the self-injury.

Because of the finely tuned match that exists between an individual and the environment, it not surprising that permanent treatment gains are the exception rather than the rule unless children are taught in a consistent manner by all significant persons in their environment, across all of their environments, in an ongoing intervention. A similar situation also may exist for the persons who provide the intervention (parents, teachers, etc.). They may acquire skills in one setting, such as in a workshop or a clinic meeting with the treatment team, but fail to use them in other settings or over time, such as working alone with the child in the child's home or school after professionals have ended their involvement.

Despite the complexities, there were many encouraging findings. What was to become the most encouraging information became available already in the first study with Beth: She was teachable. Therefore, she could acquire new, constructive behaviors, and through reversal of the effects of previous misguided intervention, she could lose acquired maladaptive behaviors. Just as importantly, Beth and all the clients we have since worked with have responded to the same laws of learning that regulate the behaviors of other living organisms. We did not have to invent treatment programs based on guesses about behavior or processes unique to "autism." The continuity in underlying learning processes allowed us to build treatment programs based on knowledge already acquired. Said differently, the autistic children appeared to be as human as the rest of us and not separate and qualitatively different organisms.

Moral Implications

Looking at the finely tuned match between individuals and their environments in another way, we suggest that the average person, possessing an essentially average nervous system, learns behaviors from the average environment behavior that enable him or her to control that environment. This learning occurs during all waking hours, all days of the year over a lifetime, allowing for continuous behavioral adaptation. The average environment, on the other hand, does not adequately teach the person with an unusual nervous system such as the autistic or mentally retarded individual. Yet there is every reason to believe that all persons, whether disabled or not, want to learn ways of controlling their environment. In the case of developmentally disabled individuals, their nervous system is so constructed that from the average environment they do not learn language, peer play, toy play, or other skills that the rest of us use to control our environment. Therefore, their control of the environment has to be sought through more primitive means, such as assaultive and self-injurious behaviors. It does not help them when others in their environment are encouraged to reward such behaviors, as we observed in Figures 12.1 and 12.2. We can understand, then, how the developmentally disabled client may have no alternative but to engage in self-injury.

From this perspective one can view self-injurious and assaultive clients as demonstrators against the inadequate and misguided treatment they have received. This treatment was, and usually is, a treatment based on ignorance, however well-meaning we are. Just like any other demonstrators against injustice, these clients certainly are entitled to convey their message, and it is important for us all to listen to their communication. An immediate danger for professional persons in this kind of situation is to provide a service whereby the self-injury would be reduced temporarily, as would happen if one failed to develop a more competent individual. This seems an inevitable outcome when we know how poorly hands-on staff are trained in most institutions serving the developmentally disabled, and when administrators work with inadequate support and enormous problems, yet are pressured to reach quick solutions.

Concluding Comments

A major implication that can be drawn from the data we have reviewed pertains to the need to treat the whole child, in order to render effective help. This certainly was not the treatment philosophy proposed when we first began this work, some 30 years ago, when we thought we could effectively help developmentally disabled children make significant gains by addressing one or a few behaviors. We have shown that numerous behaviors need to be attended to, in all significant environments by all significant persons, over a long period of time. For the majority of children who fail to be integrated into normal society, responsible treatment needs to last for a lifetime. However intensive this intervention may be, it only equals the opportunities given to more average individuals, who learn all waking hours in all environments, and over a lifetime. If disruptions occurred at any one of these points, we would expect that the behaviors of average or normal individuals also would deteriorate.

Questions often are raised about the practicality of a comprehensive program as we have described. Can such a program in fact be realistically achieved? This question, to be answered, necessitates addressing two areas. One pertains to dissemination and one to financial considerations. With regard to dissemination we believe it is possible to teach the advanced behavioral treatment procedures required of service providers over a 6-month period. This training would involve the trainee in full-time, supervised, one-to-one behavioral treatment. In addition, for at least the first 3 months of such a training program, the trainees involved would be required to familiarize themselves with basic learning theory, particularly with methods and data pertaining to discrimination learning. So far as we can determine, few such educational opportunities exist for students entering fields such as special education, clinical psychology, and speech pathology, all concerned with serving the developmentally disabled. In contrast, we find it very unlikely that a 1- or 2-day workshop (a common procedure for disseminating information at this time) would do anything but identify whether a person is interested in receiving more training or not. We estimate that the dissemination and practical use of what we now know about effective treatment lies about 30 years behind what is currently known. How long we can afford to let such a state of affairs exist is difficult to predict but it is the responsibility of all of us to help shorten the interval.

With regard to the costs of an intensive treatment program like the one we have described, one can be rather optimistic. The assignment of one well-trained special education teacher to each family with a developmentally disabled child would cost in the neighborhood of $25,000 a year. Should the intervention start early and require 3 years to be completed, the state would pay about $75,000 for each child who achieved normal functioning. This expenditure is a great savings over the approximately $2 million spent for each developmentally disabled individual requiring institutional or supervised care over a life span.

Even for the group of children who could not leave treatment after 3 years, the reduced costs of acute care still would favor intensive and early intervention.

We finish this chapter on an optimistic note: In large part because of the behavioral work on problems such as self-injury, we have made major progress in providing clients with the least restrictive environments. Clients have moved from institutions such as state hospitals to community settings. This move has had the benefit of throwing some needed light on the problems involved in providing effective treatment, as well as encouraging society to accept responsibility for providing such treatment. Another favorable sign is the move away from the global theories of autism and retardation that existed 30 years ago. The field slowly has become more data-oriented, more flexible and apt to explore alternative treatments, and more accountable for its successes and failures. Finally, the data that have been accrued to date show self-injury and other destructive behaviors to reflect the laws of behavior that affect normal or average individuals, rather than to express some abnormal, deranged, or pathological mind. This allows us to take advantage of information existing in several areas of psychology, education, medicine, and elsewhere. It brings us closer to our client to know that we are of the same kind, that we are all in this together.

References

Carr, E. G., Newsom, C. D., & Binkoff, J. A. (1980). Escape as a factor in the aggressive behavior of two retarded children. *Journal of Applied Behavior Analysis, 13*(1), 101-117.

Durand, M. V., & Carr, E. G. (1991). Functional communication training to reduce challenging behavior: Maintenance and application in new settings. *Journal of Applied Behavior Analysis, 24,* 251-264.

Favell, J. E., McGimsey, J. F., & Schell, R. M. (1982). Treatment of self-injury by providing alternative sensory activities. *Analysis and Intervention in Developmental Disabilities, 2,* 83-104.

Griffith, R., & Ritvo, E. (1967). Echolalia: Concerning the dynamics of the syndrome. *Journal of the American Academy of Child Psychiatry, 6,* 184-193.

Itard, J. M. G. (1962). *The wild boy of Aveyron* (G. Humphrey & M. Humphrey, Trans.). Englewood Cliffs, NJ: Prentice Hall. (Original work published 1894)

Lovaas, O. I. (1977). *The autistic child: Language development through behavior modification.* New York: Irvington.

Lovaas, O. I. (1987). Behavioral treatment and normal educational and intellectual functioning in young autistic children. *Journal of Consulting and Clinical Psychology, 55,* 3-9.

Lovaas, O. I., Freitag, G., Gold, V. J., & Kassorla, I. C. (1965). Recording apparatus and procedure of observation of behaviors of children in free play settings. *Journal of Experimental Child Psychology, 2,* 108-120.

Lovaas, O. I., Koegel, R. L., Simmons, J. Q., & Long, J. S. (1973). Some generalization and follow-up measures on autistic children in behavior therapy. *Journal of Applied Behavior Analysis, 6,* 131-166.

Lovaas, O. I., & Simmons, J. Q. (1969). Manipulation of self-destruction in three retarded children. *Journal of Applied Behavior Analysis, 2,* 143-157.

Lovaas, O. I., & Smith, T. (1989). A comprehensive behavioral theory of autistic children: Paradigm for research and treatment. *Journal of Behavior Therapy and Experimental Psychiatry, 20,* 17-29.

McEachin, J. J., Smith, T., & Lovaas, O. I. (1993). Long-term outocme for children with autism who received early intensive behavioral treatment. *American Journal on Mental Retardation, 97,* 359-372.

Rutter, M. (1978). Etiology and treatment: Cause and cure. In M. Rutter & E. Schopler (Eds.), *Autism: A reappraisal of concepts and treatment* (pp. 327-335). New York: Plenum.

Sapir, E. (1921). *Language: An introduction to the study of speech.* New York: Harcourt Brace.

Whorf, B. L. (1956). *Language, thought and reality.* Cambridge: MIT Press.

13

Measurement and Evaluation of Treatment Outcomes With Extremely Dangerous Behavior

RICHARD M. FOXX
GEORGE ZUKOTYNSKI
DON E. WILLIAMS

Although much has been written about interventions with self-destructive behavior and the various issues regarding its treatment, dangerous destructive behavior toward others has remained underresearched and undertreated. Although there are several possible reasons for this, one seems particularly salient. The only danger that self-destructive individuals pose is to themselves, whereas therapists and interventionists become potential victims when the individuals are aggressive toward others. Thus, although the clinical, political, philosophical, legal, and ethical issues surrounding destructive behavior toward others perhaps are less complicated and more straightforward given that the major concern is the rights of others to be protected from danger, the chosen course of action is more likely to be a restrictive environment (e.g., a forensic placement) or pharmacological intervention rather than behavioral treatment.

The greatest clinical urgency appears to be when individuals display extremely dangerous behavior toward both others and themselves because everyone is a potential victim (Foxx, Foxx, Jones, & Kiely, 1980; Martin & Foxx, 1973). This chapter describes the development and implementation of a multifaceted treatment program for Joe, a highly aggressive and self-injurious male.[1] The program was conceptualized and implemented following several strategies.

First, a hypothesis-driven treatment model was followed (Carr, Robinson, & Palumbo, 1990) in which we designed our interventions after a formal functional analysis was conducted that identified the variables that controlled Joe's destructive behaviors. Because his destructive behaviors sometimes were under multiple motivational and setting event controls and hence could not definitely be linked to specific consequences (Carr, 1977), we also conducted an in-depth analysis of antecedent and setting events such as whether the presence or absence of destructive behavior was correlated with environmental events that repeat themselves predictably across times of the day or days of a week, or with specific activities or staff (e.g., Touchette, MacDonald, & Langer, 1985).

Second, a proactive strategy was followed in which a major concern was to attempt to ensure that the stimuli that at times would control nonproblematic behaviors would be present prior to, during, and after the reduction of the target behaviors. To help determine what procedures, skills, and activities to implement when Joe was not misbehaving, we enlisted his parents as cotreatment designers (e.g., Groden, 1989). We also sought to enhance his preexisting skills.

Third, a skill-building strategy was followed in which we sought to teach new behaviors that would serve the same function as destructive behaviors by accessing the same reinforcers as well as enhancing his quality of life. A major emphasis was placed on teaching specific communication skills such as how to request relevant reinforcers. Our plan was to teach him requesting responses that would be functionally equivalent to his destructive behavior but more effective in generating reinforcers. To facilitate this process, Joe's caretakers were taught to respond consistently and rapidly to his requests so requesting behaviors ultimately would require less effort than destructive behavior (Carr et al., 1990). Joe's parents' input was sought to help train his caretakers to be knowledgeable about his communication system. Individuals selected to provide social reinforcement were those who were deemed to be functional for Joe: his parents and familiar, favorite staff because a mutual affection existed (Carr et al., 1990).

Fourth, we sought to eliminate those situations that often motivate maladaptive behavior, such as frustration and boredom, by varying tasks and actively encouraging choice making (Dyer, Dunlap, & Winterling, 1990). Similarly, because protracted periods of inactivity or a sedentary existence can lead to aggression we greatly increased Joe's activity levels. These approaches were taken in an attempt to make escape and avoidance via destructive behavior unnecessary.

Fifth, in an effort to find an effective means of controlling Joe's destructive behaviors (Van Houten et al., 1988) we followed the least restrictive treatment model (Foxx, 1982). However, it was imperative that all assessments and initial treatments be arranged to be conducted consistently and safely because Joe's dangerous behaviors, biting of others, and strength and agility made him extremely difficult to manage. This was done by employing at least three therapists and preventing escape and injuries by use of a restraint chair.

Our functional analysis clearly revealed that the vast majority of Joe's aggression was triggered by interactional or educational instructions and negatively reinforced by the postponement or termination of these events (Carr, 1977). This eliminated using positive reinforcement alone as a treatment strategy. There were several reasons for this. One, using positive reinforcement alone at the beginning of treatment would be not only extremely dangerous, but also noncompetitive with the powerful negative reinforcement that Joe had a long history of obtaining. Two, the effective use of differential reinforcement programs with an extremely aggressive individual does not simply involve dispensing positive reinforcers but also requires the skillful integration of all of the strategies and behavioral techniques described above. Yet the technology to train such subtle skills does not appear to be readily available (Foxx, 1985a, 1985b). Hence, we did not believe it was possible to adequately train everyone responsible for Joe's treatment to conduct the elaborate and lengthy differential reinforcement programs that some have stated will reduce severe aggression (e.g., LaVigna & Donnellan, 1986) but that have failed in empirical evaluations (Paisey, Whitney, Hislop, & Wainczak, in press). Three, it did not appear to be feasible to implement such programs on a 24-hour basis. Given these factors, we sought to develop Joe's responsiveness to such positive approaches over time while simultaneously bringing his destructive behavior under control. Because Joe's aggression was primarily negatively reinforced he reacted to any programming attempt as if it represented a demand. Thus, even positive programming efforts increased the likelihood that aggression would escalate and intensify. As a result, something was needed to control Joe's aggression.

A hierarchical assessment of reductive procedures (described later) revealed that contingent electric shock was most effective in suppressing aggression. Accordingly, it was used to treat destructive behavior.

Approval to use shock was obtained from Joe's parents and all appropriate parties after they had reviewed a detailed informed consent document (Foxx, Plaska, & Bittle, 1986) that addressed pertinent ethical, legal, and clinical concerns. Because Joe was the first named plaintiff in a large federal court deinstitutionalization suit against the State of Texas, the overall program and document also were reviewed by the court's expert consultant, her experts, and the plaintiff's attorney. Joe's parents witnessed the hierarchical assessment and the first three days of shock use.

Shock was viewed as a necessary, but not sufficient, part of the overall treatment effort. We believed that its use to suppress destructive behavior made desirable responses more probable and hence created a window of opportunity for replacing destructive behaviors with new ones. This process was facilitated by arranging for all preexisting and new appropriate behaviors to involve little response effort and result in the same reinforcers as destructive behaviors (e.g., escape). As discussed by Carr and colleagues (1990), the question is not whether aversive treatments are justified because nonaversive treatments have failed or whether they work at all, but rather what is done when an individual is not misbehaving. The use of shock permitted us to avoid crisis management and reactive approaches and opt instead for proactive, skill-building communication strategies by creating a situation whereby therapists could safely employ these strategies with an extremely dangerous individual.

Method

The Client

Joe, a 36-year-old blind, mesomorphic man, had been aggressive and oppositional for much of his life. His aggressive episodes typically included self-injurious behavior, destroying property, and attacking anyone who attempted to intervene. His most common and dangerous form of aggression was biting. His self-biting episodes produced severe lacerations to his limbs. His biting attacks toward others were extremely dangerous because of their intensity and unpredictability, and over the years had resulted in permanent scarring and physical damage to fingers and arms (e.g., loss of the end of a finger). Joe's strength, agility, and ability to locate people placed them at great risk whenever they attempted to assist him or physically prevent his self-abuse.

During 22 years of institutionalization (age 11 to 32), a wide variety of unsuccessful medical, custodial, and behavioral treatments had been attempted. Similar treatment failures occurred in several group homes including one that was designed specifically for Joe. In a minimally demanding environment 28 months prior to the study, Joe aggressed toward himself 12,495 times or 14.7 times per day, toward the environment 3,567 times or 4.2 times per day, and toward others 649 times or .8 times per day.

Functional Analysis

A formal functional analysis of antecedent stimuli (e.g., familiar tasks), consequences for appropriate behavior (e.g., continuous encouragement), and consequences for aggression (e.g., loud and soft verbal reprimands) revealed that Joe's aggression was primarily escape-motivated. The treatment was conducted in a special living unit at a state residential facility.

Target Behaviors

Aggression toward self included biting, teeth banging, head hitting, pinching, and head banging or attempts to do so. The behaviors were defined as follows: *self-biting*—closure of teeth on skin; *teeth banging*—forcefully striking the arm against the teeth; *head hitting*—forcefully slapping or hitting the head with the hands or fists; *pinching*—forcefully bringing the fingers together on the skin; *head banging*—forcefully striking objects with the head. Aggression toward others included biting, pinching, grabbing, and scratching others or attempts to do so. *Biting* and *pinching* were defined as above except that they pertained to aggression toward others. *Grabbing* was defined as forcefully grasping or pulling someone's body or clothing. *Scratching* was defined as raking the ends of fingers across someone's skin. Aggression toward the environment included kicking, hitting, tearing, and throwing objects and was defined as described in Foxx, McMorrow, Bittle, and Bechtel (1986).

Phase I

To implement the overall skill-building/communication strategy it was first necessary to find an event that would act as an effective punisher for aggressive behavior. Accordingly, the purpose of this phase was to

Table 13.1 Aggression by Condition

Condition	Mean Session Duration and Range (min.)	Aggressive Behaviors per Minute
Baseline	8.1 (3.7-10.0)	5.1
DRI	2.7 (1.0-6.1)	3.2
DRI + aversive noise	11.3 (7.0-15.0)	1.1
DRI + water mist	16.0 (7.7-20.7)	1.2
DRI + shock	34.3 (21.0-47.0)	.4

evaluate several procedures hierarchically sequenced according to their aversiveness. The sequence was baseline; DRI; and then DRI combined with an aversive noise, water misting, and contingent electric shock. Because Joe's aggression was primarily negatively reinforced, the evaluations included task demand situations and compliance training (see Foxx, McMorrow, et al., 1986).

Apparatus and Materials

A Hot Shot Power Mite direct stimulator (Hot Shot Products, Inc., Savage, Minnesota) was used to deliver a 1-second electric shock of up to 18.5 milliamps (ma.) to Joe's arm. Each instance of destructive behavior was followed by "no" and approximately 1 to 2 seconds of shock(s) until Joe ceased aggressing.

Data Collection and Reliability

All sessions were videotaped and interobserver agreement was assessed for 20% of them. The mean reliability across conditions and all three types of aggression ranged from 97% to 99%.

Results and Discussion

Table 13.1 shows that the shock procedure was an extremely effective consequence. It reduced total aggression by 92% of baseline. Although the aversive noise and water misting conditions reduced aggression, it was increasing in the later sessions of both. Joe's compliance increased substantially in the shock condition. Session duration averaged 34.3 minutes there versus 8.1 minutes in the baseline (a 423% increase). Joe's outbursts and self-abusive episodes also became shorter and occurred less often over the 19 shock sessions during three days, and no destructive behavior occurred during the final 8-hour assessment day. Although Joe attempted to bite several individuals, the only casualty was the senior author, who was bitten on the calf on day one of the shock contingency. Joe's on-task performance improved as did his overall demeanor. Given these outcomes there was unanimous agreement by the treatment team and parents to incorporate the shock contingency into Joe's program.

Phase II

Program Transfer, Extension, and Maintenance Program Planning

The overall program plan followed Foxx, McMorrow, and colleagues (1986) and was designed to avoid or minimize problems associated with the use of shock (Newsom, Favell, & Rincover, 1983), to produce durable treatment effects (Foxx, Bittle, & Faw, 1989), to never intermittently reinforce aggression, and to enhance generalization across therapists and settings (Foxx, 1990).

Positive Programming Strategies and Procedures

Because Phase I demonstrated that shock would control aggression, it was possible in Phase II to implement our positive programming strategies of increasing Joe's skills, communication skills, menu of potential reinforcers, self-control and patience, and choice-making opportunities and teaching him behaviors that served the same function as his aggression. Joe was paid tokens for displaying on-task behaviors, independent living skills, and social skills and taught to exchange them for preferred activities and events. Over time, Joe participated in a variety of off-unit activities including workshop, occupational, speech, and music therapy classes; swimming; gym classes; social activities; horseback riding; walking on a nature trail; and visiting the canteen.

Data Collection and Reliability

Interobserver agreement was assessed every two weeks for videotaped training sessions at the special table in the same fashion as in Phase I. It averaged 98% across the three types of aggression. When aggression occurred outside of the intensive treatment sessions, all staff present co-signed a behavior incident report.

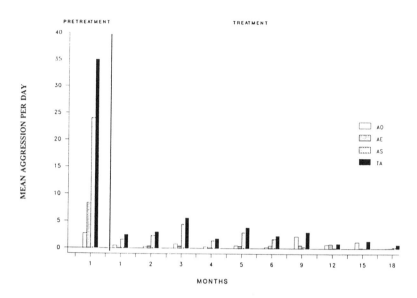

Figure 13.1. The Effects of a Multifaceted Program on Aggression

NOTE: Several custodial procedures were in effect during the pretreatment month. The symbols are as follows: TA (total aggression), or the total of AO (aggression toward others), AE (aggression toward the environment), and AS (aggression toward self). The data for months 7 through 18 are shown in 3-month blocks.

Results

As shown in Figure 13.1, a comparison of the first treatment month to the month prior to treatment revealed significant decreases in all forms of aggression: overall aggression decreased from 35 to 2.5 responses per day (a 93% reduction); aggression toward self from 24 to 1.6 responses per day (a 93% reduction); aggression toward others from 2.7 to .5 responses per day (an 81% reduction); and aggression toward the environment from 8.3 to .3 responses per day (a 96% reduction). In treatment month one, contingent shock was applied 60 times but only on 16 of 30 days (53%). In the pretreatment month, Joe injured himself 2.6 times per day (an injury report and first aid were required each time) whereas only three injuries occurred during month one (a 96% reduction).

The program has been in effect for 18 months. Figure 13.1 shows that the mean daily occurrence of all three types of aggression has remained significantly below the pretreatment month and that the trend continues to be downward. Indeed, the lowest levels of aggression have occurred in month 18, when total aggression averaged .5 times per day, and self-aggression, aggression to others, and aggression to the environment have averaged .4, .06, and .03 occurrences per day, respectively. Joe destroyed 17 personal items (e.g., clothing) in the pretreatment month versus 4 items during the past 18 months. Overall, shock has been applied 666 times and has averaged less than one shock per day during the past 15 months. On 69% of the days (373 of 537) no shock was delivered. During the past 10 months no shock was delivered on 80% of the days (ranging from 71% in month 12 to 90% in month 17).

Prior to treatment, Joe's severe aggression typically required the intervention of three or more staff members in order to prevent serious tissue damage. During the pretreatment month, emergency restraint was implemented on 10 occasions for a total of 391 minutes, whereas it has been unnecessary during the past 18 months. Currently, only one staff member typically is needed to intervene when Joe aggresses or to conduct a structured program with him. The intensity of his aggressive behavior has decreased markedly over time. No injuries to others that required medical attention have occurred since the senior author was bitten on the first treatment day.

A detailed analysis of Joe's aggression by time of day, day, setting, and antecedent events revealed some interesting findings. Because the vast majority of Joe's aggression was escape-motivated it was not surprising that aggression occurred the least on weekends (see Table 13.2) or that there also was a "honeymoon effect" on Mondays. Table 13.3 shows that 50% of Joe's aggression occurred during a 6-hour period between 8:00 a.m. and 2:00 p.m. Because this trend was apparent early in treatment, Joe's daily programmatic schedule was rearranged, whenever possible, so that his less preferred tasks and activities were presented in the afternoon. For example, Joe was enrolled in morning gym classes in the middle of month 3. During the next four months 19.5% of his aggression was displayed during this 1-hour class (range 11-23%). After this class was rescheduled to afternoons (month 7), Joe only aggressed in gym class in 4 of the 11 remaining months and his aggression averaged only 4.3%.

Although aggression occurred in 17 different settings, 68.5% of it was in the 6 settings that contained the most demands, such as his work table on the living unit. Nineteen antecedent events were identified as setting the occasion for aggression. The highest percentages of aggression were associated with instructions to perform high-demand tasks. For example, during the past 18 months, 23.3% of Joe's aggression

Table 13.2 Percentage Aggression by Day

	Mean %	Number of Months Aggression Occurred			
		Months 1-6	Months 7-12	Months 13-18	Total
Monday	11.0	6/6	2/6	2/6	10/18
Tuesday	17.6	6/6	6/6	4/6	16/18
Wednesday	17.6	6/6	5/6	5/6	16/18
Thursday	16.5	6/6	6/6	3/6	15/18
Friday	16.5	6/6	5/6	4/6	15/18
Saturday	9.9	4/6	2/6	3/6	9/18
Sunday	11.0	5/6	2/6	3/6	10/18

Table 13.3 Aggression by Time of Day

	Mean %	Number of Months Aggression Occurred			
		Months 1-6	Months 7-12	Months 13-18	Total
6 a.m.	.06	1/6	0/6	0/0	1/18
7 a.m.	6.5	5/6	3/6	2/6	10/18
8 a.m.	7.8	6/6	3/6	3/6	12/18
9 a.m.	8.4	6/6	6/6	1/6	13/18
10 a.m.	8.4	6/6	4/6	3/6	13/18
11 a.m.	8.4	6/6	6/6	1/6	13/18
12 p.m.	9.1	6/6	5/6	3/6	14/18
1 p.m.	7.8	5/6	4/6	3/6	12/18
2 p.m.	5.8	3/6	3/6	3/6	9/18
3 p.m.	4.5	4/6	2/6	1/6	7/18
4 p.m.	5.8	4/6	3/6	2/6	9/18
5 p.m.	4.5	3/6	2/6	2/6	7/18
6 p.m.	4.5	3/6	1/6	3/6	7/18
7 p.m.	2.0	0/6	3/6	0/6	3/18
8 p.m.	2.0	1/6	1/6	1/6	3/18
9 p.m.	0.0	0/6	0/6	0/6	0/18
10 p.m.	0.0	0/6	0/6	0/6	0/18
11 p.m.	0.0	0/6	0/6	0/6	0/18
12 a.m.	0.0	0/6	0/6	0/6	0/18
1 a.m.	0.6	0/6	1/6	0/6	1/18
2 a.m.	0.6	1/6	0/6	0/6	1/18
3 a.m.	2.6	3/6	0/6	1/6	4/18
4 a.m.	5.8	5/6	1/6	3/6	9/18
5 a.m.	3.9	3/6	1/6	2/6	6/18

occurred during living unit table-top activities. Similarly, during the 9 months that he has been in the facility workshop, 15.6% of all aggression has occurred there.

General Discussion

The results showed that Joe's aggressive behavior was successfully treated. This success was especially gratifying because his aggression (a) was particularly dangerous and physically damaging, (b) had been chronic and very resistant to a variety of treatments, (c) had prevented his participation in social and habilitative activities, and (d) had resulted in the routine use of emergency physical restraint by four to five large men. Joe's aggression has been maintained at low levels (i.e., more than 90% reduced from baseline) even though ever increasing demands have been placed on him to participate in new activities and environments with new therapists. He currently spends the majority of his day away from the unit, attending recreational activities and classes, running errands, and visiting the canteen. He has received no behavior control medication and has made regular home visits and trips to the community with his family.

Two programmatic components or factors appeared to play major roles in reducing Joe's negatively reinforced aggressive behavior during the initial treatment phase. First, contingent electric shock served as an aversive consequence for his escape/avoidance behaviors (i.e., aggression or SIB often led to no demands, demand reductions, or a cessation of demands). The steps taken to ensure that the shock procedure was carefully controlled followed the model and recommendations of Carr and Lovaas (1983), Foxx, McMorrow, and colleagues (1986), and Foxx, Plaska, and colleagues (1986). Second, intensive compliance training increased the probability that escape/avoidance behavior would occur yet prevented the possibility for negative reinforcement.

The long-term success achieved appears to have been due to several factors. One, Joe's aggression never produced escape from educational and vocational demands (Carr, 1977). Two, a history of appropriate responding for positive reinforcement especially with complex social contingencies was established. Hence, as Joe's behavior became increasingly appropriate over time, the density of naturally occurring positive reinforcement correspondingly increased. Three, the complexity and relevance of the tasks he was given were increased. Four, a systematic effort was made to increase Joe's self-control and patience. Five, a long-standing problem, activity avoidance via aggression, was virtually eliminated by ascertaining and responding to the communicative function of this behavior. Six, Joe's choice-making opportunities were greatly increased. Seven, we ensured that the stimuli controlling nonproblematic behavior were present throughout the treatment. Eight, Joe's parents participated in every treatment decision and phase. They served as a valuable resource regarding Joe's learning history, reinforcer preferences, and communication skills. Nine, Joe was taught request responses that were functionally equivalent to his destructive behaviors but more efficient in generating and securing reinforcers. Ten, the individuals selected to provide the most salient forms of social reinforcement were those who shared a mutual affection with Joe. Eleven, we sought to make destructive and escape and avoidance behaviors irrelevant by reducing or eliminating Joe's boredom and frustration by varying tasks and actively encouraging choice making. Twelve, the maintenance of response suppression was considered by actively programming for maintenance (Foxx et al., 1989), keeping the treatment and maintenance programs similar (Foxx & Livesay, 1984), and ensuring change agent and programmatic accountability (Foxx, McMorrow, et al., 1986). Because the most desirable long-term clinical outcome for a program that includes shock would be to discontinue it and yet continue to maintain a significant behavioral reduction, our next goal is to discontinue shock and replace it with a less intrusive procedure for Joe's infrequent aggression.

Note

1. Videotape excerpts of Joe's program were shown during Dr. Foxx's presentation at the conference where this information was first presented.

References

Carr, E. G. (1977). The motivation of self-injurious behavior: A review of some hypotheses. *Psychological Bulletin, 84,* 800-816.

Carr, E. G., & Lovaas, O. I. (1983). Contingent electric shock as a treatment for severe behavior problems. In S. Axelrod & J. Apsche (Eds.), *The effects of punishment on human behavior* (pp. 221-245). New York: Academic Press.

Carr, E. G., Robinson, S., & Palumbo, L. W. (1990). The wrong issue: Aversive versus nonaversive treatment. The right issue: Functional versus nonfunctional treatment. In

A. Repp & N. Singh (Eds.), *Perspectives on the use of nonaversive and aversive interventions for persons with developmental disabilities* (pp. 361-379). Sycamore, IL: Sycamore.

Dyer, K., Dunlap, G., & Winterling, V. (1990). Effects of choice making on the serious problem behaviors of students with severe handicaps. *Journal of Applied Behavior Analysis, 23,* 515-524.

Foxx, C. L., Foxx, R. M., Jones, J. R., & Kiely, D. (1980). Twenty-four hour social isolation: A program for reducing the aggressive behavior of a psychotic-like retarded adult. *Behavior Modification, 4,* 130-144.

Foxx, R. M. (1982). *Decreasing the behaviors of retarded and autistic persons.* Champaign, IL: Research Press.

Foxx, R. M. (1985a). Behavior mythology. In *Proceedings of the Eighth National Conference of the Australian Behaviour Modification Association* (pp. 1-26). Melbourne: Australian Behaviour Modification Association.

Foxx, R. M. (1985b). The Jack Tizzard memorial lecture. Decreasing behaviours: Clinical, ethical and environmental issues. *Australia and New Zealand Journal of Developmental Disabilities, 10,* 189-199.

Foxx, R. M. (1990). "Harry": A ten year follow-up of the successful treatment of a self-injurious man. *Research in Developmental Disabilities, 11,* 67-76.

Foxx, R. M., Bittle, R. G., & Faw, G. D. (1989). A maintenance strategy for discontinuing aversive procedures: A 52-month follow-up of the treatment of aggression. *American Journal on Mental Retardation, 94,* 27-36.

Foxx, R. M., & Livesay, J. (1984). Maintenance of response suppression following overcorrection: A 10-year retrospective examination of eight cases. *Analysis and Intervention in Developmental Disabilities, 4,* 65-79.

Foxx, R. M., McMorrow, M. J., Bittle, R. G., & Bechtel, D. R. (1986). The successful treatment of a dually diagnosed deaf man's aggression with a program that included contingent electric shock. *Behavior Therapy, 17,* 170-186.

Foxx, R. M., Plaska, T. G., & Bittle, R. G. (1986). Guidelines for the use of contingent electric shock to treat aberrant behavior. In M. Hersen, A. Bellack, & P. Miller (Eds.), *Progress in behavior modification* (Vol. 20, pp. 1-33). New York: Academic Press.

Groden, G. (1989). A guide for conducting a comprehensive behavioral analysis of a target behavior. *Journal of Behavior Therapy and Experimental Psychiatry, 20,* 163-169.

LaVigna, G. D., & Donnellan, A. (1986). *Alternatives to punishment: Solving behavior problems with non-aversive strategies.* New York: Irvington.

Martin, P. L., & Foxx, R. M. (1973). Victim control of the aggression of an institutionalized retardate. *Journal of Behavior Therapy and Experimental Psychiatry, 4,* 161-165.

Newsom, C. D., Favell, J. E., & Rincover, A. (1983). The side effects of punishment. In S. Axelrod & J. Apsche (Eds.), *The effects of punishment on human behavior* (pp. 285-316). New York: Academic Press.

Paisey, T., Whitney, R., Hislop, P., & Wainczak, S. (in press). A case study of comprehensive, non-aversive treatment of severe SIB and aggression. In R. Romanczyk (Ed.), *Self-injurious behavior: Etiology and treatment.* New York: Plenum.

Touchette, P. E., MacDonald, R. F., & Langer, S. N. (1985). A scatter plot for identifying stimulus control of problem behavior. *Journal of Applied Behavior Analysis, 18,* 343-351.

Van Houten, R., Axelrod, A., Bailey, J. S., Favell, J. E., Foxx, R. M., Iwata, B. A., & Lovaas, O. I. (1988). The right to effective behavioral treatment. *Journal of Applied Behavior Analysis, 21,* 381-384.

14

Severe Problem Behaviors of Children With Developmental Disabilities

Reciprocal Social Influences

JILL C. TAYLOR
EDWARD G. CARR

Little is known of the impact that problem behavior in people with developmental disabilities has on others. There is some indication that children with serious developmental disabilities affect overall family functioning (Schopler & Mesibov, 1984); however, the discrete effects of problem behavior per se rarely have been studied (cf., Carr, Taylor, & Robinson, 1991; Durand, 1986; Durand & Kishi, 1987). The effects of child behavior on adults—that is, child effects (Bell, 1968)—have not been adequately documented in our field.

There is an important reason that the investigation of child effects is necessary for the theoretical growth of the field of developmental disabilities. Specifically, the notion of child effects is implicit in operant theory. One assumption derived from the functional analysis literature is that problem behaviors serve a purpose, that is, enable an individual to obtain reinforcement such as adult attention or escape from a difficult

AUTHORS' NOTE: Support for preparation of this chapter was provided in part by Cooperative Agreement No. G0087C0234 from the U.S. Department of Education, "A Rehabilitation Research and Training Center on Community-Referenced Technologies for Nonaversive Behavior Management."

task (Carr, Robinson, & Palumbo, 1990; Durand, 1986). In short, child problem behaviors *cause* adults in the environment to provide access to reinforcement. Consider escape behavior (i.e., problem behavior evoked by aversive task situations) as an example. It has been assumed that escape behavior is maintained partially through negative reinforcement processes in which the termination of adult demands strengthens child behavior problems (Carr & Durand, 1985b; Iwata, 1987). Child effects also are assumed to operate in the maintenance of attention-seeking problem behavior (i.e., problem behavior exhibited under conditions of low adult attention). Here, it is the contingent presentation of adult attention on problem behavior that is thought to strengthen such behavior (e.g., Carr & Durand, 1985b). Surprisingly, although the assumptions just outlined concerning adult behavior are basic to operant theory, they have not been directly tested. Given the importance of operant theory to applied behavior analysis, such a test is warranted.

We have begun a line of programmatic research concerning the effects of the severe problem behaviors of children with developmental disabilities on adults. Our focus has been on socially motivated problem behaviors, specifically those evoked and maintained by adult-mediated stimuli. The present chapter describes escape problem behavior (that evoked by aversive task stimuli), attention-seeking problem behavior (that evoked by low levels of adult attention), and socially avoidant problem behavior (that evoked by high levels of adult attention). Thus far we have completed three studies on socially motivated problem behavior, and several more are underway. In what follows, the general findings of these studies are described.

Problem Behavior Related to Task Stimuli:
Escape Problem Behavior

Escape problem behavior may be evoked by aversive academic or task situations. Traditionally, the level of aversiveness has been defined in terms of the rate and/or difficulty of task demands (Carr & Durand, 1985a; Iwata, Dorsey, Slifer, Bauman, & Richman, 1982). Based on operant theory, escape behavior is presumed to be maintained by negative reinforcement processes in the following way. An adult presents a child with a task demand. In response the child engages in severe problem behavior, such as self-injury. This behavior, in turn, causes the adult to stop delivering task demands. In the absence of further task demands, the child ceases self-injuring or aggressing. In the scenario just described both the adult and the child are negatively reinforced: The child is reinforced by the termination of adult-delivered task demands, and the adult is reinforced by the termination of child problem behavior (Carr & Durand, 1985b; Iwata, 1987). Despite the fact that escape problem behavior has been studied for more than 15 years (Carr, Newsom, & Binkoff, 1976) and is receiving increasing systematic attention (Iwata, 1987), specific adult responses to child problem behavior have not been measured. The goal of the first study in our series on reciprocal influences (Carr et al., 1991) was to document the impact of escape problem behavior on adult teaching practices.

In contrast to traditional research in which children are the subjects, in studies of child effects, the adults are the subjects. Thus, to avoid possible confusion, the children are referred to as participants, and the adults are referred to as subjects.

Four pairs of preschool children participated in the study. Each pair included a child who exhibited significant problem behaviors in a task situation (the problem child) and a child who exhibited relatively few or no problem behaviors in a task situation (the nonproblem child). The children had been given various diagnoses including autism and developmental delay. All had mental retardation and significant language deficits.

Twelve female undergraduates pursuing careers in special education or human services served as subjects. Before entering the study, all adult subjects received standardized, criterion-based training in discrete-trial teaching (Koegel, Russo, & Rincover, 1977) and basic child-management strategies such as differential attention and extinction (Lovaas, 1981). They also were required to pass a discrete-trial performance test.

Each adult subject was assigned to a pair of children. The adult and children participated in five teaching sessions. Several common table-top preschool tasks (e.g., matching colors, labeling pictures) were identified for each child. Each adult was free to choose which child to work with, which task to present for what duration, and whether to provide a child with a play break. To ensure that the results of the study were not idiosyncratic to a particular adult subject, several adults taught each pair of children.

The results of the study fell into two categories: (a) validation of the problem and nonproblem child behavior groups and (b) child effects. The frequency of child problem behaviors distinguished the problem and nonproblem child groups. Instructional behavior (such as task commands, disciplinary commands, disapproval) presented to the nonproblem child in the pair rarely was followed by misbehavior. In contrast, adult instructional behavior presented to the problem child was followed by misbehavior the majority of the time. Finally, adult noninstructional behaviors (such as teaching the other child in the pair, preparing instructional materials) rarely evoked problem behavior in either of the children in the pair.

The data described thus far concern the child's behavior toward the adult. Especially relevant to the present discussion is the adult's behavior toward the child, that is, child effects. Results indicated that adults responded differentially to the two groups of children. Adult subjects distributed task commands unequally between the two children, presenting significantly more task commands to children from the nonproblem group than to children from the problem group. Thus the frequency of child behavior problems influenced quantitative aspects of adult-child interaction (i.e., how much the problem children were taught).

Problem behaviors also influenced the content of what was taught (i.e., the variety and type of tasks adults presented to the children). For purposes of data analysis, we divided the children's tasks into two types: tasks that were followed by problem behavior on less than 25% of the trials in which they were presented (tolerated tasks), and tasks that were followed by problem behavior on more than 25% of the trials in which they were presented (untolerated tasks). Although adults rarely taught the children from the problem group, when adults did present tasks, they used a restricted range of the tasks available to them. More specifically, adult subjects presented tolerated tasks more often than untolerated tasks. In contrast, with the nonproblem group, adult subjects presented a wider range of the tasks available.

This study tested and supported a central premise of the operant theory of problem behavior, namely, that adults and children exert reciprocal influences on one another. More specifically, regarding child effects, the study demonstrated that child behavior affects adult behavior and, furthermore, that child behavior influences adult behavior in a way that contributes to the maintenance of child misbehavior. Escape behavior served to reduce task demands. This reduction in task demands, in turn, negatively reinforced misbehavior, thereby increasing the likelihood that it would occur again in the future.

In terms of applied issues, the study demonstrated that children shape the amount and content of what they are taught. This fact implies the need for a system in which adults review the basis for curricular decisions, especially in cases where curricula are not diverse and comprehensive (i.e., heavily emphasize a particular type of instruction or task), or when items are dropped from the curriculum. This system would ensure that decisions were based on the educational needs of the child rather than on child effects.

Problem Behavior Related to Social Stimuli: Attention-Seeking and Social Avoidance

These two functional categories of problem behavior are discussed together as both are related to rates of adult attention: one form being associated with low levels of attention (attention-seeking) and the other being associated with high levels of attention (social avoidance). Attention-seeking problem behavior occurs under conditions of low adult attention (Carr & Durand, 1985a, 1985b; Durand & Crimmins, 1988; Iwata et al., 1982) and is reinforced by contingent adult attention (Iwata et al., 1982). Based on operant theory, attention-seeking behavior presumably is maintained by positive reinforcement, in the form of increased adult attention. This process is illustrated in the following example. An adult is not attending to a child. As a consequence, the child tantrums and overturns furniture. This behavior, in turn, causes the adult to attend to the child. Upon receiving adult attention, the child stops tantrumming. In the situation just described, the child is positively reinforced for tantrumming by increased adult attention, and adult attending, in turn, is negatively reinforced by the termination of child tantrums. In this manner, maladaptive adult-child interactions are maintained. A basic component of this interactive sequence, namely, how adults respond to child misbehavior, has not been systematically analyzed in the literature.

In contrast to the attention-seeking behavior profile, socially avoidant problem behavior is evoked by high levels of adult attention, both in academic task situations (Taylor & Carr, 1992a) and in social-interactive play situations (Taylor, Romanczyk, Ekdahl, & Miller, in press). The term *social avoidance* only recently has been introduced into the literature, although similar ideas have been discussed (e.g., Demchak & Halle, 1985), and data consistent with the notion have been reported (e.g., Touchette, McDonald, & Langer, 1985). Based on operant theory, socially avoidant problem behavior is presumed to be maintained by negative reinforcement processes. For example, an adult attends to a child. In response, the child screams and bangs his or her head. Screaming and head banging, in turn, cause the adult to stop attending to the child. In the absence of adult attention, the child no longer screams and head bangs. In this vignette, both the adult and the child are negatively reinforced: The child is reinforced by the reduction in adult attention, and the adult is reinforced by the termination of the child's problem behavior (Taylor & Carr, 1992a, 1992b). As in the previous example, a basic component of this interactive sequence, namely, how adults respond to child misbehavior, has not been systematically analyzed in the literature.

The second and third studies in our research program (Taylor & Carr, 1992a, 1992b) pertain to attention-seeking and socially avoidant problem behavior. The second study (Taylor & Carr, 1992a) consisted of an experimental validation procedure that served two purposes: (a) to document empirically the existence of a group of children who exhibited the socially avoidant behavior profile and (b) to validate the distinctiveness of the attention-seeking behavior profile group (AS), the socially avoidant behavior profile group (SA), and a comparison nonproblem behavior profile group (NP). It was important to establish the distinctiveness of these three groups for theoretical reasons (described later) and to lay the groundwork for the third study in our series.

In contrast to the first study described, in the second investigation the children were the subjects. Nine child subjects were involved: Three purportedly exhibited frequent, severe problem behavior under conditions of low adult attention (the AS group); three, under conditions of high adult attention (the SA group); and three purportedly exhibited a few mild problem behaviors at various times (the NP or nonproblem group). Child subjects were selected on the basis of teacher interview, teacher questionnaire, and direct observation. Subjects were elementary-school age; had received a variety of diagnoses including pervasive developmental disorder, autism, and multihandicapped; and had mental retardation as well as significant language delay.

Female undergraduate and graduate students pursuing careers in special education or clinical psychology, blind to the purpose of the study, served as experimenters. During experimental sessions, an experimenter was placed in a teaching situation with a child and presented him or her an easy matching task (i.e., preassessed to generate 100% correct responding). Easy tasks were selected to minimize escape behavior, as we were interested in the effects of adult attention, rather than aversive task situations, on child behavior.

Three experimental conditions, presented in accordance with an ABACA reversal design (Barlow & Hersen, 1984), were used to assess the effects of adult attention on the different child behavior profile groups. The A condition referred to high attention, wherein the adult provided attention to the child during the entire experimental session. In B, the low-attention condition, adult attention was reduced to 25% of the session (Durand & Crimmins, 1988; Taylor & Carr, 1992a). C referred to the contingent-attention condition, which was designed to assess the frequency with which members of each behavior profile group sought out adult attention or initiated social interactions. In this condition, adult attention was provided only contingent on child social initiations.

Results indicated that the AS, SA, and NP behavior profile groups responded differentially to adult attention. Children in the AS group (a) frequently initiated social interactions with adults (in the contingent-attention condition), (b) displayed low levels of problem behavior and high levels of compliance and work under conditions of high adult attention, and (c) exhibited high levels of problem behavior and low levels of compliance and work under low adult attention. In contrast, children in the SA group (a) rarely initiated social interactions with adults, (b) exhibited their highest level of problem behavior under high adult attention, and (c) displayed their lowest levels of problem behavior under low adult attention. Finally, the NP group also displayed a unique behavior pattern. These children (a) frequently initiated social interactions with adults and (b) exhibited low levels of problem behavior and high levels of compliance and work under all experimental conditions.

The data from the second investigation suggested (a) that there exists a group of children for whom high levels of adult attention evoke problem behavior (the SA group) and (b) that the AS, SA, and NP behavior profiles represent three empirically distinct behavior profile groups. Furthermore, by demonstrating that two unique problem behavior groups (i.e., AS and SA) are affected differentially by adult attention, these results show that adult attention interacts with child behavior profile. These data replicate and extend previous research on the operant theory of child problem behavior: The data concerning the AS group replicate previous research on this behavior profile group (e.g., Carr & Durand, 1985a; Durand & Crimmins, 1988), and the data concerning the SA children extend theory by identifying a previously undocumented behavior profile group.

The identification of the SA behavior profile group has several implications for the development of alternative reinforcement and educational strategies. For example, social stimuli, such as praise and physical contact, frequently are used as consequences for appropriate behavior and accurate task performance. However, these stimuli are not likely to function as reinforcers for children from the SA group. Instead, nonsocial stimuli, such as a brief break from adult interaction, may be more efficacious. Similarly, many educational strategies (e.g., discrete-trial teaching, incidental teaching, peer modeling) involve intense adult-child interaction. For this reason, such strategies may be ineffective or even counterproductive for children with the SA behavior profile. Alternative interactive modes and teaching strategies, such as computer-assisted instruction (e.g., Plienis & Romanczyk, 1985), merit exploration with these children.

The experimental validation also raised theoretical questions. Although adult attention affected the AS and SA groups differentially, the problem behaviors of both groups were under social control. An interesting question concerned whether the problem behaviors of both groups also exerted social control over adult behavior. That is, did misbehavior that was affected by adult attention also affect adult attention? Did the problem behaviors of the AS group increase adult attention, and did the problem behaviors of the SA group reduce adult attention? We sought answers to these questions in the third study in our research program.

As in the first child-effects study described, the adults in this investigation were the subjects. They consisted of 15 undergraduates pursuing careers in special education or human services who were blind to the purpose of the study and were unfamiliar with the child participants. Adult subjects received discrete-trial training (Koegel et al., 1977), child-management training (e.g., Lovaas, 1981), and a performance test before entering the study.

The nine children described in the experimental validation study, three from each of the AS, SA, and NP behavior profile groups, served as the child participants. These children were placed into three "trios," each consisting of a child from the AS group, a child from the SA group, and one from the NP group. Then, each adult subject was assigned to a child trio. Next, three pairs of children were constructed from each trio: One pair consisted of the child from the AS group and the child from the NP group (the AS-NP pair), one pair consisted of the child from the SA group and the child from the NP group (the SA-NP pair), and the remaining pair consisted of the child from the AS group and the child from the SA group (the AS-SA pair). Adult subjects conducted multiple teaching sessions with each pair of children in their assigned trio. The pair format was used because group instruction in the school frequently consisted of this format, particularly when a child with severe behavior problems was involved.

The results of the study fell into two categories: (a) those validating that the children exhibited their purported behavior profile (i.e., AS, SA, NP) and (b) those pertaining to child effects. Data concerning the frequency, severity, and specificity of behavior problems exhibited by the children verified their group membership and distinctiveness. The children in the AS group engaged in frequent, severe misbehavior (i.e., self-injury, aggression, tantrums) under conditions of low adult attention. In contrast, children in the SA group displayed frequent, severe problem behaviors under conditions of high adult attention. Children in the NP group, in comparison, engaged in a few mild problem behaviors such as whining or crying.

Regarding child effects, adults responded differently to the three behavior profile groups. First, the adults' initial response to child behavior problems was examined. In the AS-NP child pairs, with both the AS and NP group members, adult subjects overwhelmingly responded to child problem behavior by increasing the amount of attention given to the children and rarely responded by decreasing the amount of attention. A different pattern of initial adult responses was observed in the SA-NP pairs. Adult subjects rarely increased attention, and frequently decreased attention in response to the misbehavior of the SA group. In contrast, with the NP group, adults increased attention following most problem behavior episodes and decreased attention much less often. Another pattern of initial adult responses occurred with the AS-SA child pairs. When the AS behavior profile group misbehaved, adults frequently responded by increasing attention and infrequently by decreasing attention. In striking contrast, when children in the SA behavior profile group misbehaved, adults rarely increased attention; they decreased attention following an overwhelming majority of problem behavior episodes.

Child effects also influenced how adults distributed their attention to the children during teaching sessions. Adults gave children in the AS and NP groups high levels of attention in each teaching session and gave children in the SA behavior profile group low levels of attention. More specifically, for the AS-NP pairs, adults gave about twice as much attention (on the average) to children in the AS group than to children in the NP group. In the SA-NP pairs, however, the NP group members received much more adult attention than the SA group members. With the AS-SA pairs, adults gave children in the AS group twice as much attention as they gave to the SA group. The inequalities in attention were established within the first teaching session and were maintained over the remaining sessions. This fact suggests that child effects were powerful, immediate, and durable.

The data described so far suggest that child effects exerted powerful control over quantitative aspects of adult behavior (i.e., how much attention adults distributed to children). Child effects also influenced qualitative aspects of adult behavior (i.e., how adults attended to children). Child behavior influenced the type of task that adults presented. Recall that adults had a variety of tasks available to present to each child. Of those tasks, half required ongoing adult-child interaction (e.g., a receptive language task in which the adult asked the child to touch various objects in the classroom). These tasks were referred to as high-interaction tasks. Tasks that did not require ongoing adult-child interaction were called low-interaction tasks (e.g., a matching task in which the adult gave the child materials and required him or her to work independently). In the AS-NP pairs, adult subjects presented a higher percentage of high-interaction tasks to the members of the AS behavior profile group and presented a greater percentage of low-interaction tasks to the members of the NP behavior profile group. Within the SA-NP pairs, adults distributed a higher percentage of the high-interaction tasks to the NP children and a greater percentage of the low-interaction tasks to the SA children. Within the AS-SA pairs, adults gave a higher percentage of the high-interaction tasks to the AS group and a greater percentage of the low-interaction tasks to the SA group.

As noted, within the AS-NP child pairs, children from the AS behavior profile group exhibited frequent, severe problem behavior under low adult attention, while children from the NP group exhibited mild, infrequent problem behavior under those same conditions. If child problem behaviors are conceptualized as an aversive stimulus (punisher) for any adult behavior that they follow, then children in the AS group provided high-intensity punishment to adults when they did not attend to the children, whereas children in the NP group provided mild, intermittent punishment. Adults responded to these punishment contingencies by providing high levels of attention and high-interaction tasks to both groups of children and by exhibiting proportionately greater involvement with the AS group than the NP group.

As noted, within the SA-NP child pairs, children from the SA group frequently displayed severe problem behavior contingent on adult attention, whereas children from the NP group exhibited mild, infrequent problem behavior under conditions of no adult attention. That is, children in the SA group provided high-intensity punishment to adults when they attended to the children, whereas children in the NP group provided mild, intermittent punishment when adults ignored them. Adults responded to these punishment contingencies by decreasing attention and high-interaction tasks given to the SA group and by increasing these to the NP group.

The differential child effects generated by the AS-SA pairs were most striking and conformed to the AS and SA patterns described earlier. That is, adults received frequent, high-intensity punishment for ignoring the AS group and responded by increasing attention and high-interaction tasks. In contrast, adults received frequent, high-intensity punishment for attending to the SA group and responded by decreasing attention and high-interaction tasks.

The results of this study have several theoretical implications. Child problem behavior has a powerful impact on both quantitative and qualitative aspects of adult behavior toward children. By demonstrating that child problem behaviors have consistent, reliable effects on adult behavior and, further, that different child behavior profiles have different effects on adults, the present data support the operant theory of problem behavior.

One purpose of the present investigation was to determine whether the problem behaviors exhibited by the AS and SA behavior profile groups, in addition to being affected by adult attention, also affect it. The problem behaviors of the AS group, which occurred primarily under conditions of low adult attention, apparently punished adults for not attending to them and caused the adults to provide high levels of attention. In contrast, the misbehavior of the SA group, which occurred almost exclusively under high adult attention, apparently punished adults for attending to them, causing the adults to reduce attention. Thus adults and children constituted reciprocal social systems wherein adult attention influenced, and was influenced by, child problem behavior.

The data from the present investigation also suggest that the three different types of child pairs (the AS-NP pairs, the SA-NP pairs, and the AS-SA pairs) constituted three unique social systems, each with different effects on adults created by the combined influences of each child in the teaching pair. This fact is illustrated most clearly in the case of the NP behavior profile group. When paired with members of the AS group, members of the NP group received little adult attention. Conversely, when paired with the SA group, NP group members received much attention. The AS-NP and SA-NP pairs created different social systems with opposite child effects. Thus adult behavior may be best understood as the product of the combined child effects of each child in the teaching pair.

General Discussion

The three studies reviewed validate a central premise of operant theory: Child behavior affects adult behavior, and different child behavior profiles affect adult behavior differentially. These data also have several applied implications, including those related to assessment (i.e., functional analysis), treatment implementation, and maintenance.

First, attention to reciprocal influences and child effects may enhance functional analysis. Within the field of developmental disabilities, there has been a growing emphasis on basing interventions on functional analysis (Carr, Robinson, & Palumbo, 1990). Significantly, the literature suggests that interventions based on a thorough functional analysis tend to produce better outcomes than interventions that are not based on such an analysis (Carr, Robinson, Taylor, & Carlson, 1990). Thus, by identifying the environmental events that control child misbehavior, functional analysis may enhance treatment outcome. Nonetheless, crucial treatment variables often are overlooked in functional analysis procedures. Although such procedures identify the environmental events that affect child problem behavior, they do not determine the effects of problem behavior on the social environment (Emery, Binkoff, Houts, & Carr, 1983). For example, when a functional analysis indicates that adult behavior (such as ineffective commands) evokes misbehavior, the analysis is considered complete because the variable that controls child misbehavior (in this case, ineffective commands) has been identified. A parallel functional analysis rarely is conducted to determine the variables that maintain the adult's ineffective commands. Presumably, just as child misbehavior is a product of adult antecedents and/or consequences, adult behavior also is controlled by child antecedents and/or consequences. Thus a traditional functional analysis that provides only information about the adult antecedents and consequences of child misbehavior is incomplete and must be broadened to include the role of child behavior in maintaining ineffective adult behavior. In short, a functional analysis must be performed on both adult and child behavior. Such an analysis has been called a systems functional analysis (Emery et al., 1983). This type of functional analysis would provide more information about the full range of variables that control problem behavior. As such, it is likely to yield more effective and efficient interventions.

Child effects have other implications for assessment. Specifically, these effects may render the use of direct observation and/or questionnaires problematic. Teachers may adopt interactive and educational strategies that minimize child misbehavior. As a result, direct observation and questionnaires that focus on the child's current behavior may not capture all the variables that control child problem behavior. For this reason, systematic measurement of teacher behavior is recommended. Interviews and questionnaires should include questions pertaining to any strategies the teacher has adopted that reduce or prevent problem behavior episodes. Anecdotal data from Taylor and Carr (1992b) strongly suggest that teachers can identify such strategies as well as the reason that they adopted them (e.g., in the case of a child with the SA behavior profile, a teacher might state that low-interaction tasks were used because the child preferred to work alone). Thus interviews and questionnaires should be used in conjunction with some type of systematic manipulation of adult behavior and should target any changes in adult behavior toward the child that have occurred over time.

Second, the data from our research program indicate that children shape teacher behavior and curriculum content. This fact has implications regarding treatment implementation. Child effects may account for the fact that some children who have behavior problems early in the school year no longer misbehave by the end of the year. In some cases, it may be that the child truly no longer has a behavior problem, and the reduction in his or her misbehavior is due to the successful application of treatment procedures. However, in other cases, it may be that child effects create the appearance that the child's behavior is no longer problematic. That is, the child may have shaped his or her teacher into adopting interactive and teaching strategies that do not evoke problem behavior. In the absence of such antecedent stimuli, misbehavior may not occur. For example, a child with the AS behavior profile may teach his or her teacher to provide high rates of attention and physical contact, thus reducing the frequency of misbehavior. Conversely, the teacher of a child with the SA behavior profile may learn to present low-interaction tasks and to avoid physical contact with that child. Reductions in child problem behavior thus may be the result of child effects rather than programmatic behavior change.

Finally, knowledge of child behavior profiles and child effects also has implications for the issue of treatment maintenance. Research on treatment acceptability or social validity (e.g., Kazdin, 1981; Wolf, 1978) indicates that adults prefer interventions that pose little risk to the target child, generate few undesirable side effects, and do not disrupt the target child's environment, regardless of the efficacy of the intervention (Kazdin, 1981). If an intervention is deemed unacceptable according to these standards, adults may discontinue treatment implementation. The result is poor maintenance. Data from the first study (Carr et al., 1991) illustrate this point. Recall that when teaching strategies evoked child misbehavior, adult teaching attempts were punished and adults stopped teaching. When this outcome occurs, maintenance of academic skills is likely to be poor. Similarly, in the third study (Taylor & Carr, 1992b), adults failed to present certain types of tasks. In these examples, it is the behavior of the treatment agent (i.e., the teacher) that fails to maintain over time, and the result may be poor treatment maintenance. Traditionally, maintenance failure has been attributed to procedural inadequacies (Sulzer-Azaroff & Mayer, 1977). Although procedural inadequacies may account for many such failures, child effects also may contribute to maintenance failure. The general implication is that, when possible, interventions that generate few negative child effects should be chosen over those that generate many negative child effects. For example, assume that an educational intervention is being prescribed for a child with the SA behavior profile and that the targeted skill can be taught equally well using either a high-interaction task or a low-interaction task. In the interests of maintaining the teacher's instructional behavior, it would seem prudent, at least initially, to prescribe the low-interaction task because it generates fewer problem behaviors. In contrast, given a choice between a high- versus low-interaction task for a child with the AS behavior profile, it would seem prudent, at least initially, to use the high-interaction task because this type of task generates fewer problem behaviors for these children. In general, intervention strategies that produce few negative child effects (problem behaviors) are more likely to be implemented by adults and maintained over time. When adults persist at implementing effective intervention strategies, children are more likely to acquire and maintain skills as well as improve behaviorally.

References

Barlow, D. H., & Hersen, M. (1984). *Single case experimental design: Strategies for studying behavior change* (2nd ed.). New York: Pergamon.

Bell, R. Q. (1968). A reinterpretation of the direction of effects in studies of socialization. *Psychological Review, 75,* 81-95.

Carr, E. G., & Durand, V. M. (1985a). Reducing behavior problems through functional communication training. *Journal of Applied Behavior Analysis, 18,* 111-126.

Carr, E. G., & Durand, V. M. (1985b). The social communicative basis of severe behavior problems in children. In S. Reiss & R. Bootzin (Eds.), *Theoretical issues in behavior therapy* (pp. 219-254). New York: Academic Press.

Carr, E. G., Newsom, C. D., & Binkoff, J. A. (1976). Stimulus control of self-destructive behavior in a psychotic child. *Journal of Abnormal Child Psychology, 4,* 139-153.

Carr, E. G., Robinson, S., & Palumbo, L. W. (1990). The wrong issue: Aversive versus nonaversive treatment. The right issue: Functional versus nonfunctional treatment. In A. Repp & N. Singh (Eds.), *Current perspectives on the use of nonaversive and aversive interventions for persons with developmental disabilities* (pp. 361-379). Sycamore, IL: Sycamore.

Carr, E. G., Robinson, S., Taylor, J. C., & Carlson, J. I. (1990). Positive approaches to the treatment of severe behavior problems in persons with developmental disabilities: A review and analysis of reinforcement and stimulus-based procedures. *Monograph of the Association for Persons With Severe Handicaps, No. 4.*

Carr, E. G., Taylor, J. C., & Robinson, S. (1991). The effects of severe behavior problems in children on the teaching behavior of adults. *Journal of Applied Behavior Analysis, 24,* 523-536.

Demchak, M., & Halle, J. W. (1985). Motivation assessment: A potential means of enhancing treatment success of self-injurious individuals. *Education and Training of the Mentally Retarded, 20,* 25-38.

Durand, V. M. (1986). Self-injurious behavior as intentional communication. In K. G. Gadow (Ed.), *Advances in learning and behavioral disabilities* (Vol. 5, pp. 141-155). Greenwich, CT: JAI.

Durand, V. M., & Crimmins, D. B. (1988). Identifying the variables maintaining self-injurious behavior. *Journal of Autism and Developmental Disorders, 18,* 99-117.

Durand, V. M., & Kishi, G. (1987). Reducing severe behavior problems among persons with dual-sensory impairments: An evaluation of a technical assistance model. *Journal of the Association for Persons With Severe Handicaps, 12,* 2-10.

Emery, R. E., Binkoff, J. A., Houts, A. C., & Carr, E. G. (1983). Children as independent variables: Some clinical implications of child-effects. *Behavior Therapy, 14,* 398-412.

Iwata, B. A. (1987). Negative reinforcement in applied behavior analysis: An emerging technology. *Journal of Applied Behavior Analysis, 20,* 361-378.

Iwata, B. A., Dorsey, M. F., Slifer, K. J., Bauman, K. E., & Richman, G. S. (1982). Toward a functional analysis of self-injury. *Analysis and Intervention in Developmental Disabilities, 2,* 3-20.

Kazdin, A. (1981). Acceptability of child treatment techniques: The influence of treatment efficacy and adverse side effects. *Behavior Therapy, 12,* 493-506.

Koegel, R. L., Russo, D., & Rincover, A. (1977). Assessing and training teachers in the generalized use of behavior modification with autistic children. *Journal of Applied Behavior Analysis, 10,* 197-205.

Lovaas, O. I. (1981). *Teaching developmentally disabled children: The ME book.* Baltimore, MD: University Park.

Plienis, A. O., & Romanczyk, R. G. (1985). Analysis of performance, behavior, and predictors for severely disturbed children: A comparison of adult versus computer instruction. *Analysis and Intervention in Developmental Disabilities, 5,* 345-356.

Schopler, E., & Mesibov, G. B. (Eds.). (1984). *The effects of autism on the family.* New York: Plenum.

Sulzer-Azaroff, B., & Mayer, G. R. (1977). *Applying behavior analysis procedures with children and youth.* New York: Holt, Rinehart & Winston.

Taylor, J. C., & Carr, E. G. (1992a). Severe problem behaviors related to social interaction I: Attention seeking and social avoidance. *Behavior Modification, 16,* 305-335.

Taylor, J. C., & Carr, E. G. (1992b). Severe problem behaviors related to social interaction II: A systems analysis. *Behavior Modification, 16,* 336-371.

Taylor, J. C., Romanczyk, R. G., Ekdahl, M. M., & Miller, M. L. (in press). Escape behavior in task situations: Task versus social antecedents. *Journal of Autism and Developmental Disorders.*

Touchette, P. E., MacDonald, R. F., & Langer, S. N. (1985). A scatter plot for identifying stimulus control of problem behavior. *Journal of Applied Behavior Analysis, 18,* 343-351.

Wolf, M. M. (1978). Social validity: The case for subjective measurement or how applied behavior analysis is finding its heart. *Journal of Applied Behavior Analysis, 11,* 203-214.

PART V

Ethical Considerations in Treatments for Destructive Behavior

15

Ethics of Treatment Evaluation

Balancing Efficacy Against Other Considerations

ROBERT L. SPRAGUE

Introduction

Many ethical issues are being raised in science today, particularly concerning misconduct in science. Widespread public attention was generated in the topic of scientific ethics by a number of highly publicized cases and the publication of several books on the topic (Bell, 1992; Broad & Wade, 1982; Kohn, 1986; Panel on Scientific Responsibility, 1992). Unfortunately, a number of these highly publicized cases involve biomedical sciences, and only a few involve behavioral science, which is the main thrust to this book. A number of times I have been invited to make presentations about scientific ethics, or really the lack thereof, because I was a whistleblower in one of these cases involving developmentally disabled people (Marsa, 1992; Monson, 1991; Roman, 1988). Usually the presentations involve scientific ethics in research with severely handicapped people such as those with destructive behavior (Sprague, 1987, 1989). However, many of the issues in these cases involve issues surrounding the client in clinical experiments. With this background in mind, I discuss the issues involving balancing the efficacy of treatment with other significant interests, especially those of the client and the family.

My Personal Experience

In discussions of ethics, it seems helpful for the reader to know something of the writer's personal experience to aid in placing the writer's comments in perspective. In fact, perspective is such an important concept that it was included in the title of a book recently published on treating disturbed behavior (Repp & Singh, 1990). With the acknowledgment of this observation, I briefly outline some of my experiences that are germane to this issue.

In our society there often is a major division between the professional directing treatment and the client receiving the treatment. Of course, there are many reasons for the development of this division, which sometimes is contentious, but certainly one factor is the perspective of the individual involved. Whereas the professional who is conducting research often has career and advancement in his or her profession in mind, the client and family primarily want the best, most effective treatment that is available. Although this observation is almost a truism, nevertheless many people on both sides of the division often cannot take the perspective of the other party. One way to obtain both perspectives is to play both roles, which often is a very enlightening experience.

During the 1960s for several years my wife and I cared for foster children in our home. After several infants were placed in our home until adoptive homes could be found for them, the Illinois Department of Children and Family Services classified our home as a placement for exceptional children who had special needs. An infant who was microcephalic and epileptic was placed in our home and lived there about 3.5 years (Sprague, 1976). Although I am a university professor of psychology with a joint appointment in special education, Bethy (not her real name) taught me many things that I had not learned in my graduate education or, for that matter, in my teaching and research. For one thing, I quickly gained the perspective of the burdened parent who is searching for some type of help with a very difficult child.

Because of her seizures, I persuaded our pediatrician to refer Bethy to a children's hospital in a large nearby city for a thorough pediatric neurological workup. When we arrived at the hospital with Bethy and I saw the crib in which they planned to place her, I suggested to the nurse that Bethy was a very agile and energetic child and that she very likely would quickly climb out of the crib. The nurse coldly told us she could handle any situation. With such a rebuff of our suggestion, we told Bethy goodbye and walked to the elevator. While we were waiting for the elevator, Bethy joined us, after climbing out of the crib within 1 to 2 minutes. We took Bethy back to the nurse, who was somewhat more accepting of our suggestions during our second meeting. She agreed to place a clear plastic bubble over the crib to keep Bethy in the crib. However, after we left, for some unexplained reason somebody on the staff tied a sheet around the sides of the crib, blocking Bethy's view of the room. In our home neither her view nor her freedom of the house had been restricted. When the medical testing was completed in a few days and I returned to take Bethy home, to my amazement she was body rocking in the crib. We had never observed this pathological behavior before, and we attribute the development of the symptomatology to blocking of her vision by the hospital staff (Sprague & Newell, 1987).

For the past 12 years I have been a member of behavior management committees at facilities where mentally retarded residents are placed. The most difficult to manage cases typically are brought before such committees when the interdisciplinary treatment teams need independent assessment of their treatment plans and/or when the staff have few if any more ideas for effective treatments for the severe destructive behavior the residents often display.

One memorable case involved a tall, muscular young man who often showed aggressive behavior, sometimes in the dining room. At the request of another psychologist, I observed this man in the dining room situation. Although he was aggressive, he did not appear exceptionally difficult to handle. Later, the man was referred to a community hospital for an evaluation of an unrelated medical problem. The staff of the institution did not adequately prepare him for the journey and stay at a strange place; consequently, he became quite aggressive upon admission to the hospital. The community hospital used four-point tie-down as the first step to control his aggression. This restraint enraged him, and he became verbally very agitated and struggled violently against the restraints. The staff of the hospital then escalated this power struggle to intramuscular injections of haloperidol with rapidly increasing doses. In about 24 hours, he developed a severe case of neuroleptic malignant syndrome and nearly died. The aftermath of this episode apparently caused him to be quite unstable for a number of months after this event. In my opinion, his behavior was managed unprofessionally and inappropriately.

Adequate informed consent of the person (parent/guardian) being given the treatment is crucial. Once a person faces a very difficult medical decision with inadequate or improper information, the importance of this issue becomes very clear. After diabetic failure of her kidneys, my wife needed surgery to implant a shunt for future hemodialysis treatment. When she was still partially incoherent due to the seriousness of her illness, a nurse asked her to sign a consent form before surgery could be scheduled the next day. My wife asked me to read the form because she did not feel able to read and understand it. When I read the form, it became obvious that the form contained unacceptable exculpatory language:

> I hereby request and consent to and authorize the transfusion of blood. . . . I hereby acknowledge that . . . there is no known test for determining the existence or nonexistence of viral hepatitis in blood and that I fully understand that the transfusion of blood or components to me may result in viral hepatitis or other untoward reactions. . . . Notwithstanding such information . . . I hereby release my attending physician, Dr. _____, [the] _____ Hospital, a corporation, its personnel, and any other persons participating in my care from any responsibility whatsoever for any . . . untoward reaction caused by any such transfusion. . . . I will never sue for or on account of . . . any untoward reaction resulting from said transfusion and that this instrument may be placed as a defense to any action or other proceedings that may be brought, instituted or taken by me against the above designated parties. (Sprague, 1985, p. 10)

In reflecting on these personal experiences, some generalizations can be made. First, there is no better way of obtaining another person's perspective than by assuming a role similar to his or her role. Second, dramatic cases such as the episode of the young man taken to a community hospital can provide information about what to do and what not to do. In his case, the professionals rapidly escalated the treatment intrusiveness with little regard for other considerations. Finally, appropriate informed consent is essential.

Ethics of Human Experimentation

Nazi Treatments Shocked the World Into Concern About Research

Since the Nazi regime in Germany and its atrocities against prisoners in concentration camps, there has been great concern about human experimentation and appropriate regulations concerning such experimentation (Lifton, 1986). A brief review of some of these events will set the stage and provide background for discussing the issue of balancing values against each other. The speed with which the Nazis established their concentration camps and instituted their torture under the guise of experimentation is noteworthy. Adolf Hitler came to power in January 1933, and he suspended the constitution about one month later, in February 1933. Dachau, one of the most infamous concentration camps, established in the village of Dachau just outside Munich, opened March 21, 1933. Less than one month later, April 14, 1933, the first prisoner was shot and killed in Dachau (Distel & Jakusch, 1978).

One of the experiments conducted in the concentration camps that still causes heated controversy, even in this decade, was the investigation of methods of reviving fliers who had been chilled because of their aircraft being shot down over the North Sea. The current controversy is about whether the limited data on recovery from hypothermia, which, apparently, is available only from the Nazi experiments, is so tainted that it should not even be used today (Siegel, 1988). Because the Germans highly valued their air force and experienced pilots were in short supply, they undertook what seems on the surface to be a reasonable scientific project, namely developing treatments to save lives. However, as is abundantly evident now with most of the facts about the experiment available, the experiments constituted horrible torture because there was absolutely no attempt by the Nazi experimenters to balance the research on treatment against other humane considerations.

Approval for the medical experiment was given December 4, 1941, from the SS in Berlin (Distel & Jakusch, 1978, p. 143). Some of the letters from this period are gruesome, indeed:

Please find enclosed a summary of the results of the experiments using animal warmth for warming up, conducted on persons who have been subjected to very low temperature. At the moment I am working on experiments on human beings to prove that persons whose temperature has been reduced by dry freezing can be just as quickly warmed up as those who have been placed in cold water for [a period of time]. . . . Up to the present moment I have exposed about 30 naked persons to the open air and have reduced their body temperature within a period of 9 to 14 hours to between 27 and 29 degrees centigrade. [In regard to warming of prisoners in a sauna, the experimenter writes the following.] The least complicated solution would be for me to join the "Waffen-SS" and along with Neff to be transferred to Auschwitz. Here large scale experiments can be conducted on the re-warming of persons who have been subjected to extreme cooling in the open air. . . .
Your obedient and grateful servant
      Heil Hitler
      Yours faithfully
      S. Rascher

In another letter, bizarre thanks was given to God for cold weather:

> We have had extreme frost in Dachau recently, *thank God,* [italics added] which has enabled us to settle the question of saving air-frozen persons. Single subjects were placed outside in temperature of −6 degrees centigrade, where their body temperature fell to 25 degrees and they suffered peripheral freezing but all were revived by a hot bath. (Distel & Jakusch, 1978, p. 143)

In other documents, these deaths were reported matter-of-factly. "More than 200 experiments were carried out in which 70-80 persons died. . . . A total of 360-400 experiments were carried out on 280-300 experimental subjects 80-90 of whom died" (Distel & Jakusch, 1978, p. 143).

Lifton, in his book *The Nazi Doctors: Medical Killing and the Psychology of Genocide,* gives names and details of the physicians who willingly conducted these inhuman experiments. For whatever value it might be, Lifton noted that only one university professor was involved: "Dr. Johann Paul Kremer . . . was fifty-nine years old when he arrived there [Auschwitz] in August 1942. . . . Since 1935 an anatomy professor at the University of Munster, he was the only university professor to serve as an SS camp doctor" (Lifton, 1986, p. 292). In an attempt to explain how university-educated physicians could cooperate with such horrible experiments, Lifton develops a theory he terms "psychological . . . doubling" or the "division of the self into two functioning wholes" (Lifton, 1986, p. 418).

Moving from the Nazis to the 1960s, now consider a widely known case of clinical research with mentally retarded people that caused outrage and helped lead to the development of federal regulations in the area of human experimentation. In 1947 Dr. Saul Krugman went to New York University, and in 1954 he became a consulting physician to the Willowbrook residential facility on Staten Island, New York. Because conditions there were so crowded and unhealthy, the facility experienced tremendous problems with hepatitis. Between 1953 and 1957, 350 cases were diagnosed among the residents and 76 among the staff, giving an incidence of 25 per 1,000 among the residents and 40 per 1,000 among the staff whereas the corresponding rate in the population of the State of New York was 25 per 100,000—about 1/100th of the Willowbrook rate. Krugman developed a series of experiments to investigate this problem and obtained permission from the administration of the facility to establish a special ward for his research. He gave newly admitted children doses of pooled Willowbrook virus obtained from a large number of residents who previously had developed hepatitis. He soon discovered there were two types of hepatitis virus, and for this discovery he received acclaim from the medical community. Franz Ingelfinger, who is well-known because he was editor of *The New England Journal of Medicine,* wrote, "By being allowed to participate in a carefully supervised study . . . the patients themselves benefited" (Rothman & Rothman, 1984, p. 265). Such praise soon was vaporized by the harsh criticism of others who cited this experiment as a shocking example of lack of concern for patients and failure to follow ethical standards.

Codes Were Developed

Due to the Nazi experiments described above, nations of the world developed a code of conduct for research very soon after World War II. This code was, of course, the well-known Nuremberg Code. More relevant to the discussion here, however, is the Declaration of Helsinki:

> The Declaration of Geneva of the World Medical Association binds the doctor with the words, "The health of my patient will be my first consideration." . . .
>
> I. Basic Principles. . . .
>
> 2. Clinical research should be conducted only by scientifically qualified persons. . . .
>
> 4. Every clinical research project should be preceded by careful assessment of inherent risks in comparison to foreseeable benefits to the subject or to others. . . .
>
> II. Clinical Research Combined with Professional Care. . . .
>
> 1. [T]he doctor should obtain the patient's freely given consent after the patient has been given a full explanation. . . .
>
> 2. The doctor can combine clinical research with professional care. . . .
>
> III. Non-therapeutic Clinical Research. . . .
>
> 2. The nature, the purpose, and the risk of clinical research must be explained to the subject by the doctor. (Declaration of Helsinki, 1964, p. 473)

However, even informed consent, which is the capstone of this code, has its limitations in some situations ("Medical Treatment and Human Experimentation," 1975).

Perhaps even more important to the discussion here is the more recent Buenos Aires Oath (1988):

> Aware that, in the absence of ethical control, science and its products can damage society and its future, I pledge that my own scientific capabilities will never be employed merely for remuneration or prestige or on instruction of employers or political leaders only, but solely on my personal belief and social responsibility—based on my own knowledge and on consideration of the circumstances and the possible consequences of my work—that the scientific or technical research I undertake is truly in the best interests of society and peace. (p. 1)

Interest in Human Experimentation

Following the developments of codes, the 1970s became a decade of great interest in the ethics of human experimentation and the beginning of regulation, particularly at the federal level, to control human research. Although this is not an exhaustive list of books on the topic, an enumeration of some of the publications in this era is enlightening. Katz (1972) wrote one of the earlier books, in which he outlined some of the widely publicized cases of violation of commonly accepted standards of treatment and research that galvanized the public's attention. One of those cases was the injecting of live cancer cells into patients. For students of the history of medical methodology, Hershey and Miller (1976) wrote an ethics book that details the major advances in methodology from the application of statistical analyses to research by LaPlace in France in 1814 to the development of double blind control methods in the late 1940s. Gallant and Force (1978) added another book to the list. Specialized books began to appear written for disciplines within the broad range of clinical research. There are a number of these books, but only two are mentioned here: Bloch and Chodoff (1982) wrote a book entitled *Psychiatric Ethics,* and Dokecki and Zaner (1986) wrote the book *Ethics of Dealing With Persons With Severe Handicaps.* The crucial issue in this debate was captured by a National Academy of Sciences report (1975) entitled *Experiments and Research With Humans: Values in Conflict.* In experimentation, values are often in conflict. Principles of balancing these values are sorely needed. Even in the early 1980s the mere listing of publications in this area had grown so much that the list fills a book (Walter & Kahn, 1984).

One final consideration is needed to complete properly this discussion on research. Research is vital and needed to solve many of humankind's most pressing problems. Given this need, Haywood (1977) pointed out this important principle: "psychologists may also be guilty of unethical conduct if they fail to conduct important research" (p. 311). Thus, again the issue is not which principle to follow, but how to balance the conflict between the values expressed by the principles.

What Is Efficacy?

Principles Influencing Decisions

In an earlier version (Schroeder, Rojahn, & Oldenquist, 1989) of a recently published paper, Schroeder, Rojahn, and Oldenquist (1991) listed a number of viewpoints important in considering treatment of destructive behaviors. Because this is the best treatment of the subject that I have seen, I review the principles they listed in some detail.

1. Utilitarianism. This general principle dictates that everybody should abide by the rule that states our actions should promote the general good of humankind. Although this is a principle upon which there would be broad general agreement, often it is very difficult to obtain agreement following this rule when details of a situation are considered. An example might elucidate this problem. A general good is that every child should be educated to a level permitting the child to become a contributing member of society. But what if the education of the severely handicapped child costs 10 to 20 times that of educating the average child? It must be kept in mind also that the potential contribution of the severely handicapped child is generally less than that of the normal child even when a maximal effort is made regardless of cost. In school districts where there are limited funds, many people would strongly argue that more general good is created by a somewhat more expensive education for the normal child at the same time as providing a useful but less costly education for the severely handicapped child. Of course, this is not an idle hypothetical illustration; such arguments regularly occur under current conditions of a sluggish economy and limited tax funds.

2. Paternalism. This is the position that authorities, usually in the form of parents or administrative officials, are in a better position to decide the treatment for the severely handicapped individual than the individual him- or herself. Often this may be the case when the handicapped individual is unable to indicate his or her own wishes. However, people can indicate their wishes

in many forms other than spoken language. The behavioral reaction of handicapped people often can be an indication of their wishes.

3. Dignity. This principle is, as are most of these terms, difficult to describe operationally. But it seems to mean that each person has worth within and of him- or herself and, therefore, should be treated with respect and given as much autonomy as is possible in the situation.

4. Rights. In the United States the concept of individual rights in relation to the rights of the group has been taken almost to the extreme. There are many current examples of this. For example, does a single individual or musical group have the right to make huge sums of money by preying upon a situation? One such situation might be a musical group pandering to the sexual interests of some males by vividly describing how a female could be forced into sexual intercourse. Obviously, the right to free speech is given high value in our society. But the right to be secure also is given high value. How does society appropriately determine which right predominates in this situation?

Another example might be the right of the individual researcher to pursue and develop ideas about treatment. Does that individual consequently have the right to promote, in addition to his or her creative ideas, his or her own income and professional visibility while providing for severely handicapped people a treatment that is regarded by some in the individual's profession as worthless at best and harmful at worst? This debate occurs repeatedly. In one domain, the marketing of medication, a formal system has been developed for making these decisions—the Food and Drug Administration. However, many AIDS activists now bitterly complain that the system is stacked against them and is too cumbersome and slow to allow promising drugs on the market for those very seriously ill individuals who desperately need some form of effective treatment.

Meaning of Efficacy

Behavior Change

In this context, efficacy means an improvement or lessening of the destructive behavior displayed by the client. Improvement may take many forms that are measurable. It may mean the episodes are less violent although the frequency may stay the same. It may mean the frequency of disturbed behavior over a period of time is reduced but the intensity of the behavior is unchanged. It may be that the stimulus events associated with the onset of the disturbed behavior are limited. Of course, in the optimal situation, improvement would occur in all the above conditions.

Permanency of the Change

Efficacy implies the behavioral change will be of long duration or permanent. Sometimes treatment effects may be of very short duration. It is typical that stimulant medication for attention-deficit-disordered children lasts only 4 to 6 hours. Nevertheless, the stimulant medication is the most frequently used treatment with these children even though it has to be repeatedly administered over months or years.

On the other hand, sometimes treatments are judged ethically questionable because their effects are permanent. One of the many problems associated with the now defunct psychosurgery was that it was not reversible. In the area of birth control, some techniques are judged less useful because they are permanent, such as vasectomy for the male and tubal ligation for the female. Fortunately or unfortunately, depending upon your viewpoint, almost no behavioral treatments for destructive behavior are permanent.

Limited Side Effects

Treatments that have no or limited untoward effects are the most desirable. Perhaps no better illustration of this principle can be found than in the area of psychopharmacology, which is my research area. All medications have side effects, even the widely accepted and widely used aspirin. The task for the psychopharmacological researcher is to find medications or combinations of medications and/or other treatments that minimize side effects.

Limited Financial Cost

All treatments for destructive behavior, I will assert, are financially costly although often the client and family do not directly pay this cost. Often these high costs (up to $100,000 per year for one seriously disturbed client) are borne by taxpayers through institutional costs. Such costs may total $3.6 billion per year nationally (National Institutes of Health, 1991).

Limited Costs in Human Terms

A variety of concepts are covered under this principle. Human cost would involve excessive time and effort on the part of the family and caregivers. Another cost might be emotional in the sense that the client and family are uncomfortable with the treatment although they still may accept it. Sometimes the human cost can be placed in cultural terms (Wolfensberger, 1974). Whereas sexual discussion and openness might be acceptable to many modern U.S. parents for their teenage or young adult daughter or son, in some cultures such discussions would not be acceptable.

Considerations for Balancing

The primary issue from the perspective of balancing ethical considerations is that a multiplicity of considerations typically must be taken into account. Seldom is the situation simple, with only a few of the aspects listed below involved. Moreover, the considerations are not given equal weight by the various involved parties. Different clients with different orientations and different family backgrounds may evaluate these aspects quite differently.

Treatment Effectiveness

Treatment must be effective with minimum side effects in comparison to other appropriate treatments. Although this principle seems like a truism acceptable to almost everybody, this is not always the case for a variety of reasons. In a psychopharmacology course I teach primarily for special education graduate students, I always use the example of enuresis in this context. Bed wetting is the most common behavioral disorder among young children. There are two widely accepted treatments for the disorder. One technique is the bell and pad or buzzer blanket, which has a long history of successful treatment and which produces the highest cure rate. Another treatment is psychoactive medication that has substantial and sometimes serious side effects. It is less successful than the conditioning treatment (Stewart, 1975). Yet treatment of enuretic children with medication is far more common than treatment using the conditioning technique. The reason for this discrepancy and violation of an accepted principle is probably that parents usually seek out physicians as the first source of professional contact for the problem. It is obvious that physicians are medically trained, which usually implies they are less well-informed about behavioral techniques. This is not the only example of disregard for this principle, but perhaps it is the best example.

Reversible Effects

Effects of treatment should be reversible and return to baseline within a reasonable period of time. As noted above, some treatments are less valued because of their permanency. When a treatment is permanent, such as tubal ligation, it does not allow for the individual to make a different decision based on changed life circumstances. Fortunately or unfortunately, again depending on how you perceive this situation, the treatment of destructive behavior has few or no treatments that are permanently effective. Perhaps the only exception is institutionalization, which may have profound long-term effects on the individual if the institutionalization is of long (years) duration.

Least Intrusive Treatments

The least intrusive treatments (from a broad perspective) should be tried first. This principle, more commonly known as the least restrictive alternative, is widely applied today. Nevertheless, it is particularly appropriate for treating people with destructive behavior. All too often a decision is made to rapidly escalate the intrusiveness of the treatment when faced with destructive behavior as some of the cases cited above illustrate. Usually, but not always, this tendency toward rapid escalation is improper and should be resisted.

Promote Independence

Treatments that promote a more independent life for the client should be tried first. In the past, this principle generally has been ignored in developing plans for the mentally retarded individual with destructive behavior. Many practitioners of behavioral conditioning have downplayed the role of the environment and focused on conditioning techniques. Even people with severe disabilities usually strive for an independent manner of living in the environment although they may have very limited ability of expressing this desire. Promoting independent living wherever possible adds to the dignity of the individual, another principle always worth considering when balancing the effectiveness of treatment.

Least Interference

Treatments that have the smallest interference with daily activities are preferable. Although specialized wards and facilities for treatment of destructive behavior probably are useful, their impact on the daily life of the client should be seriously considered. There are several reasons for this concept. Perhaps the most important reason is that when an impaired individual is removed from his or her normal environment, training and learning that occur in the specialized environment may not generalize back to the normal environment. This problem has occurred numerous times when specialized housing units have been established.

Financial Cost

Treatments that financially cost less are preferable. This principle is obvious and understood by everybody except possibly by those professionals providing the expensive treatment and those families who do not directly pay for the treatment. Clearly, this principle should not be given primary importance, but neither should it be forgotten in the balancing equation. Perhaps one way in which agreement could be reached on this principle is if all the participants in the decision are provided information about the relative costs of treatment. Often physicians are not aware of the cost of medications they prescribe just as families often are not aware of the cost of treatments provided by a public organization.

Fast Results

Treatments that are effective in a shorter duration of time are generally preferable to treatments that require longer durations of time. Clearly, clients suffering from a disorder would prefer a shorter treatment time to a longer time. But as is true of all the principles listed here, this principle has to be weighed against other considerations. Generally, the client would prefer a more permanent, effective treatment even if it took a longer period of time than a quicker treatment that was not effective for as long a period of time.

Customer Acceptance

Treatments with substantial customer acceptance should be tried before other treatments. Rates of client acceptance vary from time to time, and fashionable treatments come and go. To elicit and maintain cooperation of the client and family, weight should be given to the client acceptance of various treatment modalities.

Intrusive Techniques

In severely destructive cases, it may be necessary to rapidly accelerate to intrusive treatment techniques. This principle is, of course, the opposite to the third principle above. In the balancing equation, one must consider the safety of the client, the impact of the destructive behavior, and the reaction of the caregivers in suggesting treatment plans. Although rapid escalation often is not desirable, there are situations in which rapidly moving to intrusive techniques is the best course of action.

Previous Treatment Failure

Clients with long histories of treatment failures to a variety of treatment modalities probably will require more rapid escalation to intrusive treatment techniques. It is quite apparent that a client with a long history of treatment failures usually has been exposed to many different kinds of treatments provided by a number of different professionals. In some cases, many of the direct caregivers may see the task as futile and worthless to try again. In this situation, dramatic techniques that have some promise of being effective are worth considering to try to recapture the cooperation and, more important, the enthusiasm of the caregivers.

Escalation With Older Clients

Older clients with longer histories of destructive behavior may require more rapid escalation to intrusive treatments than younger clients. In the same manner as described in the principle above, older clients are likely to be less tractable. If this is the case, more intrusive techniques may be needed.

Mechanisms for Ensuring Balanced Consideration

1. Decisions should be made by a committee. It is now generally accepted that most of the decisions involving serious destructive behavior should be made by a committee of stakeholders: those people with a decided interest in the case. As is known, rules have been developed by federal and state agencies to mandate such committees. The

committee should involve the client if practical, the client's immediate relatives who are concerned and involved with the client, and various professionals and caregivers who have an interest in the client. The size of the committee is difficult to specify, as large groups are unwieldy and very difficult to schedule on any kind of a regular basis. As is generally required, one person should be identified as the chair of the committee with administrative responsibility. A committee with one person as the leader is much more likely to accomplish its goals than in shared leadership arrangements. More important than this factor, however, is the delegation of accountability and subsequent ability to identify the accountable person. All too often, at least in academia, committees are used as a method of diffusing or, in fact, eliminating responsibility and accountability. When a person's welfare is at stake as is the case usually in such clinical cases, diffusion of accountability must be strongly resisted.

2. A hierarchy of opinion and input should be sought. In these clinical situations, absolute democratic practices probably are not the most effective manner in which difficult decisions can be made. First, it is obvious that not all the people involved have the same level of interest, commitment, emotion, and concern. Those with the highest levels of these factors, such as the client and family, should be given the most weight when a decision is being reached.

3. Most decisions will be debatable. Given that decisions about destruction behavior are quite complex with many unknowns in spite of strong opinions often held by the stakeholders, it should be expected that there seldom will be unanimous decisions. Rather, it is most likely that the decisions reached will be tentative awaiting further data or results. People of goodwill also are quite likely to perceive the situation differently from each other, largely depending upon the perspective they hold. Again, as I have stressed throughout this chapter, perspective is a crucial variable. If the participants on the committee enter into the meetings with the understanding that there probably will be differences of opinion often strongly held and believed, then split decisions should be more palatable to them.

4. Emotional appeal should be downgraded. It is easy to warn people that emotional aspects of decision making should be kept to a minimum, but it is quite a different thing to put this principle into practice. Repeating the maxim that emotional aspects should be minimized, however, might be of some value in the difficult task of balancing one principle against another in making decisions.

5. Direct experience is the most valuable. People on the committee should, hopefully, defer to those stakeholders who have direct experience with the behavior. This may mean that the professional will need to listen closely to and take the advice of the direct caregiver who has observed the destructive behavior many times and often in many situations. Particularly in initial contacts with the client and family, the professional should closely listen to the reports of the family, who usually have observed the behavior for a period of years and have observed changes in frequency and/or intensity depending on the environment. Nonprofessional direct caregivers are often a storehouse of information if questioned properly and treated as important members of the treatment team.

6. Bureaucracy should be kept to a minimum. Some paperwork and bureaucracy are inevitable when important group decisions about a client's life are being made. The frame of reference, however, always should be that the bureaucracy is to be minimized.

Summary

A brief history of societal concern about research on clinical disorders was given, beginning with the cruel Nazi experiments in the World War II concentration camps and continuing to the concerns of the 1990s. A few codes of conduct for research were cited to point out aspects of clinical research that are deemed crucial to proper ethical conduct in this area. Some background literature was cited from diverse areas in an attempt to sort out important principles to direct the delicate and difficult task of balancing principles when making treatment decisions for destructive behavior. A set of principles was listed for consideration by the reader in making important clinical decisions. The final topic concerned how decisions should be made in a committee format, as it is assumed that these important decisions always will be made by a group of stakeholders.

References

Bell, R. (1992). *Impure science: Fraud, compromise and politics influence in scientific research.* New York: John Wiley.

Bloch, S., & Chodoff, P. (1982). *Psychiatric ethics.* New York: Oxford University Press.

Broad, W., & Wade, N. (1982). *Betrayers of the truth.* New York: Touchstone.

Buenos Aires Oath. (1988, Summer). *Professional ethics report, 1.*

Declaration of Helsinki. (1964). *The New England Journal of Medicine, 271,* 473-474.

Distel, B., & Jakusch, R. (Eds.). (1978). *Concentration camp Dachau 1933-1945* (J. Vernon, R. Jakusch, & B. Distal, Eds. and Trans.). Munich: Comite International de Dachau.

Dokecki, P. R., & Zaner, R. M. (1986). *Ethics of dealing with persons with severe handicaps: Toward a research agenda.* Baltimore, MD: Paul H. Brookes.

Gallant, D. M., & Force, R. (Eds.). (1978). *Legal and ethical issues in human research and treatment.* New York: SP Medical and Scientific Books.

Haywood, H. C. (1977). The ethics of doing research . . . and of not doing it. *American Journal of Mental Deficiency, 81,* 311-318.

Hershey, N., & Miller, R. D. (1976). *Human experimentation and the law.* Germantown, MD: Aspen Systems Corp.

Katz, J. (1972). *Experimentation with human beings.* New York: Russell Sage Foundation.

Kohn, A. (1986). *False prophets.* New York: Basil Blackwell.

Lifton, R. J. (1986). *The Nazi doctors: Medical killing and the psychology of genocide.* New York: Basic Books.

Marsa, L. (1992, June). Scientific fraud. *Omni,* 38-40, 42, 44, 82-83.

Medical treatment and human experimentation: Introducing illegality, fraud, duress and incapacity to the doctrine of informed consent. (1975). *Rutgers Camden Law Journal, 6,* 538-564.

Monson, N. (1991, July/August). Misconduct in the labs. *Health Watch,* 24-33.

National Academy of Sciences. (1975). *Experiments and research with humans: Values in conflict.* Washington, DC: National Academy of Sciences Printing and Publishing Office.

National Institutes of Health. (1991). *Treatment of destructive behavior in persons with developmental disabilities* (NIH Publication No. 91-2410). Bethesda, MD: U.S. Department of Health and Human Services.

Panel on Scientific Responsibility and the Conduct of Research. (1992). *Responsible science: Ensuring the integrity of the research process.* Washington, DC: National Academy.

Repp, A. C., & Singh, N. N. (Eds.). (1990). *Perspectives on the use of nonaversive and aversive interventions for persons with developmental disabilities.* Sycamore, IL: Sycamore.

Roman, M. B. (1988, April). When good scientists turn bad. *Discover,* 50-58.

Rothman, D. J., & Rothman, S. M. (1984). *The Willowbrook wars.* New York: Harper & Row.

Schroeder, S. R., Rojahn, J., & Oldenquist, A. (1989, September). *Treatment of destructive behavior among people with mental retardation and developmental disabilities: Overview of the problem.* Paper presented at the Conference on Treatment of Destructive Behavior, Bethesda, MD.

Schroeder, S. R., Rojahn, J., & Oldenquist, A. (1991). Treatment of destructive behaviors among people with mental retardation and developmental disabilities: Overview of the problem. In *Treatment of destructive behaviors in persons with developmental disabilities* (pp. 125-171).

Siegel, B. (1988, October 30). Nazi data: A dilemma for science. *Los Angeles Times.*

Sprague, R. L. (1976). Counting jars of raspberry jam. In R. P. Anderson & C. G. Halcomb (Eds.), *Learning disability/minimal brain dysfunction syndrome* (pp. 94-125). Springfield, IL: Charles C Thomas.

Sprague, R. L. (1985, March/April). Obtaining consent in a clinical setting. *IRB, 7,* 10.

Sprague, R. L. (1987, December 14). I trusted the research system. *The Scientist,* 11-12.

Sprague, R. L. (1989, January). A case of whistleblowing in research. *Perspectives on the Professions: Ethical & Policy Issues,* 4-5.

Sprague, R. L., & Newell, K. M. (1987). Toward a movement control perspective of tardive dyskinesia. In H. Meltzer (Ed.), *Psychopharmacology: The third generation of progress* (pp. 1233-1238). New York: Raven.

Stewart, M. A. (1975). Treatment of bedwetting. *Journal of the American Medical Association, 232,* 281-283.

Walter, L., & Kahn, T. J. (Eds.). (1984). *Bibliography of bioethics.* Washington, DC: Kennedy Institute of Ethics.

Wolfensberger, W. (1974). Values in the field of mental health as they bear on policies of research and inhibit adaptive human-service strategies. In J. C. Schoolar & C. M. Gaitz (Eds.), *Research and the psychiatric patient* (pp. 104-114). New York: Brunner/Mazel.

Index

About the Editors

David B. Gray, Ph.D., is the Deputy Director of the National Center for Medical Rehabilitation Research (NCMRR), a center of the National Institute of Child Health and Human Development (NICHHD). He received his doctorate in psychology and genetics from the University of Minnesota in Minneapolis. He was instrumental in establishing the NCMRR. From 1986 to 1987 he directed the National Institute on Disability and Rehabilitation Research at the Department of Education in Washington, D.C. He has held positions at NICHHD; Rochester State Hospital and Rochester Social Adaptation Center, both in Rochester, Minnesota; New York Medical College in Valhalla, New York; and Seton Hill College in Greensburg, Pennsylvania. He has authored or coauthored numerous scientific books and articles. Recently he has been named to the national jury that selects the fourth Henry B. Betts Award Laureate. This award honors an individual who has made outstanding contributions to improving the quality of life for people with physical disabilities.

Travis Thompson is Director of the John F. Kennedy Center for Research on Human Development and Professor in the Department of Psychology and Human Development of Vanderbilt University. Thompson received his Ph.D. in Psychology from the University of Minnesota and was a N.S.F. Post Doctoral Fellow in the Psychopharmacology Laboratory at the University of Maryland. He currently holds joint appointments in the Departments of Special Education and Department of Psychology in Arts and Sciences. Thompson has held visiting positions at the University of Maryland, Cambridge University (UK), and the National Institute on Drug Abuse. He has published more than 180 articles in scientific journals and edited volumes and 18 books and has been an invited speaker in 13 countries and 26 states within the United States.

He wrote the first textbook in behavioral pharmacology and was codeveloper of the drug self-administration screening method for addiction liability of newly developed therapeutic drugs, which is used throughout the world. He has studied behavioral effects of drugs and interactions of psychological and drug treatments for behavior problems in mental retardation. He has served on national (e.g., National Institutes of Health, Food and Drug Administration, Hastings Center, National Academy of Sciences, President's Committee on Mental Retardation) and state committees concerning ethical and scientific issues vis-à-vis services for persons with developmental disabilities. He is a past president of the Divisions of Psychopharmacology & Substance Abuse and Mental Retardation & Developmental Disabilities of the American Psychological Association and recipient of the Don Hake Award of the American Psychological Association for "Exceptional Contributions to Basic Behavioral Research and Its Applications."

About the Contributors

Sharon A. Borthwick-Duffy, Ph.D., is an Associate Professor of Special Education at the University of California, Riverside (UCR), and is affiliated with the UCR Research Group at Lanterman Developmental Center (formerly Pacific State Hospital) in Pomona, California. She received her doctorate from the University of California at Riverside and is currently President of the Academy on Mental Retardation. She is an Associate Editor of the *American Journal of Mental Retardation* and serves on the editorial boards of *Mental Retardation, Education and Training in Mental Retardation,* and the *Journal on Developmental Disabilities.* Her research focuses on the education, behavior, developmental progress, and life expectancy of persons with mental retardation.

William H. Brown, Ph.D., is a Research Assistant Professor of Special Education at Vanderbilt University. He was an NICHD Research Behavioral Scientist Trainee in mental retardation and received his doctor-ate from Peabody College of Vanderbilt University. His research interests are early intervention for young children who have been severely abused and/or neglected, the development of problem behavior in children with developmental disabilities, and children's social competence.

Robert H. Bruininks, Ph.D., is Dean of the College of Education and Professor of Education Psychology at the University of Minnesota. He received his graduate training and Ph.D. degree in Education from George Peabody College (now Vanderbilt University). His research focuses on public policies, education and other forms of assistance that support individuals with substantial learning and developmental disabilities, and educational disadvantages. One of his current efforts is working with colleagues to establish the National Center on Educational Outcomes to improve the evaluation of educational and related service programs for students with disabilities. Other interests are concerned with developing dropout prevention and social skills intervention programs in collaboration with school systems, and policy and program research on deinstitutionalization and community services for citizens with developmental disabilities. He has authored and co-authored more than 105 articles in professional journals and about 25 edited books and published manuals.

Edward G. Carr, Ph.D., is currently Professor of Psychology at the State University of New York at Stony Brook. He received his doctorate in experimental psychology from the University of California at San Diego and then completed a three-year postdoctoral fellowship in clinical psychology at the University of California at Los Angeles. He has lectured widely in the United States and Europe and has served on the editorial boards of 12 scientific journals. He is a Fellow of the American Psychological Association. He has published more than 100 papers in the area of developmental disabilities in addition to the forthcoming book, *Communication-Based Intervention for Problem Behavior*.

Dawn Delaney is a Research Associate at the John F. Kennedy Center of Vanderbilt University. After earning her Ph.D. in Psychology at Western Michigan University, she did postdoctoral work in the Human Behavioral Pharmacology Laboratory of the Department of Psychiatry at the University of Vermont. Delaney's research focuses on effects of pharmacological and behavioral treatments for self-injury in mental retardation and on assessing food motivation in Prader Willi syndrome.

Lynne K. Edwards, Ph.D., is Associate Professor, Psychological Foundation, in the Department of Educational Psychology at the University of Minnesota. She specializes in experimental design and computer-intensive methods. Her recent research focuses on analysis of time-dependent observations.

Mark Egli is a Research Associate at the John F. Kennedy Center of Vanderbilt University. He earned his Ph.D. in Psychology at the University of Minnesota and spent two years as a research scientist in the Human Behavioral Pharmacology Laboratory of the Department of Psychiatry of the University of Texas Medical Center at Houston. Dr. Egli's current research is on basic mechanisms in concept learning in people with developmental delays and animal laboratory behavioral pharmacology studies.

Richard M. Foxx, Ph.D., is a Professor of Psychology at Pennsylvania State University, Harrisburg, and Clinical Adjunct Professor of Pediatrics at Pennsylvania State University College of Medicine. He has written 5 books and more than 100 scientific articles and has made 13 training films. He is codeveloper of overcorrection. He was the coeditor of *Analysis and Interventions in Developmental Disabilities* and is on the editorial boards of 8 journals. He is a Fellow of the American Psychological Association (APA), the American Psychological Society, and the Ameri- can Association on Mental Retardation. He was President of the Division on Mental Retardation and Developmental Disabilities of APA.

Robert H. Horner is a Professor of Education at the University of Oregon, Director of the Specialized Training Program, and the Oregon UAP Technical Assistance Coordinator. He has a 20-year professional history of direct service, research, program development, and training in the field of severe disabilities. For the past 6 years, Dr. Horner has served as Project Director for the Rehabilitation Research and Training Center on Positive Behavioral Support, a six-university collaboration that has played a leading role in research, training, and dissemination on positive behavioral support technology. He currently is

Associate Editor for the *Journal of Applied Behavioral Analysis* and the *American Journal on Mental Retardation* and is a past editor of the *Journal for Persons With Severe Handicaps*. Dr. Horner has been actively involved in preservice and inservice training for teachers and adult service personnel since 1977.

Kathryn G. Karsh, Ph.D., received her doctoral training in applied behavior analysis and special education. Since graduation she has been employed at the Educational Research and Services Center, where she has conducted research on nonaversive interventions for severe problem behaviors, instructional methods, and computer-assisted instruction for persons with developmental disabilities. Dr. Karsh is an author of several book chapters and journal articles and has received research grants from the National Institutes of Health and Office of Special Education.

K. Charlie Lakin, Ph.D., is Director of the Research and Training Center on Residential Services and Community Living at the University of Minnesota. His primary research interests are residential and related services for persons with developmental disabilities and public policies affecting those services.

Sheryl A. Larson is a Ph.D. candidate in Educational Psychology at the University of Minnesota. She is a Project Coordinator at the Research and Training Center on Residential Services and Community Living at the Institute on Community Integration (UAP). Current research interests focus on personnel issues and other challenges influencing community services for persons with developmental disabilities.

O. Ivar Lovaas received his Ph.D. in clinical psychology from the University of Washington and later joined the faculty at the University of California, Los Angeles. He has received an honorary Doctor of Letters, a Guggenheim Fellowship, and the Emil Kraeplin Forshung Stipendium. He is also a member of Phi Beta Kappa and a Fellow of the American Psychological Association. Since 1970, he has been investigating the effects of early and intensive behavioral intervention with developmentally disabled children, with emphasis on normalizing intellectual, educational, social, emotional and related functioning.

William E. MacLean, Jr., Ph.D., is Associate Professor of Psychology, of Special Education, and of Pediatrics at Vanderbilt University. He received his doctorate in clinical psychology from Peabody College and completed a clinical psychology internship at the University of North Carolina at Chapel Hill. His research program involves understanding the development of aberrant behavior of people with mental retardation and enhancing the coping of children with chronic physical illness. He is the editor of the forthcoming third edition of the *Handbook of Mental Deficiency, Psychological Theory and Research*.

William L. Nyhan, M.D., Ph.D., is Professor of Pediatrics at the UCSD School of Medicine in La Jolla, California. He was an undergraduate in biochemistry at Harvard University; he earned an M.D. at the Columbia University College of Physicians and Surgeons and a Ph.D. at the Uni- versity of Illinois. His work encompasses a spectrum from the direct study of metabolism and therapy at the bedside, to studies of the intermediary metabolism of small molecules, to the definition of the molecular nature of disease at the level of the enzyme protein. He first described what is now known as the Lesch-Nyhan disease and more recently has characterized a number of mutations in DNA.

Kathleen M. Olson, Ph.D., is a Project Coordinator at the University of Kansas in the University-Affiliated Program at Parsons. She received her doctorate in educational psychology from the University of Minnesota. She has more than 15 years of experience with individuals with developmental disabilities in residential and educational settings. Her research interests include developing effective strategies for staff training, the integration and empowerment of individuals with developmental disabilities, and the reduction of behavioral challenges among persons with dual diagnoses.

Alan C. Repp, Ph.D., received his doctoral training in experimental psychology and special education, with an emphasis in behavior analysis. Following gradua- tion, he worked at the University Affiliated Facility in Atlanta, where he was the director of special education. From there, he went to Northern Illinois University, where he is a Presidential Research Professor and Director of the Educational Research and Services Center. He has published more than 125 papers, primarily in the field of developmental disabilities, with a concentration on nonaversive interventions for severe problem behaviors and the application of stimulus control research to both teacher and computer-assisted instruction.

Johannes Rojahn, Ph.D., is currently Associate Professor of Psychology and Psychiatry and Coordinator of the MR/DD psychology doctoral program at the Ohio State University (OSU). He is also Academic Unit Director of the OSU University-Affiliated Program (Nisonger Center). Previously he held the posi- tions of Assistant Professor in the Psychology Department at the University of Marburg (Germany) and Assistant Professor of Psychiatry at Western Psychiatric Institute and Clinic, University of Pittsburgh Medical School. He has published more than 70 scientific articles and book chapters, many on SIB and related behavior problems. Much of his research has focused on classification and assess- ment of behavior problems and he has developed a survey and assessment instru- ment, the Behavior Problems Inventory.

Jay L. Saunders is currently a graduate student in developmental and child psychology at the University of Kansas and Director of Bluestem Technologies, which specializes in bar code hardware and software development. He received his bachelor's degree in environmental studies from the University of Kansas.

Muriel D. Saunders is currently Research Assistant at the Schiefelbusch Institute for Life Span Studies at the University of Kansas and Coordinator of the Research on Effective Group Instruction Strategies (REGIS) Project at Parsons Research Center. She received her master's degree in developmental and child psychology from the University of Kansas. She is coauthor (with H. Barrish and M. Wolf) of *The Good Behavior Game: Effects of Individual Contingencies for Group Consequences on Disruptive Behavior in the Classroom* and coeditor of *A Handbook for Scenario-Based Active Treatment*. She received the 1991 Clarissa Hug Teacher of the Year Award from the Federation of the Council for Exceptional Children.

Richard R. Saunders, Ph.D., is currently a Senior Scientist at the Schiefelbusch Institute for Life Span Studies and Courtesy Associate Professor in the Department of Human Development and Family Life, both at the University of Kansas. He also is the Administrative Coordinator at the Parsons Research Center and the Director of the Kansas Active Treatment Training Program in the University Affiliated Pro-gram at Parsons. He received his doctorate in developmental and child psychology from the University of Kansas. He has written 16 journal articles and 7 chapters and is coeditor of *A Handbook for Scenario-Based Active Treatment*. He innovated the "supported routines" approach to the treatment of aberrant behavior.

Stephen R. Schroeder, Ph.D., is currently Director of the Schiefelbusch Institute for Life Span Studies and the Kansas Center for Mental Retardation and Human Development. He is also a Professor in the Department of Human Development and Family Life as well as in the Department of Pharmacology and Toxicology. He received his doctorate in experimental and physiological psychology from the University of Pittsburgh. Most of his professional career was spent at the University of North Carolina, where his research focused on the integration of behavioral and biological studies of self-injurious behavior and on developmental neurobehavioral pharmacology and toxicology.

Tristram Smith is currently a Visiting Assistant Professor of Psychology at Drake University in Des Moines, Iowa. He serves as a member of the editorial board for *Focus on Autistic Behavior* and as a guest reviewer for many other journals. He received his doctorate in clinical psychology from the University of California at Los Angeles. For the past 10 years, he has conducted treatment and research with children who have autism and other developmental disabilities. His research has helped identify effective ways of raising intellectual functioning (as assessed by measures such as IQ tests), promoting long-lasting treatment gains, and disseminating state-of-the-art treatment approaches.

Amy N. Spiegel is a Research Assistant at the University of Minnesota in the Department of Educational Psychology. She is a doctoral student in the Measurement and Evaluation Program. She also is affiliated with the National Center on Educational Outcomes for Students With Disabilities, which is housed at the Institute on Community Integration, a University-Affiliated Program. Her research interests include educational research in applied settings, issues in developmental disabilities, and educational evaluation.

Jeffrey R. Sprague, Ph.D., is the Director of the Center for School and Community Integration at the Indiana University Institute for the Study of Developmental Disabilities in Bloomington. He received his doctorate in special education from the University of Oregon. He currently directs both state and federal demonstration and technical assistance projects related to school inclusion, transition form school to work, and supported employment for persons with developmental disabilities. He has published numerous research articles and book chapters dealing with serious problem behavior and directs a research project investigating the causes and functions of low-frequency, high-intensity behaviors. He was recognized in 1992 by TASH for distinguished contributions to nonaversive behavior management methods and research.

Robert L. Sprague, Ph.D., was a psychologist at Muscatatuck State School, Butlerville, Indiana, a facility for mentally disabled people, taught at Northern Illinois University, DeKalb, and has taught and conducted research at the University of Illinois, Urbana-Champaign, since 1964. He is a professor in seven departments located in three colleges on that campus. He has published more than 100 articles and chapters in various publications and has served on numerous federal government advisory committees. For his role in scientific integrity, he was awarded the AAAS Scientific Responsibility Award in 1989.

Wendy L. Stone, Ph.D., is an Assistant Professor of Pediatrics and Psychology and Human Development at Vanderbilt University. She received her doctorate in clinical psychology from the University of Miami. She completed her predoctoral internship at the University of North Carolina Memorial Hospital, where she received specialized training in autism at Division TEACCH. She currently coordinates a multidisciplinary clinic specializing in the diagnostic assessment of children with autism, which serves as a primary site for her National Institute of Mental Health-funded research program in early identification of children with autism.

Frank Symons is a doctoral student in Special Education at Peabody College of Vanderbilt University. He earned a B.A. (Advanced) in Psy- chology from the University of Manitoba and an M.Ed. in Educational Psychology from the University of Alberta. His current interests include the assessment and treatment of severe problem behaviors in children with or without developmental disabilities. His research focuses on methodological issues in direct observational data collected in real time.

Jill C. Taylor, Ph.D., is currently a Clinical Psychologist at the John Merck Multiple Disabilities Program at Western Psychiatric Institute and Clinic, University of Pittsburgh School of Medicine. She received her doctorate from the State University of New York at Stony Brook and did her postdoctorate work at Western Psychiatric Institute and Clinic. She has published in the *Journal of Applied Behavior Analysis, Journal of the Association for Persons With Severe Handicaps, Journal of Autism and Developmental Disorders,* and *Behavior Modification.* Her research interests include the functional analysis and treatment of socially avoidant problem behavior; reciprocal social influences in severe problem behavior; and parent, teacher, and staff training.

Richard Tessel is Professor of Pharmacology and Toxicology in the School of Pharmacy at the University of Kansas. His research interests include the use of animal models to establish neurochemical bases for the cognitive and behavioral abnormalities in individuals with central nervous dysfunction such as the developmentally disabled, as well as for the pharmacological and behavioral treatment of such individuals.

Don E. Williams, Ph.D., is currently Director of Behavioral Services at Richmond State School in Richmond, Texas. He has done extensive treatment and research with people who have developmental disabilities and severe behavior disorders. Dr. Williams is on the editorial boards of *Education and Treatment of Children* and *Research in Developmental Disabilities.*

George Zukotynski, Ph.D., is Director of the Behavior Treatment and Training Center, a community residential service of the Texas Department of Mental Health and Mental Retardation, Richmond State School, Richmond, Texas. His research and clinical interests include the treatment of self-injurious behavior, the training of self-management, parent training, and the treatment of individuals with dual diagnosis.